THE SECRET WOUND

THE SECRET WOUND

LOVE-MELANCHOLY

AND EARLY MODERN ROMANCE

Marion A. Wells

Stanford University Press, Stanford, California   2007

Stanford University Press
Stanford, California
© 2007 by the Board of Trustees of the
Leland Stanford Junior University

Printed in the United States of America

Typeset at Stanford University Press in 11/14 Garamond

FOR JOHN, THEO, AND TOBY

AND FOR MY PARENTS

Contents

Acknowledgments

This book could not have been written without the generous support of Middlebury College, whose leave policy allowed me to spend an entire year in London. The book was conceived in its present form in the British Library, where I was fortunate enough to be able to lay my hands on almost any medieval or early modern medical text that promised to contain vital information about love-melancholy.

My work is indebted to the influence of a number of scholars and friends. I would like to record here a profound debt to the late Don Fowler, Fellow and Tutor in Classics at Jesus College, Oxford, until his tragically early death in 1999. As my Classics tutor for three formative years and later as a friend, Don gave freely of his vast knowledge—so freely indeed that he shaped my thinking not only about particular classical texts but about the intellectual enterprise as a whole. My reading of Virgil in these pages is colored by the pathos of his memory. Earlier versions of some of these chapters benefited from the scrupulous attention of the late Thomas Greene, whose groundbreaking work on early modern literature informs my own work well beyond the scope of particular citations. I am greatly saddened that although he helped to shape the seed that became this book, he did not live to read it in its present form. Susanne Wofford introduced me to Spenser's poetry in an exciting graduate seminar at Yale, and I am grateful to her both for setting my course through this remarkable poem and for her continued interest in my work. I am also delighted to record my gratitude to my colleague and friend at Middlebury, John Elder, who generously read the whole manuscript in time to offer crucial advice and sorely needed encouragement. I would also like to thank Stanford University Press's readers, whose reports were models of constructive criticism and generous encouragement. I hope I have done justice to their suggestions. Jacob Risinger's painstaking work as my research assistant during the book's final revision went well beyond the call of duty; any remaining errors certainly slipped into the manuscript after it left his hands.

Thanks are also due to William McCann, whose humor and wisdom have helped to support this project—and its author—when the going got tough. Though we rarely discussed the matter of the book, our conversation nevertheless intersected with it in astonishingly productive ways.

My family also deserves my thanks—not only for their patience in the face of my periodic despair but also for their continuing interest in this seemingly interminable project. My parents and brother have my gratitude for maintaining a keen interest in the book despite their geographic distance from its author and for patiently urging its conclusion. My husband, John, has been the closest, shrewdest, and kindest of all the book's readers. His clarity of mind has been a priceless resource whose effects are invisibly present throughout these pages. My two sons, Theo and Toby, born during the course of the book's long completion phase, have helped to ensure that in my own life the terms "love" and "melancholy" remain resolutely opposed.

An earlier version of Chapter 3 appeared as "'Solvite Me': Epic, Romance, and the Poetics of Melancholy in the *Orlando Furioso*," in *Italian Studies*, Vol. 59 (Summer 2004). I am grateful to the editors for permission to reprint some of that material here.

THE SECRET WOUND

Introduction

Love-Melancholy and Early Modern Romance

> But this love of ours is immoderate, inordinate, and not to be
> comprehended in any bounds. It . . . is a wandering, extravagant, a
> domineering, a boundless, an irrefragable, a destructive passion.
> —Robert Burton, *The Anatomy of Melancholy*

> The pathological extensions of love not only touch upon but overlap
> with normal experience, and it is not always easy to accept that one
> of our most valued experiences may merge into psychopathology.
> —P. E. Mullen and M. Pathé, "The Pathological Extensions of Love"

In his *Discourse of the Preservation of Sight*, first published in 1597, the
physician André Du Laurens provides a portrait of what he calls "amorous
melancholie" that is representative of the many medieval and early modern
treatments of the topic informing his own:[1]

> [T]he man is quite undone and cast away, the sences are wandring to and
> fro, up and downe, reason is confounded, the imagination corrupted, the
> talk fond and senceless; the sillie loving worme cannot any more look upon
> any thing but his idol: all the functions of the bodie are likewise perverted,
> he becommeth pale, leane, swouning, without any stomacke to his meate,
> hollow and sunke eyed. . . . You shall finde him weeping, sobbing, sighing,
> and redoubling his sighs, and in continuall restlessness, avoyding company,
> loving solitariness, the better to feed and follow his foolish imaginations.[2]

This passage vividly captures both the psychological and the physical aspects of the disease: the sufferer's imagination is corrupted and, likewise,
"all the functions of the bodie are . . . perverted."[3] Du Laurens and his
medical colleagues describe the effects of this "violent and extreame love"
in terms of specific psychophysiological processes, usually beginning with
the perception of an object that "setteth concupiscence on fire."[4] The overheating of the spirits traveling from heart to brain disturbs the estimative
faculty, which is concerned with making judgments about the world. The

hot spirits in the middle ventricle of the brain, where the estimative faculty resides, draw heat from the anterior ventricle, causing the cooling and drying of the imaginative faculty. The fixity of the now unnaturally cold imaginative faculty activates the perseverative focus on the image (or more technically, the "phantasm") of the beloved that becomes the constitutive feature of the disease.[5] The weeping, sobbing, sighing, pallor, and agitation that Du Laurens ascribes to the sufferer are the distinctive external symptoms of this internal turmoil. As a melancholic disease, love-melancholy, as it came to be called, is also associated with a preponderance of black bile, although the exact causal relationship between melancholy and the erotic malady is controversial.[6]

As my second epigraph from a modern psychiatric source suggests, it is not always easy to distinguish clearly between "ordinary" love and pathological love, whether we call that pathological love De Clérambault's syndrome or love-melancholy.[7] Indeed, the medical writers occasionally seem to suggest that *all* love is a disease. For instance, in his *Treatise on Lovesickness* (1610) Jacques Ferrand writes that "love or erotic passion is a form of dotage, proceeding from an inordinate desire to enjoy the beloved object, accompanied by fear and sorrow."[8] This definition implies that the lover's eventual fall into melancholia is inevitable. But a number of medical texts provide a definition of the malady of love (sometimes called "amor hereos") that distinguishes it usefully from love that remains within the realm of health, and I will rely on this distinction throughout my discussion. Peter of Spain's thirteenth century commentary on the key medieval text on lovesickness, Constantine's *Viaticum*, offers the following distinction. Love falls into two categories: one that is a suffering of the heart (*passio cordis*) and not truly a disease; and one that is accompanied by "melancholic worry and depressed thought and a damaged estimative [faculty], which judges something to surpass all others." This latter form of love Peter considers "a suffering of the brain" that does constitute a disease.[9] The question is taken up by a later writer, Gerard of Solo, whose *Determinatio de amore hereos* uses Aristotelian psychology to clarify the significance of Peter's distinction.[10] As Mary Wack emphasizes, the key issue for Gerard is *time*. It is only when desire for a particular object continues over time without satisfaction that the *actio* of love results in an imbalanced complexion and becomes a *passio*, a disease. "Erotic love and lovesickness are thus the same 'action' in the technical sense of the word; but action becomes passion with time, as the somatic consequences of obsessive desire take their toll on the patient."[11] The states of ordinary love (*amor*) and lovesickness or love-melancholy (*amor hereos*) thus describe a spectrum encompassing wholly "normal" experience and extreme, delusional behavior. As we will see, medicine's assertion that a delusional disease lurks beneath the surface of a potentially ennobling passion significantly troubles the development of what Louise Fradenburg calls the "amorous subjectivity of Europe."[12]

Despite the clinical context of Du Laurens's discussion of amorous melancholy, the medical profile presented above suggests that love-melancholy is as much a cultural and poetic concept as a truly "medical" one.[13] Du Laurens's melancholic lover is vividly familiar to us from literary sources: Chaucer's Arcite, for example, whose "loveris maladye" is clearly derived in some detail from the medical texts, is also "pale, leane, swouning . . . hollow and sunke eyed."[14] Chaucer indeed actually names elsewhere a number of the doctors whose work was crucial in establishing the disease of lovesickness in the Western medical tradition.[15] This intriguing leakage between the medical and the literary traditions moves in both directions, as the very frequent recourse to Ovid's *Remedia amoris* in the medical texts indicates.[16] Even literary texts that have no pretensions to scientific or didactic status appear as corroborating "evidence" in the medical exploration of the disease of love. In his *Observationum medicinalium libri* VI (1588), François Valleriola begins his discussion of love-melancholy with an actual case study (involving a certain merchant from Arles) but moves seamlessly into an analysis of Virgil's Dido. Read through a Ficinian lens, Dido's erotic madness constitutes for this writer the paradigmatic example of the disease.[17] Virgil's portrait of Dido's madness, in its turn, is clearly indebted to Lucretius's powerful quasi-scientific discussion of the "furor" of sexual love in his *De rerum natura*. Though the exact pathways of influence between literary and medical discourses are difficult to trace, their mutual imbrication is clear. This book seeks to recover the significance of the complex literary/medical discourse of "amorous melancholy," or "love-melancholy," as it concerns the development of early modern romance.[18] I argue, in short, that the psychophysiological conception of love-melancholy available to us in the medical writing of medieval and early modern doctors provides an essential context for understanding the recurring ontological and epistemological problems raised by the genre. In particular, I demonstrate that the medical profile of the erotic melancholic, whose judgment is subverted by the obsessive thought patterns (*assidua cogitatio*) and corrupt imagination characteristic of this disease, constitutes a crucial model for the questing subject of romance.[19] The first two chapters provide a historical and theoretical account of the medical and philosophical bases of love-melancholy as a disease of the imagination. Drawing on this detailed historical material, I then turn in chapters 3 through 6 to three early modern romances: Ariosto's *Orlando Furioso*, Tasso's *Gerusalemme Liberata*, and Spenser's *Faerie Queene*, concluding with a brief consideration of the significance of this literary and medical legacy for Romanticism.

The guiding theoretical spirit in the pages that follow will be Ficino, whose dual vocation as doctor and humanist philosopher allows him to forge a powerfully syncretic theory of desire. Ficino's *De amore* (1469), which exerted an especially long-lasting influence over the poets of early modern Europe, reveals a thorough knowledge of the medical discourse on love, though it is often necessary to read against the grain of Ficino's own Christianizing/Platonizing agenda to perceive its full significance.[20] I take my own cue from the *De amore* in the first two chapters of the book, which establish a clear historical and theoretical framework for the interpretation of romance that follows. Chapter 1 examines the complex medical history that makes possible Ficino's own commentary on love-melancholy; chapter 2 explores the theoretical continuity between Ficino's original insights about the relationship between love-melancholy and grief and contemporary psychoanalytic theory. These two complementary approaches to Ficino's analysis of desire allow me to explore the ways in which this material represents a challenge to certain New Historicist claims about early modern conceptions of selfhood by positing a psychologically *theorizable* self. Nonetheless, as I emphasize throughout this discussion, this desiring self clearly makes sense only in the context of a specific medical and philosophical account of the mind.[21] My investigation of this material is intended as a contribution to ongoing studies of early modern subjectivity, responding in particular to Michael Schoenfeldt's brilliant study of inwardness, *Bodies and Selves in Early Modern England*.[22] Whereas Schoenfeldt focuses on a corporeal discourse of digestion and evacuation, stressing what he calls "a particularly physiological mode of self-fashioning," I consider more overtly "psychologically minded" texts that develop a discourse of phantasm and "spirit" to create an (albeit still ambiguously material) space of the mental.[23] It will be useful now to sketch briefly the central ideas that emerge from these opening chapters, since they organize my reading of romance as a "melancholic" genre in the remainder of the book.

Body and Soul: The "Heroic" Passion in Context

The first problem to arise in the medical writing on love-melancholy is the troubled relationship between mind and body, which is a central focus of any discussion of the "psychological" symptoms of the disease. The poetic portrait of love as a melancholic disease in the three poems I explore here intersects broadly with the erotic psychology available in the medical writing. In both contexts, the image organizing this book—the secret wound of love—serves as a figure for the disturbing vulnerability of mental functioning to bodily distemper.[24] Broadly speaking, we may understand love-melancholy as emerging from a family of concepts that includes the heated, bodily irritability of melancholia, the "strange imagination" of a quasi-Platonic ecstasy, and the psychiatric understanding of obsession made possible by an Avicennian/Aristotelian theory of the phantasm.[25] As this nexus of related "causes" suggests, love-melancholy represents for early modern medical writers and philosophers an often troubling case study in the interdependence of mind and body—or even, more controversially, the subjection of mind to body. Thus in his account of the disease Du Laurens hastens to offer suggestions on the restitution of the proper balance between mind and body when "the bodie bee fallen into such extremitie, as that it compelleth the mind to follow the temperature thereof."[26] We will encounter this basically Galenic formulation throughout the earliest texts on love-melancholy, most pointedly, perhaps, in Constantine's seminal work known as the *Viaticum*:

> Galenus: anime, inquit, virtus complexionem sequitur corporis. Unde si non eriosis succurratur ut cogitatio eorum auferatur et anima levigetur, in passionem melancholicam necesse est incidant.
>
> ["The power of the soul," Galen says, "follows the complexion of the body." Thus if erotic lovers are not helped so that their thought is lifted and their spirit lightened, they inevitably fall into a melancholic disease.][27]

As Danielle Jacquart and Claude Thomasset note, medieval writing on lovesickness is strikingly important in the history of medicine in part because it "helped to work out the links between mental states and physiological mechanisms."[28] More specifically, the medical reading of the erotic malady suggests that mental functioning is conditioned by, and thus subject to, the temper of the body. Perhaps the clearest literary illustration of this problematic among the works examined in this study is Spenser's description of Britomart's "love-sicke hart" (*Faerie Queene* 3.2.48). Chapter 6 explores in detail Spenser's depiction of the mutual influence of her "bleeding bowels" (3.2.39) and mental suffering, considering the implications of this gendering of love-melancholy as a form of hysteria for the poem's broader revision of romance.

A closer examination of the medical/philosophical context of early modern romance can illuminate the ways in which the erotic psychology of romance registers the tension between competing discourses of love in its own structure. The medical portrait of love as what Robert Burton will later call a "mad and beastly passion" is, of course, in evident tension with the Platonic view of love as an ennobling force by means of which the soul can transcend the constraints of bodily existence.[29] Although the romances I read are clearly saturated with Platonic notions of love (often filtered through Neoplatonists such as Ficino), the very fact that love-melancholy is frequently called "Knight melancholy" suggests that the erotic narrative of romance describes, at least in part, the same obsessive, maddening love that occupies the doctors.[30] Although Plato's transcendent "divine" eros begins in love of a mortal body, it should—as both the *Symposium* and the *Phaedrus* make clear—quickly move beyond love of a beautiful body toward love of an abstract and universal beauty. As Henry Staten trenchantly observes, "Plato binds the question of the sublimating of sexual love very tightly to that of the ascent to the ideal."[31] The abandonment of physical love of a particular individual is thus the index of the soul's ennoblement.

As chapter 1 demonstrates in more detail, the medical/philosophical tradition of love-melancholy engages in complex ways with this Platonic view of love. In numerous medieval texts the condition was called "heroic love" or "heroical love," in part because it was generally attributed to the nobility, but also because of the idealism implicit in this passionate attachment to the beloved.[32] Thus we sometimes find in the medical texts language that would not be out of place in a Neoplatonic treatise: "[S]ometimes the cause of this disease . . . is the delight of the rational soul in a beautiful object. For if it contemplates beauty in a form similar to itself, a rage to unite with it is kindled."[33] Despite this Platonizing language, however, the result of this "rage" ("furor") to unite with the beautiful object is not the transcendence of the body but rather a growing sexual obsession that embrutes the rational soul. The term "heroic love" thus reveals the double-sided nature of love-melancholy, which both participates in a Platonic eros that strives toward the beautiful and also remains focused on the *individual* as the source of beauty. Burton's language captures this duality nicely: "[T]his mad and beastly passion, as I have said, is named by our Physicians Heroical Love, and a more honourable title put on it, Noble Love, as Savonarola styles it, because Noble men and women make a common practice of it."[34] In a sense this tension within love-melancholy between a "mad and beastly passion" and a "noble love" highlights a contradiction within Platonic love itself, which, though it advocates a move beyond the mortal body, always begins there and may pull the lover back down toward the body.[35] The tension implicit in the medical notion of "heroic love" frequently subtends the central crises of romance. The "rage" of an Orlando or a Tancredi or even a Britomart to "unite with the beautiful object" threatens to become a potentially deadly madness that can (in Du Laurens's words) "tyrannize in commanding both minde and bodie."[36]

Fin'amor and Love-Melancholy

The connection between "heroic" love and a degrading disease of body and soul in the medical writing on love-melancholy not only suggests the danger implicit in Platonic love but also unearths the shadow side of the idealization of the beloved so central to courtly love or *fin'amor*. This shadow darkens the portrait of the lover in romance, which offers in some instances a forceful indictment of Petrarch's expansion of *fin'amor* themes in his *Canzoniere*.[37] Chapter 3 demonstrates that Orlando's descent into madness through a stylized Petrarchan dream of Angelica constitutes a critique of the deliberate choice of a phantasmic *dolce error* (sweet error) over bitter reality, which characterizes Petrarch's emotional stance in the

Canzoniere.[38] Similarly, chapter 6 interprets the house of Busirane as an allegorization of the most sinister aspects of Petrarch's poetic legacy, and in particular of the *atra voluptas*, or "dark pleasure," that he addresses directly in his *Secretum.*[39]

Though it would be unwise to generalize too freely about the diverse body of literary material that makes up the courtly love tradition, one can say with Staten that "with the fin'amor discourse of the troubadours, we are launched on the distinctively modern quest for the reconciliation of (hetero)sexual love with the protocols of idealism."[40] For Staten this reconciliation rests on the idealization of sexual love itself, or more precisely on the *foudatz* or *joi* that becomes "the highest goal of aspiration."[41] Thus, rather than encouraging a Platonic move away from the individual beloved—who can be nothing more than a mere stepping-stone toward closer contact with the divine—*fin'amor* establishes an "erotic discipline that makes a mortal beloved the untranscendable condition of joy."[42] Furthermore, the pursuit of this (sexual) joy is the "sufficient condition for the ennoblement of the self."[43] Staten thus sees this idealization of *foudatz* as a radical departure from Plato, as indeed it is. But he does not sufficiently address the continuing role of sublimation in the discourse of courtly love; though the beloved may be in herself the highest goal of aspiration, she is nevertheless by and large an object of continuing, unsatisfied *desire*. This is, as Stephen Jaeger argues, "a love with an endlessly receding goal, which finds fulfillment only in longing, striving, aspiration."[44] The joy of consummated love is not much in evidence even in Bernart's poems, which Staten takes as his point of reference. More typical is the frustration evident in a poem such as "Can vei la lauzeta mover," in which the lover compares himself to Narcissus: "I lost myself the way / Handsome Narcissus lost himself in the pool." By the poem's close, the speaker is "downcast," in "exile," and "hiding . . . from love and joy."[45] In the strain of troubadour poetry that cultivates *amor de lonh* (love from afar), this frustration is exacerbated to such a degree that the speaker's desire seems to exceed the corporeal *foudatz* of Bernard, becoming something more akin to a Platonic striving for transcendence of the mortal body.[46]

As Mary Wack has shown, the medical and "courtly" conceptions of love probably exerted a mutual influence, most evident in the crossover between medical definitions of erotic obsession (*assidua cogitatio*) and

Capellanus's description of the lover's "continual imagination of his be-loved."[47] Nonetheless, as the foregoing description of the troubadours' ide-alization of the beloved primarily as a source of continuing, anguished de-sire suggests, medical and literary treatments of such love sharply diverge in their judgment of this obsessive love. While the rarefied love of a poet like Rudel suggests—as Staten himself admits—"a sophisticated strategy of idealization and interiorization" that will ultimately ennoble the soul at the expense of the body's physical desires, the medical doctors not only predict death as the telos of love-melancholy, but a death that necessarily degrades the rational soul.[48] Asserting the untranscendable nature of the body, the medical discourse of love-melancholy interprets any form of obsessive love as a blockage of the body's natural desires and advocates resolving this blockage by any means possible, including intercourse outside marriage.[49] This highly unsentimental corrective to the "spiritualizing" tendencies of courtly love arises from the focus in the medical writing on the physi-ological underpinnings of mental activity, and offers as it were a newly somaticized view of desire.[50] The true counterdiscourse to Platonic eros is thus not the sexualized love of the troubadours, but the medical discourse of love in which the tense dialectic between body and soul unmasks a problematic tension within Platonism itself. The medical interpretation of desire as potentially harmful and degrading resonates with the portrait of eros in the romances, which permit the forces of time and mortality to pre-cipitate the psychic crisis occluded by the atemporal illusions of lyric. We need think only of the gradual disintegration of Orlando's mind, a disin-tegration that culminates, fittingly, in his destruction of the *locus amoenus* inscribed with Medoro's Petrarchan lyric. The *joi* that appears to transcend the teleological medical narrative of love-melancholy (melancholia-mad-ness-death) collapses under the pressure of time not only on the lover's mortal body but on the beloved herself as mortal creature.[51]

Romance and the Phantasms of Desire

A central feature of this psychosomatic medical portrait of love-melan-choly that informs my reading of the psychological structure of the ro-mance quest is the internalization of the beloved as a mental phantasm. The involvement of the phantasm in medical theories of desire arises from the complex amalgamation of an Aristotelian conception of the "image" or phantasm and the Stoic system of "spiritual" or "pneumatic" circulation responsible for conveying the image to the various parts of the brain.[52] As a result of the cooling and drying of the spirits in the imaginative faculty, the phantasm remains unhealthily tenacious, eventually securing all the powers of thought to itself until it finally blocks the process of sublimation so central to rational thought for writers such as Plato, Avicenna, and Ficino. The appeal of the internal phantasm directs the mind inward toward itself rather than outward toward the beloved in a turn that becomes constitutive of melancholia. The object of love, as Giorgio Agamben argues, is "not an external body, but an internal image, that is, the phantasm impressed on the phantastic spirits by the gaze."[53] The pertinence of this discourse of phantasm and spirit is apparent in all three romances but is particularly clear in Ariosto's depiction of Atlante's palace, the labyrinthine structure that has often been read as a microcosm of the poem's romance narrative. As we will see in chapter 3, the palace generates the object of desire as a phantasm that lures the lover out of the real world in an increasingly frantic search for what can never be grasped.

The corruption of the lover's ability to judge correctly the object of desire results in an improper attachment of infinite desire (a Platonic eros striving for the Good) to a particular, material object (the phantasm) that remains lodged in the imagination. As Massimo Ciavolella puts it, "[T]he Good, which should be the only true object of man's desires, is identified with the phantasma, with the image of an object of sensual desire."[54] This turn away from the actual beloved as a distinctly existing being toward a phantasm within the lover's mind is a central theme in many of the texts on love-melancholy that I examine. In Lucretius's *De rerum natura*, for instance, the deluded lover takes in the "simulacra" of the beloved in a feverish desire to internalize the beloved as a kind of food. Unlike the desire for bread and fluid, Lucretius writes, the desire for the beloved can never be fulfilled by this process of internalization but leads instead to what he calls *dira cupido* (dreadful desire). This relationship between an illusory form of "devouring" and intense love clearly has implications for a theoretical reading of the phantasmic nature of desire.

In chapter 2, I trace some of the continuities between classical and early modern theories of desire and contemporary psychoanalytic thought.[55] The notion that, as Ficino puts it, the melancholic lover continually strives to embrace something that can never be grasped resonates with the psychoanalytic view of the object of desire as intrinsically phantasmic.[56] Jean Laplanche's influential account of sexuality as a phantasmic derivative of the vital function of feeding constitutes a particularly rich point of contact between early and contemporary theories of desire: "For sexuality, it is the reflexive (*selbst* or *auto-*) moment that is constitutive: the moment of a turning back toward the self, an 'autoeroticism' in which the object has been replaced by a fantasy, by an object reflected within the subject."[57] My focus beyond these theoretical texts is, of course, the role of the phantasm in the romance quest, in which the knight errant typically, like the melancholic lover, "prefer[s] the shadow to the thing itself."[58] The ambiguous ontological status of the beloved in romance—the quasi-phantasmic quality of an Angelica or a Clorinda, or indeed a faerie queene—likewise engages the romance subject in a potentially endless, inwardly directed quest whose telos seems to be less the object itself than the phantasm within the lover's own mind. This phantasm often seems to occupy the position of the lost maternal object and thus to suggest a connection between the primitive mirroring relationship between child and mother (Lacan's Imaginary) and the regressive orality characteristic of love-melancholy. The association between the fantasy object and the mother is borne out in the early texts not only by the frequent retelling of case studies involving forbidden love of the mother but also by the way in which the object is often cast as strangely mysterious or forbidden.[59] Du Laurens is once again helpful here in his casual use of the metaphor of "weaning" to depict the lover's obsession with the "speciall object" of his affection: "[T]hey invent continually some one or other strange imagination, and have in a maner all of them one speciall object, *from which they cannot be weined* till time has worne it out" (italics mine).[60] I consider the implications of the uneasy fusion between the beloved and a lost maternal figure in detail in chapter 4, which explores the association between the dead Clorinda, Tasso's own dead mother, and the Virgilian nightingale who mourns her lost offspring. The song of the nightingale becomes, I argue, a trope for the distinctive voice of romance in the poem—plangent, seductive, and maternal.

Love-Melancholy and the "Revolt against Mourning"

My discussion of the psychoanalytic material on melancholia in chapter 2 focuses on the relationship between love and loss. Although our own automatic association between melancholia and grief is not prominent in early writing on the topic, the connection between love, loss, and melancholia finally emerges in Ficino's *De amore*.[61] In his casually brilliant interpretation of Lucretius's *De rerum natura*, Ficino uses the story of Artemisia to illustrate not only Lucretius's point—that lovers wish metaphorically to "devour" the beloved—but also, incidentally, that pathological love is linked to unbearable grief, either present or projected into the future.[62] I employ the theories of mourning and melancholia developed by Freud, Julia Kristeva, Nicolas Abraham, and Maria Torok to emphasize the useful theoretical connection between the psychoanalytic concept of melancholic "incorporation," which emphasizes the subject's inability to process fully the loss of the object, and earlier writers' emphasis on the fantasy of devouring the beloved.[63] Working between this theoretical material and the recurring patterns of romance, I argue that love-melancholy manifests itself in both contexts as an often heavily disguised resistance to mourning a lost (or inaccessible) beloved. The lost object is, as mentioned earlier, frequently cast as a version of the original lost object, the mother.[64] By contrast, Plato's doctrine of erotic transcendence urges against the exclusive love of the individual and constitutes in its most vigorous form an elaborate ritual of mourning.[65] If the lover's focus gradually moves away from the individual toward the beauty of the forms, the beloved's mortality—and thus the transitoriness of human connection—will cease to pose a continuous threat to the lover's happiness. The melancholic lover's fixation on a single beloved bespeaks a stubborn attachment to a particular, unique individual and a concomitant refusal to participate in this sublimatory form of mourning. Filone's position in Leone Ebreo's third dialogue on love (ca. 1502) may be taken as paradigmatically "melancholic" in the sense in which I use that term here: "Not the present possession [of the object], *but its continuation, is lacking*" (italics mine).[66] Love is always haunted by present or future loss and is thus never fully distinct from grief and desire.

The notion that what Freud will call a "revolt against mourning" is at the heart of the melancholic structure of romance is especially clear in chapter 5's exploration of Spenser's revision of romance.[67] Alcyon, the despairing lover from Spenser's short poem "Daphnaida," acts as a type for both Red Crosse in his despairing mode and Despair himself, who represents the telos of Red Crosse's melancholic quest. Alcyon's attitude toward the loss of his beloved Daphne exemplifies the eroticized *acedia* that imperils Red Crosse's soul: "For all I see is vaine and transitorie, / Ne will be helde in anie stedfast plight / But in a moment loose their grace and glorie" (496–68).[68] This melancholic response to beauty perceived to be "vaine and transitorie" recurs throughout the texts I examine, both theoretical and literary.[69] An inability to accept that death is the telos of any love-relationship shapes the structure of the romance narrative, which is often marked by the deliberate choice of a Petrarchan *dolce error* over bitter reality. Chapters 5 and 6 argue that Spenser explores the "melancholic" structure of romance he inherits from his Italian precursors in terms of an impulse toward despair—or, in Britomart's case, hysteria—that must be converted into a mournful purposiveness. By giving his narrative a typological structure, he elegizes it, converting the melancholic circularity of Tancredi's or Orlando's quests into a teleological process of mourning that provides what I call "figural consolation." Thus, although the poem's telos (the Glory figured by Gloriana) is beyond the scope of earthly fulfillment, the introduction of figural consolation into the narrative rehabilitates romance as a genre by deftly avoiding the tension between epic and romance that polarizes the treatment of love in Ariosto's and Tasso's poems.

Atra voluptas: The Dark Pleasures of Poetry

This complex medical/philosophical view of love as a dark, bodily force threatening to overwhelm the sovereignty of the lover's reason intersects in early modern romance with the enormously influential treatment of love in the work of Petrarch. In this book, I will focus on a particular strain of Petrarch's writing on love that appears in both the *Canzoniere* and the *Secretum* and is itself informed by the literature on love-melancholy. In the *Canzoniere*'s narrative of the speaker's tortured love for Laura, we find a delight in suffering, indeed, a willful exacerbation of grief that informs Petrarch's characteristic oxymoronic style. In his study of the relationship between the *Canzoniere* and the *Secretum*, Piero Boitani notes a detailed correspondence between the philosophical treatment of Petrarch's *acedia*-like illness in the latter and the bittersweet quality of the lyrics.[70] The deadly sin of *acedia* was particularly associated, as Siegfried Wenzel demonstrates, with the pitfalls of monastic life and denotes a spiritual lassitude, a falling away from the service of God.[71] In book 2 of the *Secretum*, Petrarch describes his sickness of the soul as a paradoxical affliction that is both tormenting and pleasurable:

> [H]ic autem pestis tam tenaciter me arripit interdum, ut integros dies noctesque illigatum torqueat, quod michi tempus non lucis aut vite, sed tartaree noctis et acerbissime mortis instar est. Et, qui supremus miserarium cumulus dici potest, sic lacrimis et doloribus pascor, atra quadam cum voluptate, ut invitus avellar.[72]

> [But this disease holds me so tenaciously sometimes that it ties me in knots and torments me for days on end. During this time, I do not see or live, but I am like one in the darkness of hell, and seem to die the most excruciating death. And the critical time of the disease could be said to be this: I so feed on the tears and pain with a kind of black pleasure that I resist being rescued from them.][73]

The melancholic humor was sometimes thought to be a partial cause of *acedia*, and the resemblance between melancholic symptoms and the various attributes of *acedia*—including torpor, mental and bodily instability, sadness—presumably encouraged the association.[74] Wenzel sees Petrarch as a pivotal figure in the gradual association of the two illnesses, arguing that Petrarch's analysis of "what [he] calls 'accidia' has been accepted as the first articulation of that bitter-sweet disgust with the world and with life which the Elizabethans were to call melancholy and the Romantics, ennui or Weltschmertz."[75] The more specific diagnosis of this malady's roots in love of a mortal woman in book 3 confirms, as George McClure suggests, the fusion of the sin of *acedia* with the disease of lovesickness.[76] Petrarch never calls his illness "melancholy" in the *Secretum*, but his interlocutor, "Augustine," does refer to him as a new Bellerophon—a figure familiar from Aristotle's list of melancholy heroes. This Bellerophon, though, is plagued by a *funesta voluptas* (morbid pleasure) that bestows on the sufferer all the symptoms of love-melancholy:

Cogita nunc ex quo mentem tuam pestis illa corrupuit; quam repente, totus in gemitum versus, eo miserarium pervenisti ut funesta cum voluptate lacrimis ac suspiriis pascereris; cum tibi noctes insomnes et pernox in ore dilecte nomen; cum rerum omnium contemptus viteque odium et desiderium mortis; tristis amor solitudinis atque hominum fuga; ut de te non minus proprie quam de Bellerophonte illude homericum dici posset.[77]

[Think of the time when that plague first entered your soul. Think how suddenly you gave yourself over to grieving and became so unhappy that you fed on tears and sighs with a morbid pleasure. You spent sleepless nights, with the name of your beloved always on your lips. You scorned everything, hating life and desiring death; and with a melancholy love of solitude, you kept yourself from other men. Homer's description of Bellerophon could just as appropriately be said of you.][78]

This concept of *atra voluptas* (dark pleasure) or *funesta voluptas* (morbid pleasure) provides a key to the particular kind of sorrow that generates the *Canzoniere*, as Boitani argues. Certain central topoi in the *Canzoniere* take on a fuller resonance against this background; for example, the motif of "feeding on tears," found in both the passages quoted above, also makes its way into the poems (see poem 134, "Pascomi di dolor").[79] Poem 35 also deploys the myth of Bellerophon, who, as in the passage from the *Secretum*, is clearly beset by a specifically erotic form of melancholia. The influence of Petrarch's fusion of the language of *acedia* and the symptoms of love-melancholy in his description of *atra voluptas* is pervasive in the romances studied here. In chapter 3 I consider Orlando's quest for Angelica in terms of a Petrarchan choice of a *dolce error* that perpetuates and intensifies his fixation on a phantasmic object. Orlando's refusal to accept the loss of Angelica produces an obsessive rage that seems to come to a symbolic end only when, through the mediation of Virgil's elegiac sixth eclogue (*solvite me*), his quest turns toward the accommodation of death. The elegization of the erotic imagination coincides, I argue, with a shift toward epic closure, a shift signaled by Ariosto's brilliant use of the Virgilian topos of the *mors immatura*, or untimely death of young warriors. In chapter 4, I argue that the language in which Tancredi's awakening to Erminia's embrace is couched suggests not (as in Ariosto's poem) that the warrior-lover will renounce the *atra voluptas* of romance for the harsh rigors of epic, but rather that romance has triumphed over epic. In Spenser's poem, Timias and Scudamour are mired in precisely the kind of erotic despair that is the object of Augustine's critique in the *Secretum*. Finally, chapter 6 interprets the house of Busirane as a complex allegorization of Scudamour's *atra voluptas*—a willfully indulged erotic suffering that holds the beloved (Amoret) prisoner by stripping her of any reality outside her lover's obsessive mind.

All four chapters on romance demonstrate that the choice of *atra voluptas* over the elegiac forms of epic is symptomatic of the "revolt against mourning" at the heart of both the psychic structure of love-melancholy and of the quest structure of romance. Petrarch's exploration of *atra voluptas* in the *Secretum* confirms the connection between erotic fixation and a refusal to acknowledge the "vaine and transitorie" nature of mortal beauty. Augustinus urges his suffering interlocutor to choose the path of Platonic transcendence, precisely in order to counteract the torment that the death of the beloved will ultimately cause him:

> [N]ecdum intelligis quanta dementia est sic animum rebus subiecisse mortalibus, que eum et desiderii flammis accendant, nec quietare noverint nec permanere valeant in finem, et crebris mortibus quem demulcere pollicentur excrucient?[80]

> [Do you not understand what folly it is to subject your soul to things of this world, things that kindle the flames of desire, that can give you no peace and cannot last? They offer the promise of sweetness but torment you with constant agitation.][81]

It is precisely the consequences of our human tendency to love the "things of this world" too much that are exposed both in the medical writing on love-melancholy and in the *dolce error* of romance. My goal in these chapters is to explore the philosophical and medical subplot of romance's story of *atra voluptas* and its attendant torments, paying due attention to the way in which this subplot gives voice to a robustly anti-Platonic insistence on the irreplaceability of the unique beloved. That this insistence may have tragic consequences is clear enough in the romances, which nonetheless only hint at the tragic potentiality of their protagonists' stories through the outlying figures of a Sir Terwin or a Fiordiligi. But Petrarch knows of what he speaks in his self-portrait as a tormented Dido, wandering like a wounded stag: "fugi enim, sed malum ubique circumferens" (I took flight, but carried my wound with me everywhere).[82] Petrarch's Virgilian simile returns us to the image that organizes the book as a whole, and that recurs in different guises in each of the texts examined here: the "secret wound," the sign precisely of the "sweetness" and "torment" of a love fixed on an embodied, mortal beloved.

CHAPTER I

From *Amor hereos* to Love-Melancholy
A Medico-Literary History

*"Amor est mentis insania qua vagatur animus per inania crebris dolori-
bus permiscens gaudia"*
—Peter of Spain, *Questiones super Viaticum* (version B)

The seventh and final speech in Ficino's *De amore* turns unwillingly to
consider the kind of love that does not adhere to the Platonic ideal of transcendence but rather remains lodged in the body, threatening to subvert
the mind's sovereignty over the body's unruly desires. In the third chapter
of this speech, Ficino argues that this kind of love is the "opposite" of
Socratic love, a form of insanity (*insania*) rather than the "divine madness" (*furor divinus*) praised by Plato as a means to knowledge. Insanity
is a bodily disease resulting from a defect of the heart and does not even
deserve the name of love:

> Cordis autem morbo eam proprie insaniam fieri arbitramur, qua affliguntur
> hi qui perdite amant. His falso sacratissimum nomen amoris tribuitur.
>
> [We think that the insanity by which those who are desperately in love are
> afflicted is, strictly speaking, caused by a disease of the heart, and that it is
> wrong to associate the sacred name of love with these.] (*De amore* 7.3, trans.
> Jayne, with minor emendation)[1]

For want of any clearer terminology, however, Ficino continues to refer
to this "insanity" as a form of love, though the anxious desire to maintain
a clear distinction between the two kinds of love is apparent throughout
the speech. In delineating the features of what he also calls "vulgar love,"
Ficino draws heavily on the medical sources with which he, as a trained
physician, was quite familiar. In these works, love always threatens to become a melancholic disease, an affliction first of the body and then, inevitably, of the mind:

Sed ne diutius de insania loquentes insaniamus, sic brevibus concludamus. Insaniae species quaedam est anxia illa sollicitudo, qua vulgares amantes diu nocte que vexantur, qui amore durante bilis incendio primum, deinde atrae bilis adustione afflicti, in furias, ignemque ruunt, et quasi caeci quo praecipitentur ignorant. . . . Hoc itaque furore homo in bestiae naturam devolvitur.

[But lest we go mad talking further about madness, let us conclude briefly thus. That anxious care by which vulgar lovers are vexed day and night is a certain species of insanity. As long as the love lasts they are afflicted first by the burning of the bile, then by the burning of the black bile, and they rush into frenzies and fire, and as if blind do not know where they are being precipitated. . . . Thus by this madness man sinks back to the nature of a beast.] (*De amore* 7.12, trans. Jayne, with minor emendation)

Before hastily turning away from the subject, as though liable to become infected by this most potent of illnesses, Ficino gives a brief synopsis of the medical writing on love as madness. "Vulgar" love gives rise to a form of mental suffering (*sollicitudo*) that is profoundly implicated in the physiology of melancholy. This chapter explores the medical history that informs this speech, pausing also to consider the broader significance for Ficino's Platonizing project of the medical interpretation of love as a powerfully disruptive psychosomatic disorder. As we will see, the medical account of love as a disease presupposes a theory of body and mind as inescapably intertwined. The implications of this theory infiltrate Ficino's erotic philosophy in subtle ways, subverting the Christianized version of Platonic eros that dominates the work. As one of the most influential texts on love for nearly two hundred years, the *De amore* is an apt text to consider before turning to early modern romance. For the complex erotic psychology of romance is undoubtedly informed by the uneasy interpenetration of medical and literary traditions that Ficino's text both illustrates and perpetuates.

Ficino's unease with the implications of the medical treatment of love-melancholy is apparent in the opening stages of the seventh speech, which purports to interpret the notoriously difficult poem by Guido Cavalcanti, *Donna me prega*. As Massimo Ciavolella has noted, Ficino distorts the meaning of this poem's discussion of sensual love to bring the poem into line with the idealizing Platonic treatment of love that his own work endorses.[2] Since Ficino is well acquainted with the medical literature on love, and in particular with Dino del Garbo's medically oriented commentary (ca. 1311) on Cavalcanti's poem, it seems unlikely that this distortion is wholly unintentional. Ficino's indebtedness to del Garbo's commentary is apparent elsewhere in the speech, when Ficino introduces the notion of love as a form of infection: "Amatoria vero contagio facile fit, et gravissima omnium pestis evadit" (The amatory infection comes into being easily and becomes the most serious disease of all, 7.5). As Sears Jayne suggests, Ficino is probably influenced here by del Garbo's description of the form of love that in his opinion is the subject of Cavalcanti's poem:

> Sed alio modo accipitur amor specialiter proprie pro passione quadam quae iam adeo est in appetitu vehementer impressa ut difficulter removeatur ab ipso, quae passio est proprie circa actus venereos inquibus actibus est furiositas et intemperantia, cum in illos actus homo inclinetur ex appetitu naturali. Et hoc modo intelligitur hic de ista passione quae dicitur amor, quae passio propter vehementem eius impressionem iam alterat corpus alteratione non naturali, unde iam quod in ipsum dicatur aegrotare eroticos, quod et auctores medicinae qui de aegritudinibus et de eorum curis determinant, tractant de hac passione, et modum etiam curationis suae, et vocatur talis passio ereos ab autoribus medicinae.

> [Love can be taken more particularly as that passion which is so vehemently impressed on the appetite that it can only be removed with difficulty. It is that passion which properly concerns venereal acts, in which there is great fury and intemperance, since man is inclined towards these acts by his natural appetite. And this is the kind of love Guido is concerned with in this poem, which because of the vehemence of its impression alters the body contrary to what is natural to it; whence the body is said to be diseased by love and is treated as such by the medical writers under the name of *amor ereos*.][3]

Although Ficino probably knew this commentary on Cavalcanti's poem— which tallies with other previous commentaries in its emphasis on a medical reading of love as disease—he chooses to suppress this reading and transforms Cavalcanti's poem into a vehicle for his own version of Platonic love.[4] By naming this form of love so precisely (*amor ereos*), del Garbo's text unearths for us a central concept in the history of the disease that will eventually become "love-melancholy." The significance of Ficino's deliberate suppression of alternative readings of Cavalcanti's poem will emerge as we look more closely at the complex medical history that informs del Garbo's reference to *amor ereos*, and it is to this history that I now turn.

From Eros to Heroic Love

Del Garbo's term for the disease of love whose vehemence alters the mind—*amor ereos*—presents considerable philological difficulty. Usually translated as "lovesickness," the term seems to have gradually emerged from Constantine's eleventh-century translation (known as the *Viaticum*) of an Arabic medical text, in which he establishes his topic as "amor qui et eros dicitur."[5] Later terms for this kind of *amor* included *heros*, *ereos*, and other formations until the term *amor hereos* became more or less standard.[6] If, as Lowes has shown, Greek medical writers originally used the word *eros* as a quasi-technical term to denote the disease of love, the aspirated form *heros* in the Latin works seems to have fulfilled an analogous function.[7] The term consistently denotes a pathological version of love that is distinct from ordinary *amor*. Johannes Afflacius's somewhat later (ca. 1100) translation of the same Arabic text consistently alters Constantine's *eros* to *heros* and his *eriosis* to *heroicus*.[8] As Mary Wack suggests, "the simplest explanation is that he [Johannes Afflacius] understood heros not only (if at all) as an aspirated form of eros, but also in its general meaning of 'hero, lord, baron.' The general meaning of the word then guided his choice of the appropriate substantive adjective, heroicus."[9] The conflation of two distinct etymological lines ("love" and "hero") seems to have provided sufficient opportunity for the coining of the hybrid term *amor hereos*.

Afflacius's text may have cemented the association between Constantine's "amor . . . eros" and the notion of a hero; certainly Gerard of Berry's commentary (ca. 1236) on the meaning of *heros* is unequivocal: "amor qui heros. Heroes dicuntur viri nobiles qui propter divicias et mollitiem vite tali pocius laborant passione" (Love [that is called] heros: Heroes are said to be noble men who, on account of riches and the softness of their lives, are more likely to suffer this disease).[10] In later writers, the growing association between this intense form of love and the term *heros* (hero) as well as *herus* (master, lord), may have been encouraged by the false etymological link between "eros" and "hero" offered in Plato's Cratylus.[11] By the mid-thirteenth century, the concept of "heroic" love seems relatively common-place, as the title of Arnaldus of Villanova's work suggests: *Tractatus de amore heroico* (ca. 1280).[12]

The concept of "heroic" love also seems to encompass the potentially emasculating subjugation of the masculine soul to a feminine love-object.[13] Arnaldus writes that heroic love is so called because it is "quasi dominalis," or like a lord, "not only because it happens to lords, but also either because it dominates by subjugating the soul [subiciendo animam] and ruling the heart of man, or because the acts of such lovers toward the desired object [rem desideratam] are like the acts of subordinates toward their own lords."[14] The subordination of the masculine lover in this scheme necessarily threatens to overturn the conventional gender hierarchy, transforming the lover into a feminized figure who is anything but "heroic" in the usual sense of the word. The gradual association of the primarily masculine disease of lovesickness with the feminine disease of hysteria confirms the fluid and unstable nature of this "heroic" conception of love, and perhaps partly explains Burton's horror of the "mad and beastly passion" that he is quick to associate with the "bestial" love of women.[15] The feminization or infantilization of the melancholic lover as a result of his obsession is also apparent in the early modern romances. Orlando's "furor" associates him with Pasiphae and, more distantly, with the figure of the maenad; Tancredi is both infantilized and feminized by his subjection to a Petrarchan *atra voluptas*; and figures such as Scudamour and Timias wallow self-indulgently in a love that subjects them to the scorn or pity of the warrior women who succor them.

Though an analysis of the complex philological history of the term *amor hereos* is beyond the scope of this study, the highly compressed account presented here does establish the emergence of a specific "technical" term to denote a love that is a distinct and medically recognized illness— "the loveris maladye / Of Hereos" (Chaucer, *Knight's Tale*, 1373–74). Of primary interest for my purposes will be the gradual convergence between the distinct illness of *amor hereos* (lovesickness, or "heroic" love) and melancholy, until the final conflation of the two disorders registered in Burton's text. For only by looking at the transformation of *amor hereos* from a condition connected only loosely to melancholy to one clearly understood as a subtype of melancholy can we appreciate the full implications of its influence on early modern romance. Since I argue for a reading of romance as a fundamentally *melancholic* genre, it will be useful to provide a brief outline of the textual transmission of the disease, highlighting the coalescence of the two apparently polarized principles of eros and melancholy.

Eros and Melancholia in Antiquity

The treatment of love in classical antiquity is divided between those who share Plato's conception of love as a transcendent force, a divine madness, and those for whom love is a symptom of somatic turbulence. Although the medieval and early modern medical community in general adopts a physiological perspective on love deriving from Galenic principles, the influence of Plato's theory of transcendent love remains considerable. In his theory, which is laid out most clearly in Diotima's lecture to Socrates in the *Symposium*, love is only secondarily a source of physical pleasure that may lead to procreation. It is primarily important as a gateway to universal beauty, which, once glimpsed, will save the lover from what Plato calls "a slavish and illiberal devotion to the individual loveliness of a single boy" (210 d).[16] Although Plato does not utterly condemn the use of love as a route to physical procreation between man and woman, he does nonetheless advocate the transcendence of the body in a gradual movement toward "the very soul of beauty" (211 d):

> And so, when his prescribed devotion to boyish beauties has carried our candidate so far that the universal beauty dawns upon his inward sight, he is almost within reach of the final revelation. And this is the way, the only way, he must approach, or be led toward, the sanctuary of Love. Starting from individual beauties, the quest for the universal beauty must find him ever mounting the heavenly ladder, stepping from rung to rung—that is, from one to two, and from two to every lovely body, from bodily beauty to the beauty of institutions, from institutions to learning, and from learning in general to the special lore that pertains to nothing but the beautiful itself—until at last he comes to know what beauty is. (211 c)

This gradual movement away from the beautiful individual toward an increasingly abstract "beauty" seems considerably more difficult to sustain in the *Phaedrus*, where the soul is continually dragged back "down" toward the desires of the body by the "bad horse," the part of the soul that "consorts with wantonness and vainglory" (253 e). The Arabic doctors, who were the first to classify obsessive love as a distinct condition, remain profoundly touched by Plato's presentation of eros, even to the extent that their term for love-melancholy, *al-'ishq*, usually rendered as *'ishk* or *ilisci*, is also used to denote a Neoplatonic striving for the good.[17] I will return to this double-sided conception of love in my consideration of Avicenna.

A classical text that is particularly important for the influence it had on the future conception of love as a melancholic disease is the pseudo-Aristotelian *Problem 30*. As Raymond Klibansky argues, Aristotelian natural philosophy first "brought about the union between the purely medical notion of melancholy and the Platonic conception of frenzy."[18] Klibansky suggests plausibly that Plato's exaltation of madness exalts by association the melancholic humor, generally understood as the principal source of madness in medical texts. Although Plato himself does not make the connection, melancholia now "began to figure as a source, however dangerous, of the highest spiritual exaltation."[19] Ficino certainly bears witness to this conflation of Platonic frenzy and a medicalized version of Aristotle's illustrious melancholia:

> Democritus quoque nullus inquit viros ingenio magnos, praeter illos qui furore quodam perciti sunt, esse unquam posse. Quod quidem noster in Phaedro probare videtur, dicens poeticas fores frustra absque furore pulsari. Etsi divinum furorem hic forte intelligi vult, *tamen neque furor eiusmodi apud physicos aliis unquam ullis praeterquam melancholicis incitatur.*
>
> [Democritus too says no one can ever be intellectually outstanding except those who are deeply excited by some sort of madness. My author Plato in the Phaedrus seems to approve this, saying that without madness one knocks at the doors of poetry in vain. Even if he perhaps intends divine madness to be understood here, nevertheless, *according to the physicians, madness of this kind is never incited in anyone else but melancholics.*][20]

Since the most powerful kind of frenzy among the four kinds that Plato discusses is the erotic, the way is prepared for the connection that *Problem 30* also establishes between melancholia and a heightened eroticism.[21] *Problem 30* is the source of much of the later work on melancholia—particularly by Rufus (fl. 98–117 AD)—that directly influences the Arabic doctors and thus the transmission of an understanding of love-melancholy to the West. Three related points emerging from this little treatise have a substantial impact on the genealogy of love-melancholy: most importantly, the connection between melancholy and heightened sexuality; the notion of melancholy as a "heroic" or "noble" disease; and the conception of melancholy as a highly *pneumatic* substance.

The connection established in *Problem 30* between melancholy and the heroic may have helped to shape the emergence of the "heroic" sickness of love, especially since the author also emphasizes the tendency of these exceptional, melancholic persons to be highly erotic. The text opens with an assertion of the natural eminence of the melancholic:

> Why is it that all those who have become eminent in philosophy or politics or poetry or the arts are clearly melancholics, and some of them to such an extent as to be affected by diseases caused by black bile? An example from heroic mythology is Heracles. . . . There are also the stories of Ajax and Bellerophon.[22]

The complex psycho-physiological profile that emerges from this text asserts a connection between the powers and dangers of a "heroic" constitution and a labile sexuality that is very closely identified with a divine "ecstasy."[23] Most melancholy persons are "lustful" (λάγνοι); "those who possess much hot black bile are elated and brilliant or erotic" (ἐρωτικοί).[24] The amorousness of the melancholic temperament is explicable in terms of the *Problem*'s pneumatic theory. The concept of pneuma, variously translated as "air," "spirit," or "breath," is in fact the concept that ties together melancholy and sexuality in the first place, and as the "spirit" of the Neoplatonic philosophers, it is the concept that permits commerce between body and soul. As a central concept in the history of the complex psychosomatic disorder of love-melancholy, it merits our brief attention here.

Though the so-called philosophers of nature before Aristotle theorized the role of the pneuma in different ways, it is, broadly speaking, a vivifying, unifying, spiritual substance that facilitates communication between different parts of the living organism.[25] It received its most influential formulation in Stoic thought, which conceived it as a subtle material substance animating the entire body. As Ruth Harvey observes, this Stoic pneumatic theory is clearly at odds with Platonic dualism: "[T]o the idea of man as an immaterial soul imprisoned in a material body is opposed the monist conception of man all made of elements, with his life itself, his breath and mover, as a subtler element."[26] Pneumatic doctrine in its various forms was central to all succeeding Greek medicine and passed by way of Galen and the Arabic doctors into the Latin West. But what in the original Stoic context was a sign of psychosomatic integration became in a religious context (whether Christian or Islamic) the sign of precisely the necessary *separation* of body and soul, which the purity of the latter required. Though originally identified with the soul, pneuma gradually came to be understood instead as the intermediary between body and soul, the most refined material substance in the body: "Spirit is a certain subtle body, which in the human body rises from the heart, and is borne in the arteries to vivify the body; this effects life, and breathing, and pulsation."[27] Arabic doctors are often notably uneasy about the integration of body and soul that they perceive in Greek medicine and philosophy. This unease is, of course, replicated in medieval and early modern Christian contexts, in which the spirit becomes an indispensable piece of psychophysiology, whose task it is to keep, as it were, the soul's hands clean.[28] As we will see, the spirit becomes especially important in Ficino's psychological theory, in which the soul perceives the image of the material object (the phantasm) in the spirit *tamquam in speculo* (as in a mirror).[29] The spirit is now the inner mirror that makes self-reflection—taken to an obsessive extreme in melancholia—possible.

According to *Problem 30*, melancholy, like wine, is a highly pneumatic substance, generating air within the organism that creates a state of tension particularly associated with the desire for sexual intercourse.[30] It is this pneumatic tension, then, that associates melancholy with a heightened eroticism often linked by analogy to drunkenness:

> Now wine too has the quality of generating air, so wine and the melancholy temperament are of a similar nature. . . . It is for this reason that wine excites sexual desire, and Dionysus and Aphrodite are rightly said to belong together, and most melancholy persons are lustful.[31]

The connection established in this text between heightened sexuality, pneumatic tension, and melancholy is a central feature of medical discussion of love-melancholy in medieval and early modern texts, though the causal relationship between these factors is sometimes reversed. Thus while *Problem 30* understands melancholy as the cause of pneumatic tension, the tradition of love-melancholy following Constantine sees pneumatic tension as a potential cause of the melancholic condition. The same tension is also responsible for the febrile creativity attributed to the illness of melancholia even to this day. *Problem 30* offers perhaps the most influential account in classical antiquity of the intuitively compelling portrait of the "inspired" melancholic:

> Many too are subject to fits of exaltation and ecstasy, because this heat is located near the seat of the intellect; and this is how Sibyls and soothsayers arise and all that are divinely inspired, when they become such not by illness but by natural temperament.—Maracus, the Syracusan, was actually a better poet when he was out of his mind (ἐκσταίη).[32]

Tasso deploys this version of the "inspired" melancholic in his own reflections on melancholia in his *Il Messaggiero*. Hoping to ally himself with the inspired heroes and poets of Aristotle's text rather than with the truly maddened Orestes or Pentheus, Tasso draws closely on Aristotle's text: "Marato poeta ciciliano allora era più eccelente ch'egli era fuor di sé, anzi quasi lontano da se stesso" (So Maratus the Sicilian poet was more excellent when he was outside himself, or rather as though distant from himself).[33] Not coincidentally, this melancholic self-alienation is precisely what overtakes Tancredi at the climax of his meeting with the phantasmic Clorinda: "va fuor di sé" (Tasso, *Gerusalemme Liberata* 13.45).

Problem 30's construal of the relationship between the imagination and melancholy is particularly important because it both hints at the eroticization of the melancholic imagination and at the same time allows for a form of "divine" (Platonic) inspiration that exceeds physical understanding. Both implications find their way into early modern writing on melancholy and love-melancholy. Jacques Ferrand's encyclopedic work on love-melancholy (1610) inherits this view of a sexualized melancholic imagination: "[T]hose who are melancholy through the adustion of pure blood also have overactive imaginations, which will quicken a man's immoderate appetites according to Aristotle in his Problems."[34] André Du Laurens emphasizes the corruption of the lover's judgment: "[T]he imagination is in such sort corrupted, as that the melancholike partie alwaies thinkes, that hee seeth that which he loveth." But the particular kinds of delusions to which the melancholic lover is subject also suggest an affinity between the eroticized imagination of the melancholic and the "inspiration" of the poet: "[H]e is alwaies in hand with the deciphering of the rare beautie therein, he seemeth to himselfe to see long golden lockes . . . a high brow, like unto the bright heavens, white and smooth, like the polished Alabaster; two starres standing in the head very cleere."[35] This description is, of course, familiar from the Petrarchan lyric tradition, in which the blazon of the beloved's body frequently deploys these very tropes. Although Du Laurens, like Ferrand, favors a pragmatic physiological explanation of the symptoms of the disease, he also concedes, again perhaps following Aristotle, that the "strange imaginations" of melancholics may exceed the reach of physiological analysis:

> Finally, we observe and finde such strange imaginations in some melancho-like men, as cannot be referred either to the complexion of the bodie, or to their condition of life: the cause thereof remaineth unknowne, it seemeth to be some secret mysterie. The old writers have thought that there is something divine in this humour.[36]

Ferrand and Du Laurens, like their medieval predecessors, probably derive their sense of the importance of the "complexion of the bodie" in the etiology of the disease from Galen (ca. 130–200). We have already seen the authority granted to Galen's assertion that "the power of the soul follows the complexion of the body" in Constantine's seminal text on love-sickness, and in general Galen's view of love as a somatic disorder prevails in Western medicine.[37] Though as Michael McVaugh observes, Galen does not classify love as a distinct disorder, his interest in Erasistratus's tale of Antiochus and Stratonice offers support for his own view of the complex interaction between mind and body.[38] Using a case study of his own—the "wife of Justus," who became enamored of the dancer Pylades—Galen argues for the psychophysiological unity that became a central and problematic feature of later depictions of love-melancholy.[39] In both these instances, the lovesick patient inadvertently revealed his or her passion through uncontrollable physical signals, such as an irregular pulse. This diagnostic tool makes its way through numerous accounts of love-melancholy, including that of Ferrand, who describes his diagnosis of the disease in a young scholar: "As I pressed him to reveal to me the external cause of his disease, an attractive girl of the house came in with a lamp as I was taking his pulse, which from that moment went through a series of changes. . . . Seeing his secret half-revealed, he confessed to the rest."[40]

The tension between a somatic conception of love (deriving from the ancient physicians) and Plato's theory of a divine, transcendent love shapes the emerging theory of love as a melancholic disease throughout later classical writing and the medieval/early modern tradition that is our primary focus. For a writer like Lucretius, the adoption of a darkly materialist conception of love as "furor" is the result of an ideological opposition to Platonic theory: the soul is a material entity and as such is literally engrossed by the desires of the body.[41] Lucretius's writing on love in the *De rerum natura* haunts the final speech of Ficino's *De amore*, as we shall see in more detail in the next chapter, and is a pervasive influence (direct or indirect) in the literary texts studied in this book. The gradual development of *amor hereos* (eventually to be called love-melancholy) as both a potentially ennobling illness *and* a disabling "beastly passion" thus charts a tricky and unstable convergence of a fundamentally divided classical tradition of love with the medico-philosophical tradition of melancholy. Each of these theories emphasizes—though with varying degrees of alarm—the mutual dependence of body and mind that is to become so prominent in later theories of love-melancholy. It is in the work of the Arabic doctors, to which I now turn, that we will find a more precise delineation of the shadowy spaces between mind and body demarcated by the disease of love.

Sollicitudo melancholica: Strange Imaginations of the Mind

As Donald Beecher has argued, "the Arab physicians of the tenth and eleventh centuries are the first on record to have accepted erotic desire as one of the anxieties of the mind that could bring on a state of melancholy."[42] Burton's list of sources confirms the psychological orientation of the Arabic physicians, emphasizing in particular Avicenna's conception of this illness as a "melancholy worry" (*sollicitudo melancholica*): "Avicenna calleth this passion Ilishi, and defines it to be a disease or melancholy vexation, or anguish of mind, in which a man continually meditates of the beauty, gesture, manners of his Mistress, and troubles himself about it."[43] In terms of the psychological inflection of writing on love-melancholy, Avicenna is perhaps the most important of the Arabic doctors, and I will return in more detail to the model of mind that provides a context for his conception of the illness as well as that of much later writers. Before Avicenna, the figure whose influence reaches the Latin West most fully is Ibn al-Jazzār (d. 979), whose chapter on the illness of love, *al-'ishq*, in chapter 20 of his Kitab *Zād al-musāfir wa-qūt al-hādir* (Provisions for the traveler and nourishment of the settled) makes its way into the West via Constantine's eleventh-century adaptation known as the *Viaticum*.[44] I will focus here on the language of Constantine's text rather than on that of his original, since it is this version that directly influences the development of the concept in the West.[45]

The work draws on Greek medical sources and approvingly cites Galen's notion that the soul follows the body's temperament. The involvement of the soul in the body's affairs (and vice versa) is perhaps the central feature of this account and inflects the entire treatise. The disease is securely located in the brain at the beginning of the treatise:

> Amor qui dicit eros dicitur morbus est cerebro contiguus. Est autem magnum desiderium cum nimia concupiscentia et afflictione cogitationum.
>
> [The love that is called "eros" is a disease touching the brain. For it is a great longing with intense sexual desire and affliction of the thoughts.][46]

This great longing remains ambiguously lodged in the mind but causally linked to rudely somatic processes. Thus the first cause of lovesickness to be mentioned is a bodily one:

> Aliquando huius amoris necessitas nimia est nature necessitas in multa humorum superfluitate expellenda. Unde Rufus: Coitus, inquid, valere videtur quibus nigra colera et mania dominantur.
>
> [Sometimes the cause of this love is an intense natural need to expel a great excess of humors. Whence Rufus says: "Intercourse is seen to benefit those in whom black bile and frenzy reign."][47]

But immediately following this grossly physical "cause" of the illness is another cause that seems to bring the disease into contact with a Platonic conception of transcendent love:

> Aliquando etiam eros causa pulchra est formositas considerata. Quam si in sibi consimili forma conspiciat, quasi insanit anima in ea ad voluptatem explendam adipiscendam.
>
> [Sometimes the cause of eros is also the contemplation of beauty. For if the soul observes a form similar to itself it goes mad, as it were, over it in order to achieve the fulfillment of its pleasure.][48]

This kind of madness seems to be a version of the medicalized Platonic ecstasy that we encountered in *Problem 30*. Certainly the notion that love is provoked by a desire for the beautiful associates it with the Platonic eros.[49] But the gradual elevation of the soul predicted in the *Symposium* or the *Phaedrus* does not occur in this context; rather, this fixation remains stubbornly attached to a single individual, fomenting the "affliction of thoughts" that gradually leads to melancholy.

Another translation of the Arabic *Zād al-musāfir*, the *Liber de heros morbo*, written a little after the *Viaticum* (ca. 1100), provides an interesting alternative to Constantine's translation of these lines:

> Huius autem herois causa aliquando est rationalis anime oblectatio in aliqua re pulcra. Quam pulcritudinem si in sibi simili conspexerit forma, furor accenditur ut ei se uniat.

> [Sometimes the cause of this disease *heros* is the delight of the rational soul in a beautiful object. For if it contemplates beauty in a form similar to itself, a rage to unite with it is kindled.][50]

This text seems more strongly Platonizing than Constantine's, emphasizing the desire on the part of the enamored soul not merely to fulfill its own pleasure but also to unite with the beautiful form. The fact that these texts offer two such different causes of the disease of "heroic" love—one robustly physical and one psychological/spiritual—clearly complicates their reception in texts whose commitment to a Platonic and/or Christianizing interpretation of love takes precedence over a therapeutic medical agenda. Thus while Ficino strives throughout his text to discriminate between a bodily *insania* and a spiritual *furor* (a divine madness), the medical texts that are among his sources present them as two sides of the same coin. The love of the individual body that can lead to worship of divine beauty can also turn into the frenzy that seeks the pleasures of the body. Mary Wack rightly comments that "it is difficult to decide [from Constantine's text] whether *amor eros* is more akin to Neo-Platonic striving for beauty or to an attack of sexual need."[51] The double face of *amor hereos* is also a feature of Avicenna's later account of love, which confirms and perpetuates the strange combination of somatic and quasi-divine elements already present in the classical conception of melancholia.

Finally, Constantine's text establishes the behavioral therapies for the disease of love that became conventional in later texts. These therapies address both the mental and the physiological aspects of the disease and include the drinking of wine, the taking of temperate baths, and the enjoyment of pleasant gardens. In fact, the reference to "luciferos . . . ortos, odoriferos et fructiferos" (bright . . . sweet-smelling and fruitful gardens") suggests a conjunction between this "cure" for love and the *locus amoenus* that is such a ubiquitous feature of medieval and early modern love poetry.[52] Though Giorgio Agamben sees the poetic trope as a "self-conscious reversal of, and defiant challenge to, the remedies of love recommended by the physicians," it seems equally likely that the influence moves fluidly in both directions, confirming our sense that medicine and literature exert a complex mutual influence.[53] Constantine's text also recommends literary and "talking" cures; the sufferer should enjoy conversation with dear friends ("colloqui dilectissimi amicis") and the recitation of poetry ("versus recitatio"). The deployment of spoken language—conversation and recitals—as a cure that soothes the body and the mind is evidence of an early awareness of the susceptibility of melancholic diseases to the power of the human voice. I address the implications of this susceptibility in the next chapter, elaborating what I take to be a latent poetics of melancholy in these early medical texts.

In the *Viaticum*, then, excessive love is not yet a form of melancholy, but is causally related to it. The "excessive thoughts" of the former condition pull the sufferer remorselessly toward the latter:

> Unde si non eriosis succuratur ut cogitatio eorum auferatur et anima levigetur, in passionem melancholica necesse est incidant.
>
> [Thus if erotic lovers are not helped so that their thought is lifted and their spirit lightened, they inevitably fall into a melancholic disease.][54]

Thought itself is implicated in the process of disease, but the exact mechanisms by which thought becomes pathological are not explored. Once Avicenna's psychological theories entered the medical discourse of the period via the twelfth-century translations of Gerard of Cremona, the vague conception of anxious *cogitatio* that appears in Constantine's text is considerably enriched, and accounts of *amor hereos* take a decisive turn inward.[55] Avicenna (980–1037), a generation younger than the author of Constantine's source for his *Viaticum*, makes the connection between *amor hereos* and melancholia more forcefully. His *Liber canonis* provides what seems to be the single most influential formulation of the disease:

> Haec aegritudo est solicitudo melancholica similis melancholiae, in quo
> homo sibi iam induxit incitationem seu applicationem cogitationis suae
> continuam super pulchritudine ipsius quarundam formarum.

> [This sickness is a melancholy worry similar to melancholy, in which a man
> is seduced into a state of excitement or continual application of thought
> over the beauty of certain forms.][56]

This psychologically oriented formulation emphasizing not only the relationship between the illness of love and melancholic anxiety but also the
role of what now resembles an obsessive form of thinking proved long
lasting. Although Avicenna does not explicitly identify the sickness of
love with melancholy, he does indicate that it has a melancholy structure
arising from the connection—also noted by Ibn al-Jazzār—between love
and worry, or *sollicitudo*. The tag *sollicitudo melancholica* is ubiquitous in
commentaries that follow Gerard's translations: Peter of Spain cites it precisely to distinguish between "ordinary" love and love-as-disorder, while
Gerard of Berry introduces his psychologically complex account of the
disorder with a discussion of the etiology of melancholy thought.[57] Dino
del Garbo's reference to Avicenna is sufficient evidence for how durable
this passage was to be in the medical treatises on love:

> [E]t istud dictum de diffinitione essentia amoris concordat cum eo quod
> auctor medicinae dicit de amore diffiniendo ipsum. Dicit enim amor est
> sollicitudo melanconica, similis melanconicae in quo homo iam sibi inducit
> incitationem cogitationis super pulchritudinem quarumdam formarum et
> figurarum quae insunt ei; deinde adiuvat ipsum ad illud desiderium eius, et
> non consequitur.

> [Furthermore what is here said concerning the definition of love agrees with
> what Avicenna gives as a definition. For he says that love is a melancholy
> worry, similar to melancholy, in which a man is led to an excitement of
> thought over the beauty of certain forms and figures until he gets a desire
> for that thing.][58]

The distinction between *sollicitudo melancholica* and "melancholia"
itself is clearly very subtle and perhaps destined to be elided by later writers. John of Gaddesden's (1280–1361) *Rosa Anglica* considers what it calls
eros (perhaps after Constantine) to be a form of melancholy: "De Genere
Melancholiae est eros, in viris et mulieribus, qui inordinate amant" (Eros

is a kind of Melancholy, [occurring in] men and women who love beyond measure).[59] Interestingly, the editor of the 1595 edition of this text adds a comment from Savonarola's fifteenth-century *Practica Major* that supports Gaddesden's conflation of eros and melancholy with Avicenna's phrase: "sic scribit: eros est *sollicitudo melancholica*, in qua quis ob amorem fortem intensumque solicitat habere rem, quam nimia aviditate concupiscit" (he writes: eros is a melancholy worry, in which someone because of strong and intense love is anxious to have a thing which he desires with too much avidity).[60] Gerard of Solo's commentary (ca. 1330–40) on Rhazes' *Liber medicinalis Almansoris* coins the term "amorereos melancholia," conflating the term *amor hereos* and using it as a modifier for melancolia.[61] By the time we reach the early modern period, the connection between lovesickness and melancholy becomes inescapable. The term "amorous melancholy" that perhaps derives from Gerard of Solo's neologism appears frequently in early modern texts, including André Du Laurens's *Discourse of the Preservation of Sight*: "Loe here the effects of this affection, and all such accidents as accompanie this amorous melancholie."[62] Jacques Ferrand's treatise on love-melancholy investigates the melancholic features of the disease in several chapters; and Daniel Sennert writes: "[t]his delirium from Love . . . is a Melancholy doting from too much love . . . and sometimes it is so vehement that it deprives a man of Reason and causeth a Delirium."[63] Burton's *Anatomy* (first published 1621) devotes the third volume to "love-melancholy," calling on Avicenna in support of his categorization: "Avicenna calleth this passion Ilishi, and defines it to be a disease or melancholy vexation."[64]

As Burton's reference to Avicenna makes clear, the influence of Avicenna's work derives in part from his use of a technical term that distinguishes extreme love from other kinds of love: *al-'ishq*, usually rendered in Latin texts as *ilisci*. The term has great currency in later discussions of love-melancholy, which increasingly favor a technical codification of pathological love as a distinct mental disease.[65] Avicenna's use of this term is particularly striking in the context of the double-edged conception of love that we have considered: love as a somatic disorder and/or a means to transcendent knowledge.[66] Avicenna uses the term *al-'ishq* both to denote a medical conception of pathological, obsessive love and to bear the weight of a Neoplatonic "motion towards perfection . . . an aspiration towards beauty."[67] His essay on precisely this philosophical content of *ilisci* describes this striving for perfection as follows:

> Every being which is determined by a design strives by nature towards its perfection, i.e., that goodness of reality which ultimately flows from the reality of the Pure Good, and by nature it shies away from its specific defect which is the evil in it, i.e., materiality and non-being,—for every evil results from attachment to matter and non-being. Therefore, it is obvious that all beings determined by a design possess a natural desire and an inborn love, and it follows of necessity that in such beings love is the cause of their existence.
>
> And this love is the source of its yearning for [the good] when it is absent . . . and of its unification with it when it is present. Therefore every being approves of what is suitable for it and yearns for it when it is not there. And the specific good is the natural propensity of a being and the recognition of the truly suitable as such. Now approval and desire, and disapproval and aversion result in a thing from the attachment to its goodness.[68]

This Neoplatonic yearning for the beautiful and the good is also characteristic, as Mary Wack points out, of the version of *al-'ishq* found in Andalusian lyric poetry, so that the same concept brings together medical, philosophical, and literary versions of a yearning that is at once ennobling *and* potentially threatening to the subject's physical and mental health.[69] That Avicenna uses the same term to denote both a melancholic "solicitude" over the beauty of a *particular* form or figure and a spiritual yearning for the pure Good indicates that melancholy arises from a misguided reorientation of spiritual desire, an attachment of infinite desire to an improper, material, *particular* object. Love-melancholy thus seems to delineate precisely the fault line that separates the material and the immaterial in the human being. This fault line runs through the imagination, whose task it is to shape sense impressions of particular objects in the world into phantasmata that can be metabolized by the estimative faculty.[70] Since the imagination is usually considered a mediating faculty necessary for both ennobling "spiritual" experiences of *exstasis* and delusional "lower" visions, it is not surprising to find that the unstable psychosomatic disease of love-melancholy is usually regarded as a byproduct of a dysfunctional imagination.[71] Though the medical texts frequently debate the exact location of the origin of the disease, the role of the imagination remains a central focus, as Donald Beecher and Massimo Ciavolella note: "[E]rotic love, in the final analysis, is a disease of the imagination, given the capacity of that faculty to create its own motions, its own principles of pleasure, and at the same time its own inferno of striving and loss, because in the imagination the object is always present to be enjoyed, yet always absent, unreal, and unattainable."[72] The focus on the corruption of the imagination and the ensuing disruption of its neighbor in the second ventricle, the power of estimation, entails a gradual psychologization of the disease.[73]

Melancholic Phantasms: The Birth of the Erotic Obsession

Avicenna's influential emphasis on the notion of a melancholic "solicitude" helps to consolidate the diagnosis of love-melancholy as a form of obsession—a fixation of thought upon a single object. Though the terms "obsessive" or "obsession" are never used—according to the *Oxford English Dictionary* the first use of the term "obsession" in a psychological context occurs in 1901—the importance of a perseverative style of thinking in the etiology of the disease becomes increasingly clear. Arnaldus of Villanova's *Tractatus de amore heroico* (ca. mid–1280s) describes the kind of thought that is constitutive of the illness of love as "assidua cogitatio non de omni sed de re desiderata" (assiduous thought not about all things but about the desired thing).[74] The term "assidua cogitatio" is repeated frequently in later treatises and seems to encompass the concept of obsession *avant la lettre*. Indeed, in this description of excessive love as a perseverative *cogitatio* over the beloved we can discern elements of our modern theories of obsessive disorders.[75] The earliest texts on melancholy (such as the pseudo-Aristotelian *Problem 30*) emphasize the humoral basis of the disease, but without providing any clear account of the genesis of psychiatric disorders within the brain. In Avicenna's *De anima* and *Canon*, the Aristotelian and Galenic models of the mind are refined and elaborated, making possible a fuller "psychological" explanation of the perseverative style of love-melancholy. Commentaries on Constantine's *Viaticum* seem to display the influence of Avicenna's eclectic psychology, moving the psychiatric analysis of lovesickness beyond Constantine's rather vague association between melancholy and *cogitationes nimias*.

Gerard of Berry's commentary, written before 1237, significantly develops the *Viaticum*'s treatment of the relation between body and soul.[76] For while Constantine's text does not venture beyond the Galenic assertion that the illness is related to *cogitationes nimias*, which directly threaten the body's health and thus indirectly, the health of the soul, Gerard explores more fully the mutual interference of body and mind. Beginning with the reference to *amor hereos* as a *sollicitudo melancolica*, Gerard's reliance on Avicenna in his commentary is pervasive:

> Amor qui heros dicit. Haec passio dicitur apud auctores sollicitudo melancolica. Est enim plurimum similis melancolie, quia tota intentio et cogitatio defixa est in pulchritudine alicuis forme vel figure desiderio coadiuvante.
>
> Causa ergo huius passionis est error virtutis estimative que inducitur per intentiones sensatas ad apprehenda accidencia insensata que forte non sunt in persona. Unde credit aliquam esse meliorem et nobiliorem et magis appetendam onmibus aliis. . . . unde si qua sun sensata non convenicencia occultantur a non sensatis intentionibus anime vehementer infixis. Estimativa ergo, que est nobilior iudex inter apprehensiones ex parte anime sensibilis, imperat imaginationi ut defixum habeat intuitum in tali persona. Ymaginativa vero concupiscibili, unde concupiscibilis hoc solum concupiscit, quia sicut concupiscibilis ymaginative obedit, ita ymaginativa estimative, ad cuius imperium cetera inclinantur ad personam quam estimativa iudicat esse convenientem, licet non sit. Ymaginativa autem virtus figitur circa illud propter malam complexionem frigidam et siccam que est in sui organo, quia ad mediam concavitatem ubi est estimativa trahuntur spiritus et calor innatus ubi estimativa fortiter operatur. Unde prior concavitas infrigidatur et desiccatur, unde remanet dispositio melancholica et sollicitudo.

[Love that is called Heros. This disease is also called a melancholic worry by medical authors. It is indeed very similar to melancholy, because the entire attention and thought, aided by desire, is fixed on the beauty of some form or figure. The cause, then, of this disease is a malfunction of the estimative faculty, which is misled by sensed intentions into apprehending non-sensed accidents that perhaps are not in the person. Thus it believes some woman to be better and more noble and more desirable than all others. Any unfitting sensations are, as a consequence, obscured by the non-sensed intentions deeply fixed in the soul. The estimative faculty, then, which is the nobler judge among the perceptions on the part of the sensible soul, orders the imagination to fix its gaze on such a person. The imaginative faculty orders the concupiscible, in fact, so that the concupiscible desires this one alone, for just as the concupiscible faculty obeys the imaginative, so the imaginative obeys the estimative, at whose command the others are inclined toward the person whom the estimative judges to be fitting, though this may not be so. Moreover, the imaginative faculty is fixated on it on account of the im-balanced complexion, cold and dry, that is in its organ, for the spiritus and innate heat are drawn to the middle ventricle, where the estimative faculty functions intensely. The first ventricle therefore grows cold and dries out, so that there remains a melancholic disposition and worry.][77]

Beecher and Ciavolella note Gerard's absorption of an Aristotelian "fusion of psychology, physiology, and physical causation" in his account of the etiology of obsessive desire.[78] The phantasm, so central to Aristotle's theory of mental functioning, also looms large in Gerard's account of the role of the imaginative faculty: "[W]hat Gerard of Berry understands quite well is the phantasmological nature of desire—that the *phantasma* plays a funda-mental role in causing emotional and mental derangements."[79] Avicenna's account of melancholy already implicates the "drying" of the spirit in the imagination and the resulting cognitive perseveration in the development of melancholy:

> [I]n melancholico fortitudo imaginationis contristantium rerum facit ei apparere, quod iam sit in actu res cuius similitudo animae representatur: et idcirco in continua perseverat tristitia. Fortitudo autem imaginationis erat propter siccitatem spiritus, quamvis rectificet motum eius. Et etiam quia intellectus a sensu et phantasia distrahitur ab actionibus rationis propter corruptionem complexionis spiritus.

> [In the melancholy man, the strength of the imagination of sorrowful things makes them appear to him, so that the thing whose likeness is represented in his soul seems to be really there, and therefore he persists in his continual sorrow. Now the strength of the imagination comes from the dryness of the spirit. . . . And it also happens because the intellect is distracted from ratio-nal actions by sense and phantasia, on account of the bad complexion of the spirit.][80]

Avicenna's account of melancholy develops the Aristotelian link between melancholia and a powerful imagination by clarifying the psychophysi-ological effect of a perseverative focus on an internal image. Perhaps tak-ing his cue from Avicenna's treatment of melancholia, Gerard attributes the polarization of the lover's thought to the fixation of the image in the imagination and prepares the way for a complex interdisciplinary study of the erotic imagination.[81]

The importance given to the imagination in Gerard's commentary and those following it is in part a function of the increasing dominance of Aristotelian psychology, in which the phantasms generated by the imagination are central to both rational and creative activity. Aristotle's statement in the *De anima* that "the soul never thinks without an image" (*De anima* 431 a) becomes a central—and controversial—tenet of medieval and early modern philosophy of mind.[82] The image is formed as a result of the sensuous appearance of the object, but crucially, as Avicenna remarks, it can be conjured in the imagination in the absence of the object. Only in this way is abstract thought possible:

> Hence (1) no one can learn or understand anything in the absence of sense, and (2) when the mind is actively aware of anything it is necessarily aware of it along with an image; for images are like sensuous contents except in that they contain no matter. (*De anima* 432 a)[83]

This thesis is taken up by materialist philosophers of the soul throughout the early modern period, giving rise, for example, to one of the central tenets of Pietro Pomponazzi's controversial treatise *De immortalite animae* (1516), which claims that the "abstraction of universals from phantasms of the imagination is fundamental to all intellective activity."[84] The phantasm thus occupies a space between the physical and the immaterial realm, between sense perceptions and reason. As Aristotle himself acknowledges, a cognitive system that rests on the physiological health of the mind is necessarily fragile

> because imagined objects remain in us and resemble the corresponding sensations, animals perform many actions under their influence; some, that is, brutes, through not having intellects, and others that is, men, because intellect is sometimes obscured by passion or disease or sleep. (*De anima* 429 a)

The uncanny power of the imagination to conjure an absent object and to keep it continually present to the mind is responsible, in the disease of love-melancholy, for the perversion of the soul's intellective activity.

Given the importance of Avicennian faculty psychology for the development of medical theories of lovesickness, it will be useful to consider his placement of the imagination and its work in the mind. The five internal powers of the soul (reduced to three in many medical texts) are the *sensus communis* and *phantasia*, often lumped together as *phantasia* or *imaginatio* (first ventricle of the brain); the *virtus cogitativa* (or, confusingly, *imagi-*

nativa) and the *virtus extimativa* (second ventricle); and the *virtus memo-rialis* (third ventricle).[85] The *sensus communis* receives images from the five external senses and compares and relates them to other such images. The *phantasia* or *imaginatio*, called by Avicenna "the forming power," receives images from the *sensus communis* and is often compared to a wax tablet or a stone on which these images are "engraved."[86] Unlike the *sensus com-munis*, the *phantasia* can recall the impression of objects to our minds in the absence of the object itself ("formans apprehendit illa duo et format ea, quamvis destructa sit res quae iam abiit," *De anima* 1.5.42). The imagina-tive or cogitative power in the second ventricle has the power to work with the phantasms located in the front ventricle, combining or dividing them in the service either of creative activity or of rational inquiry.

We come now to the faculty to which Gerard of Berry draws attention, and which is not really part of Aristotle's picture of the mind: the estima-tive faculty. This faculty is often identified with the imaginative/cogitative faculty by other medical writers, since it employs the phantasms stored there; it is also connected to memory, since it has recourse to memory's stored forms in making its judgments. Precisely because its function ties it to both imagination and memory, the estimative faculty is of primary importance in the formation of the obsessive style characterizing melan-cholic disorders, including love melancholy. It is a synthesizing faculty that attends not to the sensible appearance of the object but to what Avicenna calls the object's "intentions":

> Deinde est vis aestimationis; quae est vis ordinata in summo mediae conca-vitatis cerebri, apprehendens intentiones non sensatas quae sunt in singulis sensibilibus, sicut vis quae est in ove diiudicans quod ab hoc lupo est fu-giendum, et quod huius agni est miserendum; videtur etiam haec vis operari in imaginatis compositionem.

> [Then there is the estimative power; this is the power set in the top of the middle ventricle of the brain. It apprehends the non-sensed intentions which are in individual sensibilia; it is the power which in the sheep discerns that the wolf is to be avoided, and its own lamb to be cared for. It seems also that this power works in the compounding and dividing of imagined things.][87]

As this passage indicates, the estimative faculty is a mediating faculty in terms of both its physical location in the second ventricle and its intellectual work. For although its apprehension of the object is not as pure as that of the intellect, since it still makes use of the sensible form (or phantasm), it abstracts nonsensory information from that form. It is the last stopping place for the sensible form.[88] This information, the "intention" of the object, clearly resides in the object and concerns the *relationship* between the object and the subject. In another way, then, the estimative faculty performs a mediating function between the world and the subject. For as Dag Nikolaus Hasse argues, the "intention" is best translated as "connotational attribute," since it is an attribute perceived to be *in* the object, but which also has connotations *for* the subject.[89] The estimative faculty, then, plays a crucial role in formulating motivational feelings about the object (prompting attitudes of fight or flight, etc.).[90]

For Avicenna, desire is the product of the interaction between the imaginative and the estimative faculties: "[I]maginatio rei et concupiscentia eius, et iudicare quod delectabitur in illa si affuerit" (the imagination of some thing and longing for it and the judgment that it will please if it comes to pass, *De anima* 4.3.19). The object imagined is judged to have a positive connotational attribute, in Hasse's terms, and this judgment eventually stirs the appetite—in this case the concupiscible appetite—and provokes movement. Thus desire, when sufficiently vehement, provokes a movement toward the beloved. According to Gerard and others, the disruption of the estimative faculty that occurs in lovesickness results in precisely an *overestimation* of the beloved and a perseveration of desire: "The cause, then, of this disease is a malfunction of the estimative faculty, which is misled by sensed intentions into apprehending non-sensed accidents that perhaps are not in the person. Thus it believes some woman to be better and more noble and more desirable than all others" (Gerard of Berry, *Notule super Viaticum*, cited above).

The medical texts do not agree on the exact cause of the malfunction of the estimative faculty. For Gerard, the mistake seems to result from the estimative faculty itself, which orders the imaginative faculty to focus intensely on the beloved object. Simultaneously, the overactive estimative faculty draws in the "spiritus and innate heat," causing a cooling and drying of the first ventricle, where the phantasm becomes unnaturally rigid and fixed.[91] If the imagination is fixed, it follows that the estimative faculty will be continually faced with the same image, so that its overestimation of the object will necessarily prove self-sustaining. For Arnaldus of Villanova, excessive heat arising in the heart as a result of a pleasing perception disrupts the work of the estimative faculty and dries out the imagination. The phantasm or image of the beloved, retained in the imagination by the unnatural dryness of the anterior ventricle, feeds the desire promoted by the estimative faculty until this desire may aptly be termed obsessive: this seems to be what Arnaldus and others mean by *assidua cogitatio*.[92] Dino del Garbo's commentary provides a particularly succinct account of *amor hereos* as a perversion of knowledge: "[T]he man who has experienced such a passion cannot steadily imagine anything other than the image of his beloved, and consequently cannot steadily think about anything else, since the imaginative power serves the cogitative by representing to it the image of the thing which that power will think about and judge."[93]

Gerard of Berry's commentary, then, is representative of a complex synthesis of Aristotelian phantasmology and Avicennian faculty psychology that provides a precise analysis of the *sollicitudo melancholica* constitutive of lovesickness. The fundamental thesis that emerges from the various commentaries construes melancholic love as a product of a disruption of the mutually dependent processes of imagination and estimation. Because of the overheating of the estimative faculty and the resulting cooling of the imagination, the estimative faculty is unable to perform its proper function—that is, to judge the object's "connotational attributes" vis-à-vis the subject. Consequently, it judges the object to be superior (i.e., superior in relation to the subject) to all others, and the image of the object "remains the only 'Good' that is present to the consciousness of the lover, a perverse image of a form which can no longer become an object of knowledge."[94] The phantasm, when properly acted upon by the various powers of the mind, becomes increasingly abstract, losing its materiality by the time it passes through the estimative faculty—a process Avicenna aptly calls *denudatio*. This process of sublimation is disastrously interrupted when the estimative function is overwhelmed by the pleasing power of the phantasm conjured by the imagination and recalled by the memory. Rather than moving beyond what Plato calls a "slavish and illiberal devotion" to a particular individual, then, the lover will return unceasingly to the image of this individual lodged within his mind.

It is clear from the foregoing analysis that love-melancholy represents a subversion of the Platonic ideal of erotic transcendence. Rather than prompting the soul's flight toward the beautiful as an emanation of the Good, the phantasm replaces the Good and itself becomes the telos of the lover's search.[95] Ciavolella's formulation of this search as a kind of quest suggests a provocative parallel between the internal "wandering" of the lover and the structure of romance: "[T]he melancholy delirium which springs from this perversion of the internal senses, drags the lover into an insane quest for an image forever reflected within his own memory, into a vain, obsessive attempt to possess an object of desire that can never be reached nor seized."[96] One could hardly imagine a more apt description of the "insane quest" of an Orlando or a Tancredi. In the remainder of this chapter, I will pursue the implications of this complex medical/philosophical understanding of melancholic love for early modern notions of subjectivity. As we shall see, the derangement of the melancholy lover's ability to judge the world correctly (according to reason) draws attention to the fundamental ontological instability of the subject. As described in the medical texts, the role of the phantasm in the psychic life of the melancholy lover—its fixity in the imagination and its "domination" of the reason—emphasizes the *permeability* of the relation between body and mind, and, more radically, between self and world.[97] The loved object enters the mind as a quasi-material phantasm engraved on the spirit in the *phantasia*; the reason draws on this image in order to think; and thinking goes awry if the physical conditions of the brain are conducive to excessive dryness, coldness, or heat. In melancholic disorders the degree to which bodily functioning affects mental life is especially clear; and love-melancholy, in particular, demonstrates in turn the body's vulnerability to destabilizing factors in the external world.

"Spiritual Love": The Vulnerable Subject

Aristotle's theory of the phantasm emphasizes its role as a mediating vehicle between soul and body. It is not surprising, then, that the phantasm quickly became associated with the Stoic pneuma—the spirit whose animating work maintains the body and the soul in harmony. As Agamben has shown, the two principles were so closely associated in Neoplatonic writing that they eventually converge in Synesius's "phantastic spirit."[98]

Agamben dates the re-emergence of pneumatology to Constantine's eleventh-century translation of the Arabic medical text known as *Liber regius*, but it is Ficino—whose translation of Synesius's *De insomniis* confirms his detailed knowledge of Synesius's "phantastic spirits"—who accomplishes its most striking refinement. His theory of the spirit as a kind of internal mirror permits the elaboration of a highly complex psychology representing the culmination of the "pneumo-phantasmology" that Agamben rightly sees as the intellectual cornerstone of the period.[99] Ficino's translation of Synesius's *De insomniis* provides a good key to his own use of the mediating spirit in his later work. In this translation, the discussion of the phantastic spirit falls under three headings, each of which indicates an important aspect of the role of the phantastic spirit. These are "spiritus phantasticus est primum animae vehiculum" (the phantastic spirit is the first vehicle of the soul); "spiritus phantasticus inter aeterna, et temporalia medius est" (the phantastic spirit is the intermediary between eternal and temporal things); and "phantasticus spiritus potest purior, et impurior fieri, levior, atque gravior" (the phantastic spirit can become purer, and impurer, lighter, and heavier).[100] For Synesius, then, as for later writers (including Ficino), the phantastic spirit reflects in its lability the fragility of the human condition. It is capable through its mirrorlike reflectiveness of opening the mind to true knowledge or, conversely, of drawing the mind further into the corporeal realm.[101]

Ficino's account of the intermediary role of the spirit in *De amore* provides a particularly expansive and clear assessment of how the "subtle knot" that knits up soul and body facilitates early modern attempts to separate the mind from the toils of the body. Since Ficino's account of spirit as a kind of "mind's eye" will prove useful in assessing the later development of the relationship between his notion of "fascination" and love-melancholy, I shall quote the relevant passage at some length:

> Tria profecto in nobis esse videntur: anima, spiritus, atque corpus. Anima et corpus natura longe inter se diversa spiritu medio copulantur, qui vapor quidem est tenuissimus et perlucidus, per cordis calorem ex subtilissima parte sanguinis genitus. Inde per omnia membra diffusus animae vires accipit et transfundit in corpus. Accipit iterum per organa sensuum, corporum externorum imagines, quae in anima propterea figi non possunt, quia incorporea substantia quae corporibus praestantior est, formari ab illis per imagi-

num susceptionem non potest. Sed enim anima utique spiritu praesens imagines corporum in eo *tamquam in speculo* relucentes facile inspicit perque
illas corpora iudicat, at que haec cognitio sensus a Platonicis dicitur, dum
eas inspicit, similes illis imagines multo etiam puriores sua vi concipit in se
ipsa; huiusmodi conceptionem imaginationem, phantasiamque vocamus,
hic conceptae memoriter servantur imagines. Per has animi acies saepenu-
mero incitatur ad universales rerum ideas, quas in se continent intuendas.
ideo que unum quendam hominem et sensu cernit et imaginatione concipit.
Intellectur rationem, definitionemque hominibus omnibus communem per
innatam illi humanitatis ideam communiter contemplatur, et quae fuerint
contemplata conservat. Animo igitur formosi hominis simulacrum concep-
tum semel apud se reformatque memoriter conservanti satis esset amatum
quandoque vidisse. Oculo tamen et spiritui quae veluti specula praesente
corpore imagines capiunt, absente dimittunt, perpetua formosi corporis
praesentia opus est, ut eius illustratione continue lucescant, foveantur et
oblectentur. Igitur et isti propter indigentiam suam praesentiam corporis
exigunt et animus iis, ut plurimum, obsecutus eandem cogitur affectare.

[The soul and the body, which are by nature very different from each other,
are joined by means of the spirit, which is a certain very thin and clear vapor produced by the heat of the heart from the thinnest part of the blood.
Spread from there through all parts of the body, the spirit receives the
powers of the soul and transmits them to the body. It also receives through
the organs of the sense images of external bodies, images which cannot
be imprinted directly on the soul because incorporeal substance, which is
higher than bodies, cannot be formed by them through the receiving of
images. But the soul, being present to the spirit everywhere, easily sees the
images of bodies shining in it, *as if in a mirror*, and through those judges
the bodies. And this cognition is called by the Platonists sensation. While
looking at these, by a power of its own, it conceives within itself images like
them but much purer still. This kind of conceiving we call imagination or
fantasy. Images conceived here are stored in the memory. By these the eye of
the soul is often aroused to contemplate the universal Ideas of things which
it contains in itself. And for this reason at the same time that the soul is
perceiving a certain man in sensation, and conceiving him in the imagination, it can contemplate, by means of the intellect, the reason and definition common to all men through its innate Idea of humanity; and what it
has contemplated, it preserves. Therefore, since the soul can preserve in the
memory the image of a handsome man once it has conceived and reformed
that image within itself, the soul would be satisfied to have seen the beloved

only once. But the eye and the spirit, which, like mirrors, can receive images of a body only in its presence, and lose them when it is absent, need
the continuous presence of a beautiful body in order to shine continuously
with its illumination, and be comforted and pleased. Therefore, on account
of their poverty, the eye and the spirit require the presence of the body, and
the soul, which is usually dominated by them, is forced to desire the same
thing.] (*De amore* 6.6, italics mine)

As in Synesius's text, the spirit is conceived as a go-between, the *copula*
between body and soul.[102] Rather than receiving images from material objects directly, the soul merely looks at them in the spirit, as in a mirror
(*tamquam in speculo*). But as in both Aristotle's and Avicenna's theories of
intellection, the phantasm or image, though separated in its physicality
from the soul, is nevertheless central to its process of reflection. Given that
the soul's reflection depends on a phantasm whose origin is material, the
tension in Ficino's effort to preserve the soul's invulnerability to material
disturbance is palpable. Astonishingly, the final sentence of this passage
seems anti-Platonic in its adherence to a Galenic formulation: though the
eye and the spirit are merely the soul's instruments, their poverty necessarily affects the soul itself, which finds itself forced to submit to the body's
need to contemplate an actual, particular body. Intellection, in other
words, requires a process of sublimation that may be blocked by the physical tenacity of a particular phantasm.

Ficino's account of love-melancholy develops earlier medical accounts
of morbid love precisely by reading melancholia as a kind of "*spiritual
dissipation*" made possible by the phantasm's seductive and penetrating
power. Ficino imagines a kind of spiritual leakage into the seductive, beloved other; this dissipation naturally causes a metabolic catastrophe that
subverts the self's inner hierarchy. Ficino's account of the mechanics of
this disorder makes it abundantly clear that the psychophysiology of love-
melancholy disrupts not only this inner hierarchy but also the hierarchy
implicit in the engagement of the subject with the world:

> Animi amantis intentio in assidua amati cogitatione tota se versat. Illic
> et naturalis complexionis vis omnis intenta est. Ideo neque cibus in sto-
> macho perfecte coquitur. . . . quare membra omnia inopia cruditateque
> alimenti extenuantur et pallent. Praeterea quocumque animi assidua fertur
> intentio, illuc et spiritus qui animae sive currus, sive instrumenta sunt, ad-

volant. Spiritus in corde ex subtilissima sanguinis parte creantur. In amati imaginem phantasiae infixam ipsumque amatum amantis animus rapitur. Eodem trahuntur et spiritus. illuc evolantes assidue resolvuntur. Quapropter frequentissimo puri sanginuis fomite opus est ad consumptos spiritus re-creandos; ubi subtiliores quaeque et lucidiores partes sanguinis quotidie in reficiendos spiritibus exhalantur; propterea puro et claro sanguine resoluto, maculosus, crassus, aridus restat et ater. Hinc exiccatur corpus et squalet; hinc et melancholici amantes evadunt. Ex sicco enim crasso atroque san-guine melancholia, id est atra bilis efficitur, quae suis caput vaporibus op-plet, cerebrum siccat, animam tetris horrendisque imaginibus diu noctuque solicitare non cessat, quod Lucretio philosopho Epicureo propter amorem legimus accidisse.

[The entire attention of a lover's soul is devoted to continuous thought (*as-sidua cogitatione*) about the beloved. And to this all the force of the natural complexion is directed. For this reason the food in the stomach is not di-gested perfectly. . . . As a consequence, all parts of the body become thin and pale because of the scarcity and crudity of food. Moreover, wherever the continuous attention (*assidua intentio*) of the soul is carried, there also fly the spirits, which are the chariots, or instruments of the soul. The spirits are produced in the heart from the thinnest part of the blood. The lover's soul is carried toward the image of the beloved planted in his imagination, and thence toward the beloved himself. To the same place are also drawn the lover's spirits. Flying out there, they are continuously dissipated (*assidue resolvuntur*). Therefore there is a need for a constant source of pure blood to replace the consumed spirits, since the thinner and clearer parts of the blood are used up every day in replacing the spirits. On that account, when the pure and clear blood is dissipated, there remains only the impure, thick, dry, and black. Hence the body dries out and grows squalid, and hence lov-ers become melancholics. For from dry, thick, and black blood is produced melancholy, that is, black bile, which fills the head with its vapors, dries out the brain, and ceaselessly troubles the soul day and night with hideous and horrible images. This, we have read, happened to the Epicurean philosopher Lucretius on account of love; shaken first by love and then by madness, he finally laid hands on himself.] (*De amore* 6.9)

Ficino's description of the absorption of the lover's thought in a repeti-tive thought (an obsession) about the beloved clearly echoes the medical tradition's description of morbid love. The phrase *assidua cogitatio* may come directly from Arnaldus, with whose work Ficino was familiar. But the involvement of the dissipation of the spirits in the disease marks an important shift away from the early *Viaticum* commentaries. The flooding of the spirits to the overworked estimative faculty—resulting in the obsessive fixation of the object in the imagination—now extends beyond the confines of the lover's body. Ficino imagines a dangerous leakage of the spirits out of the subject's body toward the "original" of the phantasm, the beloved himself or herself. We note an important difference between this process and the intellectual process described earlier in which the phantasm is gradually abstracted until the soul contemplates the "idea of humanity" rather than the phantasm of a particular body. In melancholic love, rather than completing the process of sublimation, the soul reverses the process and finds itself drawn back toward the material world and to the beloved's body in particular.

The inability of the mind to fully "metabolize" the phantasm leaves the mind subject to the drawing power of the material world. The implications of this vulnerability for the ontological security of the subject are clearly enormous, as Ficino realizes. The subject is, as it were, overwhelmed by the world, in the form of the phantasm, and loses its sovereignty over its own domain.[103] Ioan Couliano describes this process as the "vampiric" draining of the subject's vitality through the phantasm, as though the beloved is first internalized—as a phantasm—and then proceeds to sap the lover of his vital energy from within.[104] Ficino takes this idea to a logical extreme in his notion that the lover actually begins to physically resemble the beloved as the spirits imprint the image on the very blood that circulates throughout the lover's body:

> Ideo nemo vestrum miretur si quem amantem audiverit amati sui similitudinem aliquam vel figuram suo in corpore contraxisse . . . vehemens cogitatio, spiritus movet interiores, atque in his excogitate rei pingit imaginem. . . . Quid mirum si usqueadeo haerentes et infixi pectore vultus ab ipsa cogitatione purgantur in spiritu, a spiritu statim in sanguine infigantur?

> [For this reason none of you should be surprised if you have heard that some lover has taken on in his own body a certain similarity of likeness to his beloved . . . the vehement thought (*vehemens cogitatio*) moves the internal spirits and paints on them an image of the thing thought about. . . . What wonder if the features are so firmly implanted and embedded in the

breast by mere thought that they are imprinted on the spirit, and by the spirit are immediately imprinted on the blood?] (*De amore* 7.8)

This physical/spiritual fusion with the beloved begins at the level of thought (the *assidua cogitatio*) and extends eventually to the body, as the phantasm promotes what amounts to a full-scale metamorphosis.[105] The ontological instability suggested by this theory is in evidence in later treatises on love-melancholy, in which the disease is credited with turning men into women, and vice versa.[106] Gender lability is but one version—perhaps the most troubling to early modern writers—of the disruption of the self brought about by the invasion of the lover by the mental phantasm of the beloved.[107]

Ficino's account of this invasion is embedded in his broader theory of fascination, which had immense influence on both literary and medical writing on love throughout the sixteenth century. This theory provides a more detailed account of how the fluid movement of the spirits through the eye—literally the gateway to the soul in this theory—brings about a contaminating spiritual exchange. When the lover sees the beloved, the spirit, which is a fine, airy (pneumatic) substance, flows into the lover's eyes and outward toward the beloved. Because the spirit contains refined elements of blood, it carries these traces of blood into the eyes of the beloved, whence it seeks the source of such spirit, the heart. The same process happens in reverse, as the lover receives the spirit of the beloved:

> Ergo quid mirum si patefactus oculus et intentus in aliquem, radiorum suorum aculeos in adstantis oculos iaculatur; atque etiam cum aculeis istis, qui spirituum vehicula sunt, sanginuem vaporem illum, quem spiritum nuncupamus, intendit? Hinc virulentus aculeus transverberat oculos; cumque a corde percutientis mittatur, hominis perculsi praecordia, quasi regionem propriam repetit; *cor vulnerat*, inque eius duriori dorso hebescit, reditque in sanguinem. Peregrinus hic sanguis a saucii hominis natura quoddamodo alienus, sanguinem eius proprium inficit, infectus sanguis aegrotat.

> [Therefore, what wonder is it if the eye, wide open and fixed upon someone, shoots the darts of its own rays into the eyes of the bystander, and along with those darts, which are the vehicles of the spirits, aims that sanguine dart which we call spirit? Hence the poisoned dart pierces through the eyes, and since it is shot from the heart of the shooter, it seeks again the heart of the man being shot, as its proper home; it *wounds the heart*, but

in the heart's hard back wall it is blunted and turns back into blood. This foreign blood, being somewhat foreign to the nature of the wounded man, infects his blood. The infected blood becomes sick.] (*De amore* 7.4, italics mine)

This account of love as a kind of optical infection carried in the fine vapor of the spirits engages with the medico-literary trope of love as a hidden or secret wound. The broader Lucretian context of this "wound" of love will be the subject of the following chapter. For now it suffices to emphasize that Ficino's theory represents a powerful synthesis of medical and literary conceptions of love, providing an essential conduit for the medical history I have outlined here. As Beecher and Ciavolella point out, "the physicians who endorsed the physiological enchantment of Ficino created the scientific basis for the love exchanges of the Petrarchan poets."[108] Evidence of the power of Ficino's theory is in its ubiquity. François Valleriola's *Observationum medicinalium libri VI* (1588) states categorically: "[C]ausa omnis et origo est oculus" (the whole cause and origin is the eye).[109] Andreas Du Laurens's influential account of what he calls "amorous melancholie" deploys Ficino's notion of fascination within the context of a metaphorical war: "Love therefore having abused the eyes, as the proper spyes and potters of the mind, maketh a way for it selfe smoothly to glaunce along through the conducting guides . . . unto the liver."[110] Jacques Ferrand remarks similarly: "The eyes are the windows by which love enters to attack the brain, the citadel of Athena; they are the true conduits by which it flows and glides into our bowels."[111] The familiarity of this trope from the Petrarchan literature of the 1590s suggests just how mutually dependent the medical and literary discourses on love have become by the end of the sixteenth century.

The Gaze of Narcissus: Love-Melancholy, Poetry, and Psychoanalysis

Ficino's elliptical remark concluding the etiology of melancholic love in the sixth speech (6.9) provides a kind of gloss on his later discussion of fascination:

Haec illis accidere consueverunt, qui amore abusi, quod contemplationis est, ad amplexus conscupiscentiam transtulerunt.

[These things (i.e., the onset of melancholic disorders) were accustomed to happen to those who, having abused love, converted what is a desire for contemplation into a desire for embrace.] (*De amore* 6.9)

This statement draws a line between the Socratic love that Ficino praises for the bulk of the treatise and the "vulgar" love to which he is about to turn in the seventh speech.[112] True love, the statement implies, is tied to the process of contemplation in which the image is "denuded" of its materiality and becomes an object of knowledge. The opposite kind of love replaces the satisfactions of contemplation with carnal satisfaction; the eye betrays the lover into desiring to touch the beloved rather than internalize his or her beauty as an image of divine beauty. This polarization of love is more clearly explicated in an earlier speech. The universe contains two Venuses—the first "embraces the splendor of divinity in herself"; the second "transfers sparks of this splendor into the Matter of the world" (2.7). The human soul contains two principles that mirror the two Venuses; the first "worships and esteems [the beauty of the human body] as an image of divine beauty," while the second "desires to procreate a form like this." Both kinds of love, Ficino writes, are virtuous.

So wherein lies the "abuse" of the latter speech?

Si quis generationis avidior contemplationem deserat, aut generationem praeter modum cum feminis, vel contra naturae ordinem cum masculis prosequatur, aut formam corporis pulchritudini animi praeferat, is utique dignitate amoris abutitur.

[If anyone, through being more desirous of procreation, neglects contemplation or attends to procreation beyond measure with women, or against the order of nature with men, or prefers the form of the body to the beauty of the soul, he certainly abuses the dignity of love.] (*De amore* 2.7)

Love-melancholy, then, is the result of a preference for the beauty of the body over the beauty of the soul—for the beauty of the merely human over the beauty of the divine. But what becomes increasingly clear in the latter stages of Ficino's text is how fragile the distinction is between two kinds of love that begin, and converge, in admiration of the beautiful *body*. Given the identical origin of both kinds of love in admiration of human beauty, it is perhaps no surprise that Ficino's account of the ascent to the One relies on the same precarious "spiritual" love that in the seventh speech is the source of a disease.[113] Ficino's account of melancholic love—unearthing as it does a medical tradition in which "eros" is a psychosomatic disease—seems to reveal a tension at the heart of Socratic love itself.[114] For Socratic love is predicated on the sublimation of bodily desire even as it depends on that desire to begin the ascent to the beautiful. Platonic eros, then, is always threatened from within by the power of the body—its desires and its beauty—to halt the process of transcendence.

This threat arises not only from the precariousness of desire but also, more radically, from the nature of thought itself. As we have seen in the medical texts on love, a desiring focus on the beloved can quickly become the *assidua cogitatio* that leads to melancholic obsession rather than the contemplation of an abstract Good. For as Ciavolella aptly emphasizes, it is precisely the element of obsessiveness that links the erotic and melancholic temperaments.[115] The condition of love-melancholy thus highlights not only the potential for "divine" love to collapse into carnal love but also—and therefore—the potential for contemplation to become melancholic fixation. Ficino's description of the connection between Platonic contemplation—which is still revered as an ennobling force—and melancholia, highlights precisely this submerged link between love-melancholy and Platonic madness:

> Contemplatio quoque ipsa vicissim assidua quadam collectione et quasi compressione naturam atrae bili persimilem contrahit. . . . Praeterea ob frequentissimum inquisitionis motum spiritus quoque moti continue resolvuntur. . . . Quod quidem Plato noster in Timaeo significat, dicens animum divina saepissime et intentissime contemplantem alimentis eiusmodi adeo adolescere potentemque evadere, ut corpus suum supra quam natura corporis patiatur exsuperet, ipsumque vehementioribus agitationibus suis aliquando vel effugiat quodammodo, vel nonnunquam quasi dissolvere videatur.

> [Contemplation itself, in its turn, by a continual recollection and compression, as it were, brings on a nature similar to black bile. . . . Moreover, on account of the repeated movements of inquiry, the spirits continually move and get dispersed. . . . My author Plato signified this in the *Timaeus*; he said that the soul contemplating divine things assiduously and intently grows up so much on food of this kind and becomes so powerful, that it overreaches its body above what the corporeal nature can endure; and sometimes in its too vehement agitation, it either in a way flies out of it or sometimes seems as if to disintegrate it.][116]

These passages from the *De vita triplici* recall in some detail the passage we have already encountered from the *De amore*, in which Ficino discusses—in negative terms—the effects of an obsessive love on the body and soul of the lover:

> Animi amantis intentio in assidua amati cogitatione tota se versat. . . . Praeterea quocumque animi assidua fertur intentio, illuc et spiritus qui animae sive currus, sive instrumenta sunt, advolant. . . . Iluc evolantes assidue resolvuntur. . . . Hinc exiccatur corpus et squalet; hinc et melancholici amantes evadunt. Ex sicco enim, crasso atroque sanguine melancholia, id est atra bilis efficitur, quae suis caput vaporibus opplet, cerebrum siccat, animam tetris horrendisque imaginibus diu noctuque solicitare non cessat.

> [The entire attention of a lover's soul is devoted to continuous thought about the beloved. . . . Moreover, wherever the continuous attention of the soul is carried, there also fly the spirits, which are the chariots, or instruments of the soul. . . . Flying out there, they are continuously dissipated. . . . Hence the body dries out and grows squalid, and hence lovers become melancholics. For from dry, thick, and black blood is produced melancholy, that is, black bile, which fills the head with its vapours, dries out the brain, and ceaselessly troubles the soul day and night with hideous and horrible images.][117]

In both contexts, Ficino uses Arnaldus's phrase *assidua cogitatio* or a variation of it to pinpoint the origin of the melancholic condition, whether of the contemplative or the erotic kind. In the first passage, Ficino's *assidue collectione* may also recall Arnaldus's *assidue recordatione*, the "continuous recollection" of the beloved through the mediation of the phantasm.[118] Whereas in the first passage this contemplation is said to engage with "divine things," in the second passage it fills the head with "hideous and horrible images."[119] In both cases, though, the melancholic dissipation of the body threatens the very life of the subject. The juxtaposition of these two passages suggests, contra Ficino's ostensible philosophical agenda, that it is the erotic nature of *all* thought that threatens the very basis of philosophical contemplation. This structural affinity between love-melancholy and the Platonic "divine" madness is apparent in the double-edged concept of "heroic love" and its Arabic forerunner, *al-'ishq*. For heroic love in the medical tradition is precisely a love that "overreaches" the power of the body, creating a "vehement agitation" that causes that body to sicken and perhaps perish. Although the object of the fixation of thought differs—in the former instance, the object is "divine" and in the latter, mortal—we have already seen how Platonic love is rooted initially in mortal beauty, while "heroic" love strains to divinize a mortal beloved. Love-melancholy thus remains the "dark" side of Platonic love, disclosing the precariousness and perhaps the incoherence of any philosophy that attempts to transcend the body altogether.

The subversion of "divine" love by what eventually becomes love-melancholy is beautifully illustrated in Ficino's allegorical interpretation of the Narcissus story. This story also deepens the significance of Ficino's account of "vulgar" or melancholic love, placing it in the context of a theory of the self that unites medical, philosophical, and, indeed, literary models of the psyche. Retelling the story from the Orphic text, Ficino recounts Narcissus's tragic distraction from the soul's true love:

> Narcissus . . . sui vultum non aspicit; propriam sui substantiam, et virtutem nequaquam animadvertit, sed umbram in aqua prosequitur, et amplecti conatur; id est, pulchritudinem in fragili corpore, et instar aquae fluentis, quae ipsius animi umbra est, admiratur. Suam quidem figuram deserit, et usu corporis non impletur. Non enim ipsum revera appetit corpus, sed sui ipsius speciem, a corporali forma quae speciei suae imago est, illectus; quemadmodum Narcissus affectat, cumque id minime advertat, dum aliud quidem cupit, aliud sequitur, desiderium suum explere non potest. Ideo in lacrimas resolutus consumitur; id est animus ita extra se positus et delaptus in corpus, perniciosis perturbationibus cruciatur, corporisque infectus sordibus quasi moritur; cum iam corpus esse potiusquam animus videatur. Quam utique mortem ut Socrates devitaret, Diotima ipsum a corpore ad animum, ab hoc in angelum, ab eo reduxit in Deum.

> [Narcissus . . . *does not look at his own face*, that is, does not notice its own substance and character at all. *But admires the reflection of it in the water and tries to embrace that*; that is, the soul admires in the body, which is unstable and in flux, like water, a beauty which is the shadow of the soul itself. *He abandons his own beauty, but he never reaches the reflection.* That is, the soul, in pursuing the body, neglects itself, but finds no gratification in the body itself; rather, seduced, like Narcissus, by corporeal beauty, which is an image of its own beauty, it desires its own beauty. And since it never notices the fact that, while it is desiring one thing, it is pursuing another, it never satis-

fies its desire. For this reason, *melted into tears, he is destroyed*; that is, when the soul is located outside itself, in this way, and has sunken into the body, it dies, as it were, since it now seems to be a body rather than a soul.] (*De amore* 6.17)

The attempt to embrace the reflection in the water seems to provide a further commentary on Ficino's earlier reference to the melancholic conversion of contemplation into the desire to embrace the beloved. In this context, however, the transaction between self and other is tellingly internalized. The beloved other is really the beauty of the lover's own soul, not to be mistaken for its shadowy reflection in the beauty of the other's body.[120] The melancholic lover, we infer, is narcissistic in the sense that he refuses to see through the material beauty of the body, as a Platonic lover would, instead remaining trapped in his fixation on a literal object that can never satisfy his desire. In the larger context of Ficino's work, this parable suggests that the melancholic lover forgoes the ennoblement of his own soul for the sake of the material phantasm that has corrupted his mind. He has been misled into believing that his desire is for a specific object rather than for knowledge that lies beyond all objects. For it is especially clear in this passage that Ficinian desire—whether or not this is recognized by the lover—is by definition always a desire for something *beyond* what is physically available.

The allegory of Narcissus suggests that Ficino's erotic theory moves considerably beyond the scope of the earlier medical writers in its philosophical and psychological interpretation of desire. Precisely insofar as it necessitates an account of the function of erotic desire as a—or perhaps *the*—organizing principle of the soul, love-melancholy becomes central to Ficino's complex account of the subject. His account of erotic love as an essentially phantasmic process centered on an internalized image is particularly compatible with psychoanalytic formulations of the self. Jacques Lacan's account of the *objet a*, for example, also interprets the desire for the object as always a desire for something beyond the immediately present object. The object is "essentially phantasmatic in nature," a "reminder that there is something else, something perhaps lost, perhaps yet to be found."[121] For Lacan, the *objet a* is a "remainder of the lost hypothetical mother-child unity" and thus exerts a potentially regressive pull on the subject away from the symbolic order toward what Mary Jacobus aptly describes as the "regressive, narcissistic, mother-identified Imaginary."[122] For Jean Laplanche, too, erotic desire is derived from the vital function of feeding and can therefore never attain an object that "has been replaced by a fantasy."[123] Agamben's account of the "phantasmic" nature of melancholia emphasizes the family resemblance between early modern and psychoanalytic conceptions of desire: "The imaginary loss that so obsessively occupies the melancholic tendency has no real object, because its funereal strategy is directed to the impossible capture of the phantasm."[124] This phantasm, then, as we have seen in Ficino's work, occupies a very similar position in early modern psychology to the shadowy *objet a* of contemporary psychoanalysis. Whether we call this "phantasmatic" object *objet a* (Lacan), *das Ding* (Freud), or the Thing (Kristeva), it is constitutive of the development of the subject as desiring being. For Kristeva, the failure to translate attachment to the Thing (the archaic object of desire) into language leads directly to a melancholic condition in which the lost object is buried within the psyche. As a result, the melancholic subject "freezes and preserves [these unpleasant affects] in a psychic inside thus constituted once and for all as distressed and inaccessible."[125] Like Ficino, Kristeva reads this story of melancholia in terms of the myth of Narcissus: "[T]his painful innerness, put together with semiotic markings but not with signs, is the invisible face of Narcissus, the secret source of his tears."[126]

I interpret Ficino's analysis of love-melancholy as a case study of the soul's potential alienation from itself in terms of his larger exploration of the nature of subjectivity that may justly be termed "psychoanalytic." There is a well-established debate about the validity of applying psychoanalytic concepts to early modern texts. Stephen Greenblatt's seminal essay on this topic argues that such concepts cannot be used to explicate early modern texts because they presuppose a model of the self that is theoretically incompatible with early modern accounts of subjectivity.[127] According to Greenblatt, the story of Martin Guerre reveals a conception of subjectivity in which the self is not the site of psychological experience and private interiority as much as a "placeholder in a complex system of possessions, kinship bonds, contractual relationships, customary rights, and ethical obligations."[128] If the self is a "*product* of the relations, material objects, and judgements" existing in a particular place and time, the "universalizing" theory of psychoanalysis will have no relevance. But Greenblatt's elision of psychic agency in the story of Martin Guerre overlooks the attempts of writers such as Ficino precisely to *theorize* the self in terms of the imperfectly understood desires and conflicts that knit together body and soul. Ficino's analysis of desire in *De amore* does posit a theorizable self arising directly from historically traceable medical and philosophical accounts of mind—most particularly from the "pneumo-phantasmology" whose history we have traced.

In this chapter we have seen how the medieval conception of "heroic" love reveals a crucial tension between the demands of body and soul not only within the disease of love but also within the Platonic conception of divine love. The medical texts' account of "heroic" love interprets obsessive love of a mortal beloved as the shadow side of Platonic love; it is a yearning that displays both an ennobling impulse toward beauty and an intoxicating desire for union with a particular beloved. The obsessive element of heroic love suggests its affinity with the "contemplative" disorder of melancholy, and in due course, as we have seen, these two conditions fuse in the disease of "love-melancholy." The tension between body and soul that is a constant feature of discussions of "love-melancholy" centers on the lover's internalization of an object as a mental phantasm, a phantasm that subsequently displaces the "true" object of love: the Good as it is reflected in the lover's own soul.

The next chapter pursues the theoretical continuity between this medieval/early modern account of melancholy love and the psychoanalytic account of melancholy as a particularly rich symptom of psychic disorder. By establishing a dialectic between psychoanalytic theory and the philosophical and medical bases of love-melancholy as a culturally specific disorder, I explore a historically distinct conception of the self that is nonetheless accessible to the psychoanalytic insights it helps to make possible. My reading of early modern romance in subsequent chapters will explore the implications of the medical account of erotic subjectivity for our understanding of the erotic "furor" that structures the romance quest. As a "heroic" quest dramatizing precisely the substitution of a phantasmic image for a transcendent Good, the romance quest reveals the influence of medicine's dark interpretation of desire as a disease of the mind. But as we will see, the links between the phantasmic interior world of love-melancholy and poetic productivity (established explicitly by Petrarch) complicate the romances' response to the psychic and moral dangers posed by the condition. For Tasso in particular, the phantasmic, enchanted world of romance is associated with the emergence of a seductive poetic voice, the *flebil canto* (mournful song) that draws Tancredi away from the epic narrative. The next chapter explores the genesis of this conception of voice in more detail, preparing the way for the re-evaluation in the romances of what I call the poetics of *atra voluptas* (dark pleasure) deriving from Petrarch's *Secretum*.

CHAPTER 2

Vulnus caecum
The Secret Wound of Love-Melancholy

Ficino's account of love-melancholy crucially expands the account of the disorder he receives from earlier medical texts by hinting at a latent association between the illness of love-melancholy and a *resistance to loss*. His tentative elaboration of the relationship between morbid love and an inability to accept the loss of a loved one in fact represents a significant development, not only of previous conceptions of melancholic love, but also of melancholy per se. As the analysis of the theories of melancholia in the preceding chapter illustrates, our automatic post-Freudian association between mourning and melancholia is not, in fact, a prominent part of the classical or medieval medical tradition that Ficino inherits.[1] Ficino's insight, of course, looks forward to psychoanalytic accounts of the intimate relationship between the illness of melancholia and the "normal" grief reaction of mourning. As we move toward an analysis of the melancholic structure of romance, this chapter will explore the theoretical continuity between the medieval medical framework that informs Ficino's account of love and psychoanalytic theory.

Two central and interlocking themes emerge from a theoretical reading of the medical tradition. First, Ficino's association of love-melancholy with excessive grief allows us to explore the vitally important function of loss in both medieval/early modern and contemporary accounts of desire. The obsessive style of love-melancholy connotes a refusal to mourn a lost object (a refusal to acknowledge its loss), and I argue in the remaining chapters of this book that it is precisely such a resistance to loss that organizes the patterns of romance. Psychoanalytic work on the distinction between mourning and melancholia will help us to elaborate more fully the theoretical import of this claim. Since Ficino's interpretation (or more accurately, revision) of Lucretius's erotic theory prompts the former's own insight into the relation between love and grief, this chapter begins with a consideration of the complex relationship between Ficino's *De amore* and book 4 of Lucretius's *De rerum natura*. Second, I consider the connection between a melancholic reaction to loss and a theory of voice that emerges in both the medieval/early modern medical tradition and modern psychoanalytic accounts of melancholia. The scattered but intriguing references to voice in the early medical literature delineate a consistent, though not fully realized, theory of the mutual imbrication of voice, language, love, and loss that allow us to pinpoint the particular relevance of the medical account of love-melancholy for the study of poetry. Using Julia Kristeva's work on melancholic language, I unearth from the medical literature a latent poetics of melancholia that achieves its most complex realization in Petrarch's *Canzoniere*. The chapter closes with an examination of some of Petrarch's lyrics through the lens of this poetic theory, considering its relevance to his account of *atra voluptas* (dark pleasure) in the *Secretum*. As I demonstrate in each of the following chapters, Petrarch's poetic deployment of *atra voluptas* provides, along with Ficino's theoretical account of love, the most influential channel for the passage of love-melancholy into early modern romance.

Lucretian Fragments: *Furor* and the Illusions of Love

Ficino's juxtaposition of a description of furious love and an anecdotal account of Artemisia's refusal to accept the death of her husband occurs in the seventh speech of the *De amore*, in the context of a dense reworking of Lucretian passages on love. The seventh speech as a whole relies heavily on—is in a sense built around—excerpts from the fourth book of Lucretius's *De rerum natura*, and his chilling portrait of lovers driven by forces beyond their control clearly informs Ficino's account of love-melancholy. In particular, Lucretius's powerful evocation of the fantasy of devouring the beloved that lies behind erotic *furor* activates Ficino's theoretically crucial account of Artemisia's devouring of her husband's ashes. This Lucretian theory of erotic illusion is obviously not couched in the language of unconscious desires. But its portrait of eros as a primitive, devouring force does anticipate contemporary psychoanalytic accounts of what Kristeva calls the "melancholy cannibalistic imagination" that struggles to block conscious acknowledgment of loss and death.[2] As I consider the theoretical links between Ficino's Lucretian erotic theory and psychoanalytic theory, I also analyze the ways in which Ficino's ambivalent deployment of Lucretius's dark materialism complicates and enriches the already potent mixture of Platonic philosophy and medical theory in his own text. For although Ficino is using Lucretius's passages to illustrate the kind of love that he regards as mistaken (vulgar, melancholic love), his references to Lucretius imply a theoretical compatibility between the two texts that is in fact wholly lacking. For Ficino, this mistaken form of eros is the shadow side of the divine love sanctioned by Plato; for Lucretius, on the other hand, *all* erotic love is destructive, uncontrollable, and degrading.

Let us begin by looking more closely at the moment in Ficino's text when he makes what appears to be an intuitive association between frenzied love and unbearable grief. The passage that promotes this intuitive step is cut and pasted from a long section of Lucretius's discussion of love in the fourth book of his *De rerum natura*. Since our analysis begins at the conjunction of Ficino's theoretical leap and his ambivalent use of Lucretius, I shall quote the relevant passage at some length:

> Id in se ipso philosophus Epicureus ille praesensit Lucretius, amantium omnium infelicissimus:
>
>> Sic igitur Veneris qui telis accipit ictus,
>> Sive puer membris muliebribus hunc iaculatur
>> Seu mulier toto iactans de corpore amorem,
>> Unde feritur, eo tendit gestitque coire:
>> Et iacere humorem in corpus de corpore ductum.
>> Adfigunt avide corpus, iunguntque salivas
>> Oris et inspirant pressantes dentibus ora
>> Nequicquam; quoniam nil inde abradere possunt,
>> Nac penetrare et abire in corpus corpore toto.
>> Nam facere interdum velle et certare videntur.
>> Usqueadeo cupide Veneris compagibus haerent,
>> Membra voluptatis dum vi labefacta liquescunt.
>
> Haec Lucretius Epicureus. Quod etiam totum in se capere amatum amantes cupiant, Artemisia Mausoli regis Cariae uxor ostendit, quae supra affectionis

humanae fidem virum suum amavisse dicitur, eiusque defuncti corpus rede-
gisse in pulverem, et aquae inditum ebibisse.

[The Epicurean philosopher, Lucretius, the most unhappy of all lovers, perceived this very thing:

> Thus, therefore, he who receives wounds from the arrows of Venus,
> whether it is a boy with girlish limbs who shoots him or a woman send-
> ing out love from her whole body, tends thither whence he is wounded
> and longs to come together; and to send out the humor drawn from his
> body into its body. . . . They hungrily form a body, and join salivas, and
> pressing lips with teeth, they breathe from each others mouths, but in
> vain, since they can rub off nothing thence, nor penetrate and pass over
> into its body with the whole body, for they sometimes seem to wish and
> to be struggling to do this. They cling passionately in the couplings of
> Venus up to the point where their parts, violently shaken for a moment
> by the force of ecstasy, melt.

This is what Lucretius the Epicurean says. That lovers desire to take the
whole beloved into themselves Artemisia, the wife of King Mausolus of
Caria, also showed, who is said to have loved her husband beyond belief
of human affection and to have ground up his body, when he died, into a
powder, and to have drunk it, dissolved in water.] (*De amore* 7.6, text and
trans. Jayne)

After quoting at length from Lucretius's description of the *furor* of love as
a frantic attempt to "devour" the lover, Ficino reaches for the further example of Artemisia, who was said to have consumed her husband's ashes.
But rather than simply confirming Lucretius's point about love-madness
as a kind of regressive oral rage, Ficino's new example extends love-melancholy to include—to be, in fact—a response to excessive grief. Artemisia's
action shows not only that "lovers desire to take the whole beloved into
themselves" but also that such a desire arises from a refusal to accept the
loss or potential loss of the beloved. We might perceive in both her absorption of her husband's ashes and the lovers' struggles to "pass over into [the
beloved's] body with the whole body" a response to the continual threat
of absence posed by the beloved's very mortality noted in Leone Ebreo's
dialogue.[3] The erotic struggle truly is, then, as Ficino implies, a struggle
against death.

Ficino's discussion of melancholic love represents in a sense the culmination of the medico-literary tradition we have been studying, and it is fitting that while earlier medical writers seem aware of Lucretius' influence, Ficino takes on the poetic as well as the philosophical legacy of this text on love. He exploits the theoretical richness of the relation between desire and devouring in Lucretius's text, deepening the psychological resonance of this relation through the reference to Artemisia as the "tomb" of her husband. But although Ficino uses Lucretius's work as though it were congruent with his own theory of love, the vast philosophical differences between these two accounts of love continually make themselves felt—in the fracturing and altering of Lucretius's lines and in the evident unease with which Ficino presents some of Lucretius's recommendations. For while Lucretius's prescription for the madness of love is "frequent coitus" (quoted by Ficino at 7.11), Ficino's Platonizing text works precisely in the opposite direction, recommending the sublimation of sexual desire in favor of the kind of "abstraction" from the particular to the general that we examined earlier. The kind of madness that leads to coitus "sinks man back to the nature of beast" (7.12) and should be transformed into an energetic return to the "One itself." For Lucretius, on the other hand, sexual desire is not in itself troublesome, since it is a function of the body's natural processes. Love, however—that is, desire for a particular person—is the result of the mind's interference with the body's natural desires, and it is this *dira lubido* (dreadful craving, 4.1046) that produces the kind of madness he describes.[4] He therefore recommends frequent coitus with what he calls *volgivagaque Venere* (freely straying Venus, 4.1071) precisely to avoid fixating on any one person in particular.

The distinction between a problematic love (for a particular person) and a natural (unproblematic) sexual desire arises from an important Epicurean doctrine, the traces of which find their way into medieval and early modern discussions of love-melancholy. Because of the reach of this doctrine and the tension its influence creates in Ficino's text, I will briefly clarify its significance here. For Epicurus (and Lucretius) pleasures fall into two basic categories: katastematic pleasure and kinetic pleasure. Katastematic pleasures are the pleasures of the "steady state" and are both natural and necessary; they include eating when hungry, drinking when thirsty, and finding warmth when cold. Kinetic pleasures are pleasures of movement and include pleasures of sensation (such as sex); they are natural but not necessary. Epicurus did not object to indulgence in kinetic plea-sure, as long as such pleasure did not become necessary; for if one suddenly desires sexual pleasure only with one person, or wishes to eat only a certain kind of food, the desire has become an obsession, and obsessions are cre-ated by the mind's interference with perception of the real world.[5] Such de-sires are both unnatural and unnecessary, and unlike the true katastematic pleasures, they are infinite in their demands. Since no actual bodily need (such as hunger) is being met, the mind's idea that it is experiencing such a need necessitates disappointment and continuing, anguished desire.

Lucretius's treatment of this doctrine in relation to sexual love indi-cates—largely through the metaphor of devouring—that the obsession of love is born of the *mind's* conversion of a kinetic pleasure into a kataste-matic one. Thus it treats sexuality not as a kinetic pleasure that is dispens-able but as a necessary pleasure (like eating) without which the lover will perish. For Lucretius (as for the many medical writers who follow at least the gist of his doctrine), passionate sexual desire for a particular person will necessarily be an infinite, anguished craving that attempts to transform the beloved into an object of katastematic desire. In psychoanalytic terms, this form of sexual desire is "propped" on the vital function of feeding, and the "real" object—food—is displaced by a phantasmic one.[6] Lucretius's use of the image of devouring is thus grounded in a philosophical doctrine, and the significance of the lovers' *dira lubido* is that it represents the mental perversion of a natural, though not necessary, desire. He represents this perversion very precisely as the transformation of an intangible image (of the beloved) into a phantasmic form of food. Interestingly, the passage that makes this perversion clearest is precisely the passage that Ficino chooses to omit from his "devouring" passage: he begins with "sic igitur Veneris qui telis accipit ictus" (4.1052), picking up the description of frenzied devour-ing at 4.1108. Between the two passages that Ficino conflates is Lucretius's crucially important clarification of the lover's fundamental ontological er-ror:

> [N]amque in eo spes est, unde est ardoris origo,
> restingui quoque posse ab eodem corpore flammam.
> quod fieri contra totum natura repugnat,
> unaque res haec est, cuius quam plurima habemus,
> tam magis ardescit *dira cuppedine* pectus.

nam cibus atque umor membris adsumitur intus;
quae quoniam certas possunt obsidere partis,
hoc facile expletur laticum frugumque cupido.
ex hominis vero facie pulchroque colore
nil datur in corpus praeter simulacra fruendum
tenvia, quae vento spes raptat saepe misella . . .
sic in amore Venus simulacris ludit amantis.

[For their hope lies in this, that from the same body from which their hot passion arises, the flame can be extinguished. Nature protests that entirely the opposite happens, and this is the one thing of which however much we have, the more the breast grows inflamed with *dreadful desire.* For food and liquid are taken inside within the limbs, and since they can occupy definite parts, *the desire for fluids and bread is thereby easily fulfilled. But from the face and beautiful complexion of a human being nothing is passed into the body to be made use of except fine images, which pitiful hope often snatches . . .* So, in love, Venus mocks lovers with images.]

(*De rerum natura* 4.1086–1101, italics mine)

Lucretius is quite explicit about the analogy between obsessive focusing on the "tenuous image" (*tenvia simulacra*) and the ingestion of food. Unlike bread and fluid, the face of the beloved produces only illusory nourishment, the *simulacra* that provide the basis of sense perception but which cannot be in any physical sense ingested. Precisely because the desire for intercourse is a kinetic and not a katastematic desire, the obsessive pursuit of the fulfillment of this desire with a particular person will produce *dira cupido* (1090).[7] On this view, Artemisia's *dira cupido* for her dead husband may be interpreted precisely as an assertion that his continuing presence is both natural and necessary for her: her need for him has been converted into what Epicurus would call a katastematic desire.

Lucretius also identifies *simulacra* with the food of love (*pabula amoris*) in an earlier passage that finds its way into two Ficinian passages that tellingly—perhaps willfully—misread their Lucretian sources. The context of the first Lucretian quotation in Ficino's text illuminates a point of contact between his and Lucretius's psychophysiology of love that is also responsible, given the ideological crosscurrents between the two texts, for considerable tension around the quotation. A second quotation from this passage is sliced away and placed later in the seventh speech, just at the point when Ficino turns from his discussion of a Lucretian *insania amoris* toward the Platonic madness that is the dominant theme of the text as a whole. The Lucretian passage in question reads as follows in its original context:

> [H]aec Venus est nobis; hinc autemst nomen Amoris,
> *hinc illaec primum Veneris dulcedinis in cor*
> *stillavit gutta et successit frigida cura.*
> nam si abest quod ames, praesto simulacra tamen sunt
> illius et nomen dulce obversatur ad auris.
> *Sed fugitare decet simulacra et pabula amoris*
> *absterrere sibi atque alio convertere mentem*
> *et iacere umorem conlectum in corpora quaeque,*
> *nec retinere, semel conversum unius amore,*
> et servare sibi curam certumque dolorem.

> [This is "Venus" to us; from this furthermore comes the name of "Love," *from this that drop of Venus' sweetness first trickled into the heart and after rose chilly care.* For the object of your love is absent, yet images of it are present and its sweet name haunts your ears. *But it is proper to shun the images and banish from oneself the food of love and also to turn the mind elsewhere and cast the gathered liquid into any bodies whatsoever, not to hold it back, having once been turned by the love of one,* and store up care for oneself and certain pain.]

> (*De rerum natura* 4.1058–1067, italics mine)

Lucretius, aware of the power of *tenvia simulacra* to become the food of love (*pabulum amoris*) that will drive the lover to obsession, advises the lover to shun images of the beloved and simultaneously to seek sexual release elsewhere.

Ficino's use of the first italicized passage indicates an unexpected convergence between his and Lucretius's physiological theories of love. Discussing the power of the spirit to contaminate the lover's blood through the process of fascination we examined earlier, Ficino writes:

> Quia subtilis, celerrime congolat in praecordia, inde facillime per venas et arterias in corpus permanat universum. Quia calidus, vehementer agit et movet, et fortius senioris sanguineum inficit, eumque in suam convertit naturam, quod Lucretius ita tetigit:
>
> > *Hinc in te primum Veneris dulcedinis in cor*
> > *Stillavit gutta, et successit frigida cura.*

Praeterea quia dulcis, fovet viscera quoddamodo, *pascit* atque oblectat.
[Because it (i.e., the spirit) is thin, it flies into the heart very quickly. From
there through the veins and arteries it easily spreads throughout the whole
body. Because it is warm, it acts and moves vigorously, it infects the blood
of the older man very powerfully, and changes it into its own nature. This
Lucretius touches on thus:

> *"Hence first that drop of Venus' honey distilled in your heart, and then came
> freezing pain."*

Moreover, because it is sweet, it comforts the viscera in some way; *it feeds*,
and pleases them.] (*De amore* 7.5, italics mine)

The work of the *simulacra* in Lucretius's discourse and the work of the
phantasms engraved on the spirit in Ficino's discourse turn out to be remarkably similar.[8] For Lucretius, *simulacrum* is a key technical term, indicating images created by the coalescence of invisible particles thrown off
by objects in the world. These images are responsible, as Robert Brown
argues, for the human capacity to perceive objects: "[T]ravelling at lightning speed in a constant succession these 'images' strike the eye when it
faces their direction and create in it a presentation (*phantasia*) by a quasi-
cinematographic effect."[9] As I have suggested, it is not the *simulacra* per
se, but rather the mind's distortion of their meaning that is responsible
for error: "[H]erein Epicurean empiricism is almost diametrically opposed
to Platonic idealism, with its distrust of the senses and elevation of intuitive intellect."[10] Ficino's absorption of a Lucretian passage on the power of
simulacra to enter the mind into his own description of the spirits' penetration of the lover's mind represents thus an extraordinary conflation of
anti-Platonic and Platonic material.[11] Ficino's Lucretianized theory of the
phantastic spirits does in fact reveal the phantasm as a highly complex link
not only between Aristotle and neo-Stoic writers like Synesius but also
between a Neoplatonic theory of mind and an empirical, materialist one.
In both Lucretius and Ficino, the phantastic spirit/*simulacrum* draws the
lover into a desiring relation with another by penetrating the lover's mind,
overthrowing as it does so the ontological security of the mind. It is thus
when Ficino describes the dissipation of the lover's self as a result of his
"infection" by the other's spirits that he reaches for Lucretian *simulacra*.

The second of these italicized passages appears toward the end of the seventh speech, as Ficino prepares to leave the medicalized treatment of love-madness behind. Immediately following the Lucretian lines about shunning images and removing oneself from the food of love, Ficino writes:

> Sed ne diutius de insania loquentes insaniamus, sic brevibus concludamus. Insaniae species quaedam est anxia illa sollicitudo, qua vulgares amantes diu nocteque vexantur, qui amore durante bilis incendio primum, deinde atrae bilis adustione afflicti, in furias, ignemque ruunt, et quasi caeci quo praecipitentur ignorant. . . . Hoc itaque furore homo in bestiae naturam devolvitur.
>
> Divino autem furore super hominis naturam erigitur, et in Deum transit.
>
> [But lest we go mad talking further about madness, let us conclude briefly thus. That anxious care by which vulgar lovers are vexed day and night is a certain species of madness. As long as the love lasts, they are afflicted first by the burning of the bile, then by the burning of the black bile, and they rush into frenzies and fire, and as if blind do not know where they are being precipitated. . . . Thus by this madness man sinks back to the nature of beast.
>
> But by the divine madness he is raised above the nature of man and passes into a god.] (*De amore* 7.12–13)

Indicating his discomfort with the Lucretian passage he has just quoted ("but lest we go mad talking about madness"), Ficino begins to convert the *insania amoris* of the medical tradition back into the Platonic eros that provides access to the divine. The movement to the divine One is a movement away from the material (the multiplicity of the body) toward the immaterial (the unity of the divine Mind): "[I]t [our soul] falls, I say, when it departs from that purity in which it is born, *embracing the body too long*."[12] It is precisely the conversion of the desire for contemplation into a desire for a literal embrace that Ficino earlier (6.9) characterizes as the cause of melancholic love; that conversion is here associated with the material "images" of love that must be set aside. But Lucretius's point is hardly that the lover should turn from the material to the immaterial: he is advocating a turn away from the particular beloved to "any bodies whatsoever."

Ficino has thus ingeniously converted his Lucretian source in order to force it into a relentlessly Platonizing theory. Lucretius advocates a rejection of devotion to a *particular* body (since this constitutes for him an obsession), and Ficino uses this advice in support of a Platonic turn away from the particular *body* toward the unity of the divine Mind. While Lucretius recommends a turn from the loved one to *volgivagaque Venere* (freely straying Venus), Ficino recommends a turn from the loved one to the One itself. Ficino does not merely advocate a banishment of the phantasmic *simulacra* then; he recommends a sublimation of them by means of the Avicennian process of *denudatio* that we examined earlier. It is precisely a failure to sublimate these images that leads to what Ficino views as the excessive grief of Artemisia, who cannot accept that her husband is merely an image of the "innate Idea of humanity" (6.6) and thus dispensable as an individual beloved.[13] Her devouring of her husband's ashes dramatizes a refusal to sublimate desire for the particular and thus demonstrates the adherence of melancholic love to the body. It constitutes for Ficino a "fall" from sight (contemplation) to touch (the embrace of the body): "Verus enim amor nihil est aliud quam nixus quidam ad divinam pulchritudinem evolandi ab aspectu corporalis pulchritudinis excitatus. Adulterinus autem, ab aspectu in tactum praecipitatio" (For true love is nothing other than a certain effort of flying up to divine beauty, aroused by the sight of corporeal beauty. But adulterous love is a falling down from sight to touch, *De amore* 7.15).

The Secret Wound

Three central issues emerge from Ficino's densely intertextual theory of love: the (latent) connection between excessive love and a refusal to accept the loss or death of the beloved; the regressive "orality" of Lucretian/Ficinian love-madness; and the role of *simulacra*/phantastic spirits in destabilizing the lover. Lucretius brilliantly uses the literary image of the hidden or secret wound to knit together these issues in his text. When Ficino imports this image into his own text, it helps to activate a further elaboration of the submerged relation between *simulacra* and the phantastic spirits while simultaneously throwing into starker relief the philosophical distance between his text and his classical source. Though Lucretius does not provide a clear causal account of what causes the wound of love, his intent to provide a grisly literalization of Hellenistic love conceits is clear. The source of this wound in Lucretius's text is implied by the metaphorical connection between the *simulacrum* as *pabula amoris* and the inner wound that worsens through "nourishment":

> [S]ed fugitare decet simulacra et pabula amoris
> absterrere sibi. . . .
> ulcus enim vivescit et inveterascit alendo,
> inque dies gliscit furor atque aerumna gravescit.

[But it is proper to shun the images and banish from oneself the food of love. . . . For the sore quickens and sets through nourishment, and from day to day derangement waxes and the affliction grows worse.]

(*De rerum natura* 4.1063–69)

> [I]nde redit rabies eadem et furor ille revisit,
> cum sibi quid cupiant ipsi contingere quaerunt
> nec reperire malum id possunt quae machina vincat:
> *usque adeo incerti tabescunt volnere caeco.*

[Then the same frenzy returns and back comes that derangement, when they seek for what it is they really desire to attain for themselves and cannot discover what contrivance will conquer the ill: *in such uncertainty do they waste away with an unseen wound.*]

(4.1115–20, italics mine)

The result of erotic obsession, or so this passage implies, is a potentially fatal sapping of energy and vitality through the psychic breach created by a futile dependence on empty images.

It is, significantly, when Ficino describes the dissipation of the lover's "self" as a result of his infection by the other's spirits that he reaches for the Lucretian figure of the "secret wound." The figure in its new context is glossed in terms of Ficino's own theory of fascination; thus the thinness and warmth of the invading spirits borne through the eye wound the lover from within:

> Illa quippe viscera dividit et discerpit; hic homini quod suum est aufert,
> et in alterius mutat naturam per quam sane mutationem eum in se quies-
> cere non permittit, sed ad eum semper, a quo infectus est trahit. Hoc ita
> Lucretius innuit:
>> Idque petit mens unde est saucia amore.
>> Namque omnes plerumque cadunt in vulnus, et illam
>> Emicat in partem sanguis unde icimur ictu.
>> Et si comminus est, hostem rubor occupat humor.

> In his carminibus Lucretius non aliter vult sanguinem hominis oculorum
> radio vulnerati in vulnerantem prolabi, quam hominis gladio caesi sanguis
> prolabitur in caedentem.

[Certainly the former [the thinness of the spirits] divides and plucks to pieces the viscera; the latter [the warmth of the spirits] takes away from the man that which is his own and changes it into the nature of the other, through which change clearly it does not permit him to rest in himself, but always draws him toward the person by whom he has been infected. This Lucretius hinted at thus:

> And the body seeks that whence the mind is wounded by love, for we all fall for the most part toward the wound, and the blood spurts out in the direction whence we are struck by the blow; and if he is nearby, the red humour seizes the enemy.

In these verses Lucretius can only mean that the blood of a man wounded by a ray of the eyes flows forward into the wounder, just as the blood of a man slain with a sword flows onto the slayer.] (*De amore*, 7.5)

Ficino develops what in Lucretius is a parodic literalization of the Hellenistic "wound of love" into a serious piece of his theory of fascination. In Lucretius's text, the "literal" wound becomes a figurative site for the exchange of body fluids in a ghastly parody of sexual intercourse. In Ficino's text, the figurative depiction of intercourse is submerged beneath an analysis of the wound as a more or less literal locus of ocular "infection." In both texts, however, the wound is the quasi-physical, quasi-psychological point at which the boundaries of the lover's "self" are breached. For Ficino, the wound marks a point of infection by the invisible, yet material spirits of the beloved other, drawing the spirits of the lover toward the beloved and draining him of his inner vitality. For Lucretius, the wound is even more clearly a site of illness, both physical and mental; it is an inward sore, much like the one that troubles Britomart after her vision of Arthegall: "[A]ll mine entrailes flow with poysnous gore, / And th'ulcer groweth daily more and more; / Ne can my running sore find remedie" (*Faerie Queene* 3.2.39).

The *vulnus caecum*, the blind or secret wound, is a crucial point of contact between literary and medical writings on love, as well as the point of contact between physical and psychological responses to love. François Valleriola's 1588 *Observationum Medicinalium libri VI* is explicitly a medical text, framing its discussion of melancholic love with a description of an actual case study. Yet Valleriola's close reading of Ficino's account of the Lucretian "wound" of love allows him to discern the occluded *poetic*

sources that may well mediate Ficino's reading of Lucretius. In the following Ficinian passage, Valleriola rightly hears an echo of Virgil's description
of Dido, wounded by a fierce love for Aeneas:

> Inquietudo quoque amantium tandiu necessario perseverat, quandiu infec-
> tio illa sanguinis per fascinationem iniecta visceribus permanens *gravi cor
> premit cura. Vulnus alit venis: caecis membra flammis adurit.*

> [Also the disquiet of lovers necessarily lasts as long as that infection of the
> blood, injected into the viscera through fascination, lasts; *it presses the heart
> with heavy care, feeds the wound through the veins, and burns the members
> with unseen flames.*] (*De amore* 7.11, italics mine)

Valleriola hears in the italicized passages a reference to the crucial Virgilian
passages depicting Dido's deadly madness: "Hoc lepido carmine summus
poetarum / Virgilius ad hunc modum expressit: At regina gravi iamdudum
saucia cura, / Vulnus alit venis, et caeco carpitur igni" (The great poet
Virgil expresses this in this way in his beautiful song: But the queen for a
long time now wounded by a deep care, nourishes the wound in her veins,
and is worn away by a hidden fire). For Valleriola, Virgil is describing
an instance of Ficinian fascination ("et paulo post, fascinationis ab amore
modu explicans").[14] Though this medico-poetic intertextuality had always
been a feature of writing on love-melancholy, the tendency to work poetic
exempla seamlessly into a "scientific" discussion is more marked in early
modern treatises.[15] Valleriola's perceptive reading of Ficino returns us to
Virgil's depiction of a love-crazed Dido that is influenced by Lucretius's
medicalized analysis of love and also exerts in its turn a significant influence on a succession of wounded lovers in both medical and poetic contexts. Perhaps the clearest instance of a fusion of the two contexts occurs in
Petrarch's self-portrait as a wounded Dido in his analysis of his deadly *atra
voluptas* in the *Secretum*: "fugi enim, sed malum meum ubique circumferens" (I fled, but carried my wound with me everywhere).[16]

Ficino's development of the ontological implications of the "secret
wound" orients his theory of melancholic love toward a fuller examination of the lover's unconscious drives. If for Lucretius the lover is deluded
by a vain conflation of katastematic and kinetic desire (the need to eat
and the erotic desire to join with the beloved), Ficino actually interprets
the unseen wound as a kind of devouring mouth. Although he omits the

passage from *De rerum natura* in which the images of the beloved are compared to empty images of food, he goes on to compare the insane lover to Artemisia, who devoured her husband's ashes. In Artemisia, then, the hidden wound takes on its full significance: her literal consumption of her husband's ashes through her mouth brings to its logical end the Lucretian identification of melancholic love (or *insania amoris*) and eating. The story of Artemisia seems to dramatize the culmination of a fantasy of *fusion* that is already present—though continually frustrated—in Lucretius's text. This conception of fusion seems to draw on the technical Stoic use of the term. Of the different kinds of mixture discussed by Chrysippus—fusion, blending, and mixture—fusion denotes the destruction of each individual substance in the process of producing a new body.[17] Although for the Stoics body and soul were blended rather than fused, food that is taken into the body is clearly fused with the body: it may not be separated from the body once digestion has taken place. Thus sexual union is fantasized not as a temporary juxtaposition of ontologically separate persons but as the permanent fusion of these persons in the creation of a new body. The inevitable failure of this fantasy in the face of the separateness of the beloved produces the madness and despair of which Lucretius speaks. For the Lucretian lover paradoxically desires the Other to such an excess that his or her irreducible Otherness represents an intolerable barrier to the desired oneness. As Martha Nussbaum aptly remarks, within the force field of Lucretian *furor* the Other virtually disappears, "becoming merely a vehicle for the lover's personal wish and, at the same time, *a permanent obstacle to its fulfillment.*"[18] Ficino's use of the story of Artemisia highlights what is at stake in the fantasy of fusion that lies behind love-melancholy. Her literal attempt to "fuse" her body with her husband's transforms the figurative "food of love" into a literal kind of food, but at the cost of turning love into a form of cannibalism.

"Some Precious Thing": Mourning and Melancholia in Psychoanalysis[19]

The image of the "secret wound" also establishes a coincidental but telling link between this classical tradition and psychoanalytic theory. Freud uses (twice) the figure of a wound to indicate just the kind of internal leakage described by Lucretius (*tabescunt volnere caeco*). "The complex of melancholia behaves like an open wound, drawing to itself cathectic energy from all sides (which we have called in the transference neuroses 'anti-cathexes') and draining the ego until it is utterly depleted."[20] The wound, to put Freud's point another way, figures an internal *psychomachia* resulting from the ego's dangerous absorption of the object: "Now the analysis of melancholia shows that the ego can kill itself only when, the object-cathexis having been withdrawn upon it, it can treat itself as an object."[21] While the medieval medical writers speak of *amor dominalis* as a love that ruthlessly subjugates the soul to the internalized object, Freud similarly sees the destructive aspects of melancholia in terms of the object's power to overwhelm the ego: "In the two contrasting situations of intense love and of suicide the ego *is overwhelmed by the object*, though in totally different ways."[22]

Without overlooking the important theoretical differences between the medieval/early modern discourse of spirit and phantasm and contemporary psychoanalytic accounts of self, I would like to turn now to Freud and other modern writers on melancholia, to explore the implications of Ficino's sophisticated theory of melancholic love. Ficino's association of the story of Artemisia's devouring of her husband's dead body with Lucretius's vivid portrait of the lover attempting to devour the beloved marks a crucial stage in the theorizing of love-melancholy. For obsessive love, love that derives its relentlessness from the inscription of a phantasm within the imaginative power of the mind, is now understood as what Freud calls in "On Transience" a "revolt against mourning."[23] In this essay Freud describes taking a walk with two companions (one of whom is a young poet) through a beautiful landscape. To Freud's surprise, his companions fail to delight in its beauty because that beauty is transient: "The idea that all this beauty was transient was giving these two sensitive minds a foretaste of mourning over its decease."[24] The melancholic attitude of these two "sensitive minds" points to the very instability of the love object that undermines for Leone Ebreo the hitherto central distinction between love and desire. All love is really desire, because the love object—as a mortal being—already contains the threat of its absence and decay.

In his later essay "Mourning and Melancholia" (1917), Freud sketches out a theoretical distinction between mourning and melancholia; this distinction, though slippery, is useful, and worth a brief summary.[25] Mourning is a teleological process undertaken by the mind "in reaction to the loss of a loved person, or to the loss of some abstraction which has taken the place of one, such as fatherland, liberty, an ideal, and so on."[26] Melancholia, on the other hand, is a more complex response to an uncertain kind of loss: "[M]elancholia is in some way related to an unconscious loss of a love-object, in contradistinction to mourning, in which there is nothing unconscious about the loss."[27] Freud later suggests that the mysterious aspects of melancholia may be due at least in part to "a regression from one type of object-choice to the primal narcissism."[28] Thus the loss of the object does not result in the ordinary process of mourning, but rather promotes an internalization of the lost object as part of the self: "[T]he result [of some form of loss] was not the normal one of withdrawal of the libido from this object and transference of it to a new one. . . . [T]he free libido . . . served simply to establish an identification of the ego with the abandoned object."[29] The defensive posture of identification would seem to ally the illness of melancholia with the trajectory of a failed Oedipal resolution, in which the (male) child identifies with an internalized maternal object rather than renouncing the mother as a love object and intensifying his identification with his father.[30]

Elsewhere, however, Freud takes a different view of this process. He recognizes this "melancholic" process of loss and identification within the ego as basic to psychic formation from the very beginning.[31] The infant's earliest experience of the world is one of loss, as a previously undifferentiated relation to another (usually the mother) gradually gives way to a recognition of a distinctly existing other. To negotiate this loss, the child internalizes the object via a process of narcissistic identification that ushers in an increasingly complex "self" where none had previously existed: "[T]he character of the ego is a precipitate of abandoned object-investments."[32] Commenting on Freud's theory of the origin of psychic structure, Jonathan Lear clarifies what is at stake in the child's relation to the earliest love-object, the mother: "The infant takes in his mother along with his mother's milk. Because the newborn infant is libidinally attached to the world primarily through his mouth, he fantasizes orally incorporating the loved object. . . . I do not reflect the world, I devour it."[33] As I shall discuss in more detail later, the concept of "incorporation" has a specific technical meaning in recent psychoanalytic writing. But it is already clear that the model of primitive identification as an attempt to "devour" the mother helps to explain the instability of ego formation in general—an instability reflected in Freud's theoretical unclarity regarding the distinction between a dangerously polarized melancholic state and the accommodation of loss constitutive of selfhood. For as Freud acknowledges, even later, more sophisticated forms of elegiac identification with a lost object involve a regression to a more primitive oral phase:

> When it happens that a person has to give up a sexual object, there quite often ensues an alteration of his ego which can only be described as a setting up of the object inside the ego, as it occurs in melancholia; the exact nature of this substitution is as yet unknown to us. It may be that by this introjection, which is a kind of regression to the mechanism of the oral phase, the ego makes it easier for the object to be given up or renders that process possible. It may be that this identification is the sole condition under which the id can give up its objects.[34]

Though, of course, neither Lucretius nor Ficino is working within a theoretical framework comparable to Freud's, both writers describe love-melancholy in terms of a furious (seemingly uncontrollable) desire to devour the beloved. This recurring topos implies that love-melancholy represents a return to a more primitive psychic state in which literal devouring and identification are indistinguishable, and in which the object, imperfectly differentiated from the self, has adopted the position of a maternal figure.[35] Indeed, Freud's observation that this kind of regressive identification may be the *only* way in which the id can give up its objects complicates our understanding of the Oedipus complex, in which the male child must renounce his claim on his mother as love-object.[36] For although he claims that in the "normal" resolution of the Oedipus complex for the boy "an intensification of his identification with his father" occurs, the internalization of the mother would in fact seem to be a necessary condition of his renunciation of her.[37]

For Freud, then—as for Ficino—the transformation of the self via the internalization of the other may in different circumstances promote either greater psychic structure or increasing fragmentation and even degradation.[38] Freud calls the successful transformation of erotic drives into psychic structure "sublimation," a theoretical move that clarifies the affinity between Freud's conception of the effects of eros on psychic development and Ficino's Platonic theory of (divine) love as a progressive dematerialization of the object.[39] Although Freud does not explicitly work through his account of the early "melancholic" or "mourning" phase and later pathological variants on it, it seems to be the case that the truly melancholic position arises from an identification that promotes psychic *tension* rather than integration. In a "good-enough" environment, the infant's absorption (via identification) of the loved object promotes the sublimation of painful feelings of loss and greater individuation in the subject; as Lear puts it, "I become I in response to the fact that there is a separate world that is not identical with me."[40] In the kind of pathological melancholy Freud describes in "Mourning and Melancholia," however, the internalized object retains a host of unmetabolized affects (notably, of course, a hatred of the object) that polarize and split the psyche, creating the self-hatred Freud diagnoses as characteristic of the disease.

Abraham and Torok deploy a useful distinction (borrowed from Ferenczi) between *introjection* and *incorporation* to clarify what is at stake in such melancholic polarization.[41] Although Freud does not distinguish between the two terms, Ferenczi maintains that in "introjection" there exists an "extension of autoerotic instincts" onto external objects, which are then included within the ego.[42] Introjection thereby introduces into consciousness drives that are mediated by the object. It is not, then, as Abraham and Torok observe, so much the *object* as the drives activated by the object that are introjected.[43] Incorporation, by contrast, occurs when the loved object is lost—either through actual death or through estrangement, separation, and so on—"before the desires concerning the object might have been freed."[44] Incorporation thus arises from a need to "recover, in secret and through magic, an object that, for one reason or another, evaded its own function: mediating the introjection of desires."[45] Because the desires surrounding the object are not absorbed or introjected into the ego, the ego develops a hidden fixation on an object that can never be fully mourned. The object retains its otherness from within what Torok and Abraham call the psychic tomb or "crypt" that holds the unconscious secret of the subject's distress.[46] Because the lost object did not fulfill its role as the mediator of desire, those early "instinctual promptings" never become desires and thus never receive "a name and the right to exist . . . in the objectal sphere."[47] The unmediated desires remain unnamed and un-nameable.

Unlike incorporation, introjection is intimately tied to referential lan-guage: instead of possessing the lost object, say the mother, the subject speaks the mother's name, recognizing as she does so the absence of the object. For Kristeva language is always an effort of translation predicated on the acceptance of loss: "To transpose corresponds to the Greek *meta-phorein*, to transport; language is, from the start, a translation, but on a level that is heterogeneous to the one where affective loss, renunciation, or the break takes place. If I did not agree to lose mother, I could neither imagine nor name her."[48] For both Kristeva and Abraham, the earliest re-sponses to deprivation prepare the way for later, more complex attitudes toward loss. Thus the child's cries and sobs are signs that she is "learning to fill the emptiness of the mouth with words. . . . [This is] the initial model for introjection."[49] Since words—or cries—replace food in the absence of the mother, it is not surprising to find that a *refusal* to accept loss is linked to a fantasy of devouring that displaces language. The metaphorical trans-lation of food into words is replaced by a fantasy of literal devouring; this fantasy is noted as a basis of the melancholic position by Kristeva: "Better fragmented, torn, cut up, swallowed, digested . . . than lost. The mel-ancholy cannibalistic imagination undertakes a repudiation of the loss's reality and of death as well."[50] The rejection of language thus constitutes a refusal of the symbolic process of substitution and displacement that promotes a *mournful* rather than a melancholic relation to a lost object.[51] Rather than "agree[ing] to lose mother," the melancholic person becomes estranged from language itself: "[M]elancholy persons are foreigners in their maternal tongue. They have lost the meaning—the value—of their mother tongue for want of losing the mother."[52] The fantasy of devouring the beloved (m)other, then, is a symptom precisely of a fixation that pre-vents the introjection of loss. In Lacanian terms, such a fixation prevents the introjection of the "*relation* between a named object and a system of named objects."[53] If such an introjection cannot take place, the subject remains within the realm of what Lacan calls the Imaginary, the dyadic, mirroring relationship with the mother's image in which the self is not fully distinct from the other.[54]

The notion that melancholic love is born of a "revolt against mourning" of the most primitive kind, a fantasized fusion with the mother, is borne out not only from the vantage point of contemporary psychoanalysis but also by accounts of the tradition in the early medical texts. We might recall Du Laurens's telling description of the lover's obsession with the "speciall object" of his affection: "[T]hey invent continually some one or other strange imagination, and have in a maner all of them one speciall object, *from which they cannot be weined* till time has worne it out."[55] There is also a persistent association—never fully theorized—between love-melancholy and an incestuous longing for the mother in many anecdotal accounts of excessive love in classical sources. Of these anecdotal reports, possibly the most popular is the story of Antiochus, son of King Seleucis, who is "overwhelmed by an infinite love" for his stepmother, Stratonice:

> [O]ut of reverence for his father, he hid the merciless wound in his heart, though he knew of the danger in that fire that consumed him. His heart enclosed the different effects; his boundless desire and his deep bashfulness reduced his body to a state of extreme sickness.[56]

This story, told by Plutarch, Valerius Maximus, and a host of other writers, illustrates the skill of Erasistratus, who, observing the young man's behavioral signs (blushing, pallor, rapid breathing) when Stratonice entered the room, diagnosed his young patient's mysterious illness without difficulty. Noting the persistence of this Oedipal drama in the medical literature of the period, Mary Wack persuasively concludes that "whether carnal or spiritual, these instances of love-madness and its somatic manifestations seem to express . . . a deep desire for an all-powerful, sovereign, nourishing 'other' who corresponds to the image of the mother from the earliest stages of psychological development."[57]

Gail Kern Paster's work on the practice of sending children out to wet nurses after birth during the early modern period provides important cultural information about the conditions that might have contributed to the apparent prevalence of the "disease" of love-melancholy during this period.[58] In fact, her reading of Leontes' inexplicable madness in *The Winter's Tale* is remarkably pertinent to any discussion of the sexualization of the child-mother relation in the form of a kind of madness: "The play enacts a narrative that roots the infant's trauma—its rage and oral deprivation—in its father's own infantile rage and jealous desire for a place near the maternal body."[59] The symptoms of love-melancholy also seem to be covertly linked to a kind of internalized maternal lack: bodily wasting suggests a fantasized "oral deprivation" that helps at one level to explain the "oral rage" of Lucretius's and Ficino's lovers.[60] Lucretius's focus on the deceptive "propping" of erotic desire on earlier oral desires therefore might seem to indicate a proto-psychoanalytic conception of the erotic object as a phantasmic version of the lost "sovereign, nourishing 'other.'" Theresa Krier's analysis of the cultural function of images of maternity in a wide variety of poetic and psychoanalytic texts broadens Wack's and Paster's historical claims, using terms that intersect usefully with mine: "Trapped in the melancholia of unperformed mourning for a fusion that we do not allow ourselves to know we have never exactly had, we consign ourselves to the pathos of nostalgia for an idealized home."[61] It is precisely this "nostalgia" for an impossible unity with a fantasized mother that subtends the development of love-melancholy in the texts studied in this book, even when the maternal nature of the object is occluded. In these medical and poetic contexts, the lover is unable to perform the "work of mourning, which relies on naming birth adequately," but instead searches insistently for an "idealized home" in the body of the Other.[62]

The Song of Orpheus: Love-Melancholy and Poetic Voice

Two related issues emerge in this psychoanalytic interpretation that provide a useful lens through which to read the medieval and early modern accounts of the relation between "voice" and love-melancholy. Kristeva and others emphasize both the centrality of a lost but inadequately mourned maternal figure in the psychic landscape of melancholia and the strange alienation of the melancholic from his or her own language. A failure to acknowledge the loss of, or necessary separation from, the mother conduces to a linguistic blockage that bars the subject from the realm of social language. This psychoanalytic account of melancholic language helps us piece together the discrete strands of a latent theory of voice in the medical tradition that centrally informs my reading of Petrarch's influential aesthetics of *atra voluptas*.

Many discussions of the *signa* or symptoms of love-melancholy focus on the lover's bizarre—and bizarrely regressive—relation to language.

Gerard of Berry, for instance, notes that the lover seems not to understand any discourse unless it pertains to the beloved:

> Ex parte anime sunt profunde cogitationes et sollicitudines, ut si aliquis de aliquo loquatur, vix intelliget, si autem de eodem, statim movetur.

> [From the soul's part are depressed thoughts and worries, so that if someone talks about something, [the patient] scarcely understands; if, however, he speaks of the beloved, he is immediately moved.][63]

The lover's "depressed thoughts and worries" block his access to ordinary discourse, narrowing his linguistic field to speech about the beloved; such speech has an immediate affective power ("he is immediately moved"). Wack notes suggestively that Hugh of St. Cher lifts this passage almost verbatim from Gerard's commentary and places it in a devotional context; mystical rapture, according to Hugh, also deprives the subject of "ordinary" language *about things that concern men* ("de hiis que inter homines fiunt"):

> [S]extum signum amoris extatici est profunda cogitatio et sollicitudo versa ad interiora, ita quod talis amorosus gerere videtur ymaginem dormientis qui evigilari non potest nisi cum de re amata fit ei mentio. Unde si cum amoroso *loquaris de hiis que inter homines fiunt, que ad rem amatam non pertinent, vix intelligere potest.* Si autem de re amata vel quod ad rem ama-tam aliquo modo pertineat statim intelligit et evigilantis gerit ymaginem eo quod tota intentio et cogitatio sua fixa est in re amata.

> [The sixth sign of ecstatic love is profound thought and worry turned in-ward, so that such a lover acts like a sleeper who cannot be awakened except by mention of the beloved. *Therefore, if you speak with the lover about those things that occupy men [lit. happen among men], which do not pertain to the beloved, he can scarcely understand you.* If however, it pertains in some way to the beloved, he at once understands and bears a wakeful aspect in that his whole attention and thought are fixed on the beloved.][64]

The analogy between mystical rapture and lovesickness suggested by Hugh's appropriation of Gerard's language indicates once again that lovesickness is a subversion of spiritual desire, an obsessive attachment to a mortal ob-ject rather than a divine one. This inappropriate attachment of an infinite desire has repercussions for the capacity of the lover to engage in ordinary discourse or, in psychoanalytic terms, fully to enter the symbolic order.

For the mediating role of language as a symbolic system is interrupted by erotic fixation. The only language that rouses the *amorosus* is the language that *pertains to* the beloved: the *res amata* is the signified of all discourse that is not impertinent—that is, nonsensical—to the lover. But whereas the silence of the divine lover in Hugh's discourse indicates a removal from "things that concern men" to the divine object of worship, the silence of the melancholic lover denotes a continuing fixation on a mortal beloved who has become an internalized, phantasmic figure.

In Bernard of Gordon's compendious treatment of the *signa amoris*, this *discours amoureux* is identified with *song*—with love lyric, in fact:

> [H]abent cogitationes ocultas et profundas cum suspiriis luctuosis. et si audiant cantillenas de separatione amoris statim incipiunt flere et tristari. et si audiant de coniunctione amoris statim incipiunt ridere et cantare.

> [They have hidden and depressed thoughts accompanied by melancholy sighs. And if they hear songs about the separation of love [sc. lovers] at once they begin to weep and become sad. And if they hear songs about the re-union of lovers they at once begin to laugh and to sing.][65]

Crucially, the songs that replace ordinary language are associated with an outpouring of nonverbal emotion in the lover: he weeps, laughs, and sings. Nearly two hundred years after the publication of *Lilium Medicinae* (1305), Robert Burton also insists on the affective plenitude suggested by the lover's wordless expressions: "sighing, sobbing and lamenting" comprise the universal language of love-melancholy.[66]

In light of the persistence in the medical literature of an intriguing connection between the lover's alienation from ordinary language, on the one hand, and his or her susceptibility to the powers of song, on the other, we should look more closely at the exact nature of this relationship between love-melancholy and language. What property do these songs have that they assuage the particular psychosomatic suffering of lovesickness? Constantine's *Viaticum* contains a helpful reflection on the subject:

> Quod melius eriosos adiuvat ne in cogitationes profundentur nimias: vinum est temperatum et odoriferum dandum *et audire genera musicorum*; colloqui dilectissimis amicis; *versus recitatio* . . . item Rufus: Non solum modo vinum temperate ebibitum aufert tristiciam, sed et alia quidem sibi similia, sicut balneum temperatum. unde fit ut cum quidam balneum ingrediantur

ad cantandum *animantur. Quidam ergo philosophi dicunt sonitum esse quasi spiritum, vinum quasi corpus, quorum alterum ab altero adiuvatur.* dicunt alii quod Orpheus dixit: Imperatores ad convivia me invitant ut ex me se delectent; ego condelector ex ipsis. Cum quo velim animos eorum flectere possim, sicut de ira ad mansuetudinem, de tristicia ad leticiam, de avaricia ad largitatem, de timore in audaciam. Hec est ordinatio organicorum muricorum atque vini circa sanitatem anime.

[What better helps erotic lovers so that they do not sink into excessive thoughts: temperate and fragrant wine is to be given; *listening to music,* conversing with dearest friends; *recitation of poetry.* . . . Again, Rufus [says]: "Not only wine, temperately drunk, relieves sadness, but indeed other similar things, like a temperate bath." Thus it happens that when certain people enter a bath they are *moved to sing. Therefore certain philosophers say that sound is like the spirit and wine like the body, each of which is aided by the other.* Others say that Orpheus said: "Emperors invite me to banquets so that they may take pleasure in me, [but] I delight equally in them; as I wish I am able to bend their spirits from anger to mildness, from sadness to joy, from avarice to liberality, from fear to boldness." This is the regulation of music and wine for the health of the spirit.][67]

Fluids—wine and water—and various kinds of voiced utterances—song, verses, speech—together permit the regulation (*ordinatio*) of the health of the soul (*circa sanitatem anime*). The tempering of the body through the addition of fluid to an excessively dry temperament in turn tempers the spirit: the modifiers *temperate* and *temperatum* emphasize that the aim of health in matters erotic is a balance between extremes of both body and mind.[68] The vehicle of the *ordinatio* of the soul is the spirit, which as we have seen mediates between mind and body. In Constantine's telling example, the soothing of the body through temperate baths produces a kind of somatic inspiration (*ad cantandum animantur*). Just as the pneumatic capacity of wine gives it its characteristic froth and its special power to energize the drinker, so the pneumatic effect of song helps to soothe and regulate the body.

It is striking, then, that the sign of the temperateness of body and soul is a *spiritual effect* arising from the harmonious blending of body and soul: the human voice. The body is like wine, Constantine writes, and wine (like melancholy), as we discovered in *Problem 30*, is a highly pneumatic (or spiritual) substance: "Now wine too has the quality of generating air, so wine and the melancholy temperament are of a similar nature. The froth which forms on wine shows that it generates air."[69] The analogy suggests that the melancholic body, like wine, produces excess pneuma that must be expelled; the by-product of an increase of melancholy in the body may be song, whose production in turn helps to return the body to a temperate state. As Aristotle argues elsewhere, the voice actually contributes to the body's regulation: "Nature employs the breath (pneuma) both as an indispensable means to the regulation of inner temperature of the living body and also as the matter of articulate voice, *in the interests of its possessor's well-being*" (*De anima* 2.8.420.20, italics mine).[70] The recitation of verses by another speaker ("versus recitatio," l. 36) is presumably effective because—as Bernard's text suggests—songs of the right kind draw the lover himself into emotional expressions that may include singing.

The voice itself, in Aristotle's theory, is the product of an inclusive process involving air (pneuma), soul, and the phantasm; only when all three elements are present can *voice* emerge:

> Voice is a kind of sound characteristic of what has soul in it; nothing that is without soul utters voice. (*De anima* 2.8.420.5)

> Voice then is the impact of the inbreathed air against the wind-pipe, and the agent that produces the impact is the soul resident in these parts of the body. Not every sound, as we have said, made by an animal is voice (even with the tongue we may merely make a sound which is not voice, or without the tongue as in coughing); what produces the impact must have soul in it and must be accompanied by an *act of imagination* [i.e., the production of a phantasm], for *voice is a sound with a meaning*. (*De anima* 2.8.420.28–34, italics mine)[71]

Voice is a sound with meaning that bears, as it were, the imprint of a soul and is made up of *pneuma* (the "matter of articulate voice"). The vehicle for this imprint of the soul is presumably the phantasm, which accompanies the pneumatic production of *voice* as opposed to mere noise. As Bruce Smith has shown, Aristotle's distinction between "voice" as meaningful sound and other kinds of "noise" remained important yet shaky for early modern writers.[72] Helkiah Crooke observes that the voice may easily slide back into a mere sound that "expresseth onelie those things that fall under Sense," and it is intuitively plausible that song and poetry might occupy a particularly slippery location on the continuum between true voice and "noise." For although poetry and song have cognitive content, it is content that eludes rational control to some extent, remaining in its rhythms and cadences closely tied to "things that fall under Sense."[73] The human voice in song therefore maintains an especially labile balance between the material and immaterial elements in its make-up. Constantine's *sonitum* seems to denote specifically the voice *in song*, especially since he goes on to discuss the power of the paradigmatic singer Orpheus to regulate the human soul with his music. But although Constantine emphasizes the positive effects of the mutual dependence of body and mind in song—"alterum ab altero adiuvatur" (each of which [body and soul] is aided by the other)—it is not difficult to imagine that this self-regulating system might prove highly unstable.

As the vehicle for the transmission of pneumatic spirit, the voice also has the potentially dangerous power to penetrate the lover's body. For if, as Ficino's discussion of fascination suggests, the penetration of the lover through the eye can prove radically destabilizing, it seems plausible that the penetration of the lover through the ear might be equally dangerous, as well as potentially curative. It is perhaps for this reason that in the poetic treatment of the relationship between song and love-melancholy, the curative power of the song is balanced by its capacity to reinforce and even exacerbate erotic fixation.[74] For both Petrarch and Tasso, the beguiling song of the nightingale, though it soothes the lover's anguish, is also a sign of his continuing, melancholic absorption in a lost object. The allusive context of the nightingale's song reinforces in Tasso's romance in particular an affiliation between the melancholic lover and Orpheus, who of course dies as a result of his love for Eurydice.[75] In the medical texts, by contrast, birdsong (particularly the nightingale's song) contributes to the curative property of the *locus amoenus*. Valescus de Taranta's *Philonium* (1418) is representative, recommending walks in "iardinos floridos ubi cantant aves et resonant philomenae" (flowering gardens where birds sing and nightingales resound).[76]

Voice in Psychoanalysis

Noting the persistence among the *signa amoris* of such preverbal modes of expression as melancholy sighs and sobbing, Wack suggests that "the lover's helplessness and inarticulateness seem those of an infant, *in-fans*, the one who cannot speak."[77] This would certainly tally with our sense that love-melancholy involves a regression to a primitive mirroring relation with the mother. But the medical texts' emphasis on the lover's powerful response to love songs indicates perhaps not that love-melancholy is entirely aphasic, but that it seeks a mode of expression closer to the affective expressions of what Kristeva has called "semiotic processes." According to Kristeva, these semiotic processes are in conflict with fully articulated language and symbolic constructs (such as ideologies and beliefs): "Discourse . . . allows itself to be changed by affective rhythm to the extent of fading into muteness. . . . [R]hythms, alliterations, condensations shape the transmission of message and data."[78] The highly affective discourse of song about separated lovers provokes a psychophysiological response in the lover presumably because it activates a psychic wound that resonates with earlier, prelinguistic experience (perhaps of separation from the mother). In Lacanian terms, the discourse of song as the medical texts present it would seem to represent the lure of the Imaginary—away from the discourse *inter homines* that constitutes ordinary social intercourse. A brief consideration of Kristeva's "semiotic" interpretation of the language of melancholia will help to reinforce the poetic significance of the medieval account of a "spiritual" discourse that is partly somatic, partly cognitive.

For Kristeva, the melancholic is characterized by a radical alienation from his own language. The failure to renounce the primary object results in a blockage in the subject's ability to symbolize experience. The "dead language" of the melancholic bespeaks the ghostly presence of a buried object that inhibits the translation of mournful affect into words:

> [M]elancholy persons are foreigners in their maternal tongue. They have
> lost the meaning—the value—of their mother tongue for want of losing
> the mother. *The dead language they speak*, which foreshadows their suicide,
> conceals a Thing [that is, the mother, or the *res amata*] buried alive. The
> latter, however, will not be translated in order that it not be betrayed; it shall
> remain walled up within the crypt of the inexpressible affect.[79]

The burial of the Thing—akin to Abraham and Torok's *incorporation* of the lost object—deprives the subject of full sovereignty over his or her language. For this reason melancholic language is characterized by a dissociation of signifiers from their referents: "The depressed speak of nothing, they have nothing to speak of: glued to the Thing (Res), they are without objects."[80] This description of a melancholic alienation from language re-calls the medieval observation that lovers are peculiarly inaccessible to or-dinary discourse—they remain (to alter Kristeva's statement a little) glued to the *res amata*. But Kristeva's account of melancholia also makes room for the regressive emotionality of the lovers' discourse noted by the earlier doctors. In her psychoanalytic account, the very power of the buried object draws to itself a host of imperfectly introjected affects, "fluctuating en-ergy cathexes, insufficiently stabilized to coalesce as verbal or other signs, acted upon by primary processes of displacement and condensation."[81] For Kristeva, these energy cathexes are "semiotic rhythms" that "convey an in-tense presence of meaning in a presubject still incapable of signification."[82] The semiotic is to be contrasted with the "symbolic," which is "identified with judgement and the grammatical sentence."[83]

As we have seen, the language that melancholy lovers understand, the song that pertains to the *res amata*, is a highly affective language that lit-erally *inspires* the lover with joy and sorrow. It is a "spiritual" voice that attests to the mutual imbrication of body and soul, eliciting in turn from the lover a "spiritual" but not fully "symbolic" outpouring of "sighing, sobbing and lamenting."[84] Like Kristeva's semiotic rhythms, the voice, so understood, testifies to bodily affects that resist full translation into the grammatical sentence. By the same token, the melancholic lover's extreme susceptibility to mournful songs indicates the subversion of his reason by somatic processes. The danger of voice in *song* is that it threatens to move away from the Aristotelian insistence on *meaning* ("for voice is a sound with a meaning") toward a less distinctively human sound. As we will see in chapter 4, the *flebil canto* (mournful song) of the nightingale heard in the enchanted wood represents a dangerously labile poetic "voice" in which the sounds of breeze and water are indistinguishably mingled with a sighing, sobbing voice. This *flebil canto*, shaped by the medical and poetic discourse of love-melancholy, emerges as the powerfully seductive voice of romance in Tasso's poem.

From a psychoanalytic perspective, the medieval medical texts' scat-tered remarks about voice begin to adumbrate a suggestive theory of the voice—and especially song—as a site of tension between the "symbolic" constructions of everyday discourse and a physiological discourse of sighs, tears, and imperfectly translated affect. This song is understood in two quite distinct ways that help to complicate our perception of the relation between literary and medical discourses on love. While the medical texts propose the voice—in particular the "recitation of poetry" and songs about lovers—as a therapy for love-melancholy, poetic treatments of song by and large emphasize the song's regressive emotional pull on the lover. Yet the medical texts themselves acknowledge the regressive impact of voice in song—the lovers respond not by snapping out of their preoccupation with the beloved but with songs, sighing, and weeping. In the context of the Aristotelian conception of true voice as "sound with meaning," the discussions of voice in the medical texts indicate that notwithstanding its capacity to soothe, the emotive quality of the voice in song might threaten to reinforce rather than reverse the lovers' slide into the infantilized position of the melancholic.

Kristeva's account underscores both the therapeutic and the dangerous aspects of melancholic voice. For her, the semiotic richness of poetry—a product of its refusal fully to "translate" the Thing into symbolic discourse—draws language toward the occluded realm of the buried object. The power of poetry lies at least in part in its hold over the lost object, whose traces therefore remain in the "semiotic processes" of prosody:

> [A]rt seems to point to a few devices that bypass complacency and, without simply turning mourning into mania, secure for the artist and the connoisseur a sublimatory hold over the lost Thing. First by means of prosody, the language beyond language that inserts into the sign the rhythm and alliterations of semiotic processes. Also by means of the polyvalence of sign and symbol, which unsettles naming and, by building up a plurality of connotations around the sign, affords the subject a chance to imagine the nonmeaning, or the true meaning, of the Thing.[85]

The affective power that song or poetry wields over the melancholic lover, on this account, derives from poetry's "sublimatory hold over the lost Thing." The lover is drawn out of his baffled, asocial silence because the song speaks directly to the "secret wound" of his or her loss. However, the song's semiotic structure also ensures that the subject will be alienated from the very language that he speaks or hears, precisely because it owes its power not to the speaker but to the buried object:

> Melancholy persons, with their despondent, secret insides, are potential exiles but also intellectuals capable of dazzling, albeit abstract, constructions. . . .

Through their empty speech they assure themselves of an inaccessible (because it is "semiotic" and not "symbolic") ascendancy over an archaic object that thus remains, for themselves and all others, an enigma and a secret.[86]

The semiotically rich yet symbolically "empty" discourse of the melancholic bears witness to the brooding power of the lost object, which, locked within a fantastic world of the lover's own making, threatens the dissolution of the subject from within.

"Note sì pietose et scorte": Petrarch and the Poetics of *atra voluptas*

Petrarch's poetry offers a particularly rich example of the relationship between poetic discourse and melancholia that allows us to trace the early medico-poetic discourse of love-melancholy to its most fully achieved form. In the poems of the *Canzoniere*, the figure of Laura, whose name is punningly associated not only with *lauro* (laurel) but also with *l'aura* (breeze, breath), represents a powerful synthesis of the pneumatic/phantasmic conception of love. Laura exerts a force that draws the poet's spirit out of him in tears and sighs, but that also "inspires" him; she is a labile, shadowy figure imperfectly distinguished from the phantasms ("l'idolo mio," Sestina 30) within the poet's own mind.[87] The tornata that closes canzone 129 beautifully illustrates the paradoxical process in which the self of the speaker is emptied out in order to permit a fantasized union with the breeze of inspiration, L/aura herself:

> Canzone, oltra quell'alpe,
> là dove il ciel è più sereno et lieto,
> mi rivedrai sovr' un ruscel corrente
> ove l'aura si sente
> d'un fresco et odorifero laureto:
> ivi è 'l mio cor et quella che 'l m'invola;
> qui veder poi l'imagine mia sola.

[Song, beyond those Alps, where the sky is more clear and happy, you shall see me again beside a running stream, where the breeze from a fresh and fragrant laurel can be felt: there is my heart, and she who steals it from me; here you can see only my image.]

This loss of self to the pneumatic "aura" that draws the speaker away from his body recalls the "spiritual" flow toward the image of the beloved—both within the lover's mind and in the actual world—described in the medical literature. In both contexts the result of this spiritual depletion is obsession, but Petrarch willingly embraces this obsession as the price of the bittersweet poetry it makes possible. In sonnet 133 we see even more clearly how the pneumatic circulation of song, words, and spirit within the metaphorical breeze both threatens the poet's life and enables his poetry:

> [E]t l'angelico canto et le parole,
> col dolce spirto ond'io non posso aitarme,
> son l'aura inanzi a cui mia vita fugge.

[And your angelic singing and your words, with your sweet spirit (*spirto*) against which I cannot defend myself, are the breeze before which my life flees.]

(*Rime Sparse* 133, trans. Durling, with minor emendation)

The quest for Laura/*l'aura* seems to represent in part a quest for poetic voice, the *dolce spirto* that in Aristotelian theory is the "matter of articulate voice." But the mysterious pneumatic song that in the medical literature offers a cure for lovesickness becomes in Petrarch's poem a more dangerous *pharmakon*—a therapy that deepens the wound it soothes. Inspiration, in this collection, involves a willed loss of self in exchange for the capture of a voice that both is and is not the poet's own.

As we saw earlier, the persistence of the *dilectoso male* (delightful sorrow) motif in Petrarch's poetry suggests a connection between the spiritual *tristitia* or *acedia* in the *Secretum* and the self-destructive, obsessive style of the *Canzoniere*.[88] The characteristic feature of Petrarch's sorrow in the *Secretum*—as in the *Canzoniere*—is its bittersweet quality; he refers to his grief as an *atra voluptas* (dark sorrow) that he indulges in spite of himself. Unable to tear himself away from this *atra* or *funesta voluptas*, Petrarch feeds compulsively on grief:

> Et (qui supremus miseriarum cumulus dici potest) sic lacrimis et doloribus pascor, atra quadam cum voluptate, ut invitus avellar.

[And (this can be said to be the supremest of miseries), I so feed on tears and griefs with a certain black pleasure that I resist being rescued from them.] (2.13.2)[89]

As Boitani suggests, the *atra voluptas* that Petrarch appears to repudiate in the *Secretum* lies behind the self-perpetuating cycle of sorrow and joy that generates the lyric poetry:

> Pascomi di dolor, piangendo rido,
> egualmente mi spiace morte et vita.
> In questo stato son, Donna, per vui.

[I feed on pain, weeping I laugh; equally displeasing to me are death and life. In this state am I, Lady, on account of you.]

(Rime Sparse 134)

The suggestive language of "feeding" on grief indicates in psychoanalytic terms that the source of Petrarchan lyric is a lost object, the buried or encrypted maternal Thing that has not been fully mourned. Recalling Kristeva's theory of melancholic language, we might interpret this incomplete mourning as the occluded source of the strangely alienated, yet brilliant language of the poems. Thus in the programmatic *canzone delle metamorfose* the speaker describes his song as "strange" to, or "estranged" from, himself: "cantava sempre, / merce chiamando con estrania voce" ("I sang always, calling for mercy with strange voice," 23.63, trans. Durling, with emendation). Melancholic language, as Kristeva argues, "ends up in asymbolia, in loss of meaning: If I am no longer capable of translating or metaphorizing, I become silent and I die."[90] This drift toward silence and "asymbolia" is apparent not only in the speaker's distance from his own *estrania voce* but in the strangely deadening effect that his impossible desire has on his words:

> Così davanti a' colpi de la morte
> fuggo, ma non sì ratto che 'l desio
> meco non venga, come venir sòle;
>
> tacito vo, ché le parole morte
> farian pianger la gente, et i' desio
> che le lagrime mie si spargan sole.

[Thus I flee before the blows of death, but not so quickly that my desire does not come with me, as it is accustomed;

I go silent; for my dead words would make people weep, and I desire my tears to be shed in solitude.]

(Rime Sparse 18)

Petrarch's evocation of his *parole morte* (dead words) suggests precisely the linguistic alienation that for Kristeva signals the ghostly presence of a buried object: "[T]he dead language they speak . . . conceals a Thing buried alive."[91]

The image of the figure that sings and "feeds" on his grief and tears as a way of sustaining the melancholy source of his inspiration draws not only on the medical/theological literature of *acedia*, but also on classical portraits of Orpheus.[92] Like the Petrarch of the *Secretum*, Ovid's Orpheus also feeds on his own tears:

> [S]eptem tamen ille diebus
> squalidus in ripa Cereris sine munere sedit;
> cura dolorque animi laacrimaeque alimenta fuere.

> [Seven days he sat there on the bank in filthy rags and with no taste of food. Care, anguish of soul, and tears were his nourishment.]

> (*Met.* 10.73–75)[93]

This transformation of tears into an illusory kind of nourishment informs Petrarch's self-consuming grief, the *atra voluptas* that both soothes and exacerbates the love-melancholy of the *Canzoniere* (*pascomi di dolor*). Ovid also connects Orpheus's melancholic absorption in his grief with the production of song. For it is after the death of Eurydice and Orpheus's refusal to accept any substitutes for his lost wife—he turns away from women and marriage altogether—that he utters the songs that fill the tenth book of the *Metamorphoses*. It is not surprising, then, to find that Petrarch associates the bittersweet plaints of his own collection directly with the song of Orpheus. In poem 311, the speaker identifies his own grief for the dead Laura with the mythical grief of the nightingale. Petrarch draws here on Virgil's *Georgic* 4, in which the laments of Orpheus are compared in a complex simile to the grief of a nightingale who has lost her children. The *miserabile carmen* of Virgil's bereft nightingale echoes behind Petrarch's poem—and indeed perhaps the whole collection:

> Quel rosigniuol che sì soave piagne
> forse suoi figli o sua cara consorte,
> di dolcezza empie il cielo et le campagne
> con tante note sì pietose et scorte,

> et tutta notte par che m'accompagne
> et mi rammente la mia dura sorte;
> ch'altri che me non ò di chi mi lagne,
> che 'n dee non credev'io regnasse Morte.

[That nightingale that so sweetly weeps, perhaps for his children or for his dear consort, fills the sky and the fields with sweetness in so many grieving, skillful notes,

and all night he seems to accompany me and remind me of my harsh fate; for I have no one to complain of save myself, who did not believe that Death reigns over goddesses.]

(*Rime Sparse* 311, trans. Durling)

As Thomas Greene has noted, in Petrarch's poem the nightingale is no longer confined to a simile; this weeping song literally suffuses the atmosphere in which the speaker moves.[94] Although the speaker is not directly compared to the nightingale, the connection between them is closer than in Virgil's text. While the earlier nightingale mourned her lost children ("amissos queritur fetus," 4.512), this nightingale has become a masculine figure mourning perhaps his children *or* his *cara consorte* (dear consort), a figure who clearly represents the lost Eurydice.[95] Petrarch's transformation of a *maternal* lament into an erotic elegy is thus clearer here than in the original Virgilian context; the nightingale is male and mourns, perhaps, a lost beloved. Unlike Virgil's simile, the particulars of whose vehicle (a female bird, lost children, and a *durus arator*" who steals them) seem deliberately distanced from its tenor, Petrarch's translation of the nightingale into the speaker's world emphasizes the connection between what Greene calls the "bittersweet affectivity of the song" and the poem itself.[96] The plangent notes of the birdsong clearly replace the speaker's own lament for Laura/Eurydice, suggesting perhaps that this identification with a maternal figure signals both a return to the semiotic rhythms of melancholic discourse and a revolt against the shocking power of *Morte*.

This poem registers some of the distance we have traveled during the course of our exploration of the theoretical bases of love-melancholy. The oxymoronic language that links grief and sweetness—the nightingale who *sì soave piagne* (so sweetly weeps)—returns us to the concept of *atra voluptas* that receives such provocative treatment in the *Secretum*. As we saw earlier, *atra voluptas* derives from a complex fusion of the sin of *acedia* and lovesickness and contributes to the literature on love-melancholy a notable emphasis on the *willful* indulgence of grief and suffering. Petrarch's development of this term seems to look both forward and backward in our history. The language of "feeding" on grief and tears that appears in both the *Secretum* and the *Canzoniere* recalls Lucretius's lovers, whose furious desire to devour each other so brilliantly conveys the phantasmic quality of the erotic object. The regressive, oral nature of desire in these texts also resonates with the psychoanalytic reading of the phantasmic object as a version of the lost, maternal object. As both Petrarch and later Tasso realize, the song of the nightingale transforms Eurydice into a maternal symbol of loss; "more than a lost object, Eurydice represents here 'the dimension of loss per se.'"[97] The lover's fierce attachment to an internalized, maternal object helps to explain, in turn, his removal from ordinary symbolic discourse; apparently unable to respond to any language that does not pertain to the beloved object, the lover is nonetheless particularly responsive to highly affective poems and songs. The labile nature of this spiritual song seems to permit its use both as a cure for love-melancholy and, paradoxically, as a way of exerting "a sublimatory hold" over the lost object that may prove destructive. But in a Petrarchan context the price of this song is a sweet grief that continues to torment him with what Augustinus calls in the *Secretum* a "plague of phantasms [*pestis . . . fantasmatum*] which are tearing apart and mutilating [his] thoughts." These phantasms, according to Augustinus, are "blocking the journey to those enlightening thoughts by which one ascends to the one and only supreme light [*summum lumen*] with their death-bringing inconstancy."[98] We have returned, then, to that foundational tension between phantasmic pleasure and transcendent eros that characterizes what the doctors sometimes called "heroic love." The obsessiveness of Petrarch's love actively blocks the "mournful" journey away from the particular beloved to the Platonic *summum lumen* at the same time as it facilitates the production of a quintessentially melancholic poetry. Our exploration of Petrarch's poetics of *atra voluptas* leads us directly to early modern romance, where we will encounter the "thousand fancies" and "sights of semblants vaine" (*Faerie Queene* 3.4.54) constitutive of the distinctive *errori* of the genre.

CHAPTER 3

Solvite me

Epic, Romance, and the Poetics of Melancholy in the *Orlando Furioso*

Recent attempts to discern in *Orlando Furioso* a self-conscious commentary on, or critique of, the romance form deployed by Boiardo and borrowed by Ariosto himself in his "continuation" of *Orlando Innamorato* have tended to focus on the figure of Atlante's enchanted palace. The palace, situated in the *profonde selve* of the poem's bosky depths, has been viewed as emblematic of the poem's own tortuous and unreliable course through a fundamentally Boiardesque terrain.[1] While the castle's structure undoubtedly represents the illusions and errors constitutive of Ariostan romance as a literary mode, the *psychological* content of this form has not been sufficiently explored.[2] Much attention has been paid to the formal qualities of romance: its labyrinthine structure, its avoidance of closure, its multiple plots, its lack of verisimilitude, and its characteristic investment in *errori* of various kinds (spiritual, mental, and geographic).[3] But I contend here that Ariosto's depiction of the structure of his romance is far more deeply engaged than has been recognized with contemporary conceptions of mind, and in particular with the psychic structure of love-melancholy. The *furor* that gives the poem its title derives in some detail from the portrait of erotic melancholia that passed through Ficino and others and helps to determine in its turn the contours and content of the "romance" elements of the poem.[4] Petrarch's self-conscious poetic exploration of the *atra voluptas* of melancholy love in his *Canzoniere* provides the literary framework for Ariosto's etiology of Orlando's *furor*. Indeed, it is the collapse of Orlando's bittersweet Petrarchan dream of Angelica that propels him into *l'amorosa inchiesta* (9.7) constitutive of the poem's romance quest. Especially in earlier editions, in which Orlando stumbles from his dream into the palace of

Atlante within a few stanzas, the palace seems to function as a continuation or intensification of the dream and *as such* as a model of the romance narrative to come.[5] If the Petrarchan dream of a phantasmic beloved is the origin of this romance quest, the interruption and gradual dismantling of that dream prompts a radical turn away from the poetry of *atra voluptas* (or what Ariosto calls *dolce pena*) toward the elegiac practices of epic.

The conclusions of this chapter will turn on a reading of the allusive moment of Orlando's "awakening" from his madness, which I interpret as generating the poem's shift toward the epic mode. This mysterious and beautiful awakening constitutes something of a crux for critics of the poem. Ariosto marks this moment with a powerful, though puzzling, allusion to Virgil's *Eclogue* 6. Orlando's first words after his wits return to him in canto 39 are *solvite me* (release me), words spoken in Virgil's poem by the satyrlike Silenus, who begs playfully to be released from "fetters made from his own garlands" (ipsis ex vinculis sertis, *Ecl.* 6.19).[6] The fact that Ariosto transfers these words directly into his own poem in their original Latin argues for the importance of the Virgilian context for understanding this complex moment.[7] I argue that Silenus's mini epic describes a transition from the madness of hopeless love (*furor*) to an elegiac acceptance of lost love that provides a vital model for Ariosto's complex negotiation of the transition from romance to epic. The figure of the wandering, demented Pasiphae epitomizes the song's focus on *furor*, and especially the *furor* of love, while the invocation of Apollo's elegy for his lost love Hyacinthus at the *Eclogue's* close engages with the epic topos of *mors immatura* (untimely death). But the sexualized violence of the *mors immatura* topos in epic suggests that even if Ariosto reads epic as an elegiac mode, the terrible costs of the transition into elegy in an epic context considerably darken what would appear to be a positive movement out of the toils of love-melancholy.

My reading of the poem against contemporary medical discourses on love and melancholy complicates the long-standing debate about the poem's generic affiliations. I will modify both Albert Ascoli's and Patricia Parker's view that epic and romance remain in uncomfortable and unresolved competition, and David Quint's view that the poem "jettisons pure romance midway in order to proceed to epic closure."[8] My contention here will be that although Ariosto does ultimately "choose" the structure of epic over romance (by concluding with a revision of the end of the *Aeneid*), this turn away from romance can never be complete precisely because romance represents for Ariosto ineradicable *psychic* forces. This is not to say that epic and romance as literary forms are therefore in *tension*, but rather that epic is inhabited by the same psychic energies that drive romance, though in a radically different guise. If romance is shaped by the madness of love that emerges from the continual focus on an internalized beloved, that madness reemerges in epic stripped of its attachment to an individual. The inhuman cruelty of Aeneas after the death of Pallas is the model for the epic *furor* that Ariosto imports into his own poem in the aftermath of Brandimarte's death, radically compromising the moral status of the epic "solution" to the errors of romance.

As we saw in chapter 1, the physical and mental debility attributed to the disease of love-melancholy contributed to its assimilation to "female" diseases (such as hysteria) and to the male lover's presumed feminization. Ariosto's treatment of Orlando's madness—especially his complex use of Pasiphae's maenadic furor as a model for Orlando's quest—reinforces this association, and draws attention to the implicit gendering of romance as a feminine genre. If the madness of Pasiphae and the feminizing symptoms of love-melancholy inscribe romance within a feminine space, the martial *furor* of epic seems clearly to belong in the normative "masculine" world of politics and male camaraderie. Fiordiligi's self-entombment with Brandimarte marks the transfer of the "feminine" melancholic obsessiveness of the romance form from Orlando to Fiordiligi and thus seems to facilitate Orlando's reintegration into the masculine world that subtends his identity as warrior. But Ariosto's darkly ironic juxtaposition of epithalamic and elegiac imagery in the treatment of Brandimarte's death constructs him, like Pallas, as a feminine and eroticized figure whose death must deepen our ambivalence about the psychological and moral costs of the choice of a "masculine," epic world. The "cure" of romance melancholy, though it brings the poem's protagonists into the political and historical "real" world, nevertheless unleashes a more dangerous form of madness not tempered by the sweet deceptions of love. The notion that romance is a melancholic, feminine form thus usefully complicates our understanding of the cultural significance of Orlando's *furor* and provides a rich contemporary context for understanding the tension between epic and romance strains in Ariosto's poem.

Atlante's Palace: Love-Melancholy and
the Form of Romance

As we have seen in the foregoing chapters, medieval and early modern writings on erotic melancholy characterize the disease primarily as a relentless focus on an internally generated phantasmic object. This focus becomes so intense, thanks to the fixity of the phantasm in the imagination and the resulting perseveration of the phantasm in the estimative faculty, that it conduces eventually to obsession, or what Arnaldus calls *assidua cogitatio*. The behavior of the knights in Atlante's palace suggests that the forces at work in the palace represent in part the obsessive pattern of an erotic *assidua cogitatio* that drives the lover into melancholy and madness.[9] The arrangement of the narrative in the 1516 and 1521 editions supports this hypothesis by indicating a temporal and genetic relationship between Orlando's obsessive love and the appearance of the palace of erotic illusion. In these editions, Orlando's dream of Angelica (which I analyze in detail later) moves within a few stanzas into the palace of Atlante.[10] Waking in tears from his terrible dream, Orlando embarks on his quest ("l'amorosa inchiesta," 9.7) only to hear the shriek ("un lungo grido," 11.83) that leads him into the palace. Since it is precisely a terrible shriek ("orribil grido," 8.83) within his dream that awakens him, the impression we have is that the phantom of Angelica leads Orlando into the place as though *back into his dream*.[11] It is no surprise, then, to find that the object of the frenzied desire of each knight is phantasmic rather than real. The mysterious voice that draws the lovers in is heard differently by each of them:

> Una voce medesma, una persona
> che paruta era Angelica ad Orlando,
> parve a Ruggier la donna di Dordona,
> che lo tenea di sé medesmo in bando.
> Se con Gradasso o con alcun ragiona
> di quei ch'andavan nel palazzo errando,
> a tutti par che quella cosa sia,
> che più ciascun per sé brama e desia.

[One and the same voice, one person that to Orlando had seemed Angelica, seemed to Ruggiero the lady of Dordogne, who kept him in banishment from himself. If that voice speaks with Gradasso or any other of those who were wandering around in the palace, it seems to all to be what each most longs for and most desires for himself.]

(*OF* 12.20)[12]

Appropriately, when the real Angelica vanishes, she does so "come fantasma al dispartir del sonno" (like a phantasm at the departure of sleep, 12.59).

When we first meet Orlando just prior to the dream sequence, he is already caught up in precisely the perseverative focus on the beloved that foretells his absorption in—and eventual subjection to—a phantasmic world:

> La notte Orlando alle noiose piume
> del veloce pensier fa parte assai.
> Or quinci or quindi il volta, or lo rassume
> tutto in un loco, e non l'afferma mai.

[In the night Orlando shares with the plaguing feathers much of his swift thought. Now to this side now to that he turns it, now brings it all together in one spot, and never keeps it still.]

(*OF* 8.71)

Orlando's skittery thought pattern ("or quinci or quindi il volta") anticipates the hither-thither movement (*di qua, di là*) of the knights in the palace that D. S. Carne-Ross rightly sees as the paradigmatic structure of the poem:[13]

> [C]orre di qua, corre di là, né lassa
> che non vegga ogni camera, ogni loggia.

[He rushes here, rushes there, and does not let up until he sees every chamber, every porch.]

(*OF* 12.9, italics mine)

Carne-Ross notes that this structure seems to allude directly to Dante's description of the tormented souls of the lustful in the second circle of the inferno. These are the souls who have subjected reason to desire ("che la ragion sommettono al talento") and are consequently carried hither and thither, downward and upward ("di qua, di là, di giù, di sù," 5.43) by a *bufera infernal* (hellish hurricane) that represents their own restless, obsessive desires.[14] Ariosto later makes quite clear the relationship between an internal world of unruly desires and its external figuration in the forest in which the palace appears:

> E quale è di pazzia segno più espresso
> che, per altri voler, perder se stesso?
>
> Vari gli effetti son, ma la pazzia
> è tutt'una però, che li fa uscire.
> Gli è come una gran selva, ove la via
> conviene a forza, a chi vi va, fallire:
> *chi su, chi giù, chi qua, qui là travia.*

[And what sign of madness is clearer than losing oneself through desire for another?

Varied are the effects, but the madness that brings them out is nevertheless all one. It is like a great forest, where of necessity the way must deceive him who goes there; *one up, one down, one here, one there goes astray.*][15]

(*OF* 24.1–2, italics mine)

The physiology of Orlando's desire clearly reflects the medical view of desire as a pneumatic-phantasmic process. We are told that the image (or phantasm) of Angelica that dominates Orlando's mind immediately before his dream, "heats up" his heart, prompting the kind of perseverative thinking characteristic of the dried-out, melancholic brain:

> La donna sua, che gli ritorna a mente,
> anzi che mai non era indi partita,
> gli raccende nel core e fa più ardente
> la fiamma che nel dì parea sopita.

[His lady, who returns to his mind,
or more truly, who never has left it,
rekindles in his heart and makes hotter
the flame that in the day seemed quenched.]

(*OF* 8.72)

As in the medical accounts of love-melancholy, the phantasm of the desired object is impressed on the mind (in the imagination or phantasia) so that it appears constantly to the memory and creates the fixation of mind conducive to melancholy.[16] This ambiguous displacement of the lady herself by an image reflects the cognitive confusion that operates in this disease. Orlando is from this point on increasingly absorbed in the image of Angelica rather than the woman herself: both the dream and the palace appear as symptoms of this fundamental imaginative distortion. Donald Beecher and Massimo Ciavolella attribute the catastrophic effects of melancholic love as described in early modern medical accounts to the corruption of the imagination, in which "the object is always present to be enjoyed, yet always absent, unreal, and unattainable."[17] The palace seems to allegorize precisely the activity of the corrupt imagination as it was understood by sixteenth-century doctors:

> [T]he imagination is in such sort corrupted, as that the melancholike partie alwaies thinkes, that hee seeth that which he loveth, running after it continually, and kissing this his idoll in the ayre, daintily intertaining and welcomming it as though it were present.[18]

For Jacques Ferrand, the ability to summon a phantasm out of thin air is characteristic of melancholia more broadly. His description of the melancholic's tendency to "fashion a thousand fantastical chimeras and imagine objects that neither exist nor ever will" also supports a reading of Atlante's palace as a figure for the "deranged imagination" of the melancholic lover.[19] Carne-Ross's observation that Orlando's "image of [Angelica] is false in the sense that the Angelica he seeks has no existence outside his own mind" is substantially enriched by placing the "psychology" of the palace within a contemporary medical conception of mind.[20] The radical implications of this reading may then emerge more fully: Angelica is quite literally no more than a phantasm who can by definition never be grasped by the increasingly self-absorbed lover. Similarly, Eugenio Donato's reading of the function of desire in Atlante's palace also makes richer sense within the context of a historically contemporary account of mind: "Atlante's palace . . . represents the interminable quest for an ever-elusive object."[21] As we have seen, this formulation matches the medical account of the deluded melancholic lover continually "running after" an internalized "plague of phantasms" (in Petrarch's terms) that block his access to true knowledge.

A characteristically melancholic potential for narcissistic absorption in the mind's figments is also a feature of Orlando's pre-dream rumination. Orlando addresses the phantasmic *donna sua* within the context of a kind of mental sparagmos in which he identifies fragmented parts of himself with the lady: she is "cor mio" (8.73); "dolce vita mia" (8.76); "speranza mia" (8.77). In the medical literature this dangerous identification with a female beloved is associated with the feminizing effects of the disease of love-melancholy, which included "a pale and wan complexion . . . palpitations of the heart, sighing, causeless fears, fainting, oppressions, suffocations, uterine fury."[22] The last of these symptoms indicates that the illness of love-melancholy is associated not only with women but in particular with female sexuality, whose dangerous lability was a feature of much earlier classical depictions of female madness as well as later accounts of "hysteria."[23] Cultural anxiety about the power of what was in fact sometimes called *femineus amor* (womanly love) thus seems to derive from a medically based assumption that a profound focus on an internal image of the beloved woman threatens at the very least a radical destabilization of the masculine ego. As Thomas Laqueur puts it in his discussion of the effect of the "one-sex" model on conceptions of masculinity: "Men's bodies . . . could sometimes come unglued. 'Effeminacy' in the sixteenth century was understood as a condition of instability, a state of men who through excessive devotion to women became more like them."[24] As we will see in more detail later, the allusion to Virgil's *Eclogue* also clearly links Orlando's quest retrospectively to the wandering of a demented Pasiphae, whose story of feminine erotic frenzy is a focus of Silenus's song.

If the illness of love-melancholy entails a feminizing of the male lover, it is not surprising that Atlante's palace should explicitly separate Orlando and his fellow knights from their duties as epic warriors. In keeping Ruggiero and a host of other knights, including Orlando, away from the dangers of battle, Atlante imprisons them in the toils of a feminizing romance structure. This is particularly clear in what I take to be the closest analogue to this episode in Boiardo's poem: the palace of Dragontina. The many echoes of the Dragontina episode in the scene in Atlante's palace (the stupefaction of the knights, the central role of Angelica in freeing them to serve her own interests, the power of her ring over the enchanted space) suggest that this episode is a primary source for Ariosto.[25] Like Circe, with whom she is closely identified, Dragontina keeps her once-virile prisoners in a condition of eroticized somnolence that symbolically unmans them.[26]

Dolce error: Orlando's Dream and
the Origin of Romance

We saw in the previous chapters that Ficino's theory of the erotic imagination emphasizes an absorption of the beloved within the lover's soul that can lead either to the sublimation constitutive of Platonic eros or to the blockage characteristic of love-melancholy. The soul is a mirror that receives within itself a reflection of the beloved with whom the lover is in a sense fused:

> Accedit quod amans amati figuram suo sculpit in animo. Fit itaque amantis animus speculum, in quo amati relucet imago.

> [There is also the fact that the lover engraves the figure of the beloved on his own soul. And so the soul of the lover becomes a mirror in which the image of the beloved is reflected.] (*De amore* 2.8)

According to the Platonic schema (as articulated by Diotima), the ultimate object of the lover's adoration is beauty that is perceived by the Intellect. The individual beloved is not significant primarily as himself but as an instantiation of a universal principle. Ficino follows this closely in his own account of "true" love:

> Amor enim fruendae pulchritudinis desiderium est. . . . Quare solo mentis intuitu contentus est, qui animi pulchritudinem expetit.

> [For love is the desire of enjoying beauty. . . . Therefore he who loves the beauty of the soul is content with the perceiving of the Intellect alone.] (*De amore* 2.9)

By contrast, the melancholic lover is one who "abuses love" (*De amore* 6.9) by wishing to embrace what should only be contemplated; he wishes to touch what truly exists only in the realm of ideas:

> Tangendi vero cupido, non amoris pars est, nec amantis affectus, sed petulantiae species, et servilis hominis perturbatio.

> [Thus the desire to touch is not a part of love, nor is it a passion of the lover, but rather a kind of lust and perturbation of a man who is servile.] (*De amore* 2.9)

Ficino's scheme helps to clarify what is at stake in Orlando's dream, which highlights the anti-Platonic fixation on a particular individual who cannot be transcended. When the visionary Angelica suddenly vanishes, only to reappear as a phantasm within the dreamlike palace, Orlando struggles precisely to grasp what can never be embraced—a phantasmic product of his own mind. It will be useful to consider this dream in its entirety:

> Parea ad Orlando, s'una verde riva
> d'odoriferi fior tutta dipinta,
> mirare il bello avorio, e la nativa
> purpura ch'avea Amor di sua man tinta,
> e le due chiare stelle onde nutriva
> ne le reti d'Amor l'anima avinta:
> io parlo de' begli occhi e del bel volto,
> che gli hanno il cor di mezzo il petto tolto.
>
> Sentia il maggior piacer, la maggior festa
> che sentir possa alcun felice amante;
> ma ecco intanto uscire una tempesta
> che struggea i fiori, ed abbattea le piante:
> non se ne suol veder simile a questa,
> quando giostra aquilone, austro e levante.
> Parea che per trovar qualche coperto,
> andasse errando invan per un deserto.
>
> Intanto l'infelice (e non sa come)
> perde la donna sua per l'aer fosco;
> onde di qua e di là del suo bel nome
> fa risonare ogni campagna e bosco.
> E mentre dice indarno:—Misero me!
> chi ha cangiata mia dolcezza in tosco?
> ode la donna sua che gli domanda,
> piangendo, aiuto, e se gli raccomanda.
>
> Onde par ch'esca il grido, va veloce,
> e quinci e quindi s'affatica assai.
> Oh quanto è il suo dolore aspro ed atroce,
> che non può rivedere i dolci rai!
> Ecco ch'altronde ode da un'altra voce:
> —Non sperar più gioirne in terra mai.—
> A questo orribil grido risvegliossi,
> e tutto pien di lacrime trovossi.

[It seemed to Orlando that on a green stream-bank all coloured with sweet-smelling flowers he was beholding the beautiful ivory and the native crimson that Love had painted with his own hand, and the two bright stars with which he fed his soul tangled in the nets of Love. I am speaking of the beautiful eyes and the beautiful face that have taken his heart from the midst of his breast.

He was feeling the greatest pleasure, the greatest joy that any happy lover can feel. But just then there rose a tempest that tore up the flowers and struck down the trees; such a one is not seen when Aquilo, Auster, and the Levant Wind are jousting. It seemed that to find some shelter he went wandering through a desert in vain.

Meanwhile the unhappy man (and he does not know how) loses the lady in the dusky air; hence on this side and on that he makes every plain and grove ring with her name. And while he is saying in vain: "Wretched me, who has changed my sweetness into poison?" he hears his lady calling for aid with tears, and asking his help.

Swiftly he goes whence the cry seems to come, and here and there strives hard. Oh, how harsh and terrible is his sorrow when he cannot see her sweet eyes again! Lo, from another direction he hears from another voice: "Do not hope to enjoy them ever more on earth." At this horrible cry he awoke and found himself all wet with tears.]

(*OF* 8.80–83)

We can certainly understand the dream as a continuation of Orlando's nighttime rumination on the internal vision of "la sua donna, che gli ritorna a mente" (his lady, who returns to his mind, 8.72). But while in Ficino's scheme the true lover's soul looks on the images within the fantasy *tamquam in speculo* (as in a mirror) without being drawn into the somatic world of the eye and spirit, which "require the presence of the body," Orlando's soul is clearly subservient to the desire for bodily presence.[27]

Ariosto's allusions to Boiardo and Petrarch in the dream sequence intensify our sense that Orlando's dream turns his gaze inward, entrancing him with the images reflected in the mirror of his mind without prompting the movement of transcendence that prevents the mind's entrapment. It is precisely this interior entrancement that produces the self-division and alienation symptomatic of melancholic love.[28] In Boiardo's poem, Orlando sees the real Angelica in just the kind of *locus amoenus* in which she appears in the dream: "Parea che l'erba a lei fiorisse intorno, / E de amor ragionasse quella riva" (The grass around her seemed to flower, / And the river's current spoke of love, *OI* 1.3.69).[29] But this is a real place, a "paradise" that Boiardo's Orlando merely believes in his astonishment to be the product of a dream:

> E non attenta ponto di svegliarla;
> Ma fiso riguardando nel bel viso
> In bassa voce con se stesso parla:
> 'Sono ora quivi, o sono in paradiso?
> Io pur la vedo, e non è ver niente,
> Però ch'io sogno e dormo veramente.'

> [He did not try to wake her, but
> Raptly gazed at her lovely face.
> In a soft voice he asked himself,
> "Am I here, or in Paradise?
> I see her, but she can't be real—
> I must be dreaming, sound asleep!"]

> (*OI* 1.3.70)

Rather than presenting the encounter between Orlando and Angelica as dreamlike, then, as Boiardo does, Ariosto presents it *as* a dream. This Petrarchan *locus amoenus* is explicitly understood as the mental space (the imagination) in which Angelica-as-phantasm may appear. This Orlando does not marvel (*mirare*) at an external object in the real world, as his Boiardesque counterpart does, but at the products of his own mind. This change underscores the notion that Orlando's quest is from the start directed inward, to the "impossible capture of the phantasm."[30] It also seems to dramatize both the tension and the crossover between literary and medical accounts of melancholic love. For this internalized *locus amoenus* seems at first to heal the lover's wound ("he was feeling . . . the greatest joy that any lover can feel"), thus apparently confirming the medical texts' view of the *locus amoenus* as curative. But the subsequent dissolution of the dream suggests both that the *locus amoenus* intensifies the sufferer's love and (contra the troubadours' idealization of such suffering) that this martyrdom is both dangerous and futile.

The ambiguous conflation of inner and outer landscapes is a central feature of Petrarch's canzone 129, a poem that seems to offer a programmatic version of the dialectic between pursuit, internalization, and loss that structures the *Canzoniere* as a whole. The similarity between this poem's bittersweet disillusionment and the sweet poison of Orlando's dream ("chi ha cangiata mia dolcezza in tosco?") suggests the importance of Petrarch's melancholic *atra voluptas* in general, and perhaps of this poem in particular, for Ariosto's conception of the origin of Orlando's quest. In 129, the speaker evinces the symptoms of a melancholic love that any onlooker, he says, would recognize as such: "'Queste arde et di suo stato è incerto'" (This man is burning with love and his state is uncertain, 129.13, trans. Durling). Just as Orlando is pulled around by his scattered thoughts, so Petrarch's speaker presents us with a scattered, fragmented mind: "De pensier in pensier, di monte in monte / mi guida Amor" ("From thought to thought, from mountain to mountain / Love guides me," 129.1–2). The poem dramatizes the connection between anguish at the absence of the beloved and pleasure at the interior conjuring of her image. This is, to be sure, the *atra voluptas* (dark pleasure) of melancholia, the *dilectoso male* whose seductive lure Petrarch deplores in the *Secretum*:

> A ciascun passo nasce un penser novo
> de la mia donna, che sovente in gioco
> gira 'l tormento ch'i' porto per lei;
> et a pena voreei
> cangiar questo mio viver dolce amaro.

[With every step is born a new thought of my lady, which often turns to pleasure the torment that I bear for her; and I would hardly wish to change this bitter, sweet life of mine.]

(*Rime Sparse* 129.17–21)

The bittersweet consolation for impossible love is to be found, it seems, within the fantastic world of the speaker's mind, where thoughts are themselves the source of pleasure. It is also clear that the poet's *atra voluptas* is decisively connected with the creation of a poetic space in which the beloved is conjured, lost, and then transformed into the stuff of poetry. Strikingly, this creative process is predicated on a radical self-alienation in which the phantasmic "error" is willingly—indeed willfully—embraced:

> Ove porge ombra un pino alto od un colle
> talor m'arresto, et pur nel primo sasso
> disegno co la mente il suo bel viso.
> Poi ch' a me torno, trovo il petto molle

de la pietate, et alor dico: 'Ahi lasso,
dove se' giunto? et onde se' diviso?'
Ma mentre tener fiso
posso al primo pensier la mente vaga,
et mirar lei et obliar me stesso,
sento Amor sì da presso
che del suo proprio error l'alma s'appaga;
in tante parti et sì bella la veggio
che se l'error durasse, altro non cheggio.

[Where a tall pine or a hillside extends shade, there I sometimes stop, and in
the first stone I see I portray her lovely face with my mind.
When I come back to myself, I find my breast wet with pity and then I say:
'Alas, where have you come to, from what are you separated?'
But as long as I can hold my yearning mind fixed on the first thought, and
look at her and forget myself, I feel Love so close by that my soul is satisfied
by its own deception; in so many places and so beautiful I see her, that, if
the deception should last, I ask for no more.]

(*Rime Sparse* 129.27–39)

Orlando, of course, portrays (*disegno*) Angelica's face on a landscape
much like this one, and he too cleaves to an "error"—the *imagin false* of
a dream.

The self-division noted in Petrarch's speaker ("onde se' diviso?") is
more radical in Orlando, whose alienation from his identity once the "dolce error" is irretrievably destroyed is tantamount to a kind of death:

[N]on son, non sono io quel che paio in viso:
quel ch'era Orlando è morto ed è sotterra.

· · · · · · · · · · ·

Io son lo spirto suo da lui diviso,
ch'in questo inferno tormentandosi erra.

[I am not, I am not the one my face makes me seem; he who was Orlando
is dead and buried.

· · · · · · · · · · ·

I am his spirit separated from him, which wanders in torment in this hell.]

(*OF* 23.128)

Petrarch's return to himself after the excursion within the deceptive landscape of the imagination is immediate: he awakens, his face wet with tears,

to ask himself, "Dove se' giunto?" Although Orlando similarly awakens in tears, the space between this moment and the true awakening to himself is coextensive with *l'amorosa inchiesta* itself. From a medical perspective, Orlando's self-alienation seems to describe the kind of "spiritual" self-evacuation diagnosed by Ficino as a precursor to love-melancholy:

> Non suppliron le lacrime al dolore:
> finir, ch'a mezzo era il dolore a pena.
> Dal fuoco spinto or il vitale umore
> fugge per quella via ch'agli occhi mena;
> ed è quell che si versa, e trarrà insieme
> e 'l dolore e la vita all'ore estreme.

[These tears were too few for my sorrow; they ceased when my sorrow was scarcely in mid-course. Driven by the fire, the vital fluid now escapes by the road that leads to the eyes, and it is that which is poured out and will bring my sorrow and my life together to their last hours.]

(*OF* 23.126)

The hemorrhaging of vital spirits ("il vitale umore") through the eyes recalls in some detail Ficino's account of the depletion of the lover's spirits as they flow unstoppably toward the interior image of the beloved (and thence outward toward the beloved's body). Finally, of course, Ficino predicts that the depleted blood will become melancholic, "ceaselessly troubl[ing] the soul day and night with hideous and terrible images" (*De amore* 6.9).[31]

For Petrarch's speaker it is precisely the shift from the *dolce error* of the phantasmic vision to the cold moment of awakening that promotes the creation of a melancholic poetic style. The enchantment and disenchantment of the landscape within the mind is quite self-conscious:

> [E]t quanto in più selvaggio
> loco mi trovo e 'n più deserto lido,
> tanto più bella il mio pensier l'adombra.
> Poi quando il vero sgombra
> quel dolce error, pur lì medesmo assido
> me freddo, pietra morta in pietra viva,
> in guisa d'uom che pensi et pianga et scriva.

[And in whatever wildest place and most deserted shore I find myself, so much the more beautiful does my thought shadow her forth. Then, when the truth dispels that sweet deception, right there in the same place I sit

down, cold, a dead stone on the living rock, like a man who thinks and
weeps and writes.]

(*Rime Sparse* 129.45–52)

This poem is written from the perspective of the poet's recantation of what
he calls his "giovenile errore" (1.3); the necessary dialectic between delusion
and disillusionment in the act of writing is thus painfully apparent to the
fully disillusioned poet whose voice lies behind the poem. The *dolce error*
is constitutive of a poetry that is nonetheless *written* from a position of
irremediable loss.[32] The willing denial of a truth that finally forces itself
on the speaker is at the heart of Ariosto's critique of Petrarchan melancholy. Whereas the structure of this lyric collection permits the speaker to
indulge repeatedly in a vain pursuit of the phantasmic image, the teleological force of Orlando's quest reveals the moral and psychological cost of
the soul's self-deception. As the medical writers predict, the extension of
Orlando's *dolce error* over time transforms the bittersweet pleasures of the
dreamworld into a degenerative madness that threatens his very life.

I have lingered over this canzone because its resonant evocation of
the seductive toils of *dolce error* informs Orlando's dream in crucial ways.
This dream is, of course, not framed by a penitent poet's renunciation of
youthful error. Orlando is thus not a poet, though his dream becomes the
stuff of lyric poetry through the actions of a narrator who, like Petrarch,
both admits to a love-madness and distances himself from it.[33] Orlando
himself remains mired in *dolce error*, wandering uncomprehendingly in
the *deserto* that follows the disappearance of the vision. Unlike Petrarch's
lyric, Orlando's vision obscures the real center of the dream by refusing
to disenchant the metaphors that sustain the dream's illusions. Though
canzone 129, like Orlando's dream, evokes a vision and its aftermath, the
true center of the lyric poem is clearly the melancholic poet, whose quasi
death alienates him from the bittersweet pleasures that saturate his language. Orlando's dream, on the other hand, metaphorizes the force behind
the destruction of the *dolce error* as *una tempesta*, a sudden, baffling storm
that destroys the beautiful vision on the stream bank. Orlando must ask
himself who is responsible for this destruction: "Misero me! / chi ha cangiata mia dolcezza in tosco?" (8.82). The transformation of the Petrarchan
sweetness into a destructive poison remains mysterious within the terms of
the dream itself. It is not until much later that the tenor of the metaphor

is revealed. When Orlando himself destroys a Petrarchan *locus amoenus* inscribed with a love lyric (written by Medoro, Angelica's lover), we realize that the storm figures both this terrible destruction and the collapse of Orlando's mind into the mania that is the telos of love-melancholy.[34]

What is striking about Orlando's dream is not that it first appears to be a kind of wish-fulfillment dream, assuaging his desire for Angelica; it is rather that it immediately stages a traumatic reenactment of the very loss that prompted his waking despair.[35] For as the echoes between this passage and the destruction of the *locus amoenus* in canto 23 indicate, Orlando's own *furor* is the occluded source of the destructive storm. In other words, it is Orlando's melancholic love that destroys the vision of the beloved that it has conjured. In its late phases Orlando's violence is explicitly compared to a tempest: "Lo scudo ruppe solo, e su l'elmetto / tempesto sì, che Dudon cadde in terra" (it broke only the shield but so like a tempest it came down on the helmet that Dudon fell to earth, 39.49). The Petrarchan *locus amoenus* at first seems to assuage Orlando's grief with the "dolce error" that fixes the mind on its own delusions. But instead of satisfying the dreamer's desire and permitting his sleep to continue, the dream transforms its *dolcezza* into its opposite, *tosco*, destroying the soothing space of the vision seemingly spontaneously. Rather than making sense of the loss that Orlando mourns before he falls asleep, the dream actually disrupts the process of sense making, repeating the original trauma and launching him into the renewed, waking suffering ("A questo orribil grido risvegliossi, / e tutto pien di lacrime trovossi") that drives him into his quest and thence into the "inferno" of madness.

As this line of inquiry will suggest, I interpret this dream as a crucial illustration of the link between a melancholic reaction to loss and the origin of the romance narrative. Though poem 129 suggests that the speaker's *dolce error* is the occluded inspiration of a coolly self-conscious poetic program, Ariosto's critique of Petrarchanism here indicates that Petrarch's melancholic style contains the seeds of psychic destruction: the *dolcezza* and *tosco* of Orlando's lament.[36] The failure to acknowledge the loss and absence of Angelica—and perhaps the instability of any love-object—promotes in this poem an inevitable disintegration into a dehumanizing madness. The closing moments of the dream confirm that a Petrarchan choice of "a plague of phantasms" over the reality of loss is the point of origin of

Orlando's romance quest. The words that prompt his anguished awakening allude to a Petrarchan source that explicitly addresses the loss of the beloved. The words that Orlando hears spoken "from elsewhere" closely echo the final line of Petrarch's sonnet 250, which records a vision of Laura informing Petrarch of her death:[37]

> Ecco ch'altronde ode da un'altra voce:
> —Non sperar più gioirne in terra mai.—
> A questo orribil grido risvegliossi . . .

[Lo, from another direction he hears from another voice:
"Do not hope to enjoy them [the sweet eyes] ever more on earth."
At this horrible cry he awoke . . .]

(OF 8.83)

> "[N]on sperar di vedermi in terra mai."

"[Do not hope ever to see me again on earth.]"

(*Rime Sparse* 250)

Petrarch's sonnet ends with the announcement that Laura is dead; but it begins with the speaker's memory of frequent visions of her in sleep: "Solea lontana in sonno consolarme / con quella dolce angelica sua vista" (Though afar, my lady was wont to console me in sleep / with her sweet angelic sight of her, 250.1–2). The "dolce *angelica* vista" who consoles Petrarch's speaker in sleep would seem to be a vital source for Angelica herself, who appears in Orlando's dream to console him, only to vanish just as Laura does at the end of sonnet 250. The speaker's resistance to the disappearance of Laura is recorded in the following poem, in which he continues to hope for sight of her: "A me pur giova di sperare ancora / la dolce vista del bel viso adorno" (I must still hope for / the sweet sight of her lovely face, 251.9–10). Orlando's lost Angelica thus appears in his dream as the distant *angelica vista* of an already lost Laura, a signifier irreparably separated from its signified. It is literally true to say with Ascoli that the prediction of death contained in the dream is misdirected, "because Angelica never does die in the poem."[38] But it is perhaps closer to the spirit of the allusion to say that it reveals the terrible truth that Angelica is no more than a ghostly phantasm that will draw Orlando into a netherworld of sweet but poisonous dreams.

The Game of Loss: Romance and the Failure to Mourn

Ariosto constructs the beginning of Orlando's romance "error," then, as an awakening into a melancholic Petrarchan world in which a phantasm is pursued in place of a real object. But whereas the self-contained, atemporal lyric allows for a discontinuous iteration of such moments of loss and despair, the narrativity of romance reveals—and is organized around—the destructive teleology of love-melancholy. Orlando's dream has, as we saw, both structural and linguistic connections to Petrarchan lyric: the *dolcezza* and *tosco* of his dream-experience seem to derive directly from the *dilectoso male* of Petrarchan discourse. But the lyric structure of the dream breaks apart under the pressure of Orlando's agony: hearing that he will "never more" be able to enjoy his beloved, he wakes into the narrative of his quest. The shift from an atemporal lyric structure to a narrative driven by the remorseless intensification of Orlando's *furor* indicates that Ariosto's critique of Petrarchism will take hold precisely at the moment at which loss enters the temporal world. For Orlando's dream stops just at the moment at which his loss of Angelica is represented as a kind of death. Rather than facilitating the transformation and introjection of this loss, then, the dream actually prompts Orlando to pursue the *imagin false* into the real world.

Jonathan Lear's discussion of how the mind processes loss provides a useful commentary on this dream's failure to accommodate the loss of Angelica/Laura.[39] Discussing Freud's celebrated elaboration of his grandson's "fort-da" game, Lear argues that the game reveals the mind's spontaneous response to external trauma: it repeats the trauma, throwing away the spool, playing with the idea of loss (not yet an "idea" at all). If the imaginative play is successful, a game emerges that stabilizes the mind's anxiety by covering over the loss in some way; if the play is not successful, the mind may begin to damage itself:

> Once the rip has occurred the child experiences internal pressure to enact the disturbance . . . there is an enactment of self-disruption: the child throws away the spool and says 'ooo'. What this disruption is for depends on what happens next. . . . Suppose the child could never get to 'da.' He would then get struck repeating 'ooo' over and over again. We would then see something that looked like a traumatic neurosis. Indeed the child might

begin to use these outbursts to attack his own mind. For the child would never be able to get a thought together if each attempt to do so was interrupted by an outburst of 'ooo'. *Rather than face the loss, the child might opt to attack his own ability to understand what has happened to him. This would be the beginning of a massively self-destructive, self-annihilating character.*[40]

The response fails because it does not produce what Lear calls a "game of loss," where the notion of a game amounts to a Wittgensteinian "form of life." The child never manages the anxiety produced by the initial loss and therefore never achieves a symbolic representation of that loss: "[T]he outcome of the game is to convert what would otherwise be a nameless trauma into a loss."[41] The game of loss necessitates the development of an imaginative space in which a *phantasmic* object can be conjured, lost, and then conjured again. Only once this space is established does it make sense to talk of a concept of loss: "[T]he name of loss requires the game of loss: it requires inventing ways of living with the loss that one has just named."[42] The process that Lear adumbrates here corresponds to—though with a different emphasis—the process of introjection, in which the loss of the object is absorbed by the ego and symbolized in words.

In a literary context the game that makes possible the introduction of the name of loss is *elegy*. Elegy is precisely the literary "form of life" that both addresses the loss of the beloved object and begins the journey toward acceptance of that loss, the movement toward "pastures new." What Orlando's dream reveals in its self-disruptive repetition of the original loss—leading to Orlando's tearful awakening—is that the Petrarchan *locus amoenus* cannot be converted into an elegiac space in which the phantasmic object can be lost and found. The "game" of loss laid out before us in Orlando's dream looks in fact rather like Lear's neurotic version of the fort-da game in which the child never gets to "da." The phantasm of Angelica is conjured, only to disappear permanently in a tempestuous rendering of the original trauma. Thus the dream cannot cover over the mind's wound but in fact propels Orlando further into a disastrous elaboration of precisely the place at which the dream fails: the moment of loss. Atlante's palace, as we have seen, appears as the inevitable intensification of the experience of an abortive game of loss. Each time the "game of loss" fails, Orlando moves closer to the final moment of madness triggered by the shepherd's narrative.

Lear stresses the importance of the imagination in the development of the game of loss (the child must be able to play with mother's absence, to *think* her as a separate object). But it is paradoxically the imaginative power of the melancholic that allows the mind to continue to deny the reality of objective loss. For the efficacy of the kind of game Lear has in mind depends on its congruence with reality:

> In being able to get to "da," the child is able to bring his experience together rather than blow it apart. The invention of the game converts this rip in the fabric of experience into an experience of loss. It creates a cultural space in which the child can play with loss: in this way he comes to be able to tolerate and name it. *This is an instance in which a way of functioning according to the pleasure principle and a way of functioning according to the reality principle get installed at the same time. . . .* It is precisely in the creation of these sorts of playful activities that a child enters the space of reasons.[43]

The successful elegiac game, initiated by the pressure of loss, turns on the capacity of the game to make reality acceptable to the mind. The melancholic response to loss, on the other hand, works by producing a phantasmic world so vivid and absorbing that the reality of objective loss need not be fully experienced: "[M]elancholy is less the regressive reaction to the loss of an object than the *phantasmic (or hallucinatory) capacity to keep it alive as a lost object.*"[44] Paradoxically, then, the melancholic sufferer does not get to "da," and thus does not arrive at a fully fledged concept of loss, but instead installs a phantasmic alternative world in the space created by the game's initial gesture ("fort"). Such a world is the *altronde* (elsewhere) constructed both within Orlando's dream and Atlante's palace.

We have arrived here at the central paradox of love-melancholy and of the romance form to which it gives shape in Ariosto's poem. For the morbid disruption of the imagination constitutive of love-melancholy provides the conditions for the development of a phantasmic world whose existence *depends on the loss of the object but whose content is rigorously anti-elegiac*. As a result of this perseverative focus on the object of love, the melancholic imagination occludes the reality of the actual object at the same time as it prevents the installation of what Lear calls the "game of loss." In place of the "fort-da" game, which for Freud and Lear represents the imaginative accommodation of loss—in my terms, the introjection of loss—we find a game whose function is continuously to re-create the loss within the subject's own mind and under the subject's control. It is not surprising, then, that unlike his Boiardesque counterpart, Orlando never knowingly encounters Angelica after his departure from Atlante's palace in pursuit of her. When he does track her down, he is that squalid *uom pazzo* who does not recognize her. Lear's commentary on the consequences of a failure even to install the concept of loss is remarkably pertinent to Orlando's disintegration: "*Rather than face the loss, the child might opt to attack his own ability to understand what has happened to him. This would be the beginning of a massively self-destructive, self-annihilating character.*"

If we return to our original discussion of the relationship between Atlante's palace and the form of romance, we might say that Atlante's palace represents romance as a form of life specifically organized to avoid the introjection of loss. David Quint has argued that Atlante's palace is a microcosm of Boiardo's romance and as such a narrative designed to defer the inevitable deaths of the poem's central protagonists.[45] Although the relationship between Boiardo's poem and the structure of Atlante's palace is indisputable, the central feature of the latter rests not merely on a literary device, but on a complex conception of melancholia that bridges literary and medical discourses. The sources of Atlante's strategies lie in the choice of *atra voluptas*, the dark pleasure of melancholy that ties Petrarchan poetry to a long history of medical and philosophical accounts of the illness:

> Questo era un nuovo e disusato incanto
> ch'avea composto Atlante di Carena,
> perché Ruggier fosse occupato tanto
> in quel travaglio, in *quella dolce pena*,
> che 'l mal'influsso n'andasse da canto,
> l'influsso ch'a morir giovene il mena.

[This was a new and unaccustomed enchantment that Atlas of Carena had devised in order that Ruggiero might so long be occupied in that labor, in *that sweet pain*, that the evil influence might pass by, the influence that is leading the youth to death.]

(*OF* 12.21, italics mine)

The *dolce pena* (sweet pain) that Ruggiero and the other knights experience in the castle seems a direct descendant of Petrarch's *atra voluptas* and of the long history of melancholic love that produces his eroticized *acedia*. What is especially provocative about this *dolce pena* is that it is explicitly deployed as a defense against death. We have hypothesized in other contexts a connection between love-melancholy and a refusal to acknowledge death, but this is the first instance in which the bitter fruits of a melancholy love actually serve as an apotropaic device to ward off death. When Orlando rushes into the palace after hearing Angelica's voice calling for aid (just as she does in his dream), he encounters the *dolcezza/tosco* of his dream in the form of Atlante's *dolce pena*. By the same token, the labyrinthine structure of romance that the palace epitomizes seems to emerge directly from Orlando's avoidance of the true meaning of Laura's prophetic words.

When Orlando circles the palace in the classic position of the melancholic, "tenendo pur a terra il viso chino" (holding his face bent over the ground, *OF* 12.14), he is enacting the psychic consequences of a failure to introject the loss of a beloved object. To enter Atlante's palace is to commit oneself to the search for an unreachable "elsewhere," the *altronde* whence Angelica's voice seems to call him:

> Ecco ch'altronde ode da un'altra voce . . .

[Lo, from elsewhere he hears from another voice . . .]

(*OF* 8.83, trans. Gilbert, with slight emendation)

> Talor si ferma, ed una voce ascolta,
> che di quella d'Angelica ha sembianza
> (e s'egli è da una parte, suona altronde) . . .

[Sometimes he stops and hears a voice like that of Angelica (and if he is in one place it sends its sound from elsewhere) . . .]

(*OF* 12.16, trans. Gilbert, with slight emendation)

As we have seen, the placement of the beloved as a phantasmic object within a permanently unreachable "elsewhere" structures the object of melancholic love as an impossible object, comparable to what Lacan will later call the *objet a*.[46] As Bruce Fink notes, the *objet a* is unreachable because it is the phantasmic remainder of a time before either subject or object existed as such: "Object (a) is the leftover of that process of constituting an object. . . . [I]t is the remainder of the lost hypothetical mother-child unity."[47] The melancholic projection of the object of desire into a phantasmic world does seem to construct the other as a quasi-maternal figure, as we have seen. Mary Wack notes that the lover often treats the object with a furious ambivalence, as though it represents a version of the "bad mother" who "acts independently of masculine control . . . [and] is fickle, disobedient, rebellious, and indulges in sexual excess."[48] The poem's portrayal of Angelica (from Orlando's perspective) as fickle and disobedient—in her sexual choice—certainly endorses the interpretation of her as at least in part a representation of the absent "bad" mother. Not only does the palace represent a resistance to loss and death, then, but it also inscribes that loss within a fantasized reenactment of the earliest loss of the mother.

Orlando's escalating madness during the course of his quest for Angelica is accompanied by both a regressive orality and a murderous violence that suggest how quickly melancholic love for the (maternal) object turns into dangerous ambivalence:

> Senza pane discerner de le giande,
> dal digiuno e da l'impeto cacciato,
> le mani e il dente lasciò andar di botto
> in quel che trovò prima, o crudo o cotto.
>
> . . . .
>
> Spesso con orsi e con cingiai contese,
> e con man nude li pose a giacere:
> e di lor carne con tutta la spoglia
> più volte il ventre empì con fiera voglia.

[Without distinguishing bread from acorns, driven by hunger and haste, he instantly let hands and teeth go at what he found first, whether raw or cooked.

. . . .

Often he fought with bears and wild boars and with his naked hands laid them low; and with their flesh, with all the hide, he many times filled his belly in fierce desire.]

(*OF* 24.12–13)

Orlando's *fiera voglia* seems to represent a literalization of the kind of *furor* that possesses Lucretius's besotted lovers, who try to turn the beloved into a phantasmic form of food. Similarly, his brutal treatment of Angelica's mare (which he eventually kills) confirms Hildegard von Bingen's striking assertion that the melancholic's "fierce desire" bespeaks a potentially murderous hatred of its female object:

The influence of the devil rages so powerfully in the passion of these men that they would kill the woman with whom they are having sexual relations if they could. For there is nothing of love or affection in them.[49]

The *desiderio insano* (insane desire, 29.70) that Orlando exhibits in his torture of the mare looks like a dramatically intensified version of the "rip in the fabric of life" first manifested by the broken dream. For the mare is clearly a substitute for Angelica herself, and the demented pleasure Orlando takes in her recalls his (equally deluded) pleasure in the dream:

> [C]on quella festa il paladin la piglia,
> qu'un altra avrebbe fatto una donzella.

[The paladin takes her with such delight as another might have done a maiden.]

(OF 29.68)

> Sentia il maggior piacer, la maggior festa
> che sentir possa alcun felice amante.

[He was feeling the greatest pleasure, the greatest joy that any happy lover can feel.]

(OF 8.81)

Orlando begins his quest as a Bellerophon figure in his dream, wandering, like Petrarch's speaker, through "i più deserti campi" (*Rime Sparse*, 35): "Parea che per trovar qualche coperto, / andasse errando invan per un deserto" (It seemed that to find some shelter he went wandering through a desert in vain, 8.81). But the repetition of certain elements of the dream in the grotesquely violent episode with Angelica's horse reveals how ugly the love-melancholy of a Bellerophon can become when not contained by the atemporal frame of lyric. Orlando has now become the mindless storm that destroys what it had previously loved. Significantly, the dream's prophetic promise that Angelica will be lost is finally fulfilled in this scene: Angelica now disappears for good from the poem.

Solvite me: The Transition from Romance Melancholy to Epic Mourning

My reading of the *Furioso* thus far has suggested that the "romance" narrative is so thoroughly entangled with Orlando's fall into melancholy and madness as to be indistinguishable from it. Thus the palace of Atlante, the paradigm of romance "error," is genetically and temporally linked to the collapse of Orlando's dream of Angelica and his emergence as a "massively self-destructive, self-annihilating character." The remainder of the chapter will argue that it is precisely when Orlando emerges from his madness—a moment marked by the allusion to Virgil's *Eclogue 6*—that the poem begins its transition toward epic closure. But the mutual implication of psychological and literary form in Orlando's madness presupposes that the transition between romance and epic will not be a purely formal, literary matter. Indeed, I suggest that in spite of the reorientation of the self implicit in epic's system of values, the newly social and political self cannot shake off the powerful psychic forces that drive the love-quest of romance—and epic, in consequence, cannot shake off its affiliation with romance.

Let us begin by considering the complex moment at which Orlando regains his lost wits. The central feature of this moment for my argument is Ariosto's striking allusion to the words of Silenus in Virgil's *Eclogue 6*: *solvite me* (release me). Though it has been argued that Seneca's *Hercules Furens* may be a source for this allusion, this strikes me as unlikely: the exact phrase is taken from the Virgilian source, and the context makes it clear that the reference is to the words of Silenus.[50] A juxtaposition of the two relevant passages seems at first to indicate mostly the differences between them:

> Poi disse, come già disse Sileno
> a quei che lo legar nel cavo speco:
> *Solvite me,* con viso sì sereno,
> con guardo sì men de l'usato bieco,
> che fu slegato; e de' panni ch'avieno
> fattir arrecar participaron seco,
> *consolandolo* tutti del dolore,
> che lo premea, di quel *passato errore.*

[Then he said, as once Silenus said to those who bound him in the hollow cave: "*Solvite me,*" with so calm a face and with a look so much less distorted than his former one that he was loosed; and they shared with him some clothes they had brought, all consoling him for the sorrow that weighed on him for that *past madness.*]

(*OF* 39.60, with minor emendation to Gilbert's translation, italics mine)

adgressi (nam saepe senex spe carminis ambo
luserat) iniciunt ipsis ex vincula sertis.
addit se sociam timidisque supervenit Aegle,
Aegle, Naiadum pulcherrima, iamque videnti
sanguineis frontem moris et tempora pingit.
ille dolum ridens "quo vincula nectitis?" inquit.
"solvite me, pueri: satis est potuisse videri.
carmina, quae voltis, cognoscite."

[Falling on him—for oft the aged one had cheated both of a promised
song—they cast him into fetters made from his own garlands. Aegle
joins their company and seconds the timid pair—Aegle, the fairest of the
Naiads—and, as now his eyes open, paints his face and brows with bloody
mulberries. Smiling at the trick, he cries: "Why fetter me? *Release me, lads;*
enough that you have shown your power. Hear the songs you crave."]

(*Ecl.* 6.18–25, trans. Loeb, with minor emendations, italics mine)

But in spite of the difference (or apparent difference) in tone between the
two passages, Ariosto's text is keyed to the central theme of Silenus's song:
the transformation of *furor* into elegiac acceptance.

Charles Segal has clarified the stark contrast between the madness
that fills the *Eclogue*'s inset stories and the cool rationality of its frame.[51]
Summarizing the dialectic between the Apollonian and Bacchic modes in
the poem he writes: "[man] can, like the poet shepherd, Tityrus, or like the
poet Gallus on Helicon, follow the 'orders' ('non iniussa cano') of Apollo
. . . Or like Pasiphae, Scylla, Tereus, he can sink into *bestial degradation
which finds its external ratification in bestial metamorphosis*" (italics mine).[52]
The figure whose "bestial metamorphosis" takes up most room in Silenus'
song is Pasiphae, and indeed her story seems to epitomize the poem's treatment of *furor*.[53] Her besotted love for the bull is described as a madness (*dementia*) that leads her to wander hopelessly (*erras*) in pursuit of a delusion.
Pasiphae's wandering, madness, and loss of humanity clearly associate her
with Orlando, and indeed Silenus's address to Pasiphae could with perfect
appropriateness be addressed to Orlando: "quae te dementia cepit?" (what
madness seized you?).

[E]t fortunatam, si numquam armenta fuissent,
Pasiphaen nivei solatur amore iuvenci.
a! virgo infelix, *quae te dementia cepit!*

> Proetides implerunt falsis mugitibus agros:
> at non tam turpis pecudum tamen ulla secuta
> concubitus, quamvis collo timuisset aratrum
> et saepe in levi quaesisset cornua fronte.
> a! virgo infelix, *tu nunc in montibus erras*:
> ille, latus niveum molli fultus hyacintho,
> ilice sub nigra pallentis ruminat herbas,
> aut aliquam in magno sequitur grege.

[*Now he solaces Pasiphae*—happy one, if herds had never been!—*with her passion for the snowy bull*. Ah, unhappy girl, *what madness seized thee*? The daughters of Proetus filled the fields with unreal lowings, but not one was led by so foul a love for beasts, albeit each had feared the yoke for her neck, and often looked for horns on her smooth brow. Ah! unhappy girl, *thou art now wandering on the hills*: he, pillowing his snowy side on soft hyacinths, under a dark ilex chews the pale grass, or courts some heifer in the great herd.]

(6.45–54, italics mine, trans. Loeb, with minor emendation)

The structural analogy between the aimless wandering that afflicts Pasiphae "even now" and her doomed *dementia* finds its psychological equivalent in later medieval accounts of love-melancholy as a wandering of the mind. "Amor est mentis insania qua vagatur animus per inania crebris doloribus permiscens gaudia" (Love is a sickness of the mind in which the spirit wanders through emptiness, mixing joy with frequent sorrows).[54] Orlando's own romance "error" seems to dramatize precisely the internalization of Pasiphae's mythical wandering.

The prominence of Pasiphae's story of "turpis . . . concubitus" in Silenus's song suggests that in ancient culture madness—and especially love-madness—was especially associated with women. As Ruth Padel comments, love-madness (or *oistros*) was often depicted as a "female, bovine, mating madness and its externalized cause: a tormenting fly."[55] Not surprisingly, then, the frenzy of *desire* in particular is often depicted as a necessarily feminizing force in Greek literature. Debra Hershkowitz recognizes this pattern in Apollonius's depiction of Heracles: "When Apollonius describes Heracles as a bull stung by a gadfly [*oistros*], he is reshaping the female tragic image of madness into a male, and arguably epic one."[56] This tension between a "female" tragic madness and a "male" epic one may also inflect the shape of Orlando's quest, especially given the other connections between Heracles and Orlando.[57] Although the importance of Heracles as a model for Orlando has been noted, the feminization of Heracles by this distinctly female *furor* has not, to my knowledge, been recognized as a significant aspect of the treatment of madness that Ariosto receives from these classical texts. The association between Orlando and a specifically feminine madness is also present in Boiardo's poem, where Orlando addresses himself at the very beginning of his madness in the words of Ovid's Medea.[58]

In his furiously destructive rampage over the countryside, Orlando also resembles the blindly driven maenads, on whose frenzy Medea's madness is clearly modeled. Hershkowitz comments that the maenad confuses conventional gender distinctions: "[S]he is at the same time hyper-feminine and masculine, possessed by divinity and possessed of violent strength and ferocity as well as heightened sexuality."[59] Orlando's "masculine" strength is, of course, in evidence throughout his mad career over the countryside. But the nature of this violence associates it strongly with maenadic and thus feminine violence. Like Agave, who unwittingly tears her own son apart in Euripides' *Bacchae*, Orlando routinely dismembers those he encounters in a kind of dark parody of Bacchic madness. We might recall that just before he encounters Angelica, he tears apart a young man, like a heron or hen "quando si vuol de le calde interiora / che falcone o ch'astor resti satollo" (whom someone wishes a falcon or hawk to gorge on its warm inwards, 29.56). If the maenad's "masculine" traits represented for classical culture a confusion of traditional gender characteristics, the "feminine" qualities of the erotic melancholic seem to have represented, as we have seen, a similar challenge to medieval and early modern culture. The framing of Orlando's quest with this prominent allusion to the *furor* of Pasiphae thus reinforces the feminization of Orlando already implied by the medical conception of love-melancholy as in some instances a *femineus amor*, and helps to construct romance as both a melancholic and a "feminine" genre.

Silenus's song about Pasiphae is presented in the *Eclogue* as a form of *consolation* for her suffering: "Pasiphaen nivei *solatur* amore iuvenci" (Now he *consoles* Pasiphae with her passion for the snowy bull, 6.46).[60] Similarly, when Orlando wakes from the "abominevol forme" of his errancy it is primarily consolation that he requires from his companions: "consolando tutti del dolore, / che lo premea, di quel passato errore" (39.60). The remainder of this chapter will demonstrate that Orlando's awakening though the echoes of Silenus's poem shifts Orlando out of the furious *errori* of romance (and simultaneously out of the "effeminate" role of maddened lover) into the renunciatory forms of epic. This argument implies a reading of epic as essentially elegiac in structure, and I shall return to this assumption in more detail. For now it is sufficient to suggest that Orlando's return to what the poem—and its literary history—designates as the "masculine" behavior of the warrior is predicated on a shift into a form of elegy characteristic of epic: the lament for the dead companion. Orlando's last significant action in the poem is the lament he gives for Brandimarte, and this lament seems calculated to signal the poem's alliance with its epic models. In particular, as we shall see, Orlando's lament recalls the lament of Aeneas for Pallas, and the Virgilian echoes here both restore Orlando's stature as epic warrior and suggest that romance modulates into epic at least in part through the action of mourning.[61] The cost of this modulation is primarily apparent, as it is in Virgil's poem, in the treatment of the tragic *mors immatura* (untimely death) topos. Like Pallas, Brandimarte is a youthful bridegroom, and his death seems to mark symbolically not only the end of Orlando's erotic obsession but also the impossibility of love in the world that the poem now inhabits.[62]

The closing lines of *Eclogue* 6 indicate that the allusion to Silenus's *solvite me* does not end with an invocation of classical stories of *furor*. Instead, the playful request for release deepens into a metaphor for psychological release: from the bonds of intense love and grief. The poem closes with an oblique reference to Apollo's loss of his beloved Hyacinthus, accidentally killed by Apollo's own discus:

> *[O]mnia quae Pheobo quondam meditante beatus*
> *audiit Eurotas iussitque ediscere laurus,*
> *ille canit* (pulsae referunt ad sidera valles),
> cogere donec ovis stabulis numerumque referre
> iussit et invito processit Vesper Olympo.

> [*All the songs that of old Phoebus rehearsed, while happy Eurotas listened and bade his laurels learn by heart—these Silenus sings.* The re-echoing valleys fling them again to the stars, till Vesper gave the word to fold the flocks and tell their tale, as he set forth over an unwilling sky.]

> (6.82–86, italics mine)

As Williams and Segal both note, the reference to Eurotas contains a covert reference to the death of Hyacinthus, since it was on the banks of the Eurotas that Apollo was said to have expressed his grief in song.[63] Since Silenus's song is thus a recapitulation of Apollo's elegiac songs for Hyacinthus, it is not primarily a song *about* tragic loves; it is quite explicitly an *elegy for* them. Not only does the reference to Apollo tie the ending of the poem back to its beginning, and back to the continuous thread of "tragic love"; more importantly it points to the role of poetry as consolation for lost love. The peacefulness of the scene evoked, "beatus Eurotas," and the serenity of the poetic practice involved, "Phoebo *meditante*," suggest the conversion of the kind of passionate *dementia* characteristic of Pasiphae's love into a necessary mourning.[64] This conversion is made possible through the meditative action of poetic performance. The act of singing about the death of a loved one is understood to transform a passionate and perhaps dangerous grief into a gentler mourning that is congruent with nature's own forms and rituals.

Elegiac Epic

Orlando's descent into the melancholic inferno that follows his dream of Angelica is coincident with his abandonment of his comrade-in-arms, Brandimarte: "Da mezza notte tacito si parte, / e non saluta e non fa motto al zio; / né al fido suo compagno Brandimarte, / che tanto amar solea, pur dice a Dio" (At midnight he goes away in silence, and he does not bid good-bye or say a word to his uncle, nor to his faithful companion Brandimarte, whom he ever loved so much, does he even say "God be with you," 8.86). For the duration of his Pasiphae-like frenzy, Orlando's obsession with Angelica obliterates his long-standing devotion to Brandimarte. Such devotion between comrades in arms is a feature of epic: the relationship between Aeneas and Pallas, which I take to be the model for this Ariostan relationship, is, of course, itself modeled on the erotic friendship between Achilles and Patroclus. As though to signal the shift in allegiance when he leaves the camp, Orlando dons black armor that he took from a Saracen he killed in battle:

> [N]on l'onorata insegna del quartiero,
> distinta di color bianchi e vermigli,

> ma portar volse un ornamento nero;
> e forse acciò ch'al suo dolor simigli:
> e quello avea già tolto a uno amostante,
> ch'uccise di sua man pochi anni inante.

[He determined to wear, not the honored device of his coat of arms, painted in white and vermilion colours, but black equipment—and perhaps that it might be like his sorrow; and he had taken that from a pasha whom with his own hand he killed a few years before.]

(*OF* 8.85)

Orlando's black armor, signifying the blackness of his melancholy, also signals the swerve away from the martial rectitude of epic toward a feminized (and pagan) romance, "l'amorosa inchiesta" (9.7).

The significance of Orlando's substitution of Angelica for Brandimarte does not become clear until Brandimarte's funeral, in canto 43. By this point in the poem Orlando has "recovered" his lost wits, and returned with renewed vigor to the battlefield. Whereas Orlando could not accept the loss of Angelica, preferring instead to enter a melancholic, interiorized world, in the epic context of Brandimarte's death he mourns his friend through elaborate funeral rites, leaving him behind to rejoin Charlemagne. As has often been noted, Ariosto models Brandimarte's death closely on the death of Pallas in the *Aeneid*.[65] What is important about this Virgilian background for my purposes is that it suggests Ariosto's direct engagement—already established by the dense allusion to Silenus's song—with the quintessentially Virgilian *mors immatura* (untimely death) topos. My argument thus far has suggested that romance as a mode is organized around an anti-elegiac refusal to acknowledge the loss of a beloved object and a subsequent internalization (incorporation) of the object within a powerful, but occluded, phantasmic world. Epic, by contrast, develops its closural strategies around the elaborate ritual acknowledgment of loss.[66] Epic's internalization of elegy frees the subject from the phantasm of the lost object and thus provides an alternative to the melancholic *aporia* of romance. Nevertheless, a consideration of the *mors immatura* topos in Virgil's and Ariosto's poems will allow us to see clearly that the act of mourning in epic is fully imbricated in the *furor* it attempts to exorcise.

The death of Pallas prompts a *furor* in Aeneas that—unlike its romance counterpart—is not only accommodated within a teleological structure but actually *promotes* the poem's movement toward its close.[67] Aeneas kills Turnus out of rageful grief, just as Orlando will kill Agramante and Gradasso in response to Brandimarte's death. We might understand the death of Pallas in Virgil's poem as the catalyst that prompts Aeneas finally to leave behind the poem's powerful "romance" episode: his sojourn in Carthage with Dido. For when Aeneas buries Pallas, he veils him in the cloak made for him by Dido: "[I]psa suis quondam manibus Sidonia Dido / fecerat et tenui telas discreverat auro/harum unam iuveni supremum maestus honorem/induit arsurasque comas obnubuit amictu" (Dido herself once with her own hands wrought [it] for him, interweaving the web with threads of gold. Of these he sadly drapes one round the youth as a last honour, and in its covering veils those locks that the fire will claim, *Aen.* 11.74–75, trans. Loeb). The verb used here of the veiling (*obnubuit*) is generally used to denote the veiling of a bride: Pallas thus becomes the (feminized) bride/groom who both replaces and symbolizes the sacrificed Dido.[68] Similarly, we might understand the loss and burial of Brandimarte as a sign of Orlando's final reconciliation to the loss of Angelica. But the result of this renunciation of the beloved object of romance is an immediate immersion on the field of battle. Like Aeneas, Orlando delivers a funeral oration praising the lost warrior's courage and stature in battle (*Aen.* 9.57–58; *OF* 43.173), and like Aeneas he turns eventually from the lost comrade back to the prospect of war.

In both texts, the dark side of the elegiac response to the death of a comrade is excessive cruelty on the battlefield. In a simile that reduces Aeneas to a deadly and unthinking force of nature, Virgil compares Aeneas's *furor* to a torrent of water or a tempest: "torrentis aquae vel turbinis atri / more furens" (raging like a brook in torrent or a black tempest, *Aen.* 10.603–4). The result of this uncontrolled *furor* is an amoral brutality that seems explicitly at odds with Aeneas's *pietas*. Thus Aeneas sardonically rejects the paterfamilias Magus's pleas for clemency, driving his sword into him "up to the hilt" ("capulo tenus applicat ensem," *Aen.* 10.536). The poem has already designated this very action as egregiously brutal: the sacrilegious Pyrrhus kills Priam in the same way ("capulo tenus abdidit ensem," *Aen.* 2.553).[69] If Pallas's death transforms Aeneas into his enemy Pyrrhus, so Brandimarte's death seems to transform Orlando into a version of this bitter, furious Aeneas. Thus we learn that Orlando's rage is stronger than his grief when he realizes that Brandimarte is dead: "[D]a piangere il tempo avea sì corto, / che restò il duolo, et l'ira uscì più in fretta" (He had so short a time for weeping that sorrow was quiet and rage came out more quickly, *OF* 41.102). Strikingly, Orlando's *crudeltade* leads him to follow Aeneas's example specifically in relation to the excessive thrust of the sword "to the hilt" when he kills Gradasso:

> Orlando lo ferì nel destro fianco
> sotto l'ultima costa; e il ferro, immerso
> nel ventre, un palmo uscì dal lato manco,
> di sangue sin all'elsa tutto asperso.

> [Orlando gave him a thrust in the right flank under the lowest rib, and the iron, plunged into his belly, came out a hand's spread from his left side, all sprinkled with blood to the hilt.]

> (*OF* 42.11)

In Ariosto's text as in Virgil's, this destructive, vengeful rage on the battlefield seems to represent the psychological cost of the elegiac foundation of epic. Aeneas's words when he concludes the funeral rites for Pallas epitomize this troubling association of elegy and renewed martial energy: "[N]os alias hinc ad lacrimas eadem horrida belli / fata vocant" (The same grim destiny of war / summons me hence to other tears," *Aen.* 11.96–97).[70]

The deepening of textual allusions associating Orlando with Aeneas suggests not only that the text is negotiating a shift from the melancholic mode of romance to the "mournful" strategies of epic, but also that this shift will entail Orlando's return to normative "masculine" behavior. The text reinforces the notion that Orlando's "escape" from the madness of his quest is also an escape from femininity by substituting Brandimarte's wife, Fiordiligi, for the melancholic Orlando of old. Fiordiligi takes on the wild grief that had previously characterized Orlando: indeed, she is explicitly compared to the maenad whose eroticized *furor* informed Orlando's earlier, Medea-like madness:

> Al tornar de lo spirto, ella alle chiome
> caccia le mani; ed alle belle gote,
> indarno ripetendo il caro nome,
> fa danno ed onta più che far lor puote:
> straccia i capelli e sparge; e grida, come

donna talor che 'l demon rio percuote,
o come s'ode che già a suon di corno
Menade corse, *ed aggirossi intorno*.

[When her spirit returns, she thrusts her hands into her hair and, vainly repeating that dear name, does as much damage and injury to her beautiful cheeks as she can; she tears her hair and scatters it, and screams as sometimes a woman does whom a wicked demon afflicts, or as was heard when long ago Maenad ran at the sound of the horn and *went whirling around*.]

(*OF* 43.158, italics mine)

The feverish circularity of this maenad's course (*aggirossi intorno*) also characterizes the basic "hither-thither" structure of the romance quest as it is epitomized in Atlante's palace: "e gli occhi indarno or quinci or quindi *aggira*" (he turns his eyes in vain to this side and that, *OF* 12.18); "l'uno e l'altro parimente *giva* / di su di giù, dentro e di fuor cercando del gran palazzo lei" (both were in the same way turning up and down, seeking her inside and outside the palace, *OF* 12.29). Fiordiligi's self-entombment also seems to dramatize an *incorporation* of Brandimarte that directly resists the elegiac work of mourning. Thus Ariosto emphasizes that her sighs and tears—both nonverbal forms of signification—are endless: "le lacrime indefesse, / ed ostinati a uscir sempre i sospiri" (her tears unremitting and her sighs determined always to come forth, *OF* 43.183). This description of Fiordiligi is reminiscent, aptly enough, of the description of Orlando as he slips into his melancholic frenzy:

Di pianger mai, mai di gridar non resta
né la notte né 'l dì si dà mai pace.
Fugge cittadi e borghi, e alla foresta
sul terren duro al discoperto giace.
Di sé si maraviglia ch'abbia in testa
una fontana d'acqua sì vivace.

[He never ceases weeping and shrieking and gives himself no peace night or day. He flees from cities and towns and lies on the hard ground out of doors in the forest. He wonders at himself that he has in his head so abundant a fountain of tears and that he can ever sigh so much.]

(*OF* 23.125)

Fiordiligi's desires, Ariosto tells us, are incommensurate with the forms of grief available to her: "né per far sempre dire uffici e messe, / mai satisfar potendo a' suoi disiri" (not being able with always saying offices and masses to satisfy her desires, *OF* 43.183). It is precisely this quality of being "beyond measure" that pulls Fiordiligi's love in a melancholic direction, and eventually necessitates her final dramatic gesture of incorporation. Finding herself unable to leave Brandimarte behind in Sicily, she eventually entombs herself with him: "nel sepolcro fe' fare una cella, / e vi si chiuse, e fe' sua vita in quella" (she had a cell made in the sepulchre, and there she shut herself up and passed her life, *OF* 43.183). As its literalization of the psychoanalytic notion of "incorporation" suggests, this moment of self-entombment might be taken as the quintessential gesture of love-melancholy—and the only possible ending to the romance form that it structures.[71]

Broken Flowers: The End of Romance

Orlando's mysterious *solvite me* refers us both to the "error" of Pasiphae, which seems retroactively to characterize Orlando's own romance quest, and to the Apollonian elegy that prefigures his entry into the mournful practices of epic. But as we have seen, the apparently positive movement from the melancholic incorporation enacted by Fiordiligi to the ritual acknowledgment of death in Brandimarte's Virgilian funeral is complicated by the reappearance of *furor* on the battlefields of epic. My final commentary on Ariosto's interpretation of his Virgilian model will return us again to the *Eclogue* and to the death of Hyacinthus that lies beneath the surface of its closing lines.

The story of Apollo and Hyacinthus recalls in a number of its particulars the story of Orlando and Brandimarte. Brandimarte is, of course, the youthful companion of the older warrior, and although the homoerotic overtones are not as clear in the later text, Orlando clearly states his love for his companion: "tornò Orlando ove il corpo fu lasciato, / che vivo e morto avea con fede amato" (Orlando when back where the body was left, which alive and dead he had loved with fidelity, *OF* 43.167). As Hyacinthus is killed by Apollo's discus, so Brandimarte is killed by Orlando's sword; both lovers feel rage, guilt, and remorse at the death of the youth. Ovid's more detailed account of the death of Hyacinthus includes a simile comparing the dead Hyacinthus to wilting or broken flowers:

> [E]rat inmedicabile vulnus.
> ut, siquis violas rigidumve papaver in horto
> liliaque infringat fulvis horrentia linguis,
> marcida demittant subito caput illa vietum
> nec se sustineant spectentque cacumine terram.

[The wound is past all cure. Just as when in a watered garden, if someone breaks off violets or poppies or lilies, bristling with their yellow stamens, fainting they suddenly droop their withered heads and can no longer stand erect, but gaze, with tops bowed low, upon the earth.]

(*Met.* 10.189–95)

The dead Brandimarte is also memorably compared to a plucked flower:

> Levossi, al ritornar del paladino,
> maggiore il grido, e raddoppiossi il pianto.
> Orlando, fatto al corpo più vicino,
> senza parlar stette a mirarlo alquanto,
> pallido come colto al matutino
> è da sera il ligustro o il molle acanto;
> e dopo a un gran sospir, tenendo fisse
> sempre le luci in lui, così gli disse . . .

[On the paladin's return, a still louder shriek was raised and the weeping redoubled. Orlando, coming near the body, without speaking stood for some time looking upon him—pale as in the evening is the privet or the soft acanthus that was cut in the morning—, and after a great sigh, holding his eyes ever fixed on him, thus he spoke . . .]

(*OF* 43.169)

Ovid's deployment of the metaphor of the fragile, broken flower in the context of the death of the beautiful youth draws on a Virgilian topos that also informs our Ariostan passage. Virgil uses the image of the cut or broken flower in the context of the *mors immatura* (untimely death) of the young, unmarried warrior.[72] Thus Euryalus, for instance, is compared to a poppy broken down by rain ("lassove papavera collo / demisere caput pluvia cum forte gravantur") or cut by the plough ("purpureus veluti cum flos succisus aratro languescit moriens," *Aen.* 9.453–57). Most significantly, Virgil uses this image in relation to the death of Pallas—the example of *mors immatura* that most clearly inflects Ariosto's treatment of Brandimarte. The "drooping hyacinth" in this passage perhaps recalls the similar story of the mythical Hyacinthus:

[H]ic iuvenem agresti sublimem stramine ponunt:
qualem virgineo demessum pollice florem
seu mollis violae seu languentis hyacinthi,
cui neque fulgor adhuc nec dum sua forma recessit,
non iam mater alit tellus virisque ministrat.

[Here they lay the youth high on his rustic bed, like a flower culled by a
girl's finger, tender violet or drooping hyacinth, whose sheen and native
grace have not yet faded, but no more does its mother earth give it strength
and nurture.]

(*Aen.* 11.67–71)

This simile of the wilting flower is originally drawn from *epithalamic*
literature, where it denotes not the death but the loss of virginity of the
beautiful youth. Thus in Catullus 62, for example, we find the same disturbing image of the plucked flower in the context of hymeneal celebration.[73] The deployment of this epithalamic topos in the context of the death
of the beautiful, unwed youth both sexualizes the death of the youth and
emphasizes the savage loss of procreative promise occasioned by the futile
losses on the battlefield. Virgil's treatment of the *mors immatura* theme in
his poem hints at a dark complicity between the elegiac treatment of loss in
epic and the brutal destruction of eros. In other words, the transition from
a melancholic absorption in erotic longing that characterizes romance to
the mournful accommodation of loss in epic is possible only through the
excision of sexuality and its replacement by a murderous *furor*. This excision is symbolized by the grimly inappropriate use of epithalamic imagery
in a funerary context. When Orlando buries Brandimarte, broken like the
"soft acanthus," the echoes of Virgil's poem indicate that the function of
elegy within this epic context is not the neutral "meditation" implied by
the *Eclogue*. In this context, elegiac accommodation is the flip side of the
uncontrolled *furor* of war: it is precisely *because* Pallas is dead that Aeneas
brings the *Aeneid* to a horrifying close with the killing of Turnus. And
although it is not Orlando who kills Rodomonte in the closing scenes of
Orlando Furioso, the tension between battle frenzy and eros is demonstrat-
ed by Rodomonte's interruption of the marriage festival of Bradamante
and Ruggiero. The poem ends not with the triumph of epithalamic celebration over war, but rather with the death of Rodomonte/Turnus in a
bleak repetition of the close of the *Aeneid*.[74]

We recall that Aeneas's hesitation over the suppliant body of Turnus turns to a savage determination to kill him only when he catches sight of the baldric of Pallas, torn from the dead youth as plunder. The baldric depicts the mythological story of the murder of fifty bridegrooms on their wedding night at the hands of their brides, the Danaids:

> rapiens immania pondera baltei
> impressumque nefas: una sub nocte iugali
> caesa manus iuvenum foede thalamique cruenti
> (quae Clonus Eurytides multo caelaverat auro).

[tearing away the belt's huge weight and the story of the crime engraved on it—the youthful band foully slain on one nuptial night, and the chambers drenched in blood—which Clonus, son of Eurytus, had richly chased in gold.]

(*Aen.* 10.496–99)

When Turnus kills Pallas during his first day in battle, then, he repeats in a dark epic key the killing of the bridegrooms on their wedding night.[75] The relationship between the destruction of sexuality and the murderous *furor* of epic is brutally clear. But when Aeneas responds to this *nefas* (crime) by murdering a suppliant Turnus, he extends the significance of Turnus's action well beyond the end of the poem. For the killing of Turnus becomes the definitive "epic" action in subsequent literary responses to the *Aeneid*, as the end of *Orlando Furioso* demonstrates. Ariosto's self-consciously Virgilian ending thus suggests that despite the epic's characteristically "mournful" introjection of loss, its "furious" end promotes not the elegiac "meditation" of pastoral, but rather a cycle of violence in which the death of Turnus is neurotically repeated throughout epic history.

When Orlando awakens from his madness into the echoes of Silenus's song, his awakening is explicitly compared to an awakening from a dream:

> Come chi da noioso e grave sonno,
> ove o vedere abominevol forme
> di mostri che non son, né ch'esser ponno,
>
> . . . .
>
> così, poi che fu Orlando d'error tratto,
> restò maraviglioso e stupefatto.

[As one who after a troublesome sleep and unpleasant dream, in which either he appears to see the abominable forms of monsters that do not exist and cannot be . . . so when Orlando was taken from madness, he was full of wonder and astonished.]

(OF 39.58)

The significance of this moment thus stretches back to include Orlando's initial dream and the intensification of the dream in the palace of Atlante: Orlando now finally emerges from the *dolce pena* of Atlante's palace. But if we expect that the transition from the *dolce pena* of romance to epic will clearly valorize epic, Ariosto's complex treatment of *furor* in his poem makes it clear that the Apollonian song of renunciation is, in an epic context, no less dangerous than Atlante's *nuovo incanto*. After Brandimarte's death, Orlando achieves the kind of detachment from life's grief that marks Petrarch's opening sonnet—he is alone now, and nothing more on earth will please him:

> Solo senza te son; né cosa in terra
> senza te posso aver più, che mi piaccia.

[I am alone without you, and without you I can have nothing further on earth that will please me.]

(OF 43.171)

> et del mio vaneggiar vergogna è 'l frutto,
> e 'l pentersi, e 'l conoscer chiaramente
> che quanto piace al mondo è breve sogno.

[and of my raving, shame is the fruit, and repentance, and the clear knowledge that whatever pleases in the world is a brief dream.]

(Rime Sparse 1)

These lines certainly bear witness to a transcendent movement away from the attachment of melancholic love that for this poem is a sine qua non of epic—nothing on earth now pleases. If we accept David Quint's suggestion that Brandimarte's death clearly anticipates Orlando's future death at Roncevaux, Orlando's lament for Brandimarte also reads like an acceptance of his own death—a self-eulogy.[76]

But in Ariosto's hands this detachment becomes frighteningly inhuman, and we cannot help but feel by the end of the poem that the elegiac cure for romance's *dolce error* has turned out to be the very poison (*tosco*) that destroyed Orlando's dream from within. At the beginning of *Eclogue* 6, Virgil explicitly distances his pastoral project from epic; others, he says, will sing of "tristia bella" (sad wars, 6.7). The introjection of grief that his pastoral poem achieves through its complex mediation ("meditabor," 6.8) on grief and loss provides a resolution to the problem of *furor* that the story of Pasiphae (among others) exemplifies. But Ariosto's exploration of epic violence in the aftermath of Orlando's "cure" suggests that the elegiac equanimity of pastoral—the dissipation of *furor*—cannot hold in this new context. For although epic achieves a painful separation from the lost object that is beyond the scope of the melancholic structure of romance, the radical excision of eros from the epic narrative produces instead the indiscriminate revenge killings that seem to be the dark flip side of obsessive love. Thus in a stunning transposition of the symbolic landscape of the dream, the literal broken flowers of the dream's pastoral *locus amoenus* ("ecco instanto uscire una tempesta / *che struggea i fiori*," *OF* 8.81, italics mine) have metamorphosed into the bodies of men, broken like flowers on the field of battle.

CHAPTER 4

Il primo error

Love-Melancholy and Romance in the
Gerusalemme Liberata

As Tasso's own letters and essays reveal, his life provides a case study of the *poëta melancholicus* whose personal struggle with melancholia is difficult to separate from the shaping of his poetic career. Recent critics have drawn attention to the complexity of the relationship between Tasso's—and his society's—view of melancholy and the tensions evident in his troubled epic project, *Gerusalemme Liberata*.[1] Analysis of the poem's "melancholic" poetics has tended to focus on the figure of Tancredi, whose obsessive love for Clorinda issues in their fight to the death and, later, Tancredi's encounter with the phantasmic Clorinda in the enchanted wood. Margaret Ferguson has considered the "melancholic" structure of Tasso's failure to extricate his own poetic career from that of his father, Bernardo Tasso, and she reads Tancredi's confused and (self-)destructive encounter with the phantasmic Clorinda allegorically, as a symptom of Tasso's own inability to "escape the family romance."[2] Lynn Enterline also considers the importance of melancholia as a figure for authorial anxiety in Tancredi's story, focusing in her account on Tasso's uneasy attempt to distinguish between melancholic phantasms of the mind and "true" visions.[3] According to Enterline, the dubious origin of the allegorical hieroglyphs in the wood gives them the same disruptive potential as the frightening visions that fill Tasso himself with melancholy.[4]

Working with these and other recent considerations of Tancredi as a melancholic figure, my discussion here will relocate Tancredi's story within the early modern medical tradition of love-melancholy and contextualize the poem's treatment of an obsessive, "fantastic" desire within the historically contemporary accounts of mind we considered earlier.[5] I will argue that while Tancredi's obsessive desire for Clorinda does lend itself to a psychoanalytic reading, it cannot be fully understood exclusively from a psychoanalytic perspective. Rather, this pattern of desire and loss draws on the profile of love-melancholy that is, as we have seen, richly supported by a complex pneumo-phantasmic theory of mind. Tancredi's love is recognizable in many of its particulars as love-melancholy: his is an obsessive fixation on a phantasmlike figure, a pleasing *sembianza* that dominates his mind, drawing him permanently away from the center of the epic action into the "romance" byways of the poem.[6] This chapter focuses on Tasso's construal of the relationship between Tancredi's love-melancholy and the poetics of romance, examining in particular the influence of the Lucretian/Ficinian model of an eroticized *furor* that seeks an impossible fusion with a quasi-maternal figure. My reading of Tancredi's erotic melancholy will suggest that unlike Ariosto, Tasso does not ultimately "cure" the melancholic form of romance by allowing his epic narrative to banish *atra voluptas* entirely. Tasso's embrace of love as a fit subject for the heroic poem in his theoretical works already suggests that this element of romance will not be extirpated from his poem as brutally as it was from Ariosto's epic.[7] However, I also demonstrate that the primarily Platonic, "noble" love that Tasso praises in his *Discourses* and elsewhere is undermined in poetic practice by precisely the dark version of "heroic" love that we have studied in its medical context.[8] To this end, I focus on the central episode in the enchanted wood, in which Tancredi's self-defeating pursuit of the phantasmic Clorinda involves him in the kind of melancholic *atra voluptas* that overwhelms Petrarch. Petrarch's conflation of psychological and poetic traditions of grief and love lies behind the seductive, plangent song that in Tasso's poem signals the resurgence of the romance imagination. Thus contextualized, the *flebil canto* in Tasso's enchanted wood emerges as an ambiguously "spiritual" voice, representing the dark forces of *atra voluptas* from which Tancredi never fully extricates himself.

Solo et pensoso: The Melancholy Poet

Tancredi's fixation on an internalized "phantasm" of Clorinda—a phantasm that finds a terrifying externality in Ismeno's enchanted wood—establishes a telling link between his ordeal as romance protagonist and Tasso's own authorial struggles. Tasso's 1583 autobiographical essay *Il Messaggiero*, which begins with a dawn visitation from a mysterious spirit, raises the epistemological question that becomes acutely important in the epic: how can one ever be sure of the objective reality of such potentially phantasmic visions? If they are not the work of dreams, they might nonetheless still be illusory, created by the awesome powers of the *virtù imaginatrice*, which can deprive the senses of their ability to distinguish true objects.[9] The particular terms of Tasso's dilemma about the nature of his own *alienazione di mente* perhaps derive from the pseudo-Aristotelian *Problem 30*, which attributes certain melancholic behaviors to "divine ecstasy" and others to specific physiological causes peculiar to the individual. But as Tasso notes in his essay, irrespective of whether one's *alienazione di mente* is caused by illness (*infirmità di pazzia*) or by a divine madness (*divino furore*), the mind is always potentially subject to falsifying visions. After entertaining the idea that his own *alienazione di mente* might be the result of a madness like that of Pentheus or Orestes, Tasso turns instead for an explanation to what he calls his *soverchia maninconia*.[10] This "excessive melancholia" is due not to a single cause—a natural disposition or an illness—but rather to both causes and is for this reason especially pernicious.

Tasso's familiarity with the Aristotelian (and Ficinian) tradition of linking melancholia and creative genius allows him to present, at least by implication, his poetic creativity as fully imbricated in his melancholic disposition. Tasso's final example of the melancholic figure in *Il Messaggiero* is Bellerophon, but as Juliana Schiesari points out, he draws not on Aristotle's Homeric Bellerophon, but on Petrarch's poem 35, which uses the figure of Bellerophon to portray the plight of the melancholic poet.[11] In the poem, the speaker is a solitary wanderer like Bellerophon, intent on avoiding contact with other human beings: "Solo et pensoso i più deserti campi / vo mesurando a passi tardi et lenti" (Alone and filled with care, I go measuring the most deserted fields with steps delaying and slow, *Rime Sparse*, 35). The source of the speaker's melancholy plight is *Amor*, who pursues him in his solitude, engaging him in the erotic discourse that is presumably the source of the poetry (*ragionando con meco*). But as we noted in the introduction, Petrarch also alludes to Bellerophon in the *Secretum*, in the context of Augustine's most detailed description of *atra voluptas* or *funesta voluptas*, the dark, morbid pleasure that Petrarch has cultivated in response to a hopeless, yet poetically productive, love:

[U]t de te non minus proprie quam de Bellerophonte illud homericum dici posset:

> qui miser in campis merens errabat alienis
> ipse suum cor edens, hominum vestigia vitans.

[Homer's description of Bellerophon could just as appropriately be used of you.

> "In the land of strangers he wandered sadly,
> eating his heart, far from the paths of men."][12]

In this context Bellerophon becomes the sign of Petrarch's folly, his self-willed surrender to the bitter pleasures of melancholic love and its attendant "plague of phantasms" that block his access to transcendent knowledge. It is precisely this morbid love of suffering that Petrarch must renounce, according to Augustine, in order to return his soul to its proper course. As we will see, the uneasy dialectic between these two allusions to Bellerophon in Petrarch's work informs Tasso's own ambivalence toward his *soverchia maninconia*. On the one hand, melancholic love is a plague (*pestis*) that corrupts Petrarch's soul, while on the other its characteristic *atra voluptas* is at the heart of the anguished poetry of the *Canzoniere*. Similarly, the melancholic figure of a Petrarchan Bellerophon constitutes in Tasso's autobiographical essay a richly ambiguous prototype for his romance protagonist Tancredi, whose obsessive quest for a phantasmic beloved is also closely tied to the discovery of an "inspired" poetic voice.

"Phantasms of Love"

When Tancredi discovers that the mysterious adversary whom he has killed is in fact the beautiful Clorinda, whose *bella sembianza* has haunted his imagination throughout the poem, he is transformed at once into the sorrowing lover par excellence. Tancredi's mourning for Clorinda defines his role throughout the remainder of the poem; unlike Ariosto's Orlando, for whom, as Elizabeth Bellamy observes, "the psychopathology of *furore* constitutes an excessive mourning for Angelica that eventually gets converted into epic purposiveness," Tancredi never enjoys a release from his melancholy.[13] But Tancredi's melancholy here merely fulfills the promise of its conception. Our first glimpse of him through God's eyes already suggests the melancholy *innamorato*: "[V]ede Tancredi aver la vita a sdegno, tanto un suo *vano amor* l'ange e martira" ("He sees Tancred holding his life in scorn, so much a vain love torments and martyrs him," 1.9, italics mine).[14] His love is characterized from the first as *un vano amor*, a futile love that leads the lover to entertain a disdain for life even before the beloved's absolute disappearance in death. For readers of Orlando's flight into the "inferno" of his *inchiesta amorosa*, the reference to Tancredi's *vano amor* here will immediately recall the earliest description of Orlando's fall away from his epic duties:

> Già savio e pieno fu d'ogni rispetto,
> e de la santa Chiesa difensore;
> or per un vano amor, poco del zio,
> e di sé poco, e men cura di Dio.

[Once he was wise and full of all regard, and a defender of the sacred Church; now, thanks to an empty love, he has little care for his uncle, little for himself, and less for God.]

(*OF* 9.1)

Tancredi has compromised his status as epic hero through his submission to an empty love that "si nutre d'affani" (nurtures itself on sorrows, 1.45), just as Petrarch feeds on tears and sorrows with a certain dark pleasure ("sic lacrimis et doloribus pascor").

The shadow of a Petrarchan *atra voluptas* around Tancredi's empty love already marks it as phantasmic in nature. Margaret Ferguson rightly notes the crucial importance of the phantasm in Tasso's writing, suggesting that for him the phantasm is "both the ghostly voice of a dead or absent person and the term he uses in an astonishing variety of ways to designate the epistemological and spiritual errors of the romance imagination itself."[15] As Ferguson goes on to suggest, the danger of the phantasm is that it obscures the distinction between "true imitations" and false products of the subject's "own frenetic mental processes."[16] But it is necessary to add to Ferguson's incisive analysis that this conception of the phantasm is embedded in a contemporary medical discourse that informs quite precisely Tasso's depiction of the psychic disturbance created in the text by Clorinda. The phantasm in Tasso's work is entirely consistent with the technical use of the term in the Neoplatonic/Aristotelian material that informs the medical texts on love-melancholy. As we saw in Synesius's *De somniis*, for example, the mediating power of what he calls the "phantastic spirit" allows the mind to receive the influence of higher, demonic forces in dreams or visions; equally it may also be responsible for pulling the mind itself downward into "lower" visions driven by bodily desires.[17] In each case the receptiveness of the "phantastic spirits" to external influences ensures that the subject is always vulnerable to a kind of spiritual lability. As in *Il Messaggiero*, the criteria for telling the difference between the two kinds of visions remain, for Tasso, eerily unstable. Thus although the dream vision of Clorinda after her death has all the trappings of a transcendent, divine vision (she is adorned with *lo splendor celeste*), this vision is, as Ferguson notes, called into question by its proximity with another, phantasmic vision of a wounded, accusing Clorinda.[18]

The status of Clorinda as "phantasm" is first established in a passage that recalls the medical account of the fixity of the phantasm in the sufferer's imagination:

> Partí' dal vinto suo la donna altera,
> ch'è per necessità sol fuggitiva;
> ma l'imagine sua bella e guerriera
> *tale ei serbò nel cor, qual essa è viva*;
> e *sempre* ha nel pensiero e l'atto e 'l loco
> in che vide, esca *continua* al foco.
>
> E ben nel volto suo la gente accorta
> legger potria: "Questi arde, e fuor di spene";
> cosí vien sospiroso, e cosí porta
> basse le ciglia e *di mestizia piene*.

[The proud lady departed from her victim, since of necessity she is a solitary fugitive*: but her lovely and warlike image he so preserved in his heart that it is alive*; and *always he has in his memory* both the gesture and the place in which he saw her, a *constant* fuel to his flame.

And by his face experienced folk could read: "This man burns, and hopelessly; in such wise he goes sighing, and in such wise carries his eyes downcast and *full of sorrow*.]

(*GL* 1.48–49, italics mine)

Tasso's language highlights the unnatural fixity of Tancredi's mental focus on Clorinda's image (*sempre*; *esca continua*), and it is, of course, just the unhealthy perseveration of the phantasm in the mind that gives the phantasm a life of its own ("tale ei serbò nel cor, qual essa è viva").[19] Like the similar description of Orlando in Ariosto's poem, this passage recalls the language of Petrarch's *Canzoniere* 129.12–13: "[O]nde a la vista uom di tal vita esperto / diria: 'Questo arde et di suo stato è incerto'" (At the sight [of my face] anyone who had experienced such a life would say: "This man is burning with love and his state is uncertain," trans. Durling). This allusion establishes a clear connection between Tancredi and the melancholic speaker of the *Canzoniere*, suggesting also a potential similarity between Tancredi's world and the phantasmic landscape of poem 129.[20] Tasso's allusion to the poem in which the speaker willfully embraces the bittersweet pleasures of self-deception (*dolce error*) indicates that Tancredi, like Orlando, will shortly slip into a phantasmic netherworld in which the lover "prefers the shadow to the thing itself."[21] The speaker's ability to conjure his beloved lady in all her splendor among the trees and stones of the landscape in poem 129 perhaps underscores Tancredi's own unconscious complicity in the creation of the phantasmic Clorinda in the wood.

Clorinda's appearances in the poem are frequently attended by references to the "marvelous." Thus when Tancredi first sees what Tasso calls her "bella sembianza" (lovely appearance, 1.47), the narrator interjects: "Oh meraviglia!" (O marvelous! 1.47). Similarly, the production of "Clorinda's" voice from the bleeding tree is heralded by the same phrase: "Oh meraviglia!" (13.41). But while I agree with Elizabeth Bellamy that "Tasso establishes Clorinda as the paradigmatic 'marvel' of the *Liberata*," I suggest that she owes her marvelous status to historically contemporary accounts of the psychophysiological status of the phantasm.[22] As we have seen, the melancholic brain provides the conditions in which the unhealthily tenacious phantasm subverts the lover's ability to judge the world accurately. The perseveration of Clorinda's *bella sembianza* in Tancredi's mind attests to the intrusion of the material world, via the mediating power of the spirits, into the psychic realm where—as in Ficino's account of love-melancholy— it destabilizes the lover's very self. Tasso's account of Tancredi's subjection to the phantasm recalls Giorgio Agamben's useful reminder that in this context the origin and object of falling in love "is not an external body, but an internal image, that is, the phantasm impressed on the phantastic spirits by the gaze":[23]

> Tancredi, a che pur pensi? a che pur guardi?
> non riconosci tu l'altero viso?

Quest'è pur quel bel volto onde tutt'ardi;
tuo core il dica, ov'è il suo essempio inciso.
Questa è colei che rinfrescar la fronte
vedesti già nel solitario fonte.

[Tancred, of what are you thinking? what are you heeding? do you not recognise the beloved face? This is in truth that beautiful countenance for which you are all on fire: *your heart can tell you, on which its image is engraven.* This is she whom you saw that day refreshing her brow in the solitary pool.]

(*GL* 3.22, italics mine)

The *bella sembianza* that meets Tancredi's gaze at the pool has been fully internalized here as *il suo essempio inciso* (its engraven image). No longer focused on the woman herself but rather on the image of her within himself, Tancredi no longer sees clearly the "real" world. The hold of the phantasm over the lover's mind gradually erodes the subject's ability to distinguish between mental objects and material ones. Thus the permeability of the mind—its capacity to be molded by a phantasm from without, and its capacity to project images onto the world—is the source of the poem's anxious relation to its own marvels. Moreover, it is Tancredi's inability to distinguish between the "real" and the "phantasmic" Clorinda in the wood that indicates most clearly the melancholic origin of what the poem designates as the "error" characteristic of the romance imagination.[24] The marvelous, then, is what we might call a phantasm-effect; disguising its origin in the perseverative activity of a febrile brain, the phantasm bears witness to an uncanny conflation of interior and exterior elements that temporarily overwhelms the subject.

If the poem uses the phantasm to demarcate the fracture between the "real" and the "marvelous" from which the *errori* of romance emerge, Clorinda's ontological ambiguity places her at the heart of the poem's exploration of romance as a mode. Even before Tancredi has embarked on the *vano amor* that will draw him away from the main epic action, Tasso's portrayal of Clorinda emphasizes the phantasm-effect that she both wields and represents in the text. Her very birth is mysteriously linked to the workings of the fantasy, for it is as a result of her mother's absorption in a painting of a white-complexioned Virgin that Clorinda herself is born white. Her birth thus draws to light the "marvelous" power of the phantasmic spirits to mediate between the world and the mind:

D'una pietosa istoria e di devote
figure la sua stanza era dipinta.
Vergine, bianca il bel volto e le gote
vermiglia, è quivi presso un drago avinta.
con l'asta il mostro un cavalier percote:
giace la fèra nel suo sangue estinta.
Quivi sovente ella s'atterra, e spiega
le sue tacite colpe e piange e prega.

Ingravida fra tanto, ed espon fuori
(e tu fosti colei) candida figlia.
Si turba; e de gli insoliti colori,
quasi d'un novo mostro, *ha meraviglia*.

[Her room was painted with a tale of piety and with figures of devotion. A virgin—her lovely face white and her cheeks crimson—is bound there, close by a dragon. A knight-at-arms is striking the monster with his lance; the beast lies slain in his own blood. There she often kneels and confesses her secret sins, and weeps and prays.

Meanwhile she becomes pregnant, and brings forth a fair-complexioned daughter (and you were she). She is distraught, and marvels [*ha maraviglia*] as at a strange monster.][25]

(*GL* 12.23–24, italics mine)

The process by which an image impressed upon the imagination of a pregnant woman may transfer itself to the fetus is described in detail by Ficino in the same section in which he describes the effect of an obsessive love-fixation on the mind of the lover:

Praegnantes saepe mulieres vinum quod avidissime cupiunt vehementer excogitant; vehemens cogitatio, spiritus movet interiores, atque in his excogitate rei pingit imaginem exprimunt. Amator autem ardentius quam praegnantes, suas cupit delicias; vehementius quoque et firmius cogitat.

[Often pregnant women think vehemently about wine which they vividly desire. The vehement though moves the internal spirits and paints on them an image of the thing being thought about. The spirits similarly move the blood, and express an image of the wine in the very soft matter of the foetus. But a lover desires his pleasures more feverishly than pregnant women desire theirs, and thinks about them more vehemently and more constantly.] (*De amore* 7.8)

In both cases, the effect of a vehement thought (*vehemens cogitatio*) on the spirits is such that it paints, as it were, the image onto the body itself (of either the fetus or the lover). Clorinda's mother is absorbed in the painting of the white virgin, and the whiteness of the image works its way, via the internal spirits of the mind, onto the child itself; thereafter, Clorinda is characterized by an uncanny whiteness that repeatedly petrifies Tancredi:

> Ed a quel largo pian fatto vicino,
> ov'Argante l'attende, anco non era,
> quando in leggiadro aspetto e pellegrino
> s'offerse a gli occhi suoi l'alta guerriera.
> *Bianche via più che neve in giogo alpino*
> *avea le sopraveste*, e la visiera
> alta tenea dal volto; e sovra un'erta,
> tutta, quanto ella è grande, era scoperta.
>
> Già non mira Tancredi ove il circasso
> la spaventosa fronte al cielo estolle,
> ma move il suo destrier con lento passo,
> volgendo gli occhi ov'è colei su 'l colle;
> *poscia immobil si ferma e pare un sasso*:
> gelido tutto fuor, ma dentro bolle.

[And he was not yet close to that broad plain where Argantes is awaiting him, when the proud warrior maiden presented herself to his eyes in a vision lovely and rare. *Her surcoat was whiter than snow on the Alpine ridge*, and she had her visor lifted from her face, and (being on rising ground) was all disclosed, how splendid she is.

Now Tancredi does not look where the Circassian is lifting up his fearsome face to the heavens, but moves his steed at a slow walk, turning his eyes where she is on her hill. *Then he stops motionless, and seems a stone*: outside all frozen, but within he boils.]

(*GL* 6.26–27, italics mine)

Both Elizabeth Bellamy and Marilyn Migiel attribute the petrifying effect of Clorinda to her castrating, Medusa-like power (associated by both critics with her androgyny).[26] My sense of Clorinda's visual impact is rather that it is symptomatic of her implication in the poem's exploration of the mental lability characteristic of love-melancholy.[27] Tancredi's rigidity seems to dramatize the obsessive circularity of the melancholic condition, which forces the lover to remain fixated on a single mental object. Like the speaker of Petrarch's 129, who sits down "pietra morta in pietra viva" (a dead stone on the living rock), Tancredi is petrified by the absorbing power of an internalized image. The mind's susceptibility to the phantasm's power becomes, in turn, the model for the oft-noted instability of the poem's epic structure, its invasion by the monsters and phantoms (such as "il fantasma orrendo," 13.25, that overwhelms Alcasto) that people the wood. As we shall see in the next section, the frenzied encounter on the battlefield between Clorinda and Tancredi intensifies our sense of Clorinda's phantasmic quality by emphasizing her overdetermined role in Tancredi's erotic imagination.

"Murderous Eros": *Furor* and the Desire for Fusion

A key concept in Lucretius's influential portrayal of the madness of love—the madness that later develops into melancholic eros—is *furor*. In their deluded attempts to join with the beloved, the lovers cause *dolorem corporis* (bodily pain):

> quod petiere, premunt arte *faciuntque dolorem*
> *corporis*, et dentes inlidunt saepe labellis
> osculaque adfligunt, quia non est pura voluptas
> et *stimuli subsunt qui instigant laedere id ipsum*,
> quodcumque est, rabies unde illaecermina surgunt.

[They tightly press what they have sought and *cause bodily pain*, and often drive their teeth into little lips and give crushing kisses, because the pleasure is not pure and *there are goads underneath which prod them to hurt that very thing*, whatever it is, from which those torments of frenzy spring.]

(*De rerum natura* 4.1079–83, italics mine)

Though Lucretius does not elaborate in this passage on the psychological underpinnings of this strange desire to hurt the beloved, his reference to hidden goads prodding the lover to act against his ostensible wishes suggests a complex conception of erotic *furor* as driven by unconscious desires. Later, of course, Lucretius's metaphorical argument transforms sexual desire into a regressive oral fury that perversely treats fine images of the human form (*tenvia simulacra*) as actual food. Tasso demonstrates a knowledge of this Lucretian theory, and quite probably of this very passage, in one of his dialogues, "La Molza overo de l'amore." His speaker remarks: "[S]'io numerassi con l'altre opinioni quella di Lucrezio, io direi che l'amore è desiderio di trasportamento: perché l'amante par che desideri di *trapassar* ne l'amata" (If I enumerated among the other opinions that of Lucretius, I would say that love is a desire for transport: because the lover seems to desire *to pass over* into the beloved).[28]

Tasso's portrayal of the final, fatal battle between Tancredi and Clorinda reads in the light of this Lucretian passage as a kind of literalization of the metaphorical language of the madness and violence of love. Now the medicalized *furor* becomes a full-blown "frenzy" or "madness," and the violence it generates produces actual, life-threatening blows:

> Tre volte il cavalier la donna stringe
> con le robuste braccia, ed altrettante
> da que' nodi tenaci ella si scinge,
> nodi di fer nemico e non d'amante.
> Tornano al ferro, e l'uno e l'altro il tinge
> con molte piaghe; e stanco ed anelante
> e questi e quegli al fin pur si ritira,
> e dopo lungo faticar respira.

[Three times the knight twines the lady in his powerful arms; and as many times she frees herself from those clinging embraces—the embraces of a fierce enemy, not a lover. They return to the sword, and the one and the other dyes his blade in many wounds; and then at last, worn out and gasping, they disengage, and after long labor breathe.]

(GL 12.57)

Though the narrator declares that these embraces are those of an enemy and not a lover, the *nodi tenaci* do suggest the closeness of an eroticized bond. The strange admixture of bloodlust and erotic passion that informs Lucretius's discourse reaches its logical conclusion here, perhaps filtered through Ficino's cento version of Lucretius's text.

I argued in chapter 2 that the earliest medical texts' predilection for retelling stories of straightforwardly incestuous desires (the story of Antiochus and Stratonice, for example) bespeaks an intuition that the pathology of love-melancholy derives from (in psychoanalytic terms) an incomplete renunciation of the earliest love object, the mother.[29] But as Freud himself acknowledges, even an apparently "successful" renunciation of the mother is made possible by an identificatory process much closer to melancholia than to the substitutive (truly elegiac) process of "mourning." The degree of identification with this altered maternal object would seem to determine the stability of the male ego.[30] The desperate desire for fusion noted in Lucretius and Ficino suggests, then, a hallucinatory repetition of an earlier "melancholic" identification with the lost mother, who was, as it were, "devoured" or incorporated rather than mourned. The beloved object is transformed into an image of the archaic mother, never fully abandoned as a source of nourishment and indistinguishable from the lover's inchoate self. Especially in light of Tasso's reference to a Lucretian "trasportamento" in *La Molta*, the *furor* of Tancredi's hostile engagement suggests a Lucretian desire for an impossible fusion with the beloved, who may also represent the lost source of nourishment, the mother. This fantasized union with the body of the mother also seems to underlie Tasso's description of the lovers' wounds as a "sanguigna e spaziosa porta" (lit. "wide and bloody doorway," 12.62); Tancredi seeks to re-create the conditions of birth, although the bloody doorway of the wounds leads not into life but into death.

This interpretation of Clorinda as a figure for a lost or inaccessible maternal body is supported by allusions in this scene both to the Amazonian non-mother Camilla, and to Tasso's own lost mother. At the very moment at which Tancredi kills Clorinda, she seems to become an overtly maternal figure. When Tancredi finally deals Clorinda the fatal blow, the wound is described in terms that create a travestied nursing scene:

> Ma ecco omai l'ora fatale è giunta
> che 'l viver di Clorinda al suo fin deve.
> Spinge egli il ferro nel bel sen di punta
> che vi s'immerge e 'l sangue avido beve;
> e la veste, che d'or vago trapunta
> le mammelle stringea tenera e leve,
> l'empie d'un caldo fiume. Ella già sente
> morsirsi, e 'l piè le manca egro e languente.

[But now behold, the fatal hour has come that owes Clorinda's life when it is past. He plunges into her lovely breast the point of his sword, that buries itself there and greedily drinks her blood, and floods with a warm stream the vestment laced with shining gold that lightly and tenderly confined her breasts. She feels herself already dying, and loses her footing, sick and languishing.]

(*GL* 12.64)

Marilyn Migiel notes the oral aggression in this scene: "Tancredi's sword is both phallic and mouth-like, for at the same time that it pierces Clorinda, it drinks her blood."[31] Blood rather than milk pours from the breast that Tancredi both wounds and—according to the implications of the metaphor—treats as a source of nourishment. Lanfranco Caretti and Migiel both recognize the echoes here of Virgil's depiction of the dying Amazon Camilla; her death is also represented as a travesty of a never-fulfilled maternal function: "[H]asta sub exsertam . . . papillam / haesit, virgineumque alte bibit acta cruorem" (the spear held fast beneath the disclosed breast, and driven deeply in drank her maiden blood, 11.818–20).[32] But while Virgil seems more interested in the perversion of Camilla's femininity in general than in the maternal/filial dynamic between her and her killer, Tasso's emphasis on the struggle between Tancredi and Clorinda indicates clearly that the sword represents a destructive conflation of sexual and filial longing. The cultural valence of the image of the nursing mother has, of course, also undergone massive revision since Virgil's portrait of the dying Camilla. As Caroline Walker Bynum observes, in medieval literature and iconography the Virgin's breast was often linked with Christ's wound, her life-giving milk with his saving blood.[33] In addition, since breast milk was understood to be transformed blood, "a human mother—like the pelican that also symbolized Christ—fed her children from the fluid of life that coursed though her veins."[34] We seem to find in Tasso's disturbing scene a literalization of the metaphorical link between breast and wound, blood and milk, a literalization that results in Clorinda's transformation into the *ancella* of God, a Christlike figure in her own right. It is, ironically, in her death that Clorinda achieves a kind of sanctified androgyny, which, like Christ's, depends on a transmutation of violence into willing (maternal) sacrifice.

This evocation of a female body deprived of its maternal function is complicated by the uncanny echoes between this scene and Tasso's autobiographical poem, the *Canzone al Metauro*.[35] This poem describes Tasso's early loss of his mother, from whom he was torn (*divelse*) amid her tears and sighs:[36]

> Me dal sen della madre empia fortuna
> Pargoletto divelse. Ah! Di que' baci,
> Ch'ella bagnò di lagrime dolenti,

Con sospir mi rimembra, e degli ardenti
Preghi, che se 'n portar l'aure fugaci,
Ch'io giunger non dovea più volto a volto
Fra quelle braccia accolto
Con nodi così stretti e sì tenaci.
Lasso! E seguii con mal sicure piante,
Qual Ascanio, o Cammilla, il padre errante.
In aspro esiglio e 'n dura
poverta crebbi in quei sì mesti errori.

[Wicked fortune snatched me, a small child, from my mother's breast. Ah, with sighs I remember those kisses, which she bathed in doleful tears, and those ardent prayers, which the fleeting breezes carried away, so that I can no longer join with her face to face, held between those arms with knots so close and strong. Alas, I followed the wandering father, like Ascanius or Camilla, with uncertain steps. I grew up in bitter exile and hard poverty in these sorrowful wanderings.][37]

(ll. 31–40)

This passage begins with a lament for the lost maternal breast, the literal source of nourishment implicitly evoked by the figurative description of Clorinda's bleeding breast. Most significantly, perhaps, the eroticized embrace between Tancredi and Clorinda (the "nodi tenaci") finds an echo here, in the "nodi cosi stretti et tenaci" that bind mother to son.[38] The *Canzone* moves beyond the loss of the mother to an enforced identification with the father: "E seguii con mal sicure piante . . . *il padre errante.*" It is this wandering (perhaps also errant) father, ambivalently mourned at the close of the poem, whom Tasso addresses in the poem's final lines ("Padre, o buon padre"). As Schiesari argues in her reading of this poem, "fathers become the addressees who legitimate [Tasso's] position in regard to them, while 'the' mother, the phantasm of the symbolic female, is internalized as the muted figure of alienation, lack, and even death."[39] The exploration of the psychological structure of romance in Tasso's epic suggests furthermore that Clorinda becomes a phantasmic figure of alienation and lack in the poem precisely to the extent that she comes to represent the lure of romance, which, in its turn, seems closely allied with the maternal Imaginary.

Margaret Ferguson's reading of this canzone endorses the notion that the poem not only provides a map for understanding the oedipal tension at play in Tasso's work, but also that "it illuminates the biographical matrix of his critical theories about the relation between romance and epic."[40] For Ferguson, "the genre of romance itself, it would seem, [is associated with] a fantasized image of [Tasso's] mother's body, conflated with mythologized images of the Neapolitan landscape in which he spent his early years."[41] According to this reading, the departure with the *padre errante* becomes a forced exile into epic. But we notice that the catalyst for this departure in the poem is *empia fortuna*, a malevolent Fortuna who drives Tasso into the *mesti errori*, the sorrowful wanderings of exile. Fortuna is, of course, commonly regarded as the engine of the *romance* form, driving Ariostan and Boiardan heroes into labyrinthine *errori*. As the source of what Boethius calls (in Chaucer's expressive translation) "aventuros welefulnesse" in human life, Fortuna—in the form of Morgana-Ventura, or Angelica, or Duessa, or Lady Fortune in the *Book of the Duchess*—generates the adventurous narrative of romance.[42] In the *Canzone*, then, Tasso explicitly associates the obligation to accompany the "padre errante" with a violent separation from the mother whose loss cannot be accommodated. But rather than reading the separation from the mother's body as a separation from romance, I understand the traumatic exile into *mesti errori* as *constitutive* of romance. The loss of the mother is precisely the impossible loss that generates the melancholic narrative of romance. Thus the yearning to return to the mother's body does not connote a desire to *return to* romance but rather *is* the form that romance takes. For if it is true that the *padre errante* is associated with Aeneas here, it is certainly the wandering, grieving Aeneas of the "romance" half of the *Aeneid*.

Tancredi's "embrace" of Clorinda thus might seem to figure his melancholic swerve away from the epic path toward the overdetermined *mesti errori* of romance. Clorinda's death, a catastrophe wrought by Tancredi's own "empia . . . mano" (12.98) rather than by *empia fortuna*, seems to repeat the death or loss of the mother, but at the same time to provide an impossible, fantasized fusion with her. One signal of the melancholic nature of Tancredi's *alienatio mentis* after his discovery of his adversary's identity is his identification with the dead Clorinda. Long before Freud noted the "identification of the ego with the abandoned object" as a constitutive feature of melancholia, Ficino theorized that the melancholic lover unwittingly transformed himself into the beloved.[43] The power of the "vehement thought" (*assidua cogitatio*) to impress itself upon the phantasmic spirits of the lover and thus to bring about a gradual likeness between lover and beloved suggests a metamorphosis analogous to, though more literal than, Freud's notion of identification.[44] We are told that Tancredi closely resembles Clorinda in certain respects at the moment of her death: "Già simile a l'estinto il vivo langue / Al colore, al silenzio, a gli atti, al sangue" (The living man lies languishing like to the dead, in color, in silence, in attitude and in blood, 12.70). Yet more strikingly, the passage concludes with a suggestion that he has in some way *fused with* Clorinda: "In sé mal vivo e morto in lei ch'è morta" (himself scarce living, and *dead in her that is dead*"). Through Clorinda's death, therefore, Tancredi has finally achieved the "fusion" with the beloved that for Lucretius is the telos of erotic *furor*.

We have already noted the mixture of love and hatred that early writers, including Lucretius, Hildegard, and Ficino, attribute to melancholic lovers.[45] For Freud this ambivalence is readily translated—through the ego's identification with the lost object—into the characteristic "lowering of self-regarding feelings that finds utterance in self-reproaches and self-revilings."[46] Similarly, Mary Wack suggests that "the depression and self-abasement characteristic of melancholy—or lovesickness—is nothing other than hostility toward the [maternal] object directed toward the self."[47] Tancredi's "self-revilings" when he wakes from his trance illustrate this internalization of ambivalence toward the lost object; his focus is not on the loss of Clorinda so much as on the newly horrifying *inner* landscape that this loss opens up:

> Vivrò fra i miei tormenti e le mie cure,
> Mie giuste furie, forsennato, *errante*;
> paventarò l'ombre solinghe e scure
> che 'l primo error mi recheranno inante,
> e del sol che scoprí le mie *sventure*,
> a schivo ed in orrore avrò il sembiante.
> Temerò me medesmo; e da me stesso
> sempre fuggendo, avrò me sempre appresso.

[I shall live then amid my torments and my sorrows—my justice-dealing furies—a *wanderer*, driven mad; I shall tremble at the dark and solitary shades that will bring before me my primal error; and I shall bear the countenance of one ashamed and in horror of the sun that discovered my *misfortunes:* I shall fear my own self and (always fleeing myself) I shall have myself always at hand.]

(*GL* 12.77, italics mine)

Tancredi's reference in this passage to his *primo error* (primal error) seems to indicate more than the killing of an adversary, though a beloved one. He styles himself here as a kind of Oedipus, torn apart by knowledge of unbearable deeds, hounded by the "furies" of his guilt. The passage is remarkable for its evocation of a psyche divided by trauma; the loss of Clorinda produces in Tancredi a split within his own self: "I shall fear my own self and (always fleeing myself) I shall have myself always at hand." The passage suggests the sudden revelation of an Oedipal crime: the killing not of a father, perhaps, but of a mother figure. The appearance of the word *errante* links Tancredi back to the *padre errante* of the *Canzone*; coupled with the word *sventure*, which also, as I have noted, evokes the romance narrative, the passage recapitulates the tragic story of the *Canzone*. Tancredi, now become the murderer of the mother, is driven into a dangerous identification with the wandering father of romance.

The Psychic Tomb: *Il bel corpo* and the Failure to Mourn

The echoes between the scene of Clorinda's death and the loss of the mother in Tasso's autobiographical *Canzone* suggest, then, that Tancredi's melancholic love for Clorinda has transformed her into a maternal object whose loss cannot be fully realized. His melancholic identification with Clorinda's *bel corpo* indicates rather that the object has become uneasily fused with his own self—hence the grammatical slippage in the stanzas surrounding the one quoted from "I" to "you."[48] As we saw in chapter 2, Nicolas Abraham and Maria Torok usefully sharpen Freud's term "identification" into two terms, "introjection" and "incorporation." Incorporation occurs when the loved object is lost—either through actual death, or through estrangement, separation, and so forth—"before the drives concerning the object might have been freed."[49] Incorporation, then, arises from a need to "recover, in secret and through magic, an object that, for one reason or another, evaded its own function: mediating the introjection of desires."[50] Because the desires surrounding the object are not introjected by the ego, the ego develops a hidden fixation on an object that can never be fully mourned. The object retains its otherness from within what Torok and Abraham call the psychic tomb or "crypt" that holds the unconscious secret of the subject's distress. The inaccessibility of this object is marked by a fantasy of devouring, which recurs not only in the psychoanalytic texts but also in Lucretius's foundational discussion of the *furor* of love.

Such a fantasy of devouring the beloved does seem to lurk beneath Tancredi's outpouring of grief for Clorinda, indicating that he, like Artemisia, has incorporated rather than introjected the lost object. Just as Artemisia's "excessive" love for her husband dramatizes the failure to introject loss through a literal *entombment* of his body, so Tancredi's ruminations about the "beloved remains" of Clorinda betray a similar fantasy of entombment:

> Ma dove, oh lasso me!, dove restaro
> le reliquie del corpo e bello e casto?
> Ciò ch'in lui sano i miei furor lasciaro,
> dal furor de le fère è forse guasto.
> Ahi troppo nobil preda! ahi dolve e caro
> troppo e pur troppo prezioso pasto!
> ahi sfortunato! in cui l'ombre e le selve
> irritaron me prima e poi le belve.
>
> Io pur verrò là dove sète; e voi
> meco avrò, s'anco sète, amate spoglie.
> Ma s'egli avien che i vaghi membri suoi
> stati sian cibo di ferine voglie,
> vuo' che la bocca stessa anco me ingoi,
> e 'l ventre chiuda me che lor raccoglie:
> onorata per me tomba e felice,
> ovunque sia, s'esser con lor mi lice.

[But where (alas, ay me!) where were they left, the relics of that chaste and lovely body!—for what my savageries left whole in it perhaps is being laid waste by the wild beasts' savagery. Ah, prey too noble! ah feast too sweet and dear, and too too precious! ah ill-starred body, against which the woods and the shadows aroused first me, and then the beasts.

Yet I shall go where you are; and shall have you with me, if you be there still, beloved spoils. But if it chance that your lovely limbs have been the food for bestial appetites, I want the same mouth to swallow me too, and the same belly enclose me that receives those limbs. Happy the tomb reverenced by me, wherever it be, if it lets me be with them.]

(GL 12.78–79)

It is striking that in this passage Tancredi's own *furor* is explicitly linked with the *furor* of wild beasts—in particular with their savage *appetites*. When Tancredi imagines the beasts' savage activities—devouring the *bel corpo* of Clorinda—we cannot but relate this fantasy back to the frenzied embrace that took place during the battle scene, and the quasi-maternal symbolism of Clorinda's death. This "sweet and dear" feast ("dolce e caro . . . pasto") reactivates the figurative transformation in that earlier scene of the blood into mother's milk, greedily "drunk" by Tancredi's sword. The final fantasy of being devoured with Clorinda, enclosed within the same *ventre* (belly *or womb*) seems to indicate the desire for fusion with the beloved (m)other so apparent in Ficino's use of Artemisia's story. In that story Artemisia's belly becomes the "tomb" of her dead husband, and this unsettling association between tomb and belly/womb perhaps also informs Tancredi's sudden turn from the enclosure of the belly to that of the tomb: "onorata per me tomba e felice" (happy tomb, and honored by me, 79.8).[51] In any case, the fact that Tancredi's fantasy of entombment with Clorinda echoes so closely Fiordiligi's tragic end suggests how far he has already strayed from the path of heroic warrior.

Tancredi's persistent fantasy of joining with Clorinda in the tomb, which is at once obdurately impenetrable and oddly internalized, suggests that Tancredi *cannot* mourn Clorinda, cannot release her as a fully distinct, now lost, object. This address to the tomb seems to prefigure in its refusal to release Clorinda the later "magical" recovery of her in the wood:

> Giunto a la tomba, ove al suo spirto
> dolorosa prigione il Ciel prescrisse,
> pallido, freddo, muto, e quasi privo
> di movimento, al marmo gli occhi affisse.
> Al fin, sgorgando un lagrimoso rivo,
> in un languido:—oimè!—proruppe, e disse:

—O sasso amato ed onorato tanto,
che dentro hai le mie fiamme e fuori il pianto,

non di morte sei tu, ma di vivaci
ceneri albergo, ove è riposto Amore;
e ben sento io da te l'usate faci,
men dolci sí, ma non men calde al core.

[Arrived at the tomb, where Heaven ordained a sorrowful prison for his living soul, pale cold and mute, and almost deprived of motion, he fixed his
eyes upon the marble. At last, releasing a stream of tears, he broke out in a
languishing Ay me!, and said, "O stone so honored and so much loved, that
holds my flames within, my tears without;

"you are the shelter not of the dead, but of live ashes wherein Love lies concealed; and truly I feel from you in my heart the accustomed flames—less
sweet, it is true, but no less warm."]

(*GL* 12.96–97, trans. Nash)

Recalling Ficino's description of the uncontrolled flow of the melancholic
lover's spirits out of his body toward the beloved object, we might understand the alienation of Tancredi's *spirto* in Clorinda's tomb as a symptom
of a similar dissipation. Tasso depicts a kind of ontological exchange between the tomb and Tancredi himself: the tomb holds Tancredi's *fiamme*,
his "flames" of love, just as it holds his *vivaci ceneri*, his "live ashes." At
the same time, however, he feels from the tomb within his own heart the
usate faci, the "accustomed flames." The tomb seems to function at least
in part as a figure for the displacement of Tancredi's own interiority into
the impenetrable, tomblike other. This picture of internal alienation recalls
Abraham and Torok's description of the function of the "psychic crypt"
within the melancholic mind: "Like a commemorative monument, the
incorporated object betokens the place, the date, and the circumstances in
which desires were banished from introjection: they stand like tombs in the
life of the ego."[52] When Tancredi proceeds to the enchanted wood, then,
the emergence of the phantasmic Clorinda seems to dramatize precisely
the magical, secret recovery of the object from within the secret "tomb"
of his own psyche. For it is surely not coincidental that Tancredi enters
the enchanted wood just after burying Clorinda: "Era il prence Tancredi
intanto sorto / a sepellir la sua diletta amica" (Meanwhile Prince Tancred

was risen to attend to the burial of his beloved, 13.32); nor that Clorinda's voice emerges "quasi di tomba," as from a tomb. The tree has taken the place of the tomb; but both tree and tomb represent the melancholic space in which the mind attempts a deadly encounter with its own phantasms.

Although the poem attributes the production of the phantasms in the wood to the magician Ismeno, the phantasms differ, as Lynn Enterline notes, according to the particular fears and needs of the person entering the wood: "[T]he phantasm . . . eerily suspends [the knight's] sense of the difference between what is inside and what outside the mind."[53] In this respect, then, the wood's function is very similar to that of Atlante's palace, in which each knight hears or sees the product of his own particular desires. Enterline reads this episode as a linguistic allegory dramatizing the "author's (and our) inability to decide whether the signs [Tancredi] sees originate with him or elsewhere."[54] But the more immediate significance of the phantasm seems to reside in the psychophysiological understanding of the mind as overwhelmed from within by a particular phantasm that skews the mind's judgment of the world and blurs the boundaries between inner and outer landscapes. Jacques Ferrand's description of the perversion of the world through the melancholic imagination is strikingly apposite here:

> [T]he imagination or the judgement . . . becomes depraved—a condition to be found in all melancholiacs insofar as they fashion a thousand fantastical chimeras and imagine objects that neither exist nor ever will. Fear and sorrow are the inseparable symptoms of this miserable passion that prevents the immortal soul from exercising its faculties and virtues.[55]

Tasso writes similarly that the knights in the wood, like innocent children, feared invisible monsters:

> cosí temean, senza saper qual cosa
> siasi quella però che gli sgomenti,
> se non che 'l timor forse a is sensi finge
> maggior prodigi di Chimera o Sfinge.

> [so did they fear, without knowing what it can be for which they feel such terror—except that their fear perhaps creates for their sense prodigies greater than chimera or sphinx.]

(*GL* 13.18)

The wood, then, seems to represent a hallucinatory space in which, to re-turn to Agamben's terms, the "impossible capture of the phantasm"—the true goal of the melancholic mode—may be attempted.[56] From this per-spective, it is particularly relevant that Ismeno is described specifically as a necromancer who raises the dead from their tombs:

> e tre scosse la verga ond'uom sepolto
> trar de la tomba e dargli il moto sòle.

[and three times he waved the wand with which he is wont to draw the bur-ied man from the tomb and give him motion.]

(*GL* 13.6)

In the light of our general discussion of romance as a melancholic mode organized around the avoidance of loss, Ismeno might be read as the spirit of romance; his power to unbury the dead works in conjunction with the romance protagonist's own "revolt against mourning." Romance draws its power, Tasso seems to imply, from the mind's melancholic preference for a phantasmic object over a real, though lost one.

We noted that a Lucretian conflation of erotic *furor* and actual vio-lence informs the lovers' martial engagement. When Tancredi returns to the tomb of Clorinda in the shape of the enchanted tree, then, it is not surprising that his "love" for her is expressed in terms of destructive blows. But the violence here also seems to reenact the blows of *empia fortuna* in the *Canzone*, so that Tancredi's failure of *pietà* (13.40) is not just a failure of pity but also of Virgilian *pietas*. His actions recall the violent disruption of the *nodi tenaci* of the maternal-filial relation in the *Canzone*, the disrup-tion that leads to Tasso's sudden engagement with the *sì mesti errori* of that autobiographical romance.[57] Tancredi's failure to carry out Goffredo's orders—to cut the trees down—suggests that this episode reenacts the au-tobiographical poem's narrative of incomplete separation from, and mel-ancholic yearning for, the mother. The notion that the tree represents a maternal object of desire is borne out by a later episode in the poem in which a similar eroticized attack occurs. Rinaldo enters the wood of en-chantment and error in order to do what Tancredi cannot bring himself to do: banish the phantasms by pitiless destruction of the trees. Now the phantasm is not Clorinda but Armida, but the description of the tree be-fore it is destroyed is strikingly relevant to the earlier scene:

Fermo il guerrier ne la gran piazza, affisa
a maggior novitate allor le ciglia.
Quercia gli appar che per se stessa incisa
apre feconda il cavo ventre e figlia,
e n'esce fuor vestita in strana guisa
ninfa d'età cresciuta (oh meraviglia!);
e vede insieme poi cento altre piante
cento ninfe produr dal sen pregnante.

[Pausing in the broad clearing the warrior then holds his gaze fixed on a greater novelty. An oak appears before him that (making its own incision) opens its hollow entrails in fertility and gives birth; and there issues out of it (O marvellous!), clothed in strange fashion, a nymph full-grown; and at the same time then he sees a hundred other trees produce from their pregnant bosoms a hundred nymphs.]

(*GL* 18.26)

If the links between Tancredi's struggle with Clorinda and his blows to her tree suggest that both scenes depict an impossible desire for fusion with the mother, the echoes with this later episode confirm that a birthing scene underlies the bloody cutting of the tree.

The phantasmic reappearance of Clorinda in the enchanted wood is therefore symptomatic of a *primo error*, although this primal error concerns not Clorinda but the maternal *bel corpo* that she becomes in Tancredi's melancholic drama. In terms of the poem's structure, the crucial point is that Tasso associates the inability to mourn, to introject rather than in-corporate the loss of the object, with a radical departure from the epic trajectory into the labyrinthine *errori* of romance. The loss of the epic trajectory is identified, naturally, with a departure from the true way of the church, as Peter's admonitions indicate: he must return to the *smar-rita strada* (12.86), the forgotten path (this phrase perhaps recalls Dante's *via smarrita*). Peter's language also recalls a Virgilian pattern in which a person seized with *furor* is called back to himself: "Misero, dove corri in abbandono / a i tuoi sfrenati e rapidi martiri?" (Wretch, where are you running, abandoned to your unbridled and ruinous agonizings? 12.88).[58] This language of "unbridled" passion, of course, also recalls Orlando's slip into madness, which is marked by a prominent pattern of such moments of unbridling. As Bartlett Giamatti argues, "Ariosto finally always sees *sfre-*

natura as leading to fragmentation of the self, to the shattered or splintered personality."[59] For Giamatti, though, the source of this fragmentation is the failure to resist the pressure of convention: "Ariosto believes that to be collected or self-contained is the result of one's being flexible and adaptable; that one controls the self by serving no overmastering ideology."[60] My reading of Ariosto's and Tasso's deployment of *sfrenatura* suggests that the fragmentation of the self results not from external pressure but rather from internal pressure; the self splinters because the mind's denial of loss divides it against itself. The archetypal figure whose abandonment to *furor* causes him literally to lose his head is thus Orpheus, who is not coincidentally also the great poet of love-melancholy. I will demonstrate that Tancredi's departure from the epic path is likewise marked by the discovery of an Orphic voice, a haunting, sirenlike voice that ultimately seems to triumph over the forces of epic in the poem.

The Song of Orpheus

The first and single most important indication that Tancredi's inability to release the beloved object, Clorinda, draws him toward a new kind of poetic voice (one associated with the "*errori*" of romance) is the simile comparing his own laments to those of the nightingale:

> Lei nel partir, lei nel tornar del sole
> chiama con voce stanca, e prega e plora,
> come usignuol cui 'l villan duro invole
> dal nido i figli non pennuti ancora,
> che in miserabil canto afflitte e sole
> piange le notti, e n'empie i boschi e l'òra.
> Al fin co 'l novo dí rinchiude alquanto
> i lumi, e 'l sonno in lor serpe fra 'l pianto.
>
> Ed ecco in sogno di stellata veste
> cinta gli appar la sospirata amica:
> bella assai più, ma lo splendor celeste
> orna e non toglie la notizia antica.

[To her on the sun's departing, to her on its return he calls with weary voice, and prays, and weeps, like the nightingale whose young as yet unfledged the hard-hearted peasant has stolen from her nest, who weeps away in pitiable song her lonely and sorrowing nights, and fills with it the woods and empty air. At last with the coming day he closes his eyes a while, and sleep insinuates itself amid their weeping.

And lo, in a dream, with starry vesture girdled, the beloved that he mourns appears to him—lovelier by far, but the heavenly splendor only adds adornment, and does not take away the old knowledge.]

(*GL* 12.90–91)

Tancredi's laments are compared here to the *miserabil canto* of the nightingale in an extraordinarily rich allusion to a complex Virgilian simile. In *Georgic* 4, when Orpheus has tried and ultimately failed to retrieve his wife, Eurydice, from the depths of the underworld, his laments are similarly compared to the *miserabile carmen* of the grieving nightingale, whose sad complaints fill the landscape:

[Q]ualis populea maerens philomela sub umbra
amissos queritur fetus, quos durus arator
observans nido implumis detraxit; at illa
flet noctem, ramoque sedens miserabile carmen
integrat, et maestis late loca questibus implet.

[Even as the nightingale, mourning beneath the poplar's shade, bewails the loss of her brood, that a churlish ploughman hath espied and torn unfledged from the nest: but she weeps all night long, and, perched on a spray, renews her piteous strain, filing the region round with sad laments.]

(*Geo.* 4.511–51, trans. Loeb)

Orpheus' loss in Virgil's poem is wholly unappeasable, and the plaintive *miserabile carmen* of the simile thus figures a lament that is truly melancholic, rather than elegiac, in nature. Orpheus's refusal to turn from Eurydice to another woman causes Peter Sacks to classify him as an unsuccessful mourner and for this reason a poor model for the elegist: "For Orpheus insists on rescuing his actual wife rather than a figure or substitute for her."[61] For this reason, it is not surprising that the maternal lament that both Tancredi and Orpheus appropriate to express their grief is not truly elegiac. In Virgil's text in particular the simile insinuates that the nightingale's lament is a timeless, endlessly repeatable song: she sings in the present tense (although the surrounding narrative is in the past), and the present participle *maerens* (grieving) bespeaks a grief that will remain "present continuous." The temporal structure of the lament is also significant: the nightingale weeps (*flet*) all night but then renews (*integrat*) her plaint, presumably in the morning. The verb *integrat*, meaning "keep entire by renewing," "recreate, refresh" (*Oxford Latin Dictionary* 1.b; 2), conveys precisely Orpheus's ongoing renewal of his grief through song.

As we saw in chapter 2, Petrarch also draws on this powerful evocation of the mutual association of passionate grief and song in poem 311 of the *Canzoniere*. In poem 336, Petrarch describes the reappearance of the dead Laura within the speaker's mind—but in a characteristic mixture of self-delusion and bitter clarity, the speaker acknowledges that her visionary appearance deceives him:

> [S]ì nel mio primo occorso onesta et bella
> veggiola in sè raccolta et sì romita,
> ch'i' grido: "Ell'è ben dessa, ancor è in vita!"
> e 'n don le cheggio sua dolce favella.
>
> Talor risponde et talor non fa motto;
> i' come uom ch'erra et poi più dritto estima
> dico a la mente mia: "Tu se' 'ngannata."

[I see her in the first encounter so chaste and beautiful, so turned inward and shy, that I cry: "That is she, she is still alive!" and I beg her for the gift of her sweet speech.

Sometimes she replies and sometimes she does not say a word; I, like one who errs and then esteems more justly, say to my mind: "You are deceived."]

(*Rime Sparse* 336)

It seems possible that Tasso's use of the Virgilian nightingale simile is mediated through Petrarch's poem, so that Tancredi's vision of Clorinda in a dream alludes to Petrarch's more self-conscious vision of the dead Laura. The Petrarchan longing to hear once again the "sweet speech" (*dolce favella*) of the dead beloved—a speech that is both seductive and deceptive—may also inform Tasso's treatment of the magical appearance of Clorinda *as* a sweet voice in the enchanted wood. The gloomy shade ("ombra funesta," 13.2) within the wood certainly evokes the *ombra* that is so fundamental a part of the landscape of the *Canzoniere*.[62]

The tension between Tancredi's two visions of Clorinda—the dream designated as "true," the vision in the wood as "false"—might be understood as dramatizing the tension between the two sides of "heroic" love. The dream seems to call on the "noble" version of love characterized as a Neoplatonic striving for the beautiful and good ("lo splendor *celeste*," italics mine, 12.91), while the seductive vision in the wood represents the power of a melancholic love that cleaves helplessly to "i vivi / del mortal mondo" (those who live in the mortal world, 12.92). Tancredi's return to Clorinda in the underworld of the wood suggests that he, like Orpheus, remains subject to what Plato calls "a slavish and illiberal devotion to the individual loveliness" of an irreplaceable beloved—and thus vulnerable to the lure of his own melancholic fantasy.[63]

The allusion to Virgil's Orpheus is remarkably apposite in this context since Tancredi, like Orpheus, has just lost his beloved. But the broader context of the allusion also highlights the fact that in both stories it is the lover's incontinent *furor* that contributes to (or even causes) the loss lamented within the simile. In Orpheus, we seem to find the paradigmatic case of the lover whose loss of his beloved is directly attributable to the driving force of his own *furor*:

> [I]amque pedem referens casus evaserat omnis,
> redditaque Eurydice superas veniebat ad auras,
> pone sequens (namque hanc dederat Proserpina legem),
> cum subita incautum dementia cepit amantem,
> ignoscenda quidem, scirent si ignoscere Manes:
> restitit, Eurydicenque suam iam luce sub ipsa
> immemor heu! victusque animi respexit. ibi omnis
> effusus labor atque immitis rupta tyranni
> foedera, terque fragor stagnis auditus Avernis.
> illa "quis et me" inquit "miseram et te perdidit, Orpheu,
> quis tantus furor?"

[And now as he retraced his steps he had escaped every mischance, and the regained Eurydice was nearing the upper world, following behind—for that condition had Proserpine ordained—when a sudden frenzy seized Orpheus, unwary in his love, frenzy meet for pardon, did Hell know how to pardon! He stopped, and on the very verge of light, unmindful, alas! and vanquished in purpose, on Eurydice, now his own, looked back! In that moment all his toil was spent, the ruthless tyrant's pact was broken, and thrice a crash was heard amid the pools of Avernus. She cried: "What madness (*furor*), Orpheus, what dreadful madness hath ruined my unhappy self and thee?"]

(*Geo.* 4.485–95, trans. Loeb)

The juxtaposition of the nightingale simile with this passage illustrates the paradox constitutive of love-melancholy. On the one hand, the condition is characterized by the kind of unremitting grief captured by the nightingale's *miserabile carmen*. Yet at the same time the lover has himself destroyed the object whose loss in fact facilitates the mind's bittersweet pursuit of its own phantasms. Orpheus becomes after this moment the archetypal grieving lover whose frenzy, weeping, and elegiac songs are the inextricably linked features of much later portraits of melancholic lovers. The nightingale simile, with its emphasis on *maestis questibus* (grieving laments) and *pianto* (weeping) suggests that instead of Eurydice, Orpheus retrieves in her place the affective song that retains, as we saw earlier, a "sublimatory hold" over the lost object.

The regressive quality of this song seems appropriate in the context of the simile's striking identification of sexual and maternal love: the *miserabil canto* is a maternal lament borrowed, as it were, by the bereft lover as his *own* song. We have noted the relationship between an ambivalent identification with the mother and the structure of love-melancholy, and indeed Schiesari reads the appropriation of the maternal position as central to Tasso's melancholic poetics. Tracing in Tasso's *Canzone al Metauro* a close identification of filial and maternal suffering, she argues that it is the identification of the mother's suffering with the poet's that engenders the poet's voice: "Tasso's melancholic mourning is focused on the mother, whose own loss is appropriated as if it were his own. . . . A symbol of permanent lack, she becomes the means through which the poet's 'loss' of her is nothing more than a pretext for the aestheticization of loss."[64] This said, the nightingale simile also works to conceal the lover's complicity in his own loss, and the disjunction between vehicle and tenor perhaps reveals the self-deception at the heart of love-melancholy. The nightingale, after all, is the victim of the *villan duro* who steals her yet unfledged (*non pennuti ancor*) offspring from the nest. The lover, on the other hand, has actually killed his beloved (in Tancredi's case) or sent her back to the underworld (in Orpheus's case). In each story it is the lover's unbridled *furor* that contributes to the permanent loss of the beloved.

The effect of Tasso's deployment of Virgil's simile here, then, is to transform Tancredi into a version of Orpheus, and at the same time to underscore the relationship between the *furor* of this love and an identification with a grieving maternal figure. The simile makes sense of Tancredi's grief because the intensity of his bond with Clorinda (the *nodi tenaci* holding them in a fatal embrace in their last battle) is already colored by the intensity of the mother-son dyad described in Tasso's autobiographical *Canzone*. In the remainder of this chapter we will see that Tancredi's appropriation of a melancholic maternal song is directly tied to the emergence of the phantasmic Clorinda in the wood. Furthermore, the retrieval of the lost object *as poetic voice* marks the culmination of the poem's exploration of the relationship between love-melancholy and romance. For it is in his melancholic return to the dead beloved and his second loss of her that Tancredi, like Orpheus, establishes himself as a figure for the poet. But it is, of course, not the voice of the epic poet that emerges here, but rather an estranged, "dead" voice, the voice of the beloved/mother, whose plaint immobilizes the epic action and drives Tancredi "fuor di sé" (13.45) into the byways of romance.

Il flebil canto: The Maternal Lament and the Return to Romance

Lately risen to bury Clorinda, Tancredi moves into the forest in an attempt to banish the *fantasma orrendo* (13.25) reputed to exist there. But as he enters what the inscription on the mysterious cypress calls the *secreta sede* of the dead, Tancredi is suddenly surrounded by a confused weeping sound that recalls the *miserabil canto* of the nightingale simile:

> Cosí dicea quel motto. Egli era intento
> de le brevi parole a i sensi occulti:
> fremere intanto udia continuo il vento
> tra le frondi del bosco e tra i virgulti,
> e trarne un suon che *flebile concento*
> par d'umani sospiri e di singulti,
> *e un non so che confuso instilla al core*
> *di pietà, di spavento e di dolore.*

[Thus spoke that inscription. He stood intent on the hidden meanings of the cryptic words: meanwhile he heard the wind continually moaning among the leaves and undergrowth of the wood, and drawing from them a sound that seems a *plaintive harmony* of human sobs and sighs, and *instills in his heart I know not what mingled sense of pity, fear and sorrow.*]

(*GL* 13.40, italics mine)

This potent mixture of weeping, sighs, and wind becomes the signature voice of the enchantments of romance in the poem.[65] Later in the poem, when Ruggiero repeats (successfully) Tancredi's attempt to exorcise the wood, a similar sound emerges as a precursor to the "marvelous" opening of the "pregnant" trees:

> Era là giunto ove i men forti arresta
> solo il terror che di sua vista spira;
> pur né spiacente a lui né pauroso
> il bosco par, ma lietamente ombroso.
>
> Passa più oltre, e ode un suono intanto
> che dolcissimamente si diffonde.
> Vi sente d'un ruscello il roco pianto
> *e 'l sospirar de l'aura* infra le fronde,
> *e di musico cigno il flebil canto*
> *e l'usignol che plora e gli risponde,*
> organi e cetre *e voci umane in rime*:
> tanti e sí fatti suoni un suono esprime.

[He came to the place where the less brave are stopped merely by the terror that rises from its appearance. Yet the grove appears neither ugly nor dreadful to him, but pleasantly shady.

He passes on, and hears a sound the while that is most pleasantly diffused; he hears the hoarse murmuring of a brook and the *breathing of the breeze* among the foliage, and the *tearful singing of the tuneful swan, and the nightingale that weeps and answers him*; organs and lyres and *human voices in harmony*; so many and such sounds one sound expresses.]

(*GL* 18.17–18, italics mine)

The "flebile concento" of "umani sospiri e . . . singulti" encountered by Tancredi reappears here in "il flebil canto" of the swan's song and, yet more significantly, the song of the weeping nightingale, "l'usignol che plora." We also find the mixing of human voice and wind in the "sospirar de l'aura." Both passages seem to insert into the "literal" narrative the highly affective voice of the nightingale simile.[66] In both cases, then, the dangerous seduction of either Clorinda or Armida—the seduction, that is, of the hero away from his *epic* goal—is associated, via the sounds of the breathing, sighing wind, and the *flebil canto* that suffuses the wood, with the *maternal* plaint of the nightingale.[67] Strikingly, it is this maternal song that confuses the

Aristotelian distinction between "sound with meaning" and mere sound, confirming our sense that this "pneumatic" song exerts a regressive power over the lover, drawing him back toward the prelinguistic (or semiotic) rhythms that defy full translation into symbolic discourse.[68]

That the hidden source of the song's power is the occluded object (the Kristevan Thing) is borne out by the resemblance between the *flebil canto* and Clorinda's dying words:

> In queste voci languide risuona
> *un non so che di flebile e soave*
> ch'al cor gli scende ed ogni sdegno ammorza,
> e *gli occhi a lagrimar gli invoglia e sforza.*

> [In this languid voice echoes *I know not what of soft and mournful sound* that descends into his heart and snuffs all sense of outrage, and *persuades and constrains his eyes to weep.*]

(GL 12.66, italics mine)

The connection between the *voci languide* that echoes "*un non so che* di flebile e soave / ch'al cor gli scende" and the later "*non so che* confuso instilla al core di pietà" is notably close; in both cases the sound is *flebile* and sinks into the hearer's heart, evoking tears in the first passage, and *pietà* and *dolore* in the second.[69] The language of the first passage in particular, with its emphasis on the mournful sound's power to evoke tears in the listener, recalls the medical discussion of the power of "pneumatic" song to penetrate the lover's body, producing tears in the otherwise "dried out" lover. It is perhaps also not coincidental that this mellifluous voice dispels Tancredi's "sdegno," his outrage or disdain; this word resonates with moments of high epic drama, notably the end of both the *Orlando Furioso* and the *Aeneid*. In Ariosto's poem Rodomonte's soul is dispatched to the underworld "sdegnosa" (and this is literally the poem's last word), while Turnus, Rodomonte's Virgilian model, is said to have a "vita . . . indignata" (a disdainful life) at his death. It is as though the power of Clorinda's "voci languide" draws Tancredi away from a repetition of a defining moment in epic—the killing of Turnus—and directs him instead towards the amorous trajectory of romance.

The mysterious voice in the wood thus clearly represents a phantasmic version of this earlier voice; it is not just the voice of Clorinda, but specifically the weeping voice of a *dying* Clorinda, now mixed with the murmuring sounds of wind in the trees. Margaret Ferguson has observed that the vision of Clorinda that eventually appears is "strikingly similar to Tasso's vision of his mother" in the *Canzone*. But even before Tancredi believes he actually sees Clorinda, her sighing and weeping already recall those of his grieving mother:

> Me del sen de la madre empia fortuna
> pargoletto divelse. Ah! di quei baci,
> ch'ella bagnò di lagrime dolenti,
> con sospir mi rimembra e de gli ardenti
> preghi che se 'n portar l'aure fugaci.
>
> (*GL* 31–35)[70]

The *ardenti preghi* carried away by a fleeing breeze (*l'aure fugaci*) seem to look forward to those of the imploring, ghostly Clorinda ("l'offesa donna sua che plori e gema") whose voice is mingled with the sighing winds.[71]

One final example of the appearance of the *miserabil canto* that I wish to associate with the poem's romance strain occurs earlier in the poem, when the mournful and lovesick Erminia arrives at the site of her pastoral retreat.[72] In view of Erminia's crucial involvement in the final stages of Tancredi's quest, it is especially significant that she is associated with the nexus of issues surrounding the "romance" voice. Tasso's description of Erminia draws directly on the Petrarchan/medical tradition of "feeding on tears" that we have explored; hers is an *atra voluptas* that will ultimately lead to the production of a *dilectoso male* Petrarchan poetics:[73]

> Cibo non prende già, ché de' suoi mali
> solo si pasce e sol di pianto ha sete.

[She takes no food at all, for she feeds herself only on her own misfortunes and is thirsty only for tears.]

> (*GL* 7.4)

Caretti points out the immediate Petrarchan subtext for this passage:[74]

> Pasco 'l cor di sospir, ch'altro non chiede,
> e di lagrime vivo, a pianger nato;
> né di ciò duolmi, perché in tale stato
> è dolce il pianto più ch'altri non crede.

[I feed my heart with sighs, it asks for nothing else, and I live on tears, born to weep; nor do I sorrow for that, for in such a state weeping is sweeter than anyone knows.]

(*Rime Sparse* 130.5–8)

But the "feeding on tears" motif also associates Erminia with Orpheus, who feeds on tears and *dolor animi* (*Met.* 10.75) prior to taking up his lyre and singing of tragic loves. This melancholic turn inward prepares us for the distinctly Orphic *miserabil canto* to which she awakens:

> Non si destò fin che garrir gli augelli
> non sentí lieti e salutar gli albori,
> e mormorar il fiume e gli arboscelli,
> e con l'onda scherzar l'aura e co i fiori.
> Apre i languidi lumi e guarda quelli
> alberghi solitari de' pastori,
> *e parle voce udir tra l'acqua e i rami*
> *ch'a i sospiri ed al pianto la richiami.*

[She did not awaken until she heard the merry birds chirping and greeting the first glimmerings of dawn, and the river murmuring and the trees, and the breeze playing with the water and the flowers. She opens her languid eyes and looks around at those solitary haunts of shepherds, *and it seems to her that she hears a voice amid the water and the branches that calls her back again to sighing and weeping.*]

(*GL* 7.5, italics mine)

Once again we encounter a mysterious, disembodied voice, half-human, half-wind or air, that draws the hearer into its own pneumatic circle of sighs and weeping.

Tasso's use of the nightingale simile seems to signal his awareness of the importance of the figure of Orpheus for this version of romance, and it is therefore plausible that the sinister aura surrounding the *flebil canto* in his poem derives in part from the end of Orpheus's story. Rejecting womankind, Orpheus is torn apart by enraged maenads, his limbs scattered over the landscape. In both Virgil's and Ovid's versions, the poet's head is swept away by the river Hebrus and produces a haunting song of death:

> [T]um quoque marmorea caput a cervice revulsum
> gurgite cum medio portans Oeagrius Hebrus
> volveret, Eurydicen vox ipsa et frigida lingua,

a miseram Euydicen! anima fugiente vocabat,
Eurydicen toto referebant flumine ripae.

[Even then, while Oeagrian Hebrus swept and rolled in mid-current that head, plucked from its marble neck, the voice itself and death-cold tongue, with fleeting breath, called Eurydice—ah, hapless Eurydice! "Eurydice" the banks re-echoed, all down the stream.]

(*Geo.* 4.523–27, trans. Loeb, with minor emendations)

Virgil's text emphasizes the disembodied nature of the voice: the odd phrase *vox ipsa* tells us that it is the voice itself that calls, rather than Orpheus. This Virgilian voice calls *anima fugiente*, with fleeting breath (or soul, presumably), suggesting once again the self-sufficiency of the pneumatic voice. Ovid's version of Orpheus's death owes a heavy debt to this Virgilian passage, and it too emphasizes the separation of voice from sentient speaker: "[F]lebile nescio quid queritur lyra flebile lingua / murmurat exanimis, respondent flebile ripae" (the lyre gave forth some mournful notes, mournfully the lifeless tongue murmured, mournfully the banks replied, *Met.* 11.52–53, trans. Loeb).[75] In each of the passages we have considered in Tasso's poem, the mysterious lamenting voice emerges amid trees and water, unconnected to any readily apparent speaker. Ovid's text contains a clear prefiguration of Tasso's *flebil canto*: the lyre, the dead or *breathless* (*ex-animis*) tongue, and the banks all whisper mournfully, *flebile*. The confusion of human and natural breaths recalls Tasso's mingling of wind and sighs; the emphasis is at once on the confusion of the sound's meaning ("nescioquid"; "un non so che confuso") and on its affective power ("flebile . . . flebile . . . flebile").

In Orpheus's story, then, the desperate (furious) quest for Eurydice ends as though inevitably in the simultaneous death of the poet and the marvelous production of a disembodied song, the continuous lament figured proleptically by the *miserabile carmen* of the nightingale. Tancredi's appropriation of the nightingale's song suggests that this displaced maternal lament is the basis for a literally "in-spired" poetic voice, the *flebil canto* that signals the listener's entrance into an enchanted romance space. These mournful sounds are notably diffuse ("dolcissimamente si diffonde," 18.18), as though the exploration of the pneumatic origin of voice figures a return to a dangerously unstable state in which boundaries of all kinds—between body and soul, self and other, mother and child—are broken down. Such an undifferentiated state seems to characterize both the underlying fantasy of love-melancholy and the "romance" spaces of Tasso's poem. The emergence of this voice *as from the tomb* seems also to suggest a magical overcoming of the boundary between the living and the dead, as though the song momentarily permits an impossible unity with the lost object: "Allor, quasi di tomba, uscir ne sente / un *indistinto gemito dolente*" (13.41, italics mine). But the price for this recapture of a lost Eurydice is the kind of "alienazione di mente" that haunts Tasso's description of his own visitation by the spirit in *Il Messaggiero*: "[V]a fuor di sé" (He is beside himself, 13.45). It is surely not by chance that Tasso declares (following Aristotle) in *Il Messaggiero* that the poet Maratus is "più eccelente ch'egli era fuor di sé."[76] The poet of romance gains the magical powers of an Oprhic *vox ipsa* only by losing himself in the *funesta voluptas* (morbid pleasure) of love-melancholy.

La medica pietosa: The Return to Romance

When Tancredi flees from the enchanted wood, he shows himself unable to overcome the power of the nightingale's song: the voice of the woman who (apparently) weeps and groans (*plora e gema*) triumphs over his ability to judge the falsity of the image.[77] The dominance of this phantasmic voice indicates his failure to enter into the discourse of epic: Goffredo has instructed him to destroy the *fantasma orrendo* in the wood because the wood is necessary for military success. As Margaret Ferguson points out, Tancredi "symbolically loses his heroic male identity when he drops his sword in fear of Ismeno's creation."[78] (It is, strikingly, a rushing wind ["impetuoso vento," 13.46] that carries this weapon of epic out of the wood, as though to symbolize the pneumatic origin of this conquering voice.) Tancredi's subjection to the seductive voice of the phantasm thus feminizes him as it signals his abandonment of the epic path. Yet in spite of Tasso's well-attested anxieties about the status of his poem as an epic, he does not "cure" Tancredi of his love-melancholy as Ariosto cures Orlando. Tancredi's last substantial appearance in the poem returns him to the infantilized position of the "romance" subject, absorbed in a Petrarchan *atra voluptas* and embraced by the figure who "more than any other brings the perspective and dynamic of romance into the *Gerusalemme Liberata*."[79] Indeed, the resolution of the Tancredi-Clorinda-Erminia story appears to prefigure what one recent critic understands as the poem's final capitulation to the romance mode.[80]

When Erminia finds the wounded Tancredi, she weeps copiously over his body, believing him dead:

> e in lui versò d'inessicabil vena
> lacrime e *voce di sospira mista* ...

[and she poured out over him tears from an inexhaustible spring, and *speech mingled with sighs*.]

(*GL* 19.105)

> Lecito sia ch'ora ti stringa e poi
> versi lo spirto mio fra i labri tuoi.
>
> Raccogli tu l'anima mia seguace,
> drizzala tu dove la tua se 'n gio.
> Cosí parla gemendo, e si disface
> quasi per gli occhi, e par conversa in rio.
> *Rivenne quegli a quell'umor vivace*
> *e le languide labra alquanto aprio:*
> *aprí le labra e con le luci chiuse*
> *un suo sospir con que' di lei confuse.*

["Allow me now to press you and then pour out between your lips my very soul.

"Receive my soul that follows, give it direction wherever yours has gone." Thus she speaks, sobbing, as it were dissolved through her eyes and seems turned into a river. *With that refreshing dew he came to himself and somewhat parted his languid lips. He parted his lips and with eyes still closed he mingled one of his sighs with those of hers.*]

(*GL* 19.108–9, italics mine)

This moment represents an extraordinary recapitulation of the elements of love-melancholy that we have traced throughout Tancredi's story. Erminia's "speech mingled with sighs" and her inexhaustible well of tears recall, of course, the *miserabil canto* of the nightingale and "Clorinda's" afflicted voice in the wood. The word "confuse" ("un suo sospir con que' di lei confuse") irresistibly reminds us of the confusion in the enchanted wood ("un non so che confuso instilla al core / di pietà," 13.40), suggesting the potential for a similar loss of self here ("fuor di sé"). In this scene the mingling ("confuse") of sighs, the drinking of tears, and the fantasy of pouring one self into another seems to refer explicitly to the Ovidian/Petrarchan motif of feeding on one's own tears, and to the Lucretian/medical metaphor of consuming the beloved. But Tancredi's response to what in the past has been a dangerous seduction away from his epic goal suggests that the poem will not, finally, endorse the relinquishing of romance in favor of epic. Rather than drawing away from the collapse of boundaries that Erminia's speech represents, Tancredi allows his body to mingle with hers.

In the context of the familiar somaticized discourse of sighs, laments, and tears, this erotic scene acquires the coloring of a Petrarchan *atra voluptas*, emphasizing in its insistence on the language of fusion/feeding a regressive return to a primitive oral identification with the mother. This suggestion is further underscored by the final position adopted by Erminia here: "Ed al suo capo il grembo indi suppone" (And then she makes of her lap a support for his head, 19.114). The fact that Erminia's position recalls in some detail that of Armida, who also holds Rinaldo's head in her lap, both enhances our sense of Tancredi's infantilization and looks forward to the renewal of the Rinaldo-Armida relationship at the very end of the poem:

> Sovra lui pende; ed ei nel grembo molle
> le posa il capo, e 'l volto al volto attolle,
>
> e il famelici sguardi avidamente
> in lei pascendo si consuma et strugge.
> S'inchina, e i dolci baci ella sovente
> liba or da gli occhi e da le labra or sugge,
> ed in quel punto ei sospirar si sente
> profondo sí che pensi: "Or l'alma fugge
> e 'n lei trapassa peregrina."

[She bends above him and he lays his head in her soft lap and lifts his face to hers;

and avidly feeding on her his ravenous gaze, is consumed and destroyed. She leans down and now from his eyes repeatedly drinks in sweet kisses, and now sucks them from his lips. And at the same moment he is heard to sigh deeply that you would think "Now his soul is leaving him and makes a pilgrimage into her."]

(*GL* 16.18–19)

Rinaldo's "avid" feeding on Armida, his own consumption by her, and the general confusion of boundaries between bodies and souls here recalls both the desperate fusion of Lucretius's lovers as well as the quieter merging of Erminia and Tancredi.[81]

In the latter episode, though, Tasso seems intent on sanctifying this fusion. Erminia's maternal succoring of Tancredi creates a vision of a kind of pietà, a vision supported by Tancredi's reference to Erminia as "medica mia pietosa" (my merciful physician, 19.114). This phrase can refer to the Virgin Mary herself, and Tancredi's restoration is staged as a kind of resurrection. It seems, then, that the poem begins to move here toward a sanctification of romance and of the psychological structure of love-melancholy that underpins it. The previously sirenlike figure, maternal, devouring, and ultimately death-bringing (Rinaldo's soul appears to leave him, and Tancredi is driven *fuor di sé*) is transformed in Erminia into the Marian *medica pietosa*. Erminia's appearance as Clorinda's substitute suggests that the fantasy of fusion with Clorinda, enunciated most clearly by Tancredi as he weeps by her tomb, is consummated here in a newly sanctified form. Tancredi's quasi-baptismal awakening under the drops of Erminia's *umor vivace* even recalls, in reverse, his desire to bathe Clorinda in his own tears:

> [N]on di morte sei tu, ma di vivaci
> ceneri albergo, ove è riposto Amore;
> e ben sento io da te l'usate faci,
> men dolci sí, ma non men calde al core.
> Deh! prendi i miei sospiri, e questi baci
> prendi ch'io bagno di doglioso umore.

[You are the shelter not of the dead, but of live ashes wherein Love lies concealed; and truly I feel from you in my heart the accustomed flames—less sweet, it is true, but no less warm. Ah! take my sighs and take these kisses that I bathe in sorrowful tears.]

(*GL* 12.97)

In Erminia's actual revival of the apparently dead Tancredi, the poem seems to provide a dramatization of precisely the (failed) fantasy of fusion/resurrection evident in Tancredi's confused conflation of his heart with Clorinda's tomb. Now, though, the "pneumatic circle" of sighs and tears ("doglioso umore" / "umor vivace") permits a Lucretian blending of souls and bodies that is integrated into the poem's larger narrative. This shift toward a revival of the Lucretian/Petrarchan melancholic tradition suggests that in the final analysis, unlike Ariosto's poem, Tasso's poem cannot authorize the restoration of the "sanity" of epic by means of a harsh acknowledgment of death and separation. Whereas Orlando awakens into an elegized awareness of the reality of loss, Tancredi lingers in the absorption of *atra voluptas*. But in spite of Tasso's sanctification of this moment of fusion, the darker implications of *atra voluptas* cannot be entirely forgotten. Tancredi's love is still directed not toward a Platonic Good, but rather remains entangled in the body of a mortal lover. Notwithstanding Tasso's theoretical commitment to a Platonic version of "heroic" love, then, the enduring power of a Petrarchan *atra voluptas* in this poem suggests that the melancholic counterpart of transcendent love—already contained within the term "heroic love"—cannot finally be extirpated from the poem.

As this sanctification of the patterns of *atra voluptas* suggests, the poem attempts to rehabilitate rather than shake off the romance patterns that earlier seemed to present such a threat to the poem's epic goal. The poem's surprising swerve toward a final embrace of romance rather than epic values is confirmed by the entirely unexpected rehabilitation of Armida at the end of the poem. As Jo Ann Cavallo argues, this rehabilitation is at odds with the epic tradition with which Tasso was intimately familiar and has disturbed the many critics intent on reading Tasso's poem as determinedly epic in purpose and structure. It makes more sense, as Cavallo argues, to see this reintroduction of romance as deliberate: "[W]hile romance was traditionally treated as a parenthesis within the epic structure, the ending of Tasso's poem gives us an opportunity to view the relation in reverse: the epic struggle to free Jerusalem was a long but nevertheless temporary effort at whose completion the knights are free to transform back to their 'natural' state."[82] That natural state, she argues, is the state of knight errant; the traditional "obstacle" to epic fulfillment (Armida, Dido, Alcina) becomes instead its goal.[83]

In terms of the melancholic structure that we have considered as the basis for Tasso's romance, the integration of Armida at the end of the poem also suggests a deliberate eschewing of the loss and mourning that characterize epic closure. Whereas Orlando's final substantial gesture in the poem is his elegy for Brandimarte, Rinaldo's last gesture is to restore Armida, embracing her as his future wife. The terms in which Armida's restoration is described make clear that the poem is reversing an epic image of loss and renunciation:

> Ella cadea, quasi fior mezzo inciso,
> piegando il lento collo; ei la sostenne,
> le fe' d'un braccio al bel fianco colonna
> e 'ntanto al sen le rallentò la gonna,
>
> e 'l bel volto e 'l bel seno a la meschina
> bagnò d'alcuna lagrima pietosa.
> Qual a pioggia d'argento e matutina
> si rabbellisce scolorita rosa,
> tal ella rivenendo alzò la china
> faccia, del non suo pianto or lagrimosa.

[She fell, like a flower half cut, letting her neck bend limply; he held her up; he made of one arm a prop for her lovely side, and meanwhile loosened her gown about her bosom.

And he bathed with a pitying tear the poor girl's lovely bosom and her lovely face. As the faded rose grows beautiful again in morning's silver shower, so she, awaking, raised her drooping face now wet with tears other than her own.]

(GL 20.128–29)

As we saw in the previous chapter, Ariosto's description of Brandimarte in death as a cut flower (the "soft acanthus," *OF* 43.169) echoes a Virgilian passage whose pathos arises from the darkly ironic use of an epithalamic trope to emphasize the horror of the death of a young, unmarried warrior. Tasso borrows the image of the cut flower only to reinsert it into an *epithalamic context*, overturning the Virgilian epic's dark revision of its meaning. Now the "epic" loss of the beautiful youth (Armida) is presented as a possibility that is deliberately avoided: though she falls "like a flower half cut," Armida rises miraculously again, "as the faded rose grows more beautiful in morning's silver shower." The sacrifice that the love-maddened Orlando is required to make in order to regain his sanity and enter into the poem's epic narrative once again is explicitly reversed here, both in the resurrection of the half-dying Armida and in the restoration of the love between her and Rinaldo. In a moment that strongly recalls the awakening of Tancredi, we seem to witness the shift from "elegiac" epic to "melancholic" romance in the magical revitalization of Armida under the *lagrima pietosa* of Rinaldo. But the very fact that this shift feels so surprising in a poem ostensibly committed to an epic structure indicates that this rehabilitation—resurrection—of the romance beloved is over-determined. The biographical plots that intersect with the fictional ones in the poem perhaps give us license to speculate that the figure of the mother, lost but not fully mourned, continues to exert a powerful hold over the poem's trajectory. The maternal "flebil canto"—echoing from Virgil's *Georgic* 4 through Tasso's own *Canzone* and into his epic—triumphs at last over the epic voice.

CHAPTER 5

Rewriting Romance

Arthur's "Secret Wound" and the "Lamentable Lay" of Elegy

Spenser's organization of Arthur's quest for the faerie queene bespeaks a deliberate transformation of the melancholic paradigm that I have argued informs the structure of romance. Rather than moving beyond melancholic romance to epic (as Orlando's quest does), or choosing the *atra voluptas* of romance over the austere, elegiac structure of epic (as Tancredi's quest does), Arthur's quest reworks romance from the inside, incorporating elegy into its very structure. This chapter begins with an examination of the ways in which Arthur's quest intersects with the melancholic structure of the poem's alternative quests. We shall see how closely his quest mirrors that of Red Crosse, whose "melancholic" wandering away from Una leads ultimately to the cave of Despair. Despair represents the telos of Spenser's spiritualized version of love-melancholy: the suicide whom Red Crosse encounters there (Sir Terwin) has killed himself because of unrequited love for a "Ladie gent" who "ioyd to see her lover languish and lament" (1.9.27). I also analyze the quest of Arthur's squire, Timias, whose obsessive, unrequited love for Belphoebe (his "sad melancholy," 4.7.38) is explicitly modeled on an Ariostan conception of love-melancholy. Finally, the chapter considers the intertextual models that illustrate Spenser's turn away from the melancholic paradigm of romance. Orlando's fateful dream of Angelica anticipates Arthur's dream of the faerie queene, insinuating the possibility that Arthur's quest might easily slip into Orlando's maddened *amorosa inchiesta* (*OF* 9.7). In a lighter vein, Chaucer's Sir Thopas dreams of the "elf-queene" before lapsing into a futile and heavily ironized "love-longynge" that threatens to undercut the gravity of Arthur's own dream of a faerie queene.

An important difference between Spenser's romance and his predecessors' is its activation of some of the theological implications of love-
melancholy. Spenser transforms love-melancholy into an eroticized version
of the medieval precursor of melancholy, *acedia*, perhaps following the
example of Petrarch's *Secretum*.[1] As we saw earlier, Petrarch's version of
love-melancholy combines the usual description of love-sorrow with an
account of *atra voluptas* that draws on the medieval sin of *acedia*. Spenser's
treatment of Red Crosse's and Timias's quests in particular emphasizes the
spiritual dimension of a melancholic subjugation of the mind to its own
phantasmic productions. In his short poem *Daphnaïda*, an imitation of
Chaucer's *Book of the Duchess*, he explores in some detail the "bitterness
of mind" (Spenser's term is "despight") that some medieval doctors diagnose as the root of *acedia*.[2] Alcyon, the despairing lover of the *Daphnaïda*,
is modeled on the mysterious Man in Black of Chaucer's poem and expresses a world-weariness that closely anticipates Red Crosse's own "deepe
despight" (1.2.6). I read Alcyon's bitter, melancholic refusal to mourn his
wife Daphne—his refusal to be reconciled to her loss—as an instantiation
of the Petrarchan *atra voluptas/acedia* which Spenser's romance will explicitly reject in favor of an elegiac stoicism.

Red Crosse's quest—and at times, Arthur's own quest—indicates the
intimate structural relationship between the psychic state of *acedia*/mel-
ancholy and the epistemological "errors" characteristic of both Spenser's
Italian models and his own romance. In particular, Archimago seems
to unleash in Red Crosse's "falsed fancy" (1.2.30) a version of what the
Secretum's Augustinus calls the "plague of phantasms [*pestis . . . fantasmatum*] that are tearing apart and mutilating [his] thoughts" (trans. mine).[3]
In his quest, Arthur narrowly avoids the "pernicious distractions" suffered
by the *acidiosus* by submitting himself to what I call the poem's "figural
consolation." Spenser organizes Arthur's dream—and, indeed, his subsequent quest—around a motto whose point is the figural unfolding of
truth: *Veritas filia temporis* (Truth is the daughter of time). Since a figural
structure is necessarily elegiac, continually replacing a lost or absent object
with a substitutive sign, it transforms romance from within into a mournful rather than a melancholic mode. This structure also acts as a corrective
to Chaucer's satiric deconstruction of romance, which takes as its starting
point the mode's potential for digression and circularity. The development

of figural consolation as the crucial mechanism of his romance constitutes Spenser's response to the inhibiting ironies of both an Ariostan *furor* and a Chaucerian "love-longynge."

"Semblants Vaine": Love-Melancholy and Despair

Like Arthur's quest, Red Crosse's quest takes a decisive turn when he dreams of a beautiful and seductive lady. But while Arthur dreams of the faerie queene for whom the poem is named (and who also, of course, figures Elizabeth), Red Crosse dreams of the false Una, imposed on his fantasy by Archimago. Arthur's dream propels him into the quest that will shape the remainder of the poem: "From that day forth I lov'd that face divine; / From that day forth I cast in carefull mind, / To seek her out with labour and long tyne" (1.9.15). Red Crosse's "false" dream, by contrast, propels him into the long error-filled journey that culminates in his sojourn in the cave of the "man of hell, that cals himselfe Despaire" (1.9.28). The language of the two scenes is strikingly close, however, and such closeness between two epistemologically opposed moments (one is a false, the other a "true" vision) necessarily worries the distinction between true and false in the poem.[4] Arthur describes his dream of the faerie queene as follows:

> For-wearied with my sports, I did alight
> From loftie steed, and downe to sleepe me layd;
> The verdant gras my couch did goodly dight,
> And pillow was my helmet faire displayd:
> Whiles every sence the humour sweet embayd,
> And slombring soft my hart did steale away,
> Me seemed, by my side a royall Mayd
> Her daintie limbes full softly down did lay:
> So faire a creature yet saw never sunny day.
>
> Most goodly glee and lovely blandishment
> She to me made, and bad me love her deare,
> For dearely sure her love was to me bent,
> As when just time expired should appeare.
> But whether dreames delude, or true it were,
> Was never hart so ravisht with delight,
> Ne living man like words did ever heare,

As she to me delivered all that night;
And at her parting said, She Queene of Faeries hight.

(1.9.13–14)

We know Red Crosse's dream is false, in the sense that we know
that Archimago produces the dream by eliciting a "fit false dream" from
Morpheus. Nevertheless, the lady offers "gentle blandishment and lovely
look / Most like that virgin true" that anticipates the "goodly glee and
lovely blandishment" offered later by the faerie queene:

Now when the ydle dreame was to him brought,
Unto that Elfin knight he bad him fly,
Where he slept soundly void of evill thought,
And with false shewes abuse his fantasy,
In sort as he him schooled privily:
And that new creature borne without her dew,
Full of the makers guile, with usage sly
He taught to imitate that Lady trew,
Whose semblance she did carrie under feigned hew.

Thus well instructed, to their worke they hast,
And coming where the knight in slomber lay,
The one upon his hardy head him plast,
And made him dreame of loves and lustfull play,
That night his manly hart did melt away,
Bathed in wanton blis and wicked ioy:
Then seemed to him his Lady by him lay,
And to him playnd, how that false winged boy
Her chast hart had subdewd, to learne Dame pleasures toy.

. . . .

In this great passion of unwonted lust,
Or wonted feare of doing ought amis,
He started up, as seeming to mistrust
Some secret ill, or hidden foe of his:
Lo there before his face his Lady is,
Under blake stole hyding her bayted hooke,
And as halfe blushing offred him to kis,
With gentle blandishment and lovely look,
Most like that virgin true, which for her knight him took.

(1.1.46–49, italics mine)

The "abuse" of Red Crosse's fantasy here illustrates the mind's vulnerability to the corruption of the fantasy that is the root of melancholic disorders: "Unto that elfin knight he bad him fly / . . . And with false shewes abuse his fantasy" (1.1.46).[5] Indeed, there is already evidence from early descriptions of Red Crosse that he may be of a melancholic disposition, ripe for Archimago's intervention: "[O]f his cheere [he] did seeme *too solemne sad*" (1.2.2, italics mine); listening to Fradubio he is "full of sad feare and ghastly dreriment" (1.2.44).[6] Although Douglas Trevor reads non-humoral sadness in Spenser's poem as a spiritual sign of "moral uprightness and Christian devotion," to be opposed to the physiologically conditioned state of melancholy, my own view is that the poem explores an unsettling continuum between the two conditions.[7] The psychological model that we have explored in earlier chapters makes it difficult to maintain a clear distinction between mind and body, since the mediating faculty—the imagination—necessarily introduces a subtle form of materiality to the mind through the phantasm. According to the medico-philosophical tradition we have studied, the imagination or fantasy is necessary for all thinking, and thus its corruption will inevitably disrupt the power of what the medieval doctors call the estimative faculty, the faculty that judges an object's "connotational attributes."[8] And indeed, after he wakes from his dream filled with "deepe despight" (1.2.6), Red Crosse is led astray precisely by his inability to judge correctly the "connotational attributes" of particular objects—notably, of course, of Una and Duessa. We will examine the significance of the melancholic structure of Red Crosse's "error," considering the implications of his subjection to a "plague of phantasms" for our interpretation of Arthur's quest.[9]

The implication of Red Crosse's own fantasy in the production of the false dream complicates the allegorization of the dream's provenance.[10] For although the dream emerges from Morpheus's sleepy underworld at Archimago's behest, Morpheus himself is described, as Donald Cheney notes, in terms that associate him with the knight: "And unto Morpheus comes, whom *drowned deepe / In drowsie fit he findes*" (1.1.4); "Unto their lodgings then his guestes he riddes: / Where when all *drownd in deadly sleepe* he findes" (1.1.36, italics mine).[11] More importantly, Morpheus also appears to be a melancholic, suffering from the fitful, troubled dreams characteristic of the cold, dry temperament:

> As one then in a dreame, whose dryer braine
> Is tost with troubled sights and *fancies weake*,
> He mumbled soft, but would not all his silence breake.
>
> (1.1.42, italics mine)

That Archimago's guests are oppressed by "the sad humour loading their eye liddes" (1.1.36) also suggests (though humor may just mean "moisture" here) that this "deadly sleepe" is a physiologically conditioned darkening of the spirit.[12] Certainly sleep and dreams were important aspects of the symptomatology of melancholia, and one sixteenth-century account of melancholic symptoms applies quite aptly to Red Crosse's mental state in the house of Archimago. André Du Laurens writes that melancholy is characterized by:

> an unseparable sadness, *which oftentimes turneth into dispayre*; he is alwaies disquieted both in bodie and spirit, he is subject to watchfulness, which doth consume him on one side, and unto sleepe, which tormenteth him on the other side: for if he think to make a truce with his passions by taking some rest, *behold so soone as he shut his eyelids, he is assayled with a thousand vaine visions, and hideous buggards, with fantasticall inventions, and dreadful dreames.*[13]

Spenser's "melancholic" Morpheus—whose very name alludes to the shape-shifting capacity of the fantasy—seems to allegorize in part Red Crosse's own increasingly melancholic fantasy, his complicity in the production of the "fantasticall inventions" that torment him. The role of Morpheus (and Archimago) in complicating the provenance of Red Crosse's dream is thus rather similar to Ismeno's role in Tasso's poem. In both cases the "magus" figure is implicated in an underworld of phantasms that exists ambiguously between the mental and the real. Such an uncanny blurring of boundaries is, of course, symptomatic of the unnatural strengthening of the fantastic capacity in melancholic diseases.

The sluggishness of the melancholic Morpheus, "drowned deepe / In drowsy fit" (1.1.40), seems to highlight the close connection between what Du Laurens calls the "unseparable sadness" of melancholy and the medieval vice of *acedia*, or sloth. For the church fathers, "torpor" is one of the *filiae acediae* (daughters of sloth): it is "the obtuse and somnolent stupor that paralyzes any gesture that might heal us."[14] Despair (*desperatio*) also belongs to this family of vices; like torpor, despair works on the sufferer's mind to produce a deadly lassitude, "a complacent sinking into one's own destruction."[15] If the disease of melancholy tends to explain the slide into despair in physiological terms, the sin of *acedia* reads the same slide in psychospiritual terms.[16] The naturally close connection between melancholia and *acedia* is widely evident in medieval religious sources, many of which diagnose the atrabilious syndrome as a potential cause of *acedia*.[17] David of Augsburg, for example, cites "bitterness of mind" that arises primarily from the melancholic humor as the main cause of *acedia*.[18] Most significantly for our purposes, though, melancholy and *acedia* share a common root in a corrupted imagination. As Giorgio Agamben notes, "the inability to control the incessant discourse of the interior phantasms is among the essential traits in the patristic characterization of sloth. . . . [T]his hypertrophy of the imagination is one of the traits that links the sloth of the fathers to the melancholic syndrome and to the love-disease of humoral medicine."[19] Red Crosse's "deadly sleepe," his submission to the "discourse of [his] interior phantasms," and his later temptation by Despair suggest that his quest reflects the complex and often imprecise fusion of *acedia*, melancholy, and despair characteristic of medieval religious and medical writing on the origin of despair.

The sexual nature of Red Crosse's dream "of loves and lustfull play" (1.1.47) eroticizes this journey toward despair, establishing an affinity between despair and love-melancholy even before we learn of Sir Terwin's suicide in Despair's cave. In fact, the exacerbation of desire that necessarily characterizes love-melancholy is also, though less obviously, a feature of the disorder's theological counterparts. For the sadness of the *acidiosus*, according to Thomas Aquinas, leads to despair because it "makes the arduous good which is hope's object look impossible to obtain."[20] *Acedia*, then, prompts the sufferer to fall away from the good not out of any lack of desire to obtain that good, but rather from a presumptuous certainty that it is out of reach. As Agamben puts it, "the *recessus* of the slothful does not betray an eclipse of desire but, rather, the becoming unobtainable of its object: it is the perversion of a will . . . which simultaneously desires and bars the path to his or her own desire."[21] In both love-melancholy and *acedia*, the sufferer yearns for, and simultaneously turns away from, a beloved object. Robert Burton trenchantly observes the family resemblance between love-melancholy and what he calls religious melancholy: "[S]ome do not obscurely make a distinct species of it, dividing Love-Melancholy into that whose object is women; and into the other, whose object is God."[22] A baffled, obsessive desire foments the "discourse of the interior phantasms" in both conditions.

Spenser creates a version of sloth/*acedia* in the figure he calls Idlenesse, the "first [of the sins] that all the rest did guyde" in Lucifera's palace. Unsurprisingly, given our interpretation of Red Crosse's "deadly sleepe," Idlenesse is described in terms reminiscent of Morpheus (and Red Crosse): "[O]f devotion he had little care, / *Still drownd in sleepe, and most of his dayes ded*; / Scarse could he once uphold his heavie hed, / To looken, whether it were night or day" (1.4.19, italics mine). An apparently paradoxical relation between Idlenesse and Contemplation betrays the kinship between Idlenesse and the spiritual sin of *acedia*: "From worldly cares himselfe he did esloyne . . . For contemplation sake" (1.4.20). But Spenser's Idlenesse also manifests the exacerbated desire that links this vice to erotic melancholy: "His life he led in lawlesse riotise; / By which he grew to grievous malady; / For in his lustlesse limbes through evill guise / A shaking fever raigned continually" (1.4.20). As A. C. Hamilton suggests, the term "lustlesse" (meaning "listless") implies that *lustfulness* has led to this condition.[23] This combination of feverish desire (the "shaking fever") and excessive inwardness (contemplation) suggests an eroticized longing that links the "grievous malady" of *acedia* to the psychosomatic *assidua cogitatio* of love-melancholy.[24]

Broadly speaking, Spenser's account of Red Crosse's "recessus" from his spiritual path seems to affirm Burton's view that *acedia*, or "religious melancholy," is a type of love-melancholy. The eroticized "grievous malady" of Idlenesse-sloth-*acedia* suggests a similar fusion of the two conditions. In both conditions, a perverse desire (driven by the uncontrolled *cogitationes* of fantasy) drives the lover away from what he loves. The "inward gall" and "deepe despight" (1.2.6) that Red Crosse feels within him at the sight of the sprights' "lewd embracement" bespeaks a spiritual depression; at the same time, his "great passion of unwonted lust" (1.1.49) suggests that his spirit is darkened by a melancholic version of eros. His erotic *acedia* produces in him both the "bitterness of mind" ("despight") characteristic of this spiritual disorder and the jealous rage ("the eye of reason was with rage yblent," 1.2.5) symptomatic of love-melancholy. Red Crosse's violent impulse toward the false Una ("he thought have slaine her in his fierce despight," 1.1.49) seems at first blush undermotivated but fits Hildegard's portrait of melancholic lovers who "would kill the woman with whom they are having sexual relations if they could."[25]

"Sorwful Ymaginacioun": Chaucer and the Literary Origins of Despair

The notion that Red Crosse's passionate withdrawal from his quest and his pursuit of Duessa should be understood as symptoms of a spiritually inflected love-melancholy is also borne out by Spenser's deployment of his Chaucerian source in the dream scene. For as many critics have noted, Spenser's Morpheus is a close relative of Chaucer's Morpheus in *The Book of the Duchess*: both are shape-shifting intermediary figures whose drowsy caves—in Chaucer's poem the cave is "as derke / As helle pitte" (*BD* 170–71)—seem to allegorize the "fantasy" of the sleeper.[26] The narrator of Chaucer's poem is suffering from a mysterious sickness—probably lovesickness—that has disrupted his imagination and driven him into "melancolye" (*BD* 51): "For sorwful ymaginacioun / Ys always hooly in my mynde. . . . And I ne may, ne nyght ne morwe, / Slepe, and thys melancolye / And drede I have for to dye" (*BD* 22–24).[27] The dream that finally comes—as though from Morpheus—also concerns love-melancholy and its cure. The central figure of the dream is the grieving Man in Black, whose overwhelming grief at the death of his beloved lady is the subject of the "compleynt" he sings when the narrator first encounters him:

> I stalked even unto hys bake,
> And ther I stoode, as stille as ought,
> That, soth to saye, he sawe me nought;
> Forwhy he henge hys hede adoune,
> And with a dedely sorwful soun
> He made a ryme X vers or twelfe
> Of a compleynt, to hymselfe.
>
> . . . .
> I went and stoode ryght at his fete
> And grette hym. But he spake noght,

> But argued with his oune thoght,
> And in hys wytte disputed faste,
> Why and how hys lyfe myght laste;
> Hym thought hys sorwes were so smerte
> And lay so colde upon hys herte.
> So throgh hys sorwe and hevy thoght
> Made hym that he herde me noght,
> For he had wel nygh lost hys mynde.
>
> (*BD* 458–64; 50211)

The complaint of the Man in Black ("with a dedely sorwful soun / He made a ryme") recalls the mournful sounds of the cave of Morpheus: "Ther were a fewe welles . . . That made a dedely slepynge soun" (162). Like Morpheus, the Man in Black is sunk in his own thoughts, self-absorbed to the point that he does not hear the speaker's greeting; even the complaint is made "to hymselfe." The Man in Black's melancholy is figured as a deadly form of sleep, a form of sleep that *is* in fact a kind of death.

Though the poem's central theme is secular love (the Man in Black's melancholy love for his dead wife), its closing image suggests that this love-melancholy has a broader "spiritual" significance. As Richard Rambuss has argued, the image of the long white castle on a hill evokes St. John's vision of the New Jerusalem:[28]

> With that me thoght that this kynge
> Gan homewarde for to ryde,
> Unto a place was there besyde,
> Which was from us but a lyte:
> A longe castel with wallys white,
> Be seynt John, on a ryche hille,
> As me mette.
>
> (*BD* 1314–20)

This movement "homewarde" toward the visionary castle suggests, in Rambuss's view, a movement away from the miseries of the world and toward a "final resolution of mourning."[29] For the vision of the New Jerusalem coincides in Revelation with a promise of perfect consolation: "God himself . . . will wipe away every tear from their eyes, and death shall be no more, neither shall there be mourning nor crying nor pain any more" (Rev. 21:3–4 RSV). Rambuss argues that the melancholy of both the narrator and his alter ego, the Man in Black, is associated with a secrecy that bespeaks a failure to accommodate loss, or even to recognize what has been lost.[30] This internal secrecy—an unsustainable defense against the reality of loss—could be considered a symptom of the melancholic process of incorporation that I discussed earlier; the lost object is buried within a psychic "crypt," whence it continues to exert an occult control over the subject. The apocalypse, in this reading, becomes a trope for "the making conscious of what has been unconscious."[31] Only once this spiritual/psychic "revelation" has taken place can the process of consolation begin. But Rambuss insists that the promise of consolation remains only a fantasy in the poem, since we return immediately after the vision of the white castle to the temporal world (as the bell strikes) and to what Chaucer calls "the processe of tyme."[32] My own view is that the homeward journey of the "king" (probably the Man in Black) represents a genuine movement away from the circularity of an obsessive (melancholic) grief toward the teleological process of mourning. The efficacy of the consolatory power of the vision is borne out by the narrator's own "awakening" into the intention to write down his dream, and the therapeutic action of unfolding his experience through writing likewise counteracts the secret pain of eight years' duration: "Thoght I, 'Thys ys so queynt a swevene / That I wol, *be processe of tyme*, / Fonde to put this swevene in ryme / As kan I best" (1324–34, italics mine). It is precisely because this turn toward writing necessitates a movement into mortal time ("be processe of tyme") that it is therapeutic; within the framework of the vision of Revelation, this "processe of tyme" suggests a gradual, mournful acceptance of the loss that portends the final end of all sorrow.

Spenser's reworking of *The Book of the Duchess* in his *Daphnaïda* provides a further indication that Red Crosse's spiritual ills have their root in a melancholic "revolt against mourning." The poem's central figure, Alcyon, suffers from a combination of spiritual depression and love-melancholy very similar not only to Red Crosse's "deepe despight" but also to Timias's "sad melancholy" when he is banished from Belphoebe's favor and to Scudamour's self-indulgent abjection. A brief analysis of Alcyon's slide from mourning into a destructive melancholia will provide a useful frame of reference for *The Faerie Queene*'s more elaborate treatment of this psychic pattern. In Chaucer's *The Book of the Duchess*, Alcyone dies from grief when she learns from a dream vision that her husband is dead. She clearly allegorizes the kind of despairing grief from which the narrator hopes to extricate the Man in Black and, implicitly, himself. Spenser's Alcyon, a kind of composite of Alcyone and the Man in Black, remains alive in bitter despair over the death of his wife, Daphne. Like the central figures of *The Book of the Duchess*, Alcyon favors cryptic, allusive references to the real object of his sorrow (Daphne is allegorized as a lioness) that indicate a deeper failure to acknowledge the reality of loss.[33] Alcyon even declares before his long narrative that "the huge anguish, which dooth multiplie / My dying paines, no tongue can well unfold" (*Daphnaïda* 73–74). Like the melancholic lovers in the medical literature, he has placed himself outside the range of normative language.

Alcyon's refusal to accept the death of his beloved Daphne turns to what the poem calls "despight." Spenser's "despight" seems to capture quite closely the notion of *amaritudo mentis*, a "bitterness of mind" and *ennui* at the root of *acedia*. Ambiguously inner and outer directed, this mixture of scorn, pride, and despairing indignation (literally "looking down upon") seems to evoke the "self-reproaches and self-revilings" noted by Freud as characteristic of melancholia.[34] As we have seen, Freud shares with earlier writers a sense that melancholic self-hatred arises from a narcissistic identification with an internalized lost object.[35] Alcyon's description of his "selfe-consuming paine" certainly evokes a process of self-absorption that drains away his vitality from within.[36] That he refers to Daphne as "she that did my vital powres supplie" seems to imply in addition that once lost, she has been assimilated as an internalized maternal object:[37]

> So doo I live, so doo I daylie die,
> And pine away in selfe-consuming paine,
> Sith she that did my vitall powres supplie,
> And feeble spirits in their force maintaine
> Is fetcht fro me, why seeke I to prolong
> My wearie daies in dolor and disdaine?
>
> (*Daphnaïda* 435–40)

Like the Ficinian lover whose spirits leak uncontrollably toward a beloved who is ambiguously both internal (engraved on the fantastic spirits) and external, Alcyon's "feeble spirits" dwindle into a melancholic self-consumption that leads remorselessly to despair. While Red Crosse's melancholic quest leads him to the cave of Despair, Alcyon's version of grief actually transforms him into a version of Despair, as a comparison of these two descriptions below suggests.

> His carelesse locks, uncombed and unshorne
> Hong long adowne, and beard all over growne,
> That well he seemd to be sum wight forlorne;
> Downe to the earth his heavie eyes were throwne
> As loathing light: and ever as he went,
> He sighed soft, and inly deepe did grone,
> As if his heart in peeces would have rent.]

(Daphnaïda 43–49)

> That darkesome cave they enter, where they find
> That cursed man, low sitting on the ground,
> Musing full sadly in his sullein mind;
> His grieisie lockes, long growen, and unbound,
> Disordred hong about his shoulders round,
> And hid his face; through which his hollow eyne
> Lookt deadly dull, and stared as astound.

(The Faerie Queene 1.9.35)

Spenser's presentation of the "self-consuming paine" of an Alcyon (or a Red Crosse) finds a useful corollary in contemporary theological, as well as philosophical/medical, discourse. In his treatise on conscience, William Perkins advises the reader on the best way to cure distress caused by melancholy:

> The way to cure melancholy is this . . . search and triall must be made whether he hath in him any beginnings of grace, as of faith and repentance, or no. If he be a carnall man, and wanteth knowledge of his estate, *then meanes must be used, to bring him to some sight and sorrow for his sinnes, that his melancholy sorrow, may be turned into a godly sorrow.*[38]

Perkins' striking phrase "godly sorrow"—and his opposition between this affect and "melancholy sorrow"—seems to translate St. Paul's distinction between two kinds of *tristitia* (sadness). As Susan Snyder has shown, Paul divides *tristitia* into two radically opposed psychospiritual conditions: *tristitia secundum Deum*, or salutary contrition, "works repentance and leads to salvation"; *tristitia saeculi*, however, is an "excess or perversion of salutary contrition" and leads to Despair.[39] It seems clear that Alcyon's relentless grief has become excessive, a "perversion" of true mourning that will lead him into sin. He neglects all other responsibilities to worship his love as a saint for whom he will do penance: "[S]he my love that was, my Saint that is" (379); more damagingly still, he "hate[s] the heaven, because it doth withold / [Him] from [his] love" (400–401). Alcyon's fixation on his beloved has turned her into an idol who blocks his access to heaven.

As the idolatrous nature of Alcyon's love suggests, the influence of Petrarch's particular brand of erotic *acedia*, his rueful yet willed indulgence of a destructive *atra voluptas*, is particularly marked in the poem. His is a *dilectoso male*, a willfully exacerbated pain for which the apt expression is precisely the "feeding on tears" that characterizes Petrarch's *voluptas dolendi*:

> For I will walke this *wandring pilgrimage*
> Throughout the world from one to other end,
> And in affliction wast my better age.
> *My bread shall be the anguish of my mind,*
> *My drink the teares which from mine eyes do raine,*
> My bed the ground that hardest I may finde;
> So will I wilfully increase my paine.
>
> (*Daphnaïda* 372–78, italics mine)

The reference here to Alcyon's "wandring pilgrimage" echoes St. Peter's description of sinful human beings as "but strangers and pilgrims, that wander to and fro in the earth."[40] But Alcyon's determination to increase his own pain suggests the "excess or perversion of contrition" that leads not to a gracious acceptance of the "evills" of the world, as Perkins advises, but rather to "melancholy sorrow." If this "wandring pilgrimage" mirrors in some measure Red Crosse's melancholic "error" after his abandonment of Una, it also indicates what may befall any of Spenser's romance protagonists, all of whom "in the wide deepe wandring arre" (1.2.1).

Alcyon's deliberately exacerbated grief dramatizes the "revolt against mourning" that has provided a theoretical link between grief and love-melancholy at least since Ficino's *De amore*. Like Artemisia, whose consumption of her husband's ashes Ficino compares to the Lucretian lovers' frantic attempts to devour each other, Alcyon cannot accept the "unstedfast . . . state" (517) of human life:

> I hate the heaven, because it doth withhold
> Me from my love, and eke my love from me.
>
> (400–401)

> For all I see is vaine and transitorie,
> Ne will be helde in anie stedfast plight
> But in a moment loose their grace and glorie.
>
> (495–98)

Like Leone Ebreo's Filone, Alcyon deplores the lack of "continuation" in the mortal beloved.[41] Alcyon's excessive and now bitter love for Daphne prohibits mourning, if by mourning we mean a process that permits the gradual removal of libidinal cathexis from the loved object.[42] It is precisely this kind of mourning that Daphne seems to recommend to Alcyon, providing him as she dies with a kind of substitute for herself: their child, Ambrosia:

> Yet ere I goe, a pledge I leave with thee
> Of the late love, the which betwixt us past,
> My yong Ambrosia, in lieu of mee
> Love her: so shall our love for ever last.
>
> (290–93)

Daphne's recommendation ("in lieu of mee / Love her") makes room for mourning by allowing the lover to accept the "vaine and transitorie" nature of the world and thus to love another in her place.

If Spenser's representation of Alcyon's willful grief confirms the close relationship between love-melancholy and the theological sin of *acedia/* despair, the Despair episode in *The Faerie Queene* also supports this connection. For the victim of Despair whom Red Crosse sees "wallowd in his owne yet luke-warme blood" (1.9.36) is Sir Terwin, an unhappy lover. As his companion Sir Trevisan tells it, Despair uses the "bitter byting griefe / Which love had launched with his deadly darts" (1.9.29) to drive him to suicide. Love-melancholy and religious-melancholy converge in Despair's cave in the state of "despight" in which the sufferer loses all hope of salvation and willfully seeks his own death:

> With wounding words and termes of foule repriefe
> *He pluckt from us all hope of due reliefe,*

That earst us held in love of lingring life;
Then hopelesse hartlesse, gan the cunning thiefe
Perswade us die, to stint all further strife.
To me he lent this rope, to him a rustie knife.

With which sad instrument of hastie death,
The wofull lover, loathing lenger light,
A wide way made to let forth living breath.

(1.9.29–30, italics mine)

At the end of the *Daphnaïda*, Alcyon similarly rejects the narrator's offer of help "as one disposed wilfullie to die" (552), thus transforming the relatively hopeful end of Chaucer's poem into a grim commentary on the power of despair. The lovesick Terwin, who lies slumped on the ground, also seems to point back to the dreaming Arthur.[43] Like Arthur, Terwin lies on the grass ("And there beside there lay upon the gras / A drearie corse," 1.9.36). Both knights also suffer from the "wounds" of love, though Arthur's remains a "secret," figurative wound ("what secret wound / Could ever find, to grieve the gentlest hart on ground?" 1.9.7), while Terwin's is a grisly literal wound: he "wallowd in his owne yet luke-warme blood, / That from his wound yet welled fresh alas" (1.9.36).[44] The juxtaposition of this love-suicide with Arthur's own account of his elegiac love for the faerie queene seems designed to indicate how perilously close is the kinship between love-melancholy and what Spenser calls the "sad remembraunce" (1.9.18) that motivates Arthur's quest.

It is against the shadows of Alcyon's "wandring pilgrimage" and the similarly melancholic journeys of Red Crosse and Sir Terwin that Arthur's quest draws its force. For Spenser makes it clear that Arthur's elegiac search for the faerie queene is precariously balanced between a "godly sorrow" and the "melancholy sorrow" that works despair. He is vulnerable to the kinds of "fancies" that beset Red Crosse and the bitter unquietness that tortures Alcyon. Thus when Florimell suddenly appears in terrified flight from the "griesly Foster" (3.1.17), he instantly pursues her, thinking her "the fairest Dame alive" (3.1.18). But as the echoes between Florimell's flight and Angelica's flight through the Ariostan forest indicate, Arthur's pursuit of this "blazing starre" (3.1.16) will threaten to draw him into the fantastic world of love-melancholy and despair:

But gentle Sleepe envyde him any rest;
In stead thereof sad sorrow, and disdaine
Of his hard hap did vexe his noble brest,
And thousand fancies bet his idle braine
With their light wings, the sights of semblants vaine:
Oft did he wish, that Lady faire mote bee
His faery Queene, for whom he did complaine:
Or that his Faery Queene were such, as shee:
And ever hastie Night he blamed bitterlie.

(3.4.54, italics mine)

Like Red Crosse in the house of Archimago, Arthur is overcome by the "sights of semblants vaine," and like Alcyon, who spends his "wearie daies in dolor and disdaine" (*Daphnaïda* 440), Arthur slips into "sad sorrow, and disdaine / Of his hard hap." And when Arthur rises after his restless night, his "heavie looke" clearly recalls the "dismall lookes" of Alcyon:

He up arose, as halfe in great disdaine,
And clombe unto his steed. So forth he went,
With heavie looke and lumpish pace, that plaine
In him bewraid great grudge and maltalent:
His steed eke seem'd t'apply his steps to his intent.

(3.4.61)

But without taking leave, he foorth did goe
With staggering pace and dismall lookes dismay,
As if that death he in the face had seene.

(*Daphnaïda* 563–65)

Veritas filia temporis: Romance, Skepticism, and Figural Consolation

The similarity between Sir Terwin's "bitter byting griefe" (1.9.29) and Arthur's "great disdaine" suggests that Arthur, like Sir Terwin and Red Crosse, is vulnerable to the discourse of Despair's "sullein mind" (for "love is sullein," 3.11.43, as we learn in the house of Busirane). I propose now to revisit the problematic dream origin of Arthur's quest in order to trace more exactly Spenser's transformation of "melancholy sorrow" into "godly sorrow," or what I will call in light of the poem's structure "figural consolation."

Two aspects of Arthur's dream seem to be at issue here. The first of these we have explored: it is the danger that the kind of "ravishment" induced by the dream will become the deadly "wallowing" of a Sir Terwin.[45] The second engages with the central epistemological problem implicit in the medical writing on love-melancholy: since the disease arises from the corruption of the imagination and a resulting distortion of the estimative power, the lover's judgment of the world, and of the beloved object in particular, is necessarily awry.[46] The juxtaposition of the false Una, delivering "gentle blandishment and lovely looke" (1.9.49), with the visionary faerie queene, who offers the similar-sounding "goodly glee and lovely blandishment" (1.9.14), raises the possibility that Arthur, like Red Crosse, has suffered an "abuse" to his fantasy and (thus) damage to his estimative faculty. How are we to interpret Arthur's unquestioning devotion to his quest when we—and even he—can see that this dream may in fact have deluded his imagination and his judgment? In what respect is Arthur's devotion to his quest superior to Red Crosse's abandonment of his, given that each is driven by what appears to be a true vision? Finally, what does it mean for Spenser's romance that it is founded on a quest undertaken in such epistemologically shaky circumstances?

In his discussion of the Despair episode, Harold Skulsky argues that Red Crosse's predicament in the cave of Despair raises *the* crucial epistemological question of the period: how does one know that one is saved?[47] As he points out, the only criteria for such knowledge—*fiducia*—turn out to be those "intuitive data" of which we believe we have "incorrigible introspective knowledge."[48] Like pain, then, fiduciary faith should be introspectively accessible. But, Skulsky argues, Red Crosse—who is Elect—does in fact lose his assurance of salvation, a turn of events in the poem that raises an unanswerable theological and epistemological question: "[H]ow does one distinguish, at any given moment, between a temporary and a permanent calling, between the confused sense of grace of the Reprobate and the imperfect faith of the Elect?"[49]

Skulsky's conception of the relevance of the *fiducia* debate to broader epistemological concerns helps to sharpen our sense of what is at stake in

Arthur's devotion to his quest:

> [T]he polemic on *fiducia* merely translates into soteriological terms the perennial question whether empirical knowledge of any domain somehow depends on *introspectible items—mental images, phantasmata, eidola, species sensibiles—items whose occurrence is beyond doubt for the person they occur to* and include signs of objective reality that are equally beyond doubt.[50]

We could understand Arthur's dream as a translation of the soteriological terms of the *fiducia* debate back into precisely the broader epistemological problematic outlined by Skulsky. Spenser emphasizes Arthur's certainty about his vision, but is also careful to indicate that this certainty might *or might not* be justified:

> For dearely sure her love was to me bent,
> As when iust time expired should appeare.
> *But whether dreames delude, or true it were,*
> *Was never hart so ravisht with delight,*
> Ne living man like words did ever heare,
> As she to me delivered all that night;
> And at her parting said, She Queene of Faeries hight.

> When I awoke, and found *her place devoyd,*
> *And nought but pressed gras,* where she had lyen,
> I sorrowed all so much, as earst I joyd,
> And washed all her place with watry eyen.
> From that day forth I lov'd that face divine;
> From that day forth I cast in carefull mind,
> To seeke her out with labour, and long tyne,
> And never vow to rest, till her I find,
> Nine monthes I seeke in vaine, yet ni'll that vow unbind.

> (1.9.14–15, italics mine)

These stanzas move delicately between equivocation and assurance: dreams *may* delude, yet Arthur's heart is "ravisht with delight"; her "place" is "devoyd," yet there is external evidence in the "pressed gras, where she had lyen," that the vision had the heft of reality.[51] Most significantly, the love of the faerie queene is tied to the unfolding of time: "As when iust time expired should appeare."

It is, I suggest, the involvement of unfolding time in Arthur's vision that provides the key to Spenser's revision of the *fiducia* debate, a revision that underwrites his conception of romance. The notion that the truth of the faerie queene's love will appear *in time* suggests the popular motto "Truth is the daughter of time" (*Veritas filia temporis*). This motto also structures the mysterious narrative of Arthur's identity, as told by Merlin:

> Him oft and oft I askt in privitie,
> Of what loines and what lignage I did spring:
> Whose aunswere bad me still assured bee,
> That I was sonne and heire unto a king,
> *As time in her iust terme the truth to light should bring.*

(1.9.5, italics mine)

This motto has a special significance in the Elizabethan period, as Fritz Saxl notes in his examination of the history of the motto.[52] During the Reformation, the motto had been used polemically to illustrate the "liberation of Christian Truth (as understood by Protestant reformers) from her captivity under the monster of Roman Hypocrisy."[53] This allegorization of Truth as the truth of the Protestant Reformers becomes yet more specific at the beginning of Elizabeth's reign. In an allegorical sideshow performed a day before her coronation, Elizabeth herself is represented as "'Temporis Filia, The Daughter of Tyme' . . . And on her brest was written her propre name, whiche was 'Veritas,' Trueth, who held a booke in her hande, upon the which was written, 'Verbum Veritatis,' the Woorde of Trueth."[54]

Spenser clearly activates the typological meaning of the motto in his text, suggesting that Arthur's quest is structured by the figural unfolding of sacred history.[55] As in figural readings of Old Testament stories, the shadow or figure of the "old" story points to the *veritas* of its fulfillment in the new:

> The fulfillment is often designated as *veritas* . . . and the figure correspond-ingly as umbra or imago; but both shadow and truth are abstract only in reference to the meaning first concealed, then revealed; they are concrete in reference to the things or persons which appear as vehicles of the meaning.[56]

Critics have noted the relevance to Spenser's text of the motto and the figural structure it implies.[57] The emphasis, though, in critical readings of the significance of the motto for the poem generally lies in the notion of *hidden*, inaccessible truth rather than in the immanence of the truth in the figure.[58] For as Erich Auerbach argues, the full meaning of the event or *figura* is always fulfilled in God, though imperfectly revealed to the human participants of history:

> In the modern view, the provisional event is treated as a step in an unbroken horizontal process; in the figural system the interpretation is always sought from above. . . . Whereas in the modern view the event is always self-sufficient and secure, while the interpretation is fundamentally incomplete, in the figural interpretation the fact is subordinated to an interpretation which is fully secured to begin with: the event is enacted according to an ideal model which is a prototype situated in the future and thus far only promised.[59]

Although Patricia Parker is right to suggest that Spenser's poem "is still within the realm of the figure," her reading focuses on the *veiling* of truth rather than the securing of truth by means of the figural interpretation required by the *figura-veritas* relationship.[60] Similarly, Elizabeth Bellamy's Lacanian reading, like David Lee Miller's, emphasizes the uncertainty of Arthur's quest: this is, according to her, "a narrative of deferral seeking an object that may not already have been there."[61] Spenser's language, on the other hand, captures precisely the dialectic between absence and presence that is constitutive of the *figura*: the faerie queene's "place" is "devoyd," yet her absent presence is beautifully captured in the "pressed gras, where she had lyen." The imprint of truth is, as it were, pressed upon the figura. We are invited to read the poem figurally, in the manner of Tyndale's reading of the Bible: "God is a spirit, and all his words are spiritual . . . if thou have eyes of God to see the right meaning of the text, and whereunto the scripture pertaineth, and the final end and cause thereof." Such a reading struggles to see the *figura* in light of the promised *veritas*, the "final end and cause" of Scripture, and in doing so to collapse the distinction between the two: "[God's] literal sense is spiritual, and all his words are spiritual."[62]

Let us consider how the figural relationship between *figura* and *veritas* urged on us both by Merlin's assurance of Arthur and by the faerie queene's promise of love informs the epistemological questions with which we began this section. Arthur's dream, bearing for him as it does an irresistible emotional truth, appears to be a version of what the Stoics called a *phantasia kataleptike*, or grasping image. Cataleptic images, as Martha Nussbaum has argued, are "certain special perceptual impressions: those which, by their own internal character, their own experienced quality, certify their own veracity."[63] Sextus Empiricus's definition of the cataleptic image emphasizes the incorrigibility of the impression: it is "one that is imprinted and stamped upon us by reality itself and in accordance with reality, one that could not possibly come from what is not that reality."[64] Spenser's use of the word "ravisht" supports the notion that Arthur's dream brings with it incorrigible knowledge: the Middle English "ravishen" means "carry up" (into heaven); transport ("into an ecstasy, or vision").[65] As Skulsky notes, the cataleptic impression also sounds a good deal like the "Pauline seal or earnest money of the Holy Spirit" by which the believer experiences *fiducia* and knows he is saved.[66] The skeptical response to such an argument posits that one can in fact be misled by sense impressions of external objects, because (for example) it may be possible to create perfectly similar replicas of objects that deceive the most acute observer.[67] We recognize this problem from Tasso's poem, though the terms of its exploration in the earlier context do not have the soteriological cast they receive in Spenser's poem. When Red Crosse is divided from himself by Archimago's "true-seeming lyes" (1.1.38), he reminds us of Tancredi, driven *fuor di sé* by his inability to conquer his fear of a phantasm that he partly knows to be false. The power of the (melancholic) mind to collude in its own deception is at the heart of Tasso's conception of romance, and Spenser's poem directly addresses this issue in its juxtaposition of the "true" and "false" visions of Arthur and Red Crosse.

Skulsky infers from Spenser's use of Archimago that "the psychology of the book of Holiness is Academic [i.e., skeptical] and not Stoic; there is no room in it for the phantasia kataleptike and hence none for assurance either."[68] In Red Crosse's case, certainly, his judgment of the world is "abused" by the images he sees both in his sleeping and waking visions of Una. Whether we understand Archimago as a demonic "man of hell" interfering with man's perception of the world, or as a figure for Red Crosse's own susceptibility to the kind of "sorwful imaginacioun" that plagues Chaucer's narrator (or some combination of the two), the impressions he receives are as false as they are compelling. But Skulsky does not consider how Arthur's "true" vision complicates this view of Spenser's poem as fundamentally skeptical. We have seen that Arthur's dream is represented in such a way as to render it epistemologically uncertain: dreams may delude, indeed. But Arthur's sudden conversion from scorner of love to devoted knight of the faerie queene bespeaks a cataleptic certainty, and one that the poem certainly endorses.

The conjunction of the two dreams suggests a revision of the terms of the debate between *fiducia* and skepticism discussed by Skulsky. Arthur's dream does not, after all, solve the epistemological problem by epistemological means: it is not because Arthur *knows* beyond any doubt that his dream is true that he pursues the quest. Indeed the shift from third-person to first-person narrative underscores the imperfection of Arthur's knowledge: "*Me seemed*, by my side a royall Mayd / Her daintie limbes full softly did lay" (1.9.13, italics mine). The notion of incorrigible first-person knowledge of introspectible items is undercut not only by Red Crosse's misfortunes but by Arthur's own dubiousness about the epistemological status of his dream: "But whether dreames delude . . ." But Arthur's *emotional* assurance is not undermined, as the following line reveals: "But whether dreames delude or true it were, / Was never *hart so ravisht* with delight" (1.9.14, italics mine). Similarly, when Arthur awakens to find "her place devoyd, / And nought but pressed gras, where she had lyen," it is his immediate emotional response to his loss that shows the way forward: "I sorrowed all so much, as earst I ioyd, / And washed all her place with watry eyen" (1.9.15). The "place devoyd" is washed with Arthur's tears as he mourns her loss. Mourning, though, leads to action:

> From that day forth I lov'd that face divine;
> From that day forth I cast in carefull mind,
> To seeke her out with labour, and long tyne,
> And never vow to rest, till her I find,
> Nine monethes I seeke in vaine yet ni'll that vow unbind.
>
> (1.9.15)

Arthur's cataleptic "delight," indubitably revealed by the dream, overrides the need for empirical knowledge. Thus Arthur's unwavering vow to "seeke her out" dramatizes what for Skulsky is the only alternative for the Christian soldier in the face of unanswerable epistemological questions: a continual performative pledging of faith to God.[69] According to Skulsky, this is what the active Christian life amounts to for Spenser: "[I]n such active pledging there is, so to say, a measure of performative or illocutionary certainty. It will not solve or get around the epistemological problem posed by the existence of Archimago, but it is quite enough to nerve Redcrosse to return from his betrothal feast to the city of fame and risk."[70] But Arthur's quest suggests a more positive appraisal of Spenser's position. There is a sense in which his "vow" *does* get around the epistemological problem posed by Archimago precisely because it sets aside the whole question of empirical knowledge. As Nussbaum argues in her discussion of cataleptic knowledge, "the cataleptic impression is not simply a route to knowing; it *is* knowing. It doesn't point beyond itself *to* knowledge; it goes to constitute knowledge."[71] Like Proust, whom Nussbaum discusses in relation to a revised kind of cataleptic knowledge, Spenser seems to have moved away from the usual kind of cataleptic impression (of objects in the world) to *emotional* impressions: knowledge of the heart. Rather than judging the truth or falsity of the dream itself, as Red Crosse appears to do, Arthur judges the truth of his inner world: he is "ravisht with delight." This impression just *is* the knowledge he needs to proceed on his quest.[72]

Stanley Cavell concludes his discussion of how we might satisfy our skepticism about whether a (seemingly human) automaton is really or only apparently human by showing that such a skepticism can never be satisfied: "Whatever can be specified, as a test of automatonity, can be built in to fail. Criteria come to an end."[73] Arthur's dream also makes clear that "criteria come to an end": the response to the dream cannot sensibly rest on any kind of "proof" that it was, or was not, "true." Arthur's response to this unknowable yet "true" vision is a kind of active mourning: he washes the "place devoyd" with his tears, filling, as it were, the space of epistemological uncertainty with a grief that moves him to activity rather than the idleness or feverishness of *acedia*. Cavell's assertion that "criteria come to an end" seems to do some justice to Spenser's complex response to the epistemological problems posed by book 1's skirmishes with dreams and visions. To put this in the medical and psychological terms we have used thus far, we might say that melancholy is revealed as a skeptical response to an unknowable world. It is, after all, Red Crosse's willingness to believe in the falseness of Una, though he knows "no'untruth" of her (1.1.53), that promotes his departure from the true quest. He is, in other words, willing to believe that she *might not* be true. This melancholic skepticism works proleptically to *produce* the loss (of truth) that he fears.[74] A mournful attitude toward the world, on the other hand, fosters an elegiac movement toward the lost object that makes room for the notion of *immanence*.

The keying of Arthur's quest to the *veritas filia temporis* motto provides a corrective to the threat of a slide into the melancholic quests of an Alcyon or a Red Crosse. It forestalls the demand to know all the truth of a situation at once because, as Auerbach shows, the figural meaning of the quest is always secured in advance: "[T]he fact is subordinated to an interpretation which is fully secured to begin with."[75] The truth of the typological quest is not transcendent but *immanent*: it informs the present event even as that event unfolds in the shadow of a more "ideal" model "which is a prototype situated in the future."[76] Gloriana's name figures the *glory* of God, which concerns God's immanence to the world; and the word "glory" itself, deriving from the Hebrew root *kbd*, "heaviness," suggests precisely the "pressed gras" that testifies to the *weight* of the faerie queene's (now absent) presence.[77] Arthur's immediate "vow" to pursue the faerie queene in the belief that "her love was to [him] bent, / As time in her just time expired should appeare" (1.9.14) is a performance of faith that sets aside the troubling epistemological questions that dog Red Crosse. The ability to proceed with the quest in the face of uncertainty and in the midst of sorrow just *is* what *fiducia* amounts to and directly responds to Alcyon's lament that "all I see is vaine and transitorie, / Ne will be helde in anie stedfast plight / But in a moment loose their grace and *glorie*" (*Daphnaïda* 495–98, italics mine). For Arthur, the glory of his vision—manifested in the lineaments of the faerie queene's "place devoyd"—"ravishes" his heart with an unwavering faith even in the absence of the beloved herself.

The structure of the dream episode also suggests how this enactment of faith responds to the danger of collapse into melancholic skepticism. For while Alcyon, as we have seen, scornfully disregards the plea of his own wife to allow another (Ambrosia) to act as a substitute for her, Arthur's dream narrative suggests that its typological structure *builds in* such substitutes. For it cannot be coincidental that Arthur tells the dream to Una in the ninth month of his quest (and the ninth canto of book 1): "Nine monethes I seeke in vaine yet ni'll that vow unbind" (1.9.15). There is a sense in which the telling of the dream narrative to Una represents a partial fulfillment of the quest, a figurative "birth," though Arthur himself may not understand this.[78] Una temporarily (here and elsewhere) stands in for

the glorious, absent faerie queene, and the force of her maieutic engagement with Arthur helps to facilitate the emergence of the identity that is
tied to unfolding time: "As time in her just terme the truth to light should
bring" (1.9.5). A figural narrative works by definition through substitution:
one event is both itself and a figure for another, absent event (or person);
in this sense the figural narrative is an essentially mournful narrative in
which the subject must learn to accept loss and substitution as a condition
of life. As Peter Sacks writes, though, "only the object as lost, and not the
object itself, enters into the substitutive sign, and the latter is accepted only
by a turning away from the actual identity of what was lost."[79] Thus the
"figural" fulfillment of the dream narrative within Arthur and Una's dialogue both consoles Arthur for his loss and also stirs within him the "sad
remembraunce" that propels him "his voyage to renew" (1.9.18).

Spenser's reorganization of the romance quest seems to reflect a response to the pathological quest of an Orlando or a Tancredi, in which the
lover is bound to a unique mortal beloved to the exclusion of all others.
For the figural structure of Arthur's quest, emphasized from its very beginning, organizes the quest around a troping process, a process in which the
"ideal" beloved object is continually mourned *and* continually replaced
by other objects that shadow her. Thus later in the poem we find another
reference to the quest as a kind of ongoing pregnancy whose "just terme"
is repetitively reached at the conclusion of each of Arthur's adventures:

> Thus when the Prince had perfectly complyde
> These paires of friends in peace and setled rest,
> Him selfe, whose minde did travell as with chylde,
> Of his old love, conceav'd in secret brest,
> Resolved to pursue his former quest.
>
> (4.10.17)

Arthur earlier complains to Una of "that fresh bleeding wound, which day
and night / Whilome doth rancle in my riven brest" (1.9.7) in words that
recall those of Alcyon: "So oft as I record those piercing words, / Which
yet are deepe engraven in my brest, / And those deadly accents, which like
swords / Did wound my heart and rend my bleeding chest" (*Daphnaïda*
295–98). But Una gently corrects Arthur: his is not a literal "bleeding wound," but a figurative, "secret" one: "Ah curteous knight (quoth
she) what secret wound / Could ever find, to grieve the gentlest hart on

ground?" (1.9.7). The "chyld" of Arthur's mind, driving his quest onward, is "conceav'd in secret brest," like the "secret wound" of which Una speaks, and seems to represent a transformation of the erotic wound into the figural power of the quest narrative. The "chyld" constitutes the telos of the pregnancy-quest, and thus signifies the reunion of Arthur and the "Glory" allegorized by the faerie queene. But the "chyld" also acts as a substitute for the absent beloved, as Daphne would like her child, Ambrosia, to replace her in Alcyon's mind. As a metaphor for a continually changing, developing being, the "chyld" of the mind captures the energy of the *figura*, which in this case figures the same perfect reunion in a variety of different forms throughout the course of Arthur's quest. Whereas Alcyon rejects Daphne's request ("in lieu of mee / Love her"), Arthur gradually fulfills the promise of "veritas filia temporis" through his determination to carry this "chyld" of the mind to its "iust terme" (1.9.5). His purposeful "travell" thus signifies the transformation of Alcyon's "wandring pilgrimage" into a teleological (because typological) *labor*.

Spenser's figural narrative works against the melancholic structure of the romance quest by introducing elegiac substitution into a narrative that naturally tends toward despair and madness. This substitution works to promote the kind of sublimation that Ficino sees as the crucial antidote to melancholic fixation, and that is also, according to Sacks, a central piece of the work of mourning:

> One of the most profound issues to beset any mourner and elegist is his surviving yet painfully altered sexuality. Although it is crucial for the mourner to assert a continued sexual impulse, that assertion must be qualified, even repressively transformed or rendered metaphorical, by the awareness of loss and mortality.[80]

The transformation of the erotic power of Arthur's "secret wound" into the figural "travell" of his ongoing quest represents a fundamental reworking of the melancholic structure of romance. We can see that this figural structure is broadly compatible with the Platonic conception of an erotic "ladder" that leads from the actual, mortal object to the divine one. Like the Platonic lover whose soul is carried by the process of *anamnesis* beyond the mortal beauty of the beloved to the divine Good, Arthur is driven onward by "sad remembraunce" of his visionary ecstasy. But the truly elegiac quality of Spenser's figures—which, after all, retain the stamp of the mourned object—seems to forbid any easy acceptance of this process of substitution. The transition from love of mortal objects—figural though they be—to desire for reunion with an abstract Glory remains difficult and always incomplete.

"Sad Melancholy" and the Elegiac Cure

The instability of the transformation from the melancholic quest to the mournful one is indicated by the implication of Arthur's quest for the faerie queene in his squire's hapless quest for Belphoebe. Timias does in fact represent a paradigmatic case of love-melancholy, as Spenser's overt imitations of the *Orlando Furioso* indicate. Dealt a sexual wound (reminiscent of Adonis's thigh wound) by the "griesly foster," Timias finds himself in the care of Belphoebe, just as Medoro wakes to find himself in the care of Angelica. Timias is "infected" by the Ficinian rays from Belphoebe's eyes, and the fateful deterioration begins:

> O foolish Physick, and unfruitfull paine,
> That heales up one and makes another wound:
> She his hurt thigh to him recur'd againe,
> But hurt his hart, the which before was sound,
> Through *an unwary dart, which did rebound*
> *From her faire eyes and gracious countenance.*
> What bootes it him from death to be unbound,
> To be captived in endlesse duraunce
> *Of sorrow and despaire* without aleggeaunce?
>
> (3.5.42, italics mine)

In light of the poem's earlier interest in the connection between despair and melancholic eros, the reference here to "sorrow and despaire" seems calculated to imply that Timias is pursuing the path of eroticized *acedia*. This implication is reinforced by the refrain "Dye rather, dye" that is repeated throughout the episode of Timias's "Malady": "If she will not, dye meekly for her sake; / Dye rather dye, then ever so faire love forsake" (3.5.47). This refrain indicates not only the tendency toward willful death characteristic of both Red Crosse and Alcyon; it also manifests in its very iteration (it is repeated five times in three stanzas) the "consuming thought" of obsession. Like Sir Terwin, Timias "lay wallowd all in his own gore" (3.5.26)—in the blood, that is, of his sexual wound. Timias presents the classic symptoms of love-melancholy: obsessive thought, paleness, wasting, despair: "the mighty ill / . . . Gan ransack fast / His inward parts, and all his entrayles wast, / That neither bloud in face, nor life in hart / Is left, but both did quite dry up, and blast" (3.5.48). The "secret wound" that becomes in Arthur's quest (under Una's tutelage) the engine of his quest, here turns into a Lucretian sickness that threatens the lover's life.

Though Spenser follows his Ariostan source closely in the description of the wound (though it is Angelica, not Medoro, who suffers the "inner" wound of love), the outcome of this episode is tellingly different. Angelica's wound grows even as Medoro's heals: "La sua piaga più s'apre e più incrudisce, / quanto più l'altra si ristringe e salda. / Il giovane si sana: ella languisce / di nuova febbre, or agghiacciata, or calda" (her wound opens wider and is more painful, the more the other contracts and grows firmer. The youth gets better; she weakens with fresh fever, now icy, now hot," *OF* 19.29). But Angelica's suit is successful, and she yields the "rose" coveted by so many love-struck knights to Medoro: "Angelica a Medor la prima rosa / coglier lasciò, non ancor tocca inante" ("Angelica let Medoro gather the first rose, untouched before," *OF* 19.33). This is hardly the mournful sublimation of elegy, nor is it the rational sublimation recommended by Ficino: Angelica follows, rather, the medical advice offered by Lucretius and countless later medical writers. But Spenser uses the "rose" device differently: Belphoebe does not offer "that sweet Cordiall, which can restore / A love-sick hart" (3.5.50) because she values that "dainty Rose, the daughter of her Morne, / More deare than life" (3.5.51). In Spenser's poem the rose represents precisely the "glory" that is the poem's ideal:

> Eternall God in his almighty powre,
> To make ensample of his heavenly grace,
> In paradize whilome did plant this flowre,
> Whence he it fetcht out of her native place,
> And did in stocke of earthly flesh enrace,
> That mortall men *her glory should admire.*
>
> (3.5.52, italics mine)

Belphoebe "shadows" Gloriana, and Gloriana, as we have seen, is in part a figure for a Platonic/Christian Good. The desire to pluck the rose, then, would demonstrate what Ficino regards as the melancholic's desire to embrace what can—or should—only be contemplated (here "admired"). Timias's love-melancholy cannot be cured by the indulgence of sexual desire (as the medical texts suggest), but rather by an elegiac acceptance that Belphoebe's "earthly flesh" is a figure for the intangible good of "heavenly grace."

Just as the lustful "foster" leads Timias to Belphoebe, and thus indirectly to his erotic fixation, so Timias's later engagement with Lust itself brings about his decline into melancholia proper. Lust represents an intensification of the frantic desire of the "foster": his conflation of sexual "deflowering" with literal "devouring" seems to allegorize precisely the regressive orality of a Lucretian/Ficinian love-madness: "He with his shamefull lust doth first deflowre, / And afterwards themselves doth cruelly devoure" (4.7.12). Timias's battle with this creature indicates an allegorical connection between them, especially since he wounds Amoret in the process of killing Lust: "Als of his owne rash hand one wound was to be seene" (4.7.35). As a result of this "lustful" interlude, Timias is banished from Belphoebe's sight and lapses at once into what Spenser does actually call "sad melancholy" (4.7.38). The structure of the episode allegorizes the "perverse Eros of the slothful" once again: because Timias desires Belphoebe too much (as his combat with Lust indicates), because he is not content merely to contemplate the rose, he falls away from what he desires into the self-destructive torpor of "sad melancholy."

Timias's decline in this episode closely mirrors the medical descriptions of advanced love-melancholy: his body wastes away, he weeps and pines, neglecting his appearance and willfully neglecting his health:

> There he continued in this carefull plight,
> Wretchedly wearing out his youthly yeares,
> Through wilfull penury consumed quight,
> That like a pined ghost he soone appeares.
> For other food then that wilde forrest beares,
> Ne other drinke there did he ever tast,
> Then running water, tempred with his teares,
> The more his weakened body so to wast:
> That out of all mens knowledge he was worne at last.
>
> (4.7.41)

The salient feature of Spenser's description of Timias's melancholy is his emphasis on its willfulness; his is "wilful penury"; he "wilfully did cut and shape" his garments to conform to his newly distressed state; and he drinks water "tempred with his teares" in a gesture reminiscent of the speaker of the *Secretum*. The destructive nature of this self-fashioning indicates that we are once again in the vicinity of despair: he intends to "wast his wretched daies in wofull plight; / So on him selfe to wreake his follies own despight" (4.7.39). The language of "despight" recalls both Red Crosse and Alcyon, and indeed the description of Timias's once "faire lockes" as "uncomb'd, uncurl'd, and carelesly unshed; / That in short time his face they overgrew, / And over all his shoulders did despred" (4.7.40) recalls not only Alcyon but the type of all these figures, Despair himself. And when Arthur comes across his squire, he finds "this wretched man, / Spending his daies in dolour and *despaire*" (4.7.43, italics mine). Indeed when Timias finally encounters Belphoebe again, she diagnoses his condition as one of "wilfull woe" in terms that closely approximate the church fathers' conception of *acedia*:

> But if through inward griefe or wilfull scorne
> Of life it be, then better doe advise.
> For he whose daies in wilfull woe are worne,
> The grace of his Creator doth despise,
> That will not use his gifts for thanklesse nigardise.
>
> (4.8.15)

Timias's relation to language also places him within the medical tradition of love-melancholy. As we saw earlier, many medical writers report that the melancholic lover does not understand ordinary discourse *inter homines*, and this is exactly the case when Arthur attempts to engage Timias in conversation:

> But to his speech he aunswered no whit,
> But stood still mute, as if he had beene dum,
> Ne signe of sence did shew, ne common wit,
> As one with griefe and anguishe overcum,
> And unto every thing did aunswere mum.
>
> (4.7.44)

And just as melancholic lovers are said to respond only to language that pertains to the *res amata*, so Timias responds joyfully to any reference to "Belphoebe": "Yet saw he often how he wexed glad, / When he it heard, and how the ground he kist, / Wherein it written was, and how himselfe he blist" (4.7.46). We noted above that although "the lover's helplessness and inarticulateness seem those of an infant, *in-fans*, the one who cannot speak," the melancholic lover does in fact respond to songs, and in particular to songs about separated lovers.[81] The song's pneumatic power allows it to penetrate the lover's physical and linguistic isolation and to create the conditions for a cure of the disease. But we also noted the potential danger of the song's regressive pull back toward the object to whose hidden existence it gives voice. Tasso's *flebil canto* is clearly represented as a quasi-maternal lament that actually calls the lover back to a melancholic position: "[E] parle voce udir tra l'acqua e i rami / ch'a i sospiri ed al pianto la richiami" (it seems to her that she hears a voice amid the water and the branches that calls her back again to sighing and weeping, *GL* 7.5).

Spenser's use of song in this episode is quite different from Tasso's— perhaps consciously so. Like Tancredi, Timias hears an alluring song as he enters the forest in which Belphoebe lives:

> Beside the same a dainty place there lay,
> Planted with mirtle trees and laurels greene,
> In which the birds song many a lovely lay
> Of gods high prayse, and of their loves sweet teene,
> As it an earthly Paradize had beene.

> (3.5.40)

Although this shady grove is reminiscent of Tasso's wood, the "lovely lay" of the birds clearly has a different resonance here. Rather than singing a version of the nightingale's *miserabile carmen*, with its mingled sounds of wind, trees, and human plaint, this song is in honor of "gods high prayse" as well as "loves sweet teene." As a result, Tasso's sinister enchanted wood gives way to an "earthly Paradize," a sacred space in which Timias will eventually be restored to grace. Similarly, the song that actually begins Timias's cure is quite different from the Tassoan *flebil canto*. The singer of this curative song is a turtle Dove whose "lamentable lay" so works on the almost autistically isolated Timias that he pours forth "plenteous teares":

> Till on a day, as in his wonted wise
> His doole he made, there chaunst a turtle Dove
> To come, where he his dolors did devise,
> That likewise late had lost her dearest love,

Which losse her made like passion also prove.
Who seeing his sad plight, her tender heart
With deare compassion deeply did emmove,
That she gan mone his undeserved smart,
And with her dolefull accent beare with him a part.

Shee sitting by him as on ground he lay,
Her mournfull notes full piteously did frame,
And thereof made a lamentable lay,
So sensibly compyld, that in the same
Him seemed oft he heard his owne right name.
With that he forth would poure so plenteous teares,
And beat his breast unworthy of such blame,
And knocke his head, and rend his rugged heares,
That could have perst the hearts of Tigres and of Beares.

(4.8.3–4)

The song in this instance is not merely a love song, but an elegy; it is a "lamentable lay" that mourns the loss of the dove's "dearest love." It is this elegy that begins the work of mourning for Timias, drawing him back to himself ("him seemed oft he heard his owne right name") and into the social world: "[A]t the last of all his woe and wrong / Companion she became, and so continued long" (4.8.5). Unlike the *flebil canto*, which draws the listener more deeply inward, compounding the melancholic power of the phantasm, this song is genuinely elegiac. The dove's sadness does not produce a self-indulgent *atra voluptas*, but rather an empathetic sadness: "with her mournfull muse / Him to recomfort in his greatest care" (4.8.5). His response is thus not to sink back into wordless sighs and laments, but gradually to move into the symbolic realm of discourse. In his voiceless fixation on one name, "Belphoebe," Timias had become less than human, unable to converse with Arthur or to speak his own grief. It is when Timias finally finds his voice—led to his interlocutor by the dove—that his long anguish draws to an end: "[E]ftsoones he brake / His sodaine silence, which he long had pent, / And sighing inly deepe, her thus bespake" (4.8.16). The lover's newfound voice represents the beginning of liberation from the spiritual fixity of the melancholic condition. In accordance with Spenser's rehabilitation—as opposed to extirpation—of romance, then, he interestingly incorporates the medical cure for love-melancholy that in both Ariosto's and Tasso's poems becomes a site of peculiar danger to the lover. This *locus amoenus* thus returns the power of song (and particularly birdsong) to a context that recalls Valescus da Taranta's curative "iardinos floridos ubi cantant aves et resonant philomenae."[82]

Timias's "sad melancholy" fills out the relationship between eros and despair first indicated by the presence of Sir Terwin in Despair's cave and the eroticization of Red Crosse's *acedia*. His proximity to Arthur develops what we might understand as the melancholic frame (also inhabited by Red Crosse) that sharpens the structure of Arthur's alternative quest. The "cure" of Timias's love-melancholy also supports the notion that Spenser's revision of romance entails the introduction of elegy into a fundamentally melancholic narrative. The elegization of Arthur's quest is, as I have argued, tied to the figural structure of his quest; loss is mitigated by the promise that love, and truth, will appear "in time's just terme." It is significant, then, that when Arthur leaves Timias without recognizing him, he leaves him "in languor to remaine, / *Till time for him* should remedy provide" (4.7.47, italics mine).

Revelation: Figural Consolation and the Ends of Romance

Spenser's deployment of a figural structure to underpin his romance gives his own poem a sacred structure.[83] Like the *figurae* of the Old Testament, which are certainly not merely allegorical, Spenser's figures command a fuller significance (the biblical *sensus plenior*) by virtue of their imbrication in the structure of salvation history: the "eternal thing is already figured in them [i.e., the *figurae*]."[84] Spenser's use of a figural narrative to elegize the melancholic structure of romance extends to his deployment of literary intertexts, which become *figurae*: older, less complete forms of romance that will be renewed and fulfilled in his own poem. I will close this chapter with a brief consideration of the relationship between Spenser's poem and two texts that leave their stamp on Arthur's quest: Chaucer's *Tale of Sir Thopas* and Ariosto's *Orlando Furioso*. In each case these texts are invoked—as figures—to be transformed within this newly elegiac structure, just as the *flebil canto* is invoked only to be transformed into the curative "lamentable lay."

When Arthur responds to Una's questions by telling the story of his dream, he retells the dream of Sir Thopas, who, like Arthur himself, dreams of a faerie queene with whom he instantly becomes enamored:

> O seinte Marie, benedicite!
> What eyeleth this love at me
> To bynde so soore?
> Me dremed al this nyght, pardee,
> An elf-queene shal my lemman be
> And slepe under my goore.
> An elf-queene wol I love, ywis,
> For in this world no womman is
> Worthy to be my make
> In towne:
> Alle othere wommen I forsake,
> And to an elf-queene I me take
> By dale and eek by downe!
>
> (1975–86)

Since the *Tale of Sir Thopas* is told by "Chaucer" himself, this allusion stages a direct engagement with Chaucer's own persona—however parodic and foolish he may be—rather than with one of the pilgrims. Arthur re-dreams, unwittingly of course, the dream of his literary predecessor, his "me seemed" echoing Sir Thopas's "me dremed," so that his dream seems to stage less an incursion of the supernatural into the poem than a deliberate encounter with the "well of English undefyled," "Dan Geffrey" himself. This allusion, though often noted, has not been sufficiently explained. Why should Spenser, at what must be regarded as a crucial moment in his poem, allow his readers to hear the ghostly laughter of Chaucer's pilgrims?

Bishop Hurd, in his remarkable *Letters on Chivalry and Romance*, sees exactly the difficulty caused by Chaucer's parody:

> His rime of Sir Topaz, in the Canterbury tales, is a manifest banter on these books [that is, on romance], and may be considered as a sort of prelude to the adventures of Don Quixot. I call it a manifest banter: for we are to observe that this was Chaucer's own tale, and that, when in the progress of it the good sense of the Host is made to break in upon him, and interrupt him, Chaucer approves his disgust and, changing his note, tells the simple

instructive tale of Meliboeus, *a moral tale virtuous*, as he chuses to characterize it; to shew, what sort of fictions *were most expressive of real life*, and most
proper to be put into the hands of the people.[85]

The *Tale of Sir Thopas*, by exaggerating an essential feature of romance,
spells its end as a serious literary form, and the path between Sir Thopas
and Don Quixote is not long. But between Chaucer and Cervantes, Spenser must find his way, and for Bishop Hurd this "manifest banter" at the
expense of romance represents Spenser's main poetic challenge.

> This ridicule, we may suppose, hastened the fall both of Chivalry and ro-
> mance. At least from that time the spirit of both declined very fast, and at
> length fell into such discredit, that when now Spenser arose, and with a
> genius singularly fitted to immortalize the land of faery, he met with every
> difficulty and disadvantage to obstruct his design.[86]

The allusion to Chaucer's parodic tale in *The Faerie Queene* thus concerns not only the status of romance but also the relationship between
Spenser and his great English precursor. An analogous moment in the
text is the "completion" of *The Squire's Tale*; Spenser precedes this tricky
bit of "overgoing" with a reverent invocation to Chaucer as the source of
his inspiration: "[T]hrough infusion sweete / Of thine owne spirit, which
doth in me survive, / I follow here the footing of thy feete, / That with thy
meaning so I may the rather meete" (4.2.34). Unlike this allusion to *The
Squire's Tale*, the allusion to *Thopas*, though clear, is unadvertised: Spenser
chooses not to mention it in the *Letter to Raleigh*, though he does refer to
a good number of his sources, and the effect of Arthur's first-person account of the dream, his unknowing "me seemed," is to lend the allusion
an unwitting air. This indicates, I think, that the allusion to *Thopas* will
constitute no straightforward completion of a text in the style of a revered
precursor, but a radical revision of that text.

In fact, Spenser's allusion to Chaucer's tale draws deliberate attention
to the very working of romance. Sir Thopas's tale is easily recognizable as
a parody of the metrical romances popular at the time and includes many
literary devices characteristic of such texts. But the element that Chaucer
singles out for ridicule as, presumably, both constitutive of romance as a
genre and the basis of its hopeless failure, is its *pointlessness*.[87] The host's
blunt interruption of the tale has a particular aesthetic agenda:

"By God," quod he, "for pleynly, at o word,
Thy drasty rymyng is nat worth a toord!
Thou doost noght elles but despendest tyme.
Sire at o word, thou shalt no lenger ryme."

(929 ff., italics mine)

The accusation that "thou doost noght elles but despendest tyme" is not an idle one, and indeed it coincides with many contemporary accounts of romance as an "endlesse worke." This then, seems to be the crux of Spenser's complex allusion. The dialogue established by the allusion between Chaucer's parody and Spenser's grand romance has at its center nothing less than the engine of romance itself: *time.*

The host's complaint about "Chaucer's" romance is that it is without a discernible point: "[T]hou doost noght elles but despendest tyme." It is not difficult to see that the structure of Arthur's dream of the faerie queene counters this directly by placing the *veritas filia temporis* motto at its center. The poem is not a romance without end or goal, but is underpinned by a typological structure that guarantees its participation in the "general end" referred to in the *Letter.* The dream is a *figura,* bringing forth in the text a version of an end and prefiguring a greater one. We can also see that the typological framework serves the interest of a poet's struggle against literary belatedness. In the direct confrontation with Chaucer's spirit in book 4, Spenser represents himself as stepping into the poetic footing of a poet whose traces "wicked Time" threatens to erase:

But wicked Time that all good thoughts doth waste,
And workes of noblest wits to nought out weare,
That famous moniment hath quite defaste . . .

. . . .

Then, pardon, O most sacred happie spirit,
That I thy labours lost may thus revive,
And steale from thee the meede of thy due merit,
That none durst ever whilest thou wast alive,
And being dead in vaine yet many strive:
Ne dare I like, but through infusion sweete
Of thine owne spirit, which doth in me survive,
I follow here the footing of thy feete,
That with thy meaning so I may the rather meete.

(4.2.33–34)

This passage represents an emulative tradition of allusion, envisaging a seamless continuity within literary history in which the guiding spirit of the literary forefather is sweetly present in the work of the successor. But even here references to stealing the "meede" of that precursor's due merit hint at a struggle for poetic supremacy, and at another, more subversive use of allusion. The metapoetic implication of the use of *veritas filia temporis* motto within the allusive context of Arthur's dream is that Spenser's version of the tale is truer and more complete than the earlier one. The reading of literary texts then becomes an exercise in reading figurally: we are asked to see Spenser's text as fulfilling and annulling the work of his precursor rather than merely following the footing of his feet. Like a literary New Testament, Spenser's poem claims to complete and fulfill the earlier text whose figures it now triumphantly reads as merely anticipating its own.[88]

The biblical grounding of Arthur's dream is indicated not only by its structural analogy with the *figurae* of the New Testament but also by its echoes of one of Spenser's earlier "vision" poems whose relation to the book of Revelation is overt. It is precisely the organization of Arthur's dream as a revelatory figura that differentiates it not only from the comic vision of Sir Thopas, but also from the much darker vision of Orlando, whose madness stems directly from his dream of Angelica. If that dream works closely with (and indeed quotes from) a Petrarchan sonnet, Arthur's dream is keyed to a sonnet whose Petrarchan tone belies its biblical content. The sonnet in question is poem 4 of the *Complaints*, published with *The Ruines of Time* in 1591, just a year, that is, after the publication of the first edition of the first three books of *The Faerie Queene*. The vision described in this poem provides a key to our reading of the relationship between Orlando's and Arthur's dreams:

> Looking aside I saw a stately Bed,
> Adorned all with costly cloth of gold,
> That might for anie Princes couche be red,
> And deckt with daintie flowres, as if it shold
> Be for some bride, her joyous night to hold:
> Therein a goodly Virgine sleeping lay;
> *A fairer wight saw never summers day.*
> I heard a voyce that called farre away

And her awaking bad her quickly dight,
For lo her bridegrome was in readie ray
To come to her, and seeke her loves delight:
With that she started up with cherefull sight,
When suddeinly both bed and all was gone,
And I in languor left there all alone.

(*Complaints* 4, italics mine)

This sonnet provides a sacred context for Arthur's dream of the faerie queene: the line "A fairer wight saw never summers day" closely echoes "So faire a creature yet saw never sunny day," and the "royall Mayd" of the epic poem clearly figures the "goodly Virgine" of this sonnet. The disappearance of the faerie queene when Arthur wakes is thus rewritten as the departure of the Virgin—the church—to her sacred marriage with the Lamb. This, then, provides a clearer fulfillment of the *figura* of Arthur's dream, inscribing the figural truth of that poem within the sacred book of Revelation. The situation of the speaker ("I in languor left there all alone") is ambiguous: the "langour" recalls the plight of Timias when Arthur leaves him "in languor to remaine, / *Till time for him* should remedy provide" (4.7.47, italics mine). But the context of Revelation suggests that this vision shortly precedes the coming of "a new heaven and a new earth" (Rev. 21:1): the promise accompanying this vision is precisely that sadness and mourning will be at an end:

> I heard a great voice from the throne saying, "Behold, the dwelling of God is with men. He will dwell with them, and they shall be his people, and God himself will be with them; *he will wipe away every tear from their eyes, and death shall be no more, neither shall there be mourning* nor crying nor pain any more, for the former things have passed away." (Rev. 21:2—4 RSV, italics mine).

The "languor" of the speaker suggests the possibility of a slide into melancholy or despair; but the allusive context confirms the *elegiac* role of the *figurae* themselves. Though they pass away, like the faerie queene and the "Virgine," they promise the perfect consolation recorded here: "[N]either shall there be mourning, nor crying nor pain any more."

Spenser's use of what we might call figural consolation as the context for the romance vision contrasts directly with Ariosto's deployment of Orlando's dream. The points of contact between these two dreams are striking and sharpen the differences between them. Most obviously, both Orlando and Arthur embark on their quests as a direct result of a dream; but while Orlando's *amorosa inchiesta* (*OF* 9.7) amounts to a parodic revision of Aeneas's heroic quest (also undertaken as the result of a dream vision), Arthur's quest is both amorous *and* heroic. Arthur's quest, as we have seen, raises the possibility that "dreames may delude," only to explore the deeper truth of a cataleptic emotional knowledge. But Orlando undertakes his quest with the reader's knowledge of its phantasmic falsehood: "Senza pensar che sian l'imagine false / quando per tema o per disio si sogna" (Without considering that images may be false when one dreams in fear and in desire, *OF* 8.84). Both Orlando and Arthur wake to find that their beloved has vanished, and both weep:

> A questo orribil grido risvegliossi,
> e tutto pien di lacrime trovossi.

> [At this horrible cry he awoke, and found himself all wet with tears.]
>
> (*OF* 8.83)

> When I awoke, and found her place devoyd,
> And nought but pressed gras, where she had lyen,
> I sorrowed all so much, as earst I joyd,
> And washed all her place with watry eyen.
>
> (*Faerie Queene* 1.9.15)

But while Orlando's love is explicitly said to be "un vano amor" that distances him from God: "or per un vano amor, poco del zio, / e di sé poco, e men cura di Dio" (now, because of a vain love, he cares little for his uncle and little for himself and less for God, *OF* 9.1), Arthur's quest, as we have seen, is tied to the structure of sacred history and unfolds accordingly. Thus it is appropriate that the terrible cry that awakens Orlando (*questo orribil grido*) seems to find its sacred counterpart in the holy voice of Spenser's sonnet. In the former case the voice speaks directly from Petrarch's *Canzoniere* 250, while the latter echoes the "great voice from the throne" (Rev. 21), the voice of Christ himself:

> Ecco ch'altronde ode da un'altra voce:
> —Non sperar più gioirne in terra mai.—

[Behold from elsewhere he hears another voice: "Do not hope to enjoy them any more on this earth."]

(OF 8.83)

> I heard a voyce that called farre away
> And her awaking bad her quickly dight,
> For lo her Bridegrome was in readie ray
> To come to her, and seeke her loves delight.

(Complaints 4)

Whereas Orlando plunges into an inferno-like labyrinth without center or circumference, Arthur embarks on a quest whose linear unfolding is guaranteed by its figural structure. The melancholic madness that overcomes Orlando is thus circumvented by the mournful process of figural consolation; it is mournful both because it acknowledges the "passing away" of all things and because it promotes the perfect consolation that only a removal to the heavenly city can provide. In Spenser's revision of romance, it is precisely this "Godly sorrow" that underpins his protagonists' "travell" through a world that "changeth ever too and fro" (*Daphnaïda* 429). But the weight of "sad melancholy" (*Faerie Queene*, 4.7.38) on the questing mourners nonetheless suggests that Spenser's sympathies, in some measure, lie with the anguished Alcyon.

CHAPTER 6

The "Love-sicke Hart"
Female Love-Melancholy and the Romance Quest

When Britomart and Glauce first enter Merlin's cave they attempt, for reasons that the text does not quite make clear, to conceal both Britomart's identity and their knowledge of the real cause of what Glauce refers to as her charge's "deepe engraffed ill" (3.3.18). Glauce invokes the inward space of Britomart's body as the invisible site of a mysterious suffering, cloaking the real cause with obfuscating rhetoric:

> But this *sad evill*, which doth her infest,
> Doth *course of naturall cause* farre exceed,
> And *housed is within her hollow brest*,
> That either seemes some *cursed witches deed*,
> Or *evill spright, that in her doth such torment breed.*
>
> (*Faerie Queene* 3.3.18, italics mine)

Merlin is not deceived; he has no difficulty either in reading through Britomart's disguise or in discerning the nature of her complaint: "Glauce, what needs this colourable word, / To cloke the cause, that hath it selfe bewrayd?" (3.3.19). Britomart's body is immediately legible to Merlin, under whose gaze her illness "bewray[s]" itself. And indeed Glauce herself has diagnosed Britomart's mysterious sickness as love in the previous canto, "Aye me, how much I feare, least love it bee" (3.2.33), and has tried unsuccessfully to extirpate it. The poet provides a yet more precise reference to the source of Britomart's suffering as her "*love-sicke hart*" (3.2.48), for as the detailed descriptions of her physical and mental symptoms clearly demonstrate, Britomart is suffering from the female form of lovesickness or love-melancholy.[1] Glauce's superstitious fear and horror of the tenacious power of this condition reflect attitudes in contemporary discussions of female sexuality during this period, which sometimes record instances of the sexual contamination of young girls by witches or the devil.[2]

This chapter begins with a close look at Spenser's descriptions of Britomart's psychosomatic suffering, juxtaposing them with contemporary medical accounts of female love-melancholy (sometimes suggestively called "uterine fury") and its treatment, to clarify the cultural and poetic significance of Britomart's "love-sick hart." For if, as Michael Schoenfeldt has convincingly argued, "bodily condition, subjective state, and psychological character are in this earlier regime fully imbricated," Britomart's "subjective state" is, to a greater degree even than that of her lovesick male counterparts, deeply "engraffed" in her body.[3] My investigation explores the significance of Spenser's use of the recognizable disease of love-melancholy as the catalyst of Britomart's quest. To this end I will focus on two episodes that demonstrate most fully the new orientation of Spenser's romance: Britomart's encounter with Merlin, whose prophetic discourse marks the transformation of the "hysterical" element of her condition into an elegiac acknowledgment of her procreative destiny; and her victory over the dark eros of Busirane that this transformation makes possible. In exploring these questions, I argue that Britomart's quest necessitates a reevaluation of female love-melancholy that implicitly revises misogynist contemporary accounts of the female body as a dangerous and even maddening influence on the mind. At the same time, the organization of the quest around the vicissitudes of Britomart's procreative destiny contributes to the revision of the romance form itself. Like Arthur's quest, Britomart's quest deploys a typological structure that counters the open-ended labyrinthine structure of Ariostan romance. But whereas the unfolding of Arthur's quest relies on the tropes of childbirth and pregnancy, Britomart's quest depends on her body's literal embodiment of the *iust terme* of providential time.

Women in Love

A brief consideration of early modern conceptions of female love-melancholy will help us to place Britomart's condition in its proper context. Female love-melancholy gradually came to be regarded as including a range of specifically "female" sexual disorders, prominent among them "uterine fury," or hysteria.[4] The focus in these medical texts on the womb as the mysterious, hidden source of both power and sickness is reflected in Spenser's use of uterine symbolism at key moments of Britomart's story.[5] The reference in the quoted stanza to Britomart's "hollow brest" recalls Merlin's mirror, "round and hollow-shaped" (3.2.19), in which Britomart first views Arthegall, and even the withdrawn space of her father's closet where the mirror is kept apart from all other eyes. Both mirror and closet seem to symbolize a specifically female space of interiority associated with the womb. Susanne Wofford points out that the word "closet" is "one of the early examples in English of a term for an inner moral and emotional self, located by analogy inside the body," noting its use elsewhere in the poem to denote the specifically feminine inner space of the womb ("The loving mother, that nine monethes did beare, / In the deare closet of her painfull side, / Her tender babe" (3.2.11).[6] The potentially problematic assimilation of female psychology and female physiology in this figure is abundantly clear. But as we will see, the complex crossing of bodily and psychic forces in the "closet" of Britomart's interior self will in fact suggest the power of female physiology to promote a noble quest that is fully coincident with "eternall providence" (3.3.24).

The application of the disease of erotic melancholy to women has something of a chequered history in early medical literature. As Mary Wack has observed, despite the tendency in the history of medicine to assume that love-melancholy is a male disease, there is no shortage of literary examples of women suffering from the disease.[7] Sappho's famous description of erotic love establishes her as the paradigmatic female sufferer of the disorder that ancient writers simply called love-madness.[8] Her description of the state of intense love is strikingly physical and anticipates much later psychosomatic treatments of the disease in both literary and medical texts:

> [M]y tongue is broken and thin fire
> runs like a thief through my body.
> My eyes are dead to light, my ears
> pound, and sweat pours down over me.
> I shudder, I am paler than grass.[9]

It is precisely Sappho's evocation of the fusion of mental and physical in this experience of erotic mania that Longinus praises: "Don't you wonder at how, under the same emotional experience, she seeks out soul and body, hearing and tongue, sight and color, all departing as if they were someone else's?"[10]

Wack traces the medical tradition's interest in the female experience of lovesickness to the influence of Peter of Spain (*Quaestiones*, ca. 1246–72), who attempted to draw fine distinctions between male and female sexual pleasure, on the basis that love-sickness was directly tied to the intensity of sexual pleasure.[11] As Wack notes, Peter of Spain's interest in women's experience of love was in fact an early hint of an increasing association between women and love-melancholy. By the time Jacques Ferrand writes his seminal work on the disease, women are understood to be the primary victims of what had hitherto been a largely male disorder:

> According to Strabo and Suidas, Sappho the poetess, forlorn for her love of Phaon hurled herself from the Leucadian rock into the sea, *for women are more frequently and more grievously troubled by these ills than are men*. Such love gives rise to a pale and wan complexion, joined by a slow fever that modern practitioners call amorous fever, to palpitations of the heart, swelling of the face, depraved appetite, a sense of grief, sighing, causeless tears, insatiable hunger, raging thirst, fainting, oppressions, suffocations, insomnia, headaches, melancholy, epilepsy, madness, uterine fury, satyriasis, and other pernicious symptoms that are, for the most part, without mitigation or cure other than through the [established medical] remedies for love and erotic melancholy, based on the teachings of Hippocrates toward the end of his book on the diseases of young women and in his book on generation.[12]

Ferrand reveals the most significant medical source of the gendering of love-melancholy in his reference to Hippocrates. Hippocratic writing on the centrality of the womb (in particular unruly movement of the womb) in the etiology of female disease of *all* kinds was the basis of the (Galenized) sixteenth-century gynecology on which writers like Ferrand drew in their study of love-melancholy.[13] It also seems likely that the existing body of theory on female hysteria provided a natural resource for writers, such as Peter of Spain, whose focus on the sexual organs as the origin of the disease of love-melancholy gradually transformed it into a "lower" illness associated with women. As Wack argues, this "decline in the localization of *amor hereos* may help to account for its transformation from a heroic malady to a 'hysteric affliction.'"[14]

In any case, we can see in this shift toward a sexual etiology of love-melancholy the hazy outline of later distinctions between a predominantly masculine, intellectual (and positively valorized) melancholia, and a predominantly feminine, bodily (and negatively valorized) hysteria. The crucial point that emerges from Ferrand's text as from other contemporary accounts of "uterine furor" is that the association between women and love-melancholy led to a much greater emphasis on the *bodily* conditions for the disease and hence a (gendered) polarization of its psychological and physical manifestations. For this reason, the disease is increasingly likely to be seen as an almost inevitable vicissitude of female physiology rather than as a potentially ennobling mental preoccupation. If the earliest conceptions of *amor hereos* as a "heroic" disease emphasized the dual nature of an illness that manifested itself both as a Neoplatonic striving for the beautiful and as a degrading sexual obsession, this "feminization" of the disease seems to begin the process of splitting apart these two poles.[15]

If, as the dominant Hippocratic gynecological theories would seem to imply, the female subject is understood as *intrinsically* susceptible to the derangements of love-melancholy, we can begin to see how the disease might, in this period, seem to threaten the very notion of a stable self. For as Schoenfeldt has noted, "it is the disordered, undisciplined self, subject to a variety of internal and external forces, that is the site of subjection, and the subject of horror."[16] The litany of disorders attributed by Ferrand to the lovesick woman (*"grief, sighing, causeless tears, insatiable hunger, raging thirst, fainting, oppressions, suffocations, insomnia, headaches, melancholy, epilepsy, madness, uterine fury, satyriasis, and other pernicious symptoms"*) provides a profile of precisely the kind of disordered self that might well be considered the "subject of horror" for early modern commentators.[17] In light of this consideration of the cultural context of female love-melancholy, let us now consider how Spenser deals with both the somatic and the psychic effects of Britomart's "love-sicke hart."

Love-Melancholy in the Body: Britomart's "Bleeding Bowels"

In his essay on the somatogenesis of love in early modern medicine, Donald Beecher draws attention to the intricate crossing of physical and psychic causes that we have already noted in early modern medical writing on love-melancholy.[18] A Galenic emphasis on the role of the humors in the origin of the disease merges seamlessly with a basically Aristotelian focus on the role of phantasms in creating the psychological conditions for melancholic disorders. This crossing is evident in Spenser's depiction of Britomart's love-melancholy, which manifests itself both in her "fantasticke sight / Of dreadfull things" (3.2.29) and in her graphically described bodily distress, located in her "bleeding bowels" (3.2.39). Though controversy about the original site of love-melancholy in men is evident in the medical texts (head, liver, testicles, and so on), most writers favor the "psychological" explanation, though the psyche in question is certainly conditioned by the humoral state of the body. Medical discussion of female melancholy moves in the opposite direction, probably influenced, as I have suggested, by existing theories about the subjection of women's health (mental and physical) to uterine disorder. The fact that, as Beecher notes, female love-melancholy was not clearly distinguished from a variety of "hysterical" diseases conduces to a tendency to focus on the role of the sexual organs in the disruption of mental stability. Unsurprisingly, women emerge from these texts as more fully conditioned by their sexuality than men.

A treatise on uterine furor (or what the author calls "suffocation of the mother") provides a useful context in which to consider the implications of Britomart's sufferings. This treatise, written by Edward Jorden in 1603, actually grows out of a case of "suffocation" suffered by a young girl, Mary Glover. Jorden was called to testify in a case brought against an older woman, Elizabeth Jackson, who was thought to have bewitched the girl. (Glauce's defensiveness about Britomart's possession by an "evil spright" should perhaps be understood in light of this tendency to assign responsibility for the disease to women labeled as "witches.") Jorden's position, influenced by the writings of Gabriel Harvey on the subject, is that these symptoms are all fully explicable in terms of the disruptiveness of the womb to physical and mental health.

> The passive condition of womankind is subject unto more diseases and of other sortes and natures then men are: and especially in regarde of that part from whence this disease which we speake of doth arise [i.e., the womb]. For whatsoever straunge accident may appeare in any of the principall funtions of mans bodie, either animall, vitall, or naturall, the same is to bee

sene in this disease, by reason of the communitie and consent which this part hath with the braine, heart, and liver, the principall seates of these three functions. And *hereupon the symptoms of this disease are sayd to be monstrous and terrible to beholde,* and of such a varieitie as they can hardly be comprehended within any method or boundes. Insomuch as they which are ignorant of the strange effects which naturall causes may produce, and of the manifold examples which our profession of phisicke doth minister in this kind, have sought above the Moone for supernaturall causes: *ascribing these accidents either to diabolicall possession, to witchcraft, to the immediate finger of the Almightie.*[19]

There is much here that is significant for understanding Spenser's presentation of Britomart's predicament. Most importantly, Jorden's Galenic/ Hippocratic theory that the "communitie and consent" between the womb and the other major organs of the body is the organizing feature of female physiology speaks to Spenser's organization of Britomart's vision in relation to various hollow spaces of intrauterine enclosure. In particular, the "communitie" that Jorden asserts exists between the womb and the three main seats of love-melancholy (liver, heart, and brain) provides a contemporary medical context for understanding the relationship between Britomart's "bleeding bowels," her "love-sicke hart," and her "fantasticke sight." The centrality of the womb in this system ensures a full-scale overthrow of physical and mental health, should the healthy functioning of the womb cease. It is perhaps not surprising, then, that Jorden regards the prospect of such an overthrow with scarcely concealed horror: "[A]nd hereupon the symptoms of this disease are sayd to be monstrous and terrible to beholde, and of such varietie as they can hardly be comprehended within any method or boundes."

Glauce also invokes the language of monstrosity when she accuses Britomart of making a "monster of [her] mind" (3.2.40), and indeed the latter's description of her physical suffering does indicate a radical poisoning of the mind through the body, and vice versa:

> Nor man it is, nor other living wight;
> For then some hope I might unto me draw,
> But th'only shade and semblant of a knight,
> Whose shape or person yet I never saw,
> Hath me subiected to loves cruell law:

The same one day, as me misfortune led,
I in my fathers wondrous mirrhour saw,
And pleased with that seeming goodly-hed,
Unwares the hidden hooke with baite I swallowed.

Sithens it hath infixed faster hold
Within my bleeding bowels, and so sore
Now rankleth in this same fraile fleshly mould,
That all mine entrailes flow with poysnous gore,
And th'ulcer groweth daily more and more;
Ne can my running sore find remedie,
Other then my hard fortune to deplore,
And languish as the leafe falne from the tree,
Till death make one end of my dayes and miserie.

(3.2.39)

One critic has plausibly suggested that this description of Britomart's "bleeding bowels" refers to the sudden and perhaps traumatic (from Britomart's point of view) onset of menstruation.[20] But Spenser's language of disease (her entrails "flow with poysnous gore," her body is poisoned by "an ulcer" and "running sore") allows us to be more specific. The taxonomical proximity of love-melancholy and hysteria ensures that the former disease, like the latter, comes to be associated in female sufferers with a variety of uterine disorders. If Britomart's language suggests a menstrual disorder symptomatic of love-melancholy, it is not surprising that she regards her blood with horror, as a source of pollution. For as Peggy McCracken remarks, although menstrual blood is the sign of fertility, it is also "in many medieval discourses . . . a polluting blood, a feature of the imperfect female body whose imperfections mirror the perfections of the male body."[21] It is also interestingly connected to psychological disorders in a further demonstration of the seemingly unavoidable imbrication of female sexuality and female mentality. Jacquart and Thomasset note that the retention of menstrual blood was thought to be particularly dangerous because it "contained a mixture of the four humours; when melancholy was overabundant in it, its spreading to the brain could lead to serious disorders of the reason."[22]

The emphasis on the maintenance of a balance in the body between excess and depletion of certain key substances is central to Jorden's account of uterine furor. In this respect the treatise illustrates clearly Schoenfeldt's contention that "the body is in this regime a dynamic and porous edifice continually producing superfluous excrements which must be removed."[23] However, it also makes clear that the discourse of love-melancholy renders the female body especially volatile, subject as it is to an unruly organ whose products are ambiguously both nourishing and potentially toxic. The ambivalence with which these products are treated is particularly clear in Jorden's analysis of the role of blood in the female system:

> *Blood is that humor wherwith we are nourished*: without which the infant in the mothers wombe could neither grow and increase in bignesse, nor yet live: and therefore it was necessarie that those that were fit for generation, should be supplied with sufficient store of this humour. . . . *But this provision of nature is oftentimes defective: as when it is cut off by violent causes, and the part left destitute of this familiar humor.* . . . As the want and scarsitie of bloud may procure grief, *so the abundance and excesse thereof doth more commonly cause it, where the patients do want those monethly evacuations which should discharge their bodies of this superfluitie.* . . . *But if this blood wanting his proper use doe degenerate into the nature of an excrement, then it offendeth in qualitie as well as in excesse*, and being detayned in the bodie, causeth divers kinds of symptoms, according to the qualitie and degree of the distemperature thereof.[24]

The excess of blood in Britomart's "bleeding bowels" suggests perhaps the "want of due and monethly evacuation" that Jorden deems essential for the well-being of the female body.[25] Most medical authors agree that passionate love arises from a copious—but presumably not dangerously imbalanced—supply of blood.[26] In this case, the dependency of the female metabolism on a particularly shaky balance between "scarsitie of bloud" and its "abundance and excesse" makes women's vulnerability to the slide from nonpathological love into erotic melancholy seem incontrovertible. Ferrand makes an explicit connection between the role of the heart in the genesis of love-melancholy and the obstruction of the blood in the womb. In his account the womb is responsible for the perturbation of the very center of the body's pneumatic functioning:[27]

> Agreeing with Aristotle, we may believe the heart to be the true seat of passionate love. The authority of Hippocrates further confirms the point where he says in his On the Diseases of Young Women that women are troubled

by fear, sorrow, anxiety, and distraction when the superfluous blood that each month should be excreted through the canals destined by nature for that purpose is retained in the body because these canals become obstructed. *Such blood overflows the womb and rises to the heart where it causes fear, sorrow, and madness, symptoms that accompany melancholy as the shadow does the body.*[28]

Britomart's own language suggests her awareness of an imbalance of blood in her body: "For no usual fire, no usuall rage / It is, O Nurse, which on my life doth feed, / And *suckes the bloud, which from my hart doth bleed*" (3.2.37, italics mine). Overall, then, we understand that female blood symbolizes precisely the delicate balance between excess and depletion so central to early modern notions of health. Thus although Elizabeth Bellamy is right to note the *symbolic* importance of female wounds in book 3, the full significance of the poem's emphasis on female blood only emerges against the background of this medical view of the volatility of the female body and (thus) the lability of female psychological states.[29]

The second cause of suffocation mentioned in Jorden's treatise is the accumulation of seed. For like blood, "nature," or sperm, is perfect when properly balanced, but deadly when retained in the body.[30] This symptom is related to the balance of blood in the body, since blood was thought to be "the material cause of seed."[31] The want of what Schoenfeldt quite aptly calls (in relation to digestion) bodily "solubility" in respect of "nature" threatens once again the health of the womb, producing corrupt, toxic matter:[32]

> [T]he other substance which most commonly is found culpable of this disease, is nature or sperma: which besides the suspition of superfluitie in some persons, may also receive divers sortes of alteration, and likewise corruption, able to work most strange and grievous accidents in our bodies. For as it is a substance of greatest perfection and puritie so long as it retayneth his native integrity, *so being depraved or corrupted, it passeth all the humours of our bodie, in venom and malignitie . . . a substance so pure and full of spirits as this is, must needes prove most malitious unto the bodie when it is corrupted.*[33]

Because seed is a highly pneumatic substance ("so full of spirits"), it places the organism under intense pressure when it is retained.[34] Aristotle's *Problemata* make an important connection between melancholia and a desire for intercourse, a connection that rests in part on the pneumatic quality of melancholia and semen: "Why are the melancholic inclined to sexual intercourse? It is because they are full of breath and semen is an emission of breath. Those therefore who have a quantity of semen which is full of breath must often desire to be purged of it; for by this means they are relieved."[35] Britomart's furious sighs suggest that she is also dangerously "full of breath": "Sorrow is heaped in thy hollow chest, / Whence forth it breakes in sighes and anguish rife, / As smoke and sulphure mingled with confused strife" (3.2.32).

The corruption of female seed is crucially related in the medical texts to *chastity*. As Jacquart and Thomasset note, the disease of suffocation was associated primarily with widows and virgins. Just as the obstruction of the proper "canals" intended for the removal of superfluous blood leads to the noxious corruption of the blood, so a failure to release seed through intercourse leads, on this view, to the transformation of this pure, pneumatic substance into a kind of poison:

> The cause of this passion is the abundance of sperm or its corruption. It occurs when women are deprived of union with a man: the sperm increases, becomes corrupt and begins to resemble a poison. Widows suffer particularly from it, especially if they have had several children. Likewise, young girls suffer from it when they reach the age [of puberty] without knowing any man, for the sperm accumulates to be expelled, just as in men, as the action of nature requires.[36]

The connection between chastity and suffocation is, of course, particularly pertinent to our reading of Britomart's suffering, since she is the allegorical representative of Chastity. Her description of her sufferings also sounds remarkably similar to the description of "poison" in these medical texts: "[A]ll mine entrailes flow with poysnous gore, / And th'ulcer groweth daily more and more; / Ne can my running sore find remedie" (3.2.39). Britomart is cast here as one of the young girls mentioned by Constantine who "reach the age of puberty without knowing any man."[37]

Not only does the retention of seed threaten the body with internal corruption, however; it also threatens a monstrous transformation of woman into man. Thanks primarily to the Aristotelian notion of woman as an "imperfect" man, women's sexual physiology was considered to be fundamentally labile, vulnerable to the excess heat produced by love-melancholy. Once again Hippocrates is Ferrand's source:

Hippocrates seems to attribute to passionate love the power to transform women into men when he explains how in the city of Abdera, Phaetusa, who loved Pytheus her husband dearly, but who was not able to enjoy him due to his long absence, therewith became a man with body hair, a masculine voice, and a beard.[38]

The kind of metamorphosis that attends the love-madness of Ovidian heroines (Glauce refers to Byblis, Myrrha, and Pasiphae) finds its medical analogue in the alleged transformation of woman into man.[39] When Britomart first looks into Merlin's mirror, she intends to look only at herself: "Her selfe a while therein she vewd in vaine" (3.2.22); eventually, however, she sees the image of a male knight: "Eftsoones there was presented to her eye / A comely knight, all arm'd in complete wize, / Through whose bright ventayle lifted up on hye / His manly face, that did his foes agrize" (3.2.24). Britomart's figurative androgyny is, of course, already a part of her story: disguised as a male knight, she defeats Guyon and (unwittingly) seduces Malecasta. Bellamy reads Britomart's absorption in the figure of Arthegall in terms of secondary narcissism: "Arthegall is, as the (phallic) ego ideal, what the androgynous and combative Britomart 'would like to be.'"[40] But the medical texts seem to authorize a more radical reading of the episode: Britomart's nascent "furor" threatens quite literally to "make a monster" of both mind and body, transforming her into the male knight she sees as a reflection of herself.

Love-Melancholy in the Mind: "Fantasticke Sight of Dreadfull Things"

The difficulty of distinguishing between mental and physical causes of love-melancholy is as apparent in Spenser's text as in the medical literature. For even before we reach Britomart's own physical descriptions of her "bleeding bowels," Spenser physicalizes her emotional/imaginative experience of her vision. Though it is Britomart's sight of Arthegall that initiates her love-melancholy ("By strange occasion she did him behold, / And much more strangely gan to love his sight," 3.2.18), sight here, as in Valleriola's and Ficino's texts, has profoundly material effects on the body. We might recall that Ficino's theory of fascination, in which the mind looks (*tamquam in speculo*) upon the image conveyed through the eye to the phantasmic spirits, depends upon the notion of a quite literal optical infection:

> [T]he ray extends as far as that person opposite, and that along with the ray he emanates a vapour of corrupt blood, by the contagion of which the eye of the observer is infected. Aristotle writes that women, when the menstrual blood flows down, often soil a mirror with bloody drops by their own gaze. (*De amore* 7.4)

The reference here to Aristotle's fable about the effect of menstruation on the woman's gaze may inflect Spenser's treatment of Britomart's "sight." After all, the "round and hollow shaped" mirror (3.2.19) is itself an image of her own "hollow" body (3.2.32), and the relationship between her "bleeding bowels" and the power of this vision suggests perhaps that *bodily* forces shape the vision that she sees. It is, perhaps, the infecting power of her blood that eroticizes the image in the first place. The circular structure of the relationship between mind and body ensures that the mental image thus constructed will, in its turn, exacerbate the bodily state that first conditioned it.

The potentially noxious effect of uterine forces on the imagination (or fantasy) is a feature of the medical literature that we have been considering. For Jorden, the corruption of the imagination is so central to the disease of "suffocation" as to be virtually constitutive of it:

> This depravation of the internal sences, is so ordinary in the fits of the Mother, as Horatius Augenius Epistola 6 seems to make it of the essence of this disease, that the imagination is ever depraved in it.[41]

Ferrand, once again relying on Hippocrates, writes in yet more graphic terms of the disastrous effect of uterine furor on the inward wits:

> [T]he acute inflammation drives them out of their wits, the putrefaction makes them homicidal, the blackness of the condition causes frights and starts, and the pressure around the heart brings on a desire to strangle themselves. The most inward reason, troubled and anguished by the corruption of the blood, in turn, becomes perverted.[42]

The "hidden hooke" that Britomart "unwares . . . swallowed" (3.2.38) corrupts both her body and her mind, just as Ficino's lover is corrupted from within by the invisible ray emanating from the beloved. As a result, she manifests, like the lover in countless medical treatises, a mysterious mental affliction: "Sad, solemne, sowre, and full of fancies fraile / She woxe; yet wist she neither how nor why" (3.2.27).

The immediate source of Britomart's "fancies fraile" is the phantasm of Arthegall: "Tho gan she to renew her former smart, / And thinke of that faire visage, written on her hart" (3.2.28–29). Like Orlando, who is plagued by inward visions of Angelica as he tosses restlessly on his bed, and like Tancredi, who bears the "essempio inciso" (*GL* 3.2) within his heart, Britomart is focused on an internal image—one that is explicitly said to be *written* on her heart. This writing is clearly linked to the "deepe *engraffed* ill" (3.3.18) that Britomart attempts to conceal within her body, but that is in fact written *on it*—"bewrayd" in part by her helpless blushing in Merlin's presence. As we saw in chapter 1, the phantasm inscribed within the lover's soul may, under certain conditions, radically undermine the working of the very capacities of judgment and reason it is designed to serve. Du Laurens's deployment of the metaphor of an engraving or "stampe" in the mind also indicates how a perseverative style of mind may take hold:

> [I]n melancholike persons, the braine may seeme to have gotten a habit, and therewithall the humour which is drie and earthie, *having set his stampe in a bodie that is hard, suffereth not it selfe easily to be blotted out.*[43]

As the medical accounts of love-melancholy have shown us, the inscription of a phantasm in an increasingly retentive imaginative faculty is responsible for the gradual development of melancholic symptoms:

> They desire solitariness, because they using to bee busie and earnestly following their imagination, doe feare to bee drawne away by others their presence, and therefore doe avoide it: *but the cause of such their uncessant perseverance in their imaginations, is because their spirits are grosse, and as it were immoveable.*[44]

Among the often-recorded results of this "uncessant perseverance" of the imagination are insomnia and a susceptibility to unruly thoughts and images. Britomart herself is subject to both of these symptoms:

> But sleepe full farre away from her did fly:
> In stead thereof sad sighs, and sorrowes deepe
> Kept watch and ward about her warily,

That nought she did but wayle, and often steepe
Her daintie couch with teares, which closely she did weepe.

And if any drop of slombring rest
Did chaunce to still into her wearie spright,
When feeble nature felt her selfe opprest,
Streight way with dreames, and with fantasticke sight
Of dreadfull things the same was put to flight,
That oft out of her bed she did astart,
As one with vew of ghastly feends affright.

(3.2.28–29)

Britomart's restless agitation fits Du Laurens's description of "melanchol-icke folke [who] both sleeping and waking may be haunted with a thou-sand vaine inventions."[45] Drawing perhaps on Du Laurens, Ferrand also addresses the tendency of lovers to suffer from insomnia in terms that cor-respond very closely to Spenser's description of Britomart's wakefulness:

> The insomnia that troubles lovers, making them more melancholy, sad, lean and dry . . . *is caused by the diverse fantasies that run through their brains,* never leaving the soul in peace, thereby making the brain cold and dry. . . . If at times they fall into a light sleep sent by nature to repair the animal spir-its dissipated by the violence of the imagination and the excessive waking, such *sleep is accompanied by a thousand fantasms and horrible dreams from which they awake more miserable, sad, pensive, more fearful and sorrowful,* in-deed more grieved by sleep than by waking.[46]

The general portrait Spenser creates of Britomart's "love-sick" state cor-responds to Ferrand's description of Canace, an Ovidian heroine whose love-sickness is also diagnosed by her nurse: "Canace became pale, lean, wanting appetite, insomniac, complaining without cause; by these signs her nurse knew she was in love."[47] As we will see presently, it is not coin-cidental that Britomart is so closely modeled on an *epyllion* heroine whose sexual "furor" poses such danger to herself and her family.

Britomart's own account of herself as a version of the besotted Narcissus also emphasizes her melancholic subjugation to "fantasticke sight"; like Tancredi, she is only partly convinced of the reality of what she sees, yet remains hopelessly entranced by it:

> But wicked fortune mine, though mind be good,
> Can have no hope of end, nor hope of my desire,
> But feed on shadows, whiles I die for food,
> And like a shadow wexe, whiles with entire
> Affection, I doe languish and expire.
> I fonder, then Cephisus foolish child,
> Who having vewed in a fountaine shere
> His face, was with the love thereof beguild;
> I fonder love a shade, the bodie farre exiled.
>
> (3.2.44)

The final line of this stanza in particular seems to associate Britomart with the melancholic lover who "prefers the shadow to the thing itself," who prefers, that is, the internalized phantasm to the actual love object. Like Lucretius's lovers (and like Narcissus), Britomart "feed[s] on shadows" in a hopeless attempt to *incorporate* her beloved as a part of herself. The Lucretian trope of "feeding" on images of love (the *pabula amoris* that should be shunned) is—as in Lucretius's text—linked directly to the "wound" of love:

> A thousand thoughts she *fashioned in her mind*,
> And in her *feigning fancie* did pourtray
> Him such, as fittest she for love could find,
> Wise, warlike, personable, curteous, and kind.
>
> With such *selfe-pleasing thoughts her wound she fed*,
> And thought so to beguile her grievous smart;
> *But so her smart was much more grievous bred,*
> *And the deepe wound more deepe engord her hart,*
> That nought but death her dolour mote depart.
>
> (3.4.5–6, italics mine)

Britomart's "selfe-pleasing thoughts" also evoke the regressive self-absorption of the Petrarchan lover who worsens his own pain ("but so her smart was much more grievous bred") with the "willful woe" of the *acidiosus*.[48]

The Wound of Love

As the quoted passage suggests, the image that best figures the complex conditioning of the mind through bodily suffering, and of the body through the "fantasticke sight" of the mind, is the wound of love. Unlike Arthur's "secret wound," Britomart's wound is both literal and figurative. Although she does suffer from the metaphorical wound that "the false Archer, which that arrow shot / So slyly" (3.2.26), this wound finds its physical correlative in her "bleeding bowels."[49] As we have noted, these "bleeding bowels" suggest a literal, physical bleeding peculiar to her female physiology. Indeed, the use of the image of a female wound to denote a medically grounded conception of the self as a profoundly material substance seems to build on, but also to develop, Lucretius's influential discourse on love. His treatment of the wound of love, as we saw in chapter 2, parodies and literalizes the traditional Hellenistic "wound of love":

> But it is proper to *shun the images and banish from oneself the food of love* . . . For *the sore quickens and sets through nourishment*, and from day to day derangement waxes and the affliction grows worse. (4.1063–69, italics mine)

The physicality of this wound is palpable, since the lover's body wastes away, or bleeds, or feels pain. But it is at the same time an "unseen" wound that cannot be located in any internal organ or understood without reference to the "psychological" state of "furor." Britomart's decidedly material wound locates the experience of love more firmly in the body, in a move that would seem to be in line with contemporary medical emphasis on the disruptive power of female physiology.[50] Notwithstanding this medical view of the female body as potentially toxic, Spenser's treatment of Britomart's wound suggests that it is precisely the inescapable materiality of the female self that transforms a wasteful, even sinful erotic disease into a dynamic source of procreative energy.

Literary Love-Therapy: From Epyllion to Romance

The best remedy for suffocation or hysteria, as Jacquart and Thomasset note, was thought to be intercourse sanctioned by marriage: "If the suffocation comes from a retention of sperm, the woman should together with and draw up a marriage contract with some man."[51] Ferrand makes the same recommendation on the basis of Hippocratic authority: "Hippocrates states this view explicitly toward the end of his treatise *On the Diseases of Young Women*: 'all young women taken by this disease should be forthwith married.'"[52] Whereas both Orlando and Tancredi disappear into increasingly phantasmic, unreal quests, which paradoxically alienate the "real" beloved object, Britomart's quest will shift decisively away from an absorption in the "feigning fancie" of her mind toward precisely the marriage that represents the telos of the *medical* narrative of love-melancholy. This identification of the course of Britomart's quest with the onset and cure of the "furor" of love-melancholy suggests that Spenser's revision of romance will in part be modeled on the conversion of a circular (melancholic) narrative into a teleological (mournful) one. Whereas Ariosto's psychological model for romance is the melancholic narrative that leads only to madness, Spenser's poem transforms that model by introducing the medical cure that is also the paradigmatic *literary* ending: marriage. At the same time, Merlin's reinterpretation of Britomart's "love-sicke hart" as the instigator of a procreative role fully coincident with the "streight course of heavenly destiny" (3.3.24) integrates the Virgilian telos of nation-building into this romance narrative.

Spenser's treatment of this episode suggests that a new interpretation of the signs of melancholy will provide the "cure" for an Ariostan style of romance. Glauce's hermeneutic method, we infer, is inappropriate. As we saw earlier, her choice of herbs with which to cure her charge associates her with the practice of witchcraft, and the reference to Britomart's "miscarriage" ("for feare least blame / Of her miscarriage should in her be fond," 3.3.52) hints that her interference in Britomart's illness is unlawful.[53] Thus although she is able to "read" the signs of love-melancholy in Britomart ("But if that love it be, as sure I read / By knowen signes and passions, which I see," 3.2.33), her interpretation of those signs as a sickness to be immediately "undone" is not condoned by the narrator:

> And that old Dame said many an idle verse,
> Out of her daughters hart fond fancies to reverse.
>
> So thought she to undoe her daughters love:
> But love, that is in gentle brest begonne,
> No idle charmes so lightly may remove.
>
> (3.2.48, 51)

Britomart's plight here looks forward to Amoret's suffering in the house of Busirane: on that occasion, it will be Britomart who constrains Busirane to "reverse" his "charmes" and "sad verse" (3.12.36). But Glauce's "idle verse" and "idle charmes" are helpless against the strength of love "that is in gentle brest begonne." Her interpretation of Britomart's distress suggests that love is inexorable, deadly, something to be "removed" or "reversed" at all costs: "Aye me, how much I feare, least love it bee" (3.2.33). This attitude is reinforced by the generic form of the episode: Spenser's treatment of the onset of Britomart's desperate love and Glauce's attempts to heal her is modeled closely on the pseudo-Virgilian epyllion *Ciris*. Merlin's prophetic discourse, on the other hand, which reveals to Britomart the extent and fortunes of the race she will breed with Arthegall, derives from an epic tradition of prophetic-historic discourse, such as the one Anchises delivers to Aeneas in the underworld.

The epyllion is perhaps the ancient form most clearly dedicated to depicting the experience of sexual desire, often a *feminine* sexual desire that has catastrophic results both for the lover herself and for her immediate social context.[54] It is perhaps also significant that, as Georgia Brown has shown, the 1590s saw an explosion of interest in erotic epyllia that tended to focus specifically on "stories of shameful sexuality."[55] Spenser's clear shift into the epyllion mode would thus have alerted his readers not only to the episode's likely focus—sexuality, and female sexuality in particular—but also to the potentially transgressive nature of this material. Epyllion combines the focus on personal, intense mental states characteristic of lyric with a concern for the wider social context central to epic. The language of erotic madness that we saw for instance in Sappho's lyric is transferred to a context in which such an extreme state will cause havoc on a broader social scale. Because the epyllion focuses not just on the lineaments of erotic madness and the individual suffering it brings, but also on the resulting conflict between the individual and her society, it is unsurprising that shame, as Brown argues, is such a prominent theme of the genre. Thus the women to whom Glauce refers all appear in epyllia or epyllion-style narratives, and all are women ruined by catastrophic desire: Pasiphae, Myrrha, and Biblis. Given the focus on the experience of passionate desire, epyllia tend toward naturalistic, physiologically based descriptions influenced by the medical language of madness. Thus in *Ciris*, Scylla is struck by a wasting disease that runs through her viscera just as Britomart's illness runs through her bleeding bowels:

> [A]tque ubi nulla malis reperit solacia tantis
> tabidulamque videt labi per viscera mortem,
> quo vocat ire dolor, subigunt quo tendere fata,
> fertur et horribili praeceps impellitur oestro . . .

[And when for ills so great she finds no comfort, and sees slow-wasting death steal through her entrails, she is carried where her anguish summons her to go, where the fates compel her to hasten, and by awful goading-madness is driven headlong.]

(Ciris 181–84, trans. Loeb, with minor emendations)

As we saw earlier, the term *oistros* for a peculiarly female madness is heavy with connotations: "[O]istros is female, bovine, mating-madness and its externalized cause: a tormenting fly."[56] It is precisely this visceral, female frenzy that overtakes both Britomart and Scylla (*horribili oestro*); the word marks the madness as bestial, a madness that by its very nature threatens to drive the woman out of her (human) mind and into another form.

The animalistic sexuality of the epyllion heroine is ultimately stronger than *pietas*, the virtue that underpins epic: Scylla's love for Minos, a love that has swept her away by its furor ("novo correpta furore," 130), is destructive to nation and family. By staging a clash between the medical pathology of erotic madness and the exigencies of the social world (the epic context), the ancient epyllion creates a kind of anti-epic. But the fact that even Britomart's name may derive from the chaste daughter of Scylla's nurse (Britomartis) suggests a reevaluation—from within the romance form—of both the form and the content of female passion. Whether Britomart becomes more like the maddened Scylla of the epyllion or the chaste Britomartis is made to depend on how the poem uses and interprets its epyllion sources. And it is Merlin, as surrogate poet figure and *magister amoris*, who steps in to reinterpret the nature of Britomart's "deepe engraffed ill" even as he redirects the course of the epyllion toward a Virgilian telos: the founding of a race and nation.

Within the context of Merlin's prophetic discourse, female love-madness is represented no longer as a maddening force that runs directly counter to the values of *pietas*, but rather as a vital source of energy that propels

Britomart toward her predestined goal. Merlin's reevaluation of epyllion passion pivots on a new interpretation of those very bodily symptoms that terrify Britomart and her nurse. Placing her suffering in a new, epic context, he reinterprets, in particular, the symbolic import of female blood:

> Most noble Virgin, that by fatall lore
> Has learn'd to love, let no whit thee dismay
> That hard begin, that meets thee in the dore,
> And with sharpe fits thy tender hart oppresseth sore.
>
> For so must all things excellent begin,
> And eke enrooted deepe must be that Tree,
> Whose big embodied braunches shall not lin,
> Till they to heavens hight forth stretched bee.
> For from thy wombe a famous Progenie
> Shall spring, out of the auncient Troian blood,
> Which shall revive the sleeping memorie
> Of those same antique Peres, the heavens brood,
> Which Greeke and Asian rivers stained with their blood.

> (3.3.21–22)

Britomart's bodily distress is no longer a sign of a deadly illness, then, but the guarantee of her connection to an ancient epic lineage. The blood within Britomart's "bleeding bowels" is now read through its connection to "the auncient Troian blood" as a sign of the figural dimension of Britomart's quest rather than an indication of the toxic powers of the womb. The unfolding of time within the "constant terme" of history guarantees that the "wandring eye" of Britomart's desire will turn out to be fully congruent with "the streight course of heavenly destiny" (3.3.24). As testimony to her reproductive powers, her blood is a sacred sign of her body's place in providential history.

The reevaluation of female blood in this episode is inaugurated by a striking moment that underscores the generic shift from epyllion to epic. When Merlin effortlessly reads through Britomart's disguise to the "cause [of her illness] that hath it selfe bewrayd" (3.3.18), Britomart produces an expansive literary blush:

> The doubtfull Mayd, seeing her selfe descryde,
> Was all abasht, and her pure yvory
> Into a cleare Carnation suddeine dyde;

> As faire Aurora rising hastily,
> Doth by her blushing tell, that she did lye
> All night in old Tithonus frosen bed,
> Whereof she seems ashamed inwardly.
>
> (3.3.20)

The excess of blood in Britomart's "bleeding bowels" now seems to rush to her face in this sexualized blush, confirming the nature and origin of her "deepe engraffed ill"; associated here with Aurora, Britomart seems proleptically ashamed of a sexual encounter that is yet to come. As Brown argues, blushing—because of its association with both shame and sexuality—is "an integral part of the action" of the epyllion.[57] Britomart's allegiance with epyllion heroines, and with their potentially shameful, or shameless, sexuality, is exposed in this *telling* blush.

But Merlin's discourse of course suggests that the energy of female sexuality that in the eypllion becomes a dangerous "furor," will in this context be translated into the "excellent" beginning of her romance quest. His interpretation of Britomart's embodied passion places the driving obsession of love-melancholy within a teleological narrative that provides precisely the "cure" of marriage. As a result of this shift, Britomart's blush may be read retrospectively not as the sign of a transgressive, private emotion, but rather as an indication of Britomart's unwitting association with the dynastic figures of epic. The language of her blush, in fact, echoes Virgil's description of Lavinia's famous blush quite closely, and may therefore indicate Spenser's conscious manipulation of generic markers in this scene.[58] Similarly, Merlin's discourse places Britomart's womb within the unfolding of history according to "the full time prefixt by destiny" (3.3.40), so that the seemingly chaotic suffering of her "fraile fleshly mould" is drawn within the framework of a typological narrative. This typologization of the body ensures that Britomart's "bleeding bowels" are now interpreted in the context of the figural unfolding of "Briton blood" (3.3.48) from "the auncient Troian blood" (3.3.22) to the "royall Virgin" (3.3.49), whose appearance in Merlin's discourse marks the contemporary culmination of his vision. The true meaning of Britomart's passion can only be understood in the context of what Spenser calls "the great volume of Eternitie" (3.3.4) in which the "fruits of matrimoniall bowre" are seen to "unfold by dew degrees and long pretense" (3.3.4). The rehabilitation of epyllion passion within the context of providential romance thus represents generically the transformation of the womb from the source of sickness and corruption to that "sacred mould / Of [Britomart's] immortal wombe" (3.4.11).

We saw in our discussion of Arthur's quest that Spenser's use of a figural structure reorganizes the melancholic quest—a quest beset by phantasms and by self-absorbed grief—into a mournful one. The figural narrative, I argued, is essentially elegiac because it necessarily works through substitution and repetition, operating against the melancholic fixation on a single, lost object. In Arthur's quest, pregnancy becomes a trope for the figural quest: the "chylde / conceav'd in secret brest" (4.9.17) drives him onward, beyond the "terme" of each completed adventure, closer each time to the birth or fulfillment of the *figura* of the faerie queene. Britomart's quest uses pregnancy both as a trope and as a literal fulfillment of promise within the procreative female body. Thus Britomart's "immortal wombe" situates her within a figural narrative that involves the production of literal offspring, her "famous Progenie" (3.3.22), but that also emphasizes loss and substitution as a condition of this birth. Merlin's account of the birth of Britomart's heir emphasizes the immediate substitution of the child for the father. The son will activate the memory of the displaced father, just as the new "progenie" emerging from Britomart's blood will activate the "sleeping memorie / Of those same antique Peres, the heavens brood" (3.3.22) in a dramatization of typological fulfillment:

> Long time ye both in armes shall beare great sway,
> Till thy wombes burden thee from them do call,
> And his last fate him from thee take away,
> Too rathe cut off by practise criminall
> Of secret foes, that him shall make in mischiefe fall.
>
> With thee yet shall he leave for memory
> Of his late puissaunce, his Image dead,
> That living him in all activity
> To thee shall represent.
>
> (3.3.28–29)

Like Ambrosia, whom Daphne hopes Alcyon will love "in lieu" of herself, Britomart's son appears to "represent" Arthegall to her as "his Image dead." The whole of Merlin's historical discourse turns on the revolution from one "terme," or historical event, to the next, just as Arthur's quest labors toward its "just terme." Each stage in this discourse represents a fuller revelation of the truth that underpins the vision, so that the narrative ends with a resurgence of "Briton bloud": "Tho when the terme is full accomplishid, /there shall a sparke of fire. . . . Be freshly kindled in the fruitful Ile / Of Mona" (3.3.48). But the final fulfillment of the figures of history cannot be represented within the present moment, and Merlin's discourse thus ends on the cusp between veiling and full revelation: "But yet the end is not" (3.3.50).

What is crucial here is Merlin's introduction of figural mourning as a structuring principle of Britomart's narrative. Recognizing the "iust revolution" of time within his narrative, she feels both grief for the losses of her people and hope for the future: "The Damzell was full deepe empassioned, / Both for his griefe, and for her peoples sake, / Whose future woes so plaine he fashioned" (3.3.43). Her movement into an elegized narrative tempers the fury of her love-melancholy, preparing her for losses to come. It is, as we shall see in the next section, Britomart's absorption of Merlin's elegiac perspective that distinguishes her from the melancholic, despairing Scudamour, and that consequently permits her to conquer the house of Busirane.

"Sweet Consuming Woe": Overcoming Love-Melancholy in the House of Busirane

Our first encounter with Scudamour sets the scene in precise terms for Britomart's encounter with the nightmarish projection of love-melancholy that constitutes the house of Busirane. Scudamour's symptoms invoke those of Sir Terwin in the cave of Despair and of Alcyon, the grief-stricken lover who cannot relinquish his dead beloved, Daphne. As in these portraits of the suicidal lover and the Man in Black who hates the "vaine and transitorie" world (*Daphnaïda* 495), Spenser creates in Scudamour a figure in whom the spiritual disorder of *acedia* and the *atra voluptas* of Petrarchan love lyric converge. We saw earlier that the Petrarch of the *Secretum* suffers from *tristitia*, or *acedia*, a self-absorbed suffering that is nevertheless sweet: "And thus I feed on tears and grief, with a sort of dark, gloomy pleasure."[59] Though Augustine condemns this attitude of mind in the *Secretum*, *atra voluptas* is nonetheless the aesthetic and psychological cornerstone of the

Canzoniere. Scudamour's stance is likewise characterized by its self-absorbed, willful suffering:

> Faire Britomart so long him followed,
> That she at last came to a fountaine sheare,
> By which there lay a knight *all wallowed*
> *Upon the grassy ground*, and by him neare
> His haberieon, his helmet, and his speare.
>
> (3.11.7, italics mine)

Scudamour has the physical lassitude of the slothful, wallowing languorously on the ground, the cold, earthy element of melancholy. A characteristic sign of *acedia* is torpor, "the obtuse and somnolent stupor that paralyzes any gesture that might heal us."[60] Scudamour's deadly torpor recalls that of Sir Terwin, whose inability to wrest himself from Despaire's grasp proves fatal:

> And him beside there lay upon the gras
> A d... corse, whose life away did pas,
> *All wallowd in his owne yet luke-warme blood*,
> That from his wound yet welled fresh alas.
>
> (1.9.36, italics mine)

Spenser's own portrayal of the slothlike Idleness emphasizes that *acedia* is not merely a physical stupor, but combines physical enervation and exacerbated desire: "His life he led in lawlesse riotise; / By which he grew to grievous malady; / For in his lustlesse limbes through evill guise / A shaking fever raigned continually" (1.4.20). As Agamben has argued, the constitutive feature of *acedia* is in fact an agonized desire that presumptuously forestalls its own progress toward the desired object. Thus "it is the perversion of a will that wants the object, but not the way to it, and which simultaneously desires and bars the path to his or her own desire."[61] One of the "daughters" of *acedia*, then, is pure *desperatio*: "the dark and presumptuous certainty of being already condemned beforehand and the complacent sinking into one's own destruction, as if nothing, least of all divine grace, could provide salvation."[62] Spenser emphasizes the willfulness of Scudamour's anguish, the self-inflicted abjection that rejects out of hand the possibility of succor:

With great indignaunce he that sight forsooke,
And downe againe himself disdainfully
Abiecting, th'earth with his faire forhead strooke:
Which the bold Virgin seeing, gan apply
Fit medcine to his griefe, and spake thus courtesly.

(3.11.13)

Spenser's allegorization of Scudamour's psychic state clearly suggests that he both "desires and bars the path to his own desire." The causal relationship between Scudamour's own "burning torment" (3.11.27)—characteristic of love-melancholy—and the wall of fire that actually prevents him from entering Busirane's house is the clearest instance of the "perversion of will" central to *acedia*:

Whom whenas Scudamour saw past the fire,
Safe and untoucht, he likewise gan assay,
With greedy will, and envious desire,
And bad the stubborne flames to yield him way.
. . . .
With huge impatience he inly swelt,
More for great sorrow, that he could not pas,
Then for the burning torment, which he felt,
That with fell woodnesse he effierced was,
And wilfully him throwing on the gras,
Did beat and bounse his head and brest full sore.

(3.11.26–27)

The qualities of rancor and impatience are traditionally associated with those suffering from *acedia*, and Scudamour's "huge impatience" and "fell woodnesse" clearly contribute to the paradoxically self-defeating nature of his "envious desire."[63]

The appearance of the unhappy lover Sir Terwin "wallowd in his owne blood" in Despaire's cave has already established love-melancholy as an eroticized version of *acedia*. Scudamour's abjection further clarifies the relationship between the spiritualized eroticism of Petrarchan poetics and the psychological complex of melancholia/*acedia*/love-melancholy. For as several critics have noted, the "penning" of Amoret in Busirane's house while Scudamour languishes outside suggests an allegory of Petrarchan poesis ("My Lady and my love is cruelly pend / In doleful darkenesse from the vew of day," 3.11.11).[64] But the allegory is more specific than this. Scudamour's self-abjection indicates that the house may be a projection of that *atra voluptas* that turns a real woman into a phantasm and desire into a field of loss in which a "wilful anguish" (3.12.43, 1590) continually renders the desired object unobtainable.[65] Thus Spenser emphasizes Scudamour's connection not only to erotic desire but very precisely to the form of *despair* condemned by Augustine in the *Secretum*. In the 1590 version of the ending of book 3, Britomart "left Sir Scudamour in great distresse / Twixt dolour and despight halfe *desperate*" (3.12.43), and in the 1596 version Scudamour's presumption of his inability to achieve what he desires prompts him to leave before Britomart emerges:

> But he sad man, when he had long in drede
> Awayted there for Britomarts returne,
> Yet saw her not nor signe of her good speed,
> *His expectation to despaire did turne.*
>
> (3.12.45, 1596, italics mine)

Scudamour's language also recalls the language of the despairing Red Crosse:

> At last breaking into bitter plaintes
> He said: O soveraigne Lord that sit'st on hye,
> And raignst in blis emongst thy blessed Saintes,
> How suffrest thou such shamefully cruelty,
> So long unwreaked of thine enimy?
> Or hast thou, Lord, of good mens cause no heed?
> Or doth thy iustice sleepe, and silently?
> What booteth then the good and righteous deed,
> If goodnesse find no grace, nor righteousnesse no meed?
>
> (3.11.9)

Britomart, seeing the "ghastly fit, / threatning into his life to make a breach" (3.11.12), reacts much as Una does when Red Crosse, into whose conscience Despaire's rhetoric has "made a secret breach" (1.9.48), threatens suicide. Una reminds her interlocutor of the power of grace against despair:

> In heavenly mercies hast thou not a part?
> Why shouldst thou then despeire, that chosen art?
> Where iustice growes, there grows eke greater grace,
> The which doth quench the brond of hellish smart.
>
> (1.9.53)

Britomart reaches for a similar lesson, perhaps reflecting in her reference to "high providence" her own lessons in Merlin's cave:

> Ah gentle knight, whose deepe conceived griefe
> Well seemes t'exceede the powre of patience,
> Yet if that heavenly grace some good reliefe
> You send, submit you to high providence,
> And ever in your noble hart prepense,
> That all the sorrow in the world is lesse,
> Then vertues might, and values confidence,
> For who nill bide the burden of distresse,
> Must not here thinke to live: for life is wretchednesse.
>
> (3.11.14)

Britomart attempts to introduce into Scudamour's perspective the elegiac mournfulness that has altered her own relationship with erotic melancholy: "for life is wretchednesse." Her subjection to Merlin's doctrine of "divine foresight" has taught her to interpret both the pain of her "bleeding bowels" and the vision in the womblike mirror in terms of divine providence. Thus she is to be comforted *in time* "through hope of those, which Merlin had her told / Should of her name and nation be chiefe, / And fetch their being from the *sacred* mould / Of her *immortal wombe, to be in heaven enrold*" (3.4.11, italics mine). Like Arthur, whose sorrow leads to the performative "vow" to find the faerie queene ("And never vow to rest, till her I find," 1.9.15), Britomart's soldierly attitude permits her to accept loss and suffering ("the burden of distresse") and to pursue her goal nonetheless. Scudamour's reaction, "let me dye, that ought" (3.11.19), recalls by contrast the relentless melancholy of Alcyon, who rejects the narrator's help "as one disposed willfullie to die" (*Daphnaïda* 552), and of Timias, whose refrain "dye, rather, dye" echoes through three stanzas of a highly stylized Petrarchan lament (3.5.45–47).

When Britomart plunges through the fire that seems to represent Scudamour's own self-defeating "burning torment" into the house of Busirane, we suspect that the house itself will allegorize and explore the condition of erotic melancholy that has governed book 3 thus far. Perhaps the most compelling indication that this is the case is Spenser's portrait of the cupid who rules this space. After a long ekphrastic passage depicting "Cupids warres" (3.11.28), the poet provides a telling account of cupid's own involvement in the suffering he promulgates: "Ne did he spare sometime to pricke himselfe, / that he might tast the sweet consuming woe" (3.11.45). The self-inflicted nature of cupid's "sweet consuming woe" suggests that this version of eros is allied to that of the *acidiosus*: its melancholic nature is indicated by the "woe" that, though "sweet," is nonetheless "consuming." The range of imagery associating love-melancholy with a turn inward— the lover "feeds" on his own tears, his own sorrow—culminates in this vision of an autoerotic self-wounding.[66] Like Britomart, whose gaze turns first on herself, and like Scudamour, whose "deepe conceived griefe" is exacerbated by his own "greedy will" (3.11.26), Cupid turns inward to "taste" the oxymoronic delights of passion. The latent imagery of feeding here ("taste") also connects this movement to the Lucretian trope of heightened sexuality as a fantasized form of feeding.

This displacement of a real object by an internally generated, phantasmic figure on which the lover hopelessly "feeds" is at the heart of love-melancholy in the texts we have studied. The house of Busirane provides a brilliant externalization of the obsessive interior world of the erotic melancholic, furnished as it is with the various "phantasies" (3.12.26) generated by the melancholic imagination.[67] Quite appropriately, then, the poet declares during his description of Saturn that "love is sullein, and Saturnlike seene" (3.11.43). The clear connection between the "idle shewes" everywhere apparent in the house of Busirane and the dominance of a "Saturnlike" eros is supported by the poem's earlier portrait of Phantastes, who demonstrates Aristotle's contention that melancholics are "apt to follow their imagination":[68]

> All those were idle thoughts and fantasies,
> Devices, dreames, opinions unsound,
> Shewes, visions, sooth-sayes, and prophesies;
> And all that fained is, as leasings, tales and lies.

Emongst them all sate he, which wonned there,
That hight Phantastes by his nature trew;
A man of yeares yet fresh, as mote appeare,
Of swarth complexion, and of crabbed hew,
That him full of melancholy did shew;
Bent hollow beetle browes, sharpe staring eyes,
That mad or foolish seemd: one by his vew
Mote deeme him borne with ill disposed skyes,
When oblique Saturne sate in the house of agonyes.

(2.9.51–52)

This melancholic Phantastes would clearly be at home in the house of Busirane, whose household god is the "Saturnlike" figure of love. The decisive connection between sexuality, melancholia, and a hyperactive imagination that emerges in the very earliest sketches of love-melancholy seems to lie behind the "straunge characters" of Busirane's art as it appears in the rooms through which Britomart passes. Many of the Ovidian stories represented in the tapestries in the first room portray love as a degrading transformation, a perversion of self that is allegorized by the transformation of a god into a beast. That this transformation is driven by melancholic forces is suggested not only by the figure of Saturn himself "that to a Centaure did him selfe transmove" (3.11.43), but by Neptune, whose pose recalls Scudamour's:

The God himselfe did pensive seeme and sad,
And hong adowne his head, as he did dreame:
For privy love his brest empierced had,
Ne ought but deare Bisaltis ay could make him glad.

He loved eke Iphimedia deare,
And Aeolus faire daughter Arne hight,
For whom *he turnd him selfe into a steare,*
And fed on fodder, to beguile her sight.

(3.11.41–42, italics mine)

The emphasis throughout these ekphrastic stanzas on a god's transforming or "transmoving" himself into a bestial form in order to embrace a beloved mortal woman might usefully be glossed by Ficino's central statement about the conditions that create melancholic love: "[H]aec illis accidere consueverunt, *qui amore abusi,* quod contemplationis est, ad amplexus concupiscentiam transtulerunt" (these things were accustomed to happen to those who, *having abused love,* converted what is a desire for contemplation into a desire for embrace," italics mine).[69] In the previous chapter Ficino calls the power that twists the soul away from the good of contemplation an evil demon, *kakodaemon*:

> [V]erum secundus ideo dictus est malus, quia propter abusum nostrum saepe nos turbat, et animum a praecipuo eius bono, quod in veritatis speculatione consistit, avertit maxime, et ad mysteria viliora detorquet.

> [The second impulse only becomes evil—earning its name *kakodaemon*—by means of our abuse, as a result of which it often disturbs us and powerfully diverts the soul from its chief good, which consists in the contemplation of truth, and twists it to baser purposes.] (*De amore* 6.8, trans. Jayne)

The *abuse* in Busirane's name might seem to indicate a specifically Ficinian abuse in which the soul is twisted toward the literalness of an embrace, the "base mysteries" of the body ("ad mysteria viliora detorquet").[70] As Ficino argues, the love of the voluptuous man provokes an immediate descent "from sight to touch." Busirane then appears to represent the *kakodaemon*, the impulse to touch what can only be contemplated, that is allegorically connected to Scudamour's perverse "despight." He is, it would seem, precisely the kind of "deplorable spirit" of which Synesius warns, a spirit that enters the labile fantasy, forcing the soul downward into the false visions sponsored by the base, material world. The state of Scudamour's psyche thus finds close correlatives within the house. We find his "wilful" degradation not only in the mythical metamorphoses of the first room, but also in the masque, which contains figures who allegorize aspects of Scudamour's melancholic pose. *Griefe* (allied with *Fury*) is represented "downe hanging his dull head, with heavy chere" (3.12.16), leaving those he attacks "in wilfull languor and consuming smart, / Dying each day with inward wounds of dolours dart" (3.12.16).[71]

As we have repeatedly seen in both medical and literary texts, the internalization of the image of the beloved signals the displacement of the real woman by a mental phantasm. Like Narcissus, who attempts an impossible union with his own image, the melancholic lover pursues an inwardly generated phantasm, a shadow that will necessarily elude him.

If we accept that the house of Busirane allegorizes the inner workings of the melancholy lover's mind, beset by wavering fantasies and degraded by its increasing materiality, the capture of Amoret would seem to represent the process of internalizing—or more precisely, incorporating—the lost object as just such a phantasm. Busirane thus acts as a sinister alter ego for Scudamour, spiriting away the beloved whom he desires only as an inaccessible object of his own mind. It is not entirely surprising, then, that Scudamour's initial seizure of Amoret is cast in rather violent terms that link it to Busirane's rupture of the wedding ceremony. In his own account of his seizure of Amoret, Scudamour twice refers to her as "spoyle" (4.10.55; 4.10.58), and emphasizes Amoret's desire to gain her freedom from him:

> She often prayd, and often me besought,
> Sometime with tender teares to let her goe,
> Sometime with witching smyles: but yet for nought,
> That ever she to me could say or doe,
> Could she her wished freedome fro me wooe.
>
> (4.10.57)

It is similarly appropriate, in the light of our earlier discussion of the figure of Orpheus as the archetypal melancholic lover, that Scudamour should compare himself to Orpheus as he draws Eurydice toward the upper world:

> No less did Daunger threaten me with dread,
> When as he saw me, maugre all his powre,
> That glorious spoyle of beautie with me lead,
> Then Cerberus, when Orpheus did recoure
> His leman from the Stygian Princes boure.
>
> (4.10.58)

Like Orpheus, Scudamour loses his Eurydice to a "furor" that facilitates the imaginative creation of a house of fantasy/underworld whose primary role is to prevent the satisfaction of desire. The anonymous lover in the temple to Venus refers to this "furor" in his Lucretian song: "Soone as with fury thou doest them inspire, / In generation seeke to quench their inward fire" (4.10.46). Scudamour, we infer, is similarly inspired by a "fury" that first provokes the capture of Amoret and then conspires to render her yet more desirable as a lost object "pend / In dolefull darkenesse from the vew of day" (3.9.11). The intervention of Busirane at the wedding feast "*before the bride was bedded*" (4.1.3, italics mine) confirms our sense that Busirane's rapture of Amoret is crucially timed to forestall the sexual consummation that would "cure" Scudamour's melancholy. For Lauren Silberman is surely right to suggest that Amoret's imprisonment is not attributable, as some critics have suggested, to her unwillingness to "bed" Scudamour, but rather to her *willingness* to do so. It is because "she Scudamore will not denay" (3.11.11) in the sense of say 'no' to, that Scudamour/Busirane forcibly removes her.[72]

The final tableau in the house of Busirane—the use of Amoret's "living bloud" to figure the "straunge characters of his art"—seems to represent a devastating critique of Cupid's "sweet consuming woe," that is, of Petrarchan *atra voluptas*. We saw earlier that within the force field of Lucretian *furor* the Other virtually disappears as a distinctly exisiting being, "becoming merely a vehicle for the lover's personal wish and, at the same time, *a permanent obstacle to its fulfillment*."[73] Amoret's disappearance into the house of Busirane seems to offer an indictment of Scudamour's Petrarchan desire along similar lines; she is, impossibly, both the object of his desire and—as an autonomous being with independent desires—the obstacle to its fulfillment. Scudamour's continuing desire for total possession of Amoret is therefore expressed vicariously, through Busirane's attempt to transform Amoret into the poetic "beloved," a phantasmic Angelica:

> With living bloud he those characters wrate,
> Dreadfully dropping from her dying hart,
> Seeming transfixed with a cruell dart.
>
> (3.12.31)

Just as Petrarch's Laura does not exist independently of *l'aura* and *lauro*, the breeze and the laurel that symbolize poetic inspiration, so Amoret is in danger of being transformed into a figment of the poet's own mind. That Amoret is poised here between her existence as an independent being and a "phantasmic" existence in Scudamour's melancholic mind is indicated by the allegorical connection between the "sweet consuming woe" that torments Cupid and his followers (including Scudamour) and Amoret's own "consuming paine" (3.12.21). As writers from Hildegard to Freud have noted, the melancholic exacts a punitive revenge on the object of its desires when that object has been narcissistically assimilated with the self:

> If the object-love, which cannot be given up, takes refuge in narcissistic identification, while the object itself is abandoned, then hate is expended upon this new substitute-object, railing at it, depreciating it, making it suffer and deriving sadistic gratification from its suffering.[74]

Scudamour's own self-abjection is but the other side of his/Busirane's torture of Amoret, and Scudamour's broken heart (he groans "as if his hart were peeces made," 3.11.8) is reflected in Amoret's "dying hart" (3.12.31). Quite appropriately, then, Britomart frees Amoret by literally undoing the "bloudy lines" (3.12.36) that hold Amoret a prisoner within the love poet's own psyche.

In her critique of Agamben's account of melancholia, Juliana Schiesari notes that it fails to explore the gendering of melancholia that is apparent in the medical, literary, and philosophical development of the disease.[75] She looks specifically for answers to the question as to "how this metaphysics of melancholia interlocks with its gendering, with the masculine subjectivity that bemoans an absent object."[76] Spenser's portrait of Britomart's erotic melancholy and its intersection with Scudamour's "desiring fantasy" seems to address precisely the questions that Schiesari raises. The construction of the house of Busirane suggests that Scudamour's self-directed "despight" feeds on a specifically masculine, narcissistic identification with a feminine other who is forcibly placed in the role of the "lost object." Busirane's violent constraint of Amoret—both poetic and erotic—thus dramatizes the impossible embrace of a lost/phantasmic object (Ficino's "abuse") constitutive of melancholia. More specifically, the violent use of Amoret as the literal matter of Britomart's art, the source of the bloody ink with which he writes the "straunge characters of his art" (3.12.31), constitutes a shocking disclosure of the relationship between this "abuse" and the bittersweet poetics of Petrarchan *atra voluptas*. Britomart's reversal of Busirane's "charmes" is thus predicated on the reinterpretation of female sexuality that her sojourn with Merlin makes possible. In extricating Amoret from her captivity and healing her "riven bowels gor'd" (3.12.38), Britomart continues the healing of her own "bleeding bowels" even as she demonstrates by example the sterility of Scudamour's languid despair.

It is striking that when Britomart releases Amoret from the house of Busirane—from her status as mere phantasm—Scudamour's response oscillates in the two versions of the ending between a Lucretian fantasy of fusion and a "despairing" refusal of the beloved. The 1590 version uses the image of the hermaphrodite to represent the ecstatic reunion of Amoret and Scudamour. Numerous critics read this ending as an endorsement of eros, and even as a figure for the union of Arthegall and Britomart.[77] John Watkins's reading of this moment is representative: "Busirane might agree with Golding that the Salmacis and Hermaphroditus story proves that 'idlenesse / Is cheefest nurce and cherisher of all voluptuousnesse' (Epistle, ll. 113–14). Spenser himself endorsed that interpretation in tracing the origin of the fountain that emasculates Redcrosse. But at the end of the 1590 poem, he reads it differently as a tribute to matrimony."[78] My own view is that there are numerous reasons to believe that Spenser's use of the hermaphrodite image in book 3 has not changed substantially from his use of it in the earlier book. The hermaphrodite appears instead to function as the culminating image of erotic melancholy in the book. Indeed, Golding's reference to "idleness" reminds us that the early medical writers attributed the onset of love-melancholy in aristocratic patients precisely to the voluptuous idleness of their lives. Spenser's own erotic masque is appropriately introduced by "Ease," who brings on stage the "minstrals," "wanton Bardes," and "Rymers impudent" who sing "a lay of loves delight" (3.12.5); this "delitious harmony" induces the kind of somnolent stupor that overcomes Amoret and Scudamour: "[T]he rare sweetnesse of the melody / The feeble senses wholly did confound, / And the fraile soule in deepe delight nigh dround" (3.12.6). Unlike the therapeutic "lamentable lay" that draws Timias out of his "sad melancholy," this song bears a close resemblance to the dangerously sensual Tassoan *flebil canto*, or, closer to home, to the "melodious sound, / Of all that mote delight a daintie eare" (2.12.70) that greets Guyon and the Palmer in the Bowre of Bliss.

Like Lucretius's maddened lovers who attempt a kind of mutual devourment, these lovers also attempt an impossible fusion. Scudamour runs to Amoret with "hasty egernesse, / Like as a Deare, that greedily embayes / In the cool soile, after long thirstinesse" (3.12.44, 1590), and the two lovers are locked in a mutual attempt to "despoil" each other of "loves bitter fruit" (3.12.47, 1590). Lucretius's description of the lovers' frenzy constitutes an apt commentary on this "greedy" embrace:

> They hungrily form a body, and join salivas, and pressing lips with teeth, they breathe from each other's mouths, but in vain, since they can rub off nothing thence, nor penetrate and pass over into its body with the whole body. (*De rerum natura* 7.6)

I argued earlier that the basic fantasy behind this Lucretian vision is the fantasy of fusion, in its technical Stoic sense. Fusion (as opposed to blending or mixture) denotes the absolute destruction of each individual substance in the process of producing a new body. What is desired by the Lucretian lovers, then, is not just a temporary juxtaposition (mixing) of discrete bodies, but the permanent dissolution of each body into a new one: Hermaphroditus, or, in this case, Scudamoret.

> But she faire Lady overcommen quight
> Of huge affection, did in pleasure melt,
> And in sweete ravishment *pour out her spright*:
> No word they spake, nor earthly thing they felt,
> *But like two senceles stocks in long embracement dwelt.*
>
> Had ye them seene, ye would have surely thought,
> That they had beene that faire Hermaphrodite,
> Which that rich Romane of white marble wrought,
> And in his costly Bath causd to bee site:
> *So seemd those two, as growne together quite.*
>
> (3.12.45–46, 1590, italics mine)

It is difficult to believe, in light of the medical and philosophical context that we have considered, that Spenser intends his depiction of these "senceles stocks" as a "tribute to matrimony."[79] Read in conjunction with the 1596 ending, this fantasy of fusion seems to highlight precisely the condition of erotic melancholy that desires an impossible union with the beloved even as that union is willfully denied. For the "wilfull anguish" (1590, 3.12.43) that Scudamour experiences in the first ending turns to "despaire" in the second ending, prompting him to leave the house of Busirane before Amoret emerges. This is indeed the "perversion of a will that . . . simultaneously desires and bars the path to his or her own desire":[80]

> But he, sad man, when he had long in drede
> Awayted there for Britomarts returne,

Yet saw her not not signe of her good speed,
His expectation to despaire did turne,
Misdeeming sure that her those flames did burne.

(3.12.45)

The juxtaposition of these two endings suggests that Britomart's emergence with Amoret from the house of Busirane coincides with the poem's
movement beyond the obsessive passion that has imprisoned Amoret within the "loathed layes" (1590, 3.12.44) of her lover and his dark alter ego.
The breaking of Amoret's "hart-binding chaine"—and, by implication, of
Britomart's—requires that they move into a space beyond both the fantasy
of fusion with the beloved and the despair that necessarily accompanies
that fantasy. The trajectory of book three indicates that it is precisely the
bodily *furor* of female love-melancholy that begins the process of transforming the masculine forms of melancholy that entrap both lover and
beloved in the "wilfull anguish" of *atra voluptas*. Once her own potentially
destructive "furor" is cured by Merlin's integration of her love-quest within
the typological structure of "divine foresight" (3.3.2), Britomart's love-melancholy is transformed into a positive source of energy that frees the romance form from its debt to a paralyzing Petrarchan aesthetic. Merlin's
prophetic interpretation of Britomart's blood (her "bleeding bowels") as
the source of the renewal of "Briton bloud" (3.3.48) provides a powerful
model for an elegiac romance in which hope for the future is balanced
by loss. In its reinterpretation of female blood, it also offers a critique of
Busirane's use of Amoret's "living bloud" as a sign of the "sweet consuming
woe" (3.11.45) that prevents Amoret and Scudamour from entering a true
marriage.

"The End and All the Long Event": Romance Transfigured

John Watkins and Susanne Wofford are both right to insist that Britomart's
triumph over Busirane should not be read in terms of her own increasingly
perfect understanding of her role.[81] As Watkins points out, Spenser "repeatedly reminds us of her failures as an interpreter. . . . '[she] could not con-
strue it / By any ridling skill, or commune wit'" (3.11.54).[82] Nevertheless,
the organization of Britomart's quest around the bodily power of her "immortal wombe" does draw her gradually closer to a full unveiling of the

"terme" or end of her quest. The climax of her quest in Isis church represents the translation of numerous earlier figures in a moment of revelation
that supersedes, but mirrors, Britomart's encounters with both Merlin and
Busirane. The wound imagery that has governed Britomart's quest from
the start, surfacing in the red and white of her blush in Merlin's cave and
the "sanguine red" of Amoret's wound, appears in Britomart's dream as a
sign of mature sexuality and marriage:

> Her seem'd, as she was doing sacrifize
> To Isis, deckt with Mitre on her hed,
> And linnen stole after those Priestes guize,
> All sodainely she saw transfigured
> *Her linnen stole to robe of scarlet red,*
> And Moone-like Mitre to a Crowne of gold,
> That even she her selfe much wondered
> At such a chaunge, and ioyed to behold
> Her selfe, adorn'd with gems and iewels manifold.
>
> (5.7.13, italics mine)

The shift from white to red now has the character of a transfiguration, as
though the earlier instances of this pattern are now fulfilled in the image
of Britomart as Isis, goddess, wife, mother, and symbol of fertility. Thus
although Watkins disputes the notion that we see in Britomart's quest "a
linear progression from girlish ignorance toward a mature understanding
of sexuality," this moment develops Britomart's vision of herself markedly
from the moment when she first views herself in Merlin's mirror.[83] The
emphasis in the stanza on "chaunge" and transfiguration, coupled with
the remarkable use of the dream narrative to allow Britomart to "behold
/ Her selfe," suggest that indeed Britomart's movement toward marriage
does involve a movement toward greater self-consciousness. Rather than
watching blankly as the mysterious "masque" of Cupid passes before her
eyes, Britomart now regards "her selfe," as though she is momentarily both
audience and actor.

Most significantly for my argument, Britomart's mysterious vision of
"her selfe" as Isis culminates in the final transfiguration of the "hysterical"
disease that afflicts her at the beginning of her quest. The figural connection between her "bleeding bowels" and production of a sacred race is
confirmed by the mystical *hieros gamos* presented in the dream. As a dream

of pregnancy and conception ("she soon enwombed grew, / And forth did bring a Lion of great might," 5.7.16), it is this vision, rather than the image of the hermaphrodite at the end of book 3 that represents Spenser's tribute to marital sexuality. The vision is also construed by the priest as revelatory, as a kind of figural "terme" to the whole of Britomart's quest. Tellingly, Britomart's dream discourse reveals her hidden "royall blood" to the priest, just as her blush revealed the truth about her "bleeding bowels" to Merlin:

> Magnificke Virgin, that in queint disguise
> Of British armes doest maske thy royall blood,
> So to pursue a perillous emprize,
> How couldst thou weene, through that disguized hood,
> To hide thy state from being understood?
> Can from th'immortall Gods ought hidden bee?
> They doe thy lingage, and thy Lordly brood;
> They doe thy sire, lamenting sore for thee;
> They doe they love, forlorne in womens thraldome see.
>
> The end whereof, and all the long event,
> They doe to thee in this same dreame discover.
>
> (5.7.21–22)

The notion that the dream discourse reveals to Britomart "the end . . . and all the long event" of her quest for Arthegall indicates the degree to which her quest, like Arthur's, is structured in terms of figural revelation. Unlike the labyrinthine errors of Orlando or Tancredi, the "long event" of Britomart's wandering finds an "end" in this vision: an end "deeply engraffed," as promised, in the productivity of her "immortall wombe." And in the transfiguration of Britomart from virgin warrior to wife, mother and queen within the hieroglyphic figure of the dream, we seem also to behold the transfiguration of romance itself.

Britomart's dream of pregnancy in Isis church is tied tightly to her "reversal" of Busirane's power in book three. The conversion of an "hysterical" epyllion narrative to a typological one permits her both to counter the male version of love-melancholy in the house of Busirane and as a result to fulfill a bodily role that is perfectly congruent with her "heavenly destiny" (3.3.24). The vision of a "Magnificke Virgin" becoming "enwombed" within the Temple of Isis seems to offer a radical reconciliation of the hitherto fractured versions of love as either a bodily, tormenting ill or a transcendent force that moves the lover toward God/Goodness. Whereas Plato (and Ficino) fastidiously separates physical procreation with a woman from intellectual procreation with a male lover, Spenser seems to conflate bodily pregnancy with mental inspiration (the "wondrous vision," 5.7.12) in this complex dream sequence. The priest's therapeutic interpretation of her dream (uttered under the influence of "heavenly fury," 5.7.20) also exalts Britomart's physical role within the scope of a sacred history:

> Then shalt thou take him to thy loved fere,
> And ioyne in equall portion of they realme.
> And afterwards a sonne to him shalt beare,
> That Lion-like shall shew his powre extreame.
> So blesse thee God, and give thee ioyance of thy dreame.
>
> (5.7.23)

Two literary versions of female subjectivity are thus transformed by Britomart's travails over the course of her quest: the hysterical, dangerous heroine of the epyllion; and the passive, absent beloved of lyric, forever "transfixed with a cruel dart" (3.12.31). A new female agent emerges, one whose bodily sufferings are no longer the source of civic chaos, but rather the origin of the "Briton bloud" (3.3.48) that produces the poem's historical "faerie queene." Britomart's "fury," reoriented by the elegiac acceptance of loss necessitated by her reproductive destiny, breaks open the dark phantasmic world of Petrarchan love lyric. By stripping the romance love quest of its debt to Petrarchan *atra voluptas*, Spenser seems explicitly to revise his Ariostan and Tassoan sources. The timeless stasis of Petrarchan melancholia, associated by both Ariosto and Tasso with the labyrinthine *error* of romance, gives way in Spenser's poem to a figural structure that accommodates the pathos of loss through the travails of an embodied self deeply embedded in time.

Conclusion

La Belle Dame Sans Merci: Romance and the Dream of "Language Strange"

As Ian McEwan's fictional depiction of an "enduring love" that is dangerously obsessive and utterly phantasmic suggests, the more extreme versions of love-melancholy are readily recognizable in our modern erotic disorders, in spite of the quite different conception of obsessive illness that supports their diagnosis.[1] The power of the mind—under the pressure of desire—to people the world with phantasms is as compelling a topic for McEwan as it was for Ariosto. I will not attempt, in the pages that remain, to give a full account of how the tradition of love-melancholy gradually metamorphoses into its current forms. Rather, I wish to end with a text that is clearly indebted to the melancholic tradition preceding it at the same time as it subtly turns its interpretation of the "furor" of love in a new and powerfully influential direction. Using Keats's *La Belle Dame Sans Merci* as my focus, I will argue that Keats's poetry is representative of the Romantic poets' recuperation of the melancholic structure of early modern romance as the vehicle for their passionate engagement with the internal world of the imagination.

La Belle Dame Sans Merci belongs to a family of poems that explore the beautiful and sometimes fatal consequences of a passionate love for an otherworldly, phantasmic woman. I am thinking here primarily of *Endymion* and *Lamia*, though as we will see, the sonnet "On a Dream after Reading of Paolo and Francesca" also treats very similar material. *La Belle Dame* reaches back in tone and form to its roots in medieval ballad, but its Spenserian language suggests the intervening influence of early modern romance. Keats's knowledge of Burton's *Anatomy* is well attested and may also inflect his portrait of melancholic love in this poem as it does more evidently elsewhere. In short, the sweet yet sinister pleasures that this poem depicts seem entirely Keatsian, and yet we can also hear in the faery's seductive "language strange" a distilled form of the voice of *atra voluptas* that we have traced from Petrarch to Spenser. From this belated, though archaizing perspective, then, we may hope to apprehend more closely the power of a tradition whose effects still linger with us.

A poem written probably a month earlier than *La Belle Dame* provides striking evidence of Keats's attraction to the dangerous mixture of languor, bitterness, and delight that infuses Petrarch's *atra voluptas*. "When the melancholy fit shall fall," advises the speaker of the *Ode on Melancholy*, "glut thy sorrow on a morning rose" (1.15), or "feed deep, deep upon [thy mistress'] peerless eyes" (l. 20). This voracious sorrow, of course, reminds us of Petrarch's own indulgent self-consumption, and its source is remarkably similar: the necessary transience of earthly beauty and happiness. For Keats's melancholy dwells not just with beauty, but specifically with "beauty that must die." The bitter pleasure of melancholy dwells precisely in the knowledge that what one loves cannot last; yet this is, so the poem implies, the very finest pleasure of all. Like Spenser's Alcyon, Keats is deeply preoccupied with the "vaine and transitorie" nature of the things of the world. But whereas Spenser distances himself from Alcyon's self-destructive "despight," Keats—like Petrarch—shows no sign of renouncing the "aching Pleasure" (l. 23) to be had in experiencing joy in the very moment of its evanescence. On the contrary, the taste of lost joy is precisely what excites the poet's "palate fine."[2]

The melancholic pleasures of loss—this time specifically the loss of love—are also central to *La Belle Dame*. The "haggard and woe begone" knight announces himself from the beginning of the poem as the type of the melancholic lover—alone, pale, and consumed from within by a feverish passion for an object now seemingly forever out of reach. The distinction between the present tense of the lover's ongoing torment ("And this is why I sojourn here") and the past tense of the encounter with the lady ("I met a Lady in the Meads") is poignantly absolute. As this frame material indicates, the poem clearly borrows some of the romance topoi that illustrate the mutual influence of medical and literal portraits of the melancholy lover. Most significantly, the beloved belongs to a phantasmic otherworld: she is a "fairy's child," she sings a "fairy's song" and leads the hapless lover to her "elfin grot." As we will see in more detail later, the knight's beloved recalls the "faerie queene" whom Arthur encounters only once, in a dream, but who ceaselessly inhabits his waking thought thereafter. Unlike the faerie queene, though, this phantasmic lady has a sinister cast that allies her with Ismeno's phantasmic Clorinda. She is entrancingly beautiful, but all too reminiscent of those Circe-like figures who tempt their suitors into an erotic/aesthetic "bowre of blis" only to destroy them:

> She took me to her elfin grot,
> And there she gaz'd and sighed deep,
> And there I shut her wild wild eyes
> With kisses four.
>
> (29–32)

Finally, the lady's otherworldly qualities have a vaguely maternal feel—she feeds the knight and "lull[s]" him to sleep—as though this figure's dangerous nurturance of the knight represents in part the eroticized appeal of the lost mother who seems so often to inhabit the beloved object.

As Susan Gubar and Sandra Gilbert point out, the feeding of the knight with "roots of relish sweet/And honey wild and manna dew" (25–26) seems connected with her honeyed language of love: "And sure in language strange she said / I love thee true—" (27–80).[3] This "language strange" is the latest version we have encountered of the mysterious and imperfectly semanticized melancholic discourse that "discloses an unfulfilled mourning for the maternal object."[4] It is "strange" primarily from the perspective of the knight, for whom perhaps it seems to promise, along with love and nurturance, the "ideal home" of the lost mother.[5] In Kristevan terms, this language is strange because it yearns to "discover, in the mother tongue, a 'total word, new, foreign to the language' (Mallarmé), for the purpose of capturing the unnameable."[6] The lady's "language strange," like her "faery's song," seems to represent the poem's own straining toward a distinctively melancholic Petrarchan voice, the *estrania voce* (estranged voice) whose source is the morbid pleasure (*funesta* or *atra voluptas*) of the poet's longing for an inaccessible Laura.[7] Such a longing is the precondition, or so Keats's own vision of Petrarch suggests, of the poet's access to "the face of Poesy":

> Petrarch, outstepping from the shady green,
> Starts at the sight of Laura; *nor can wean*

His eyes from her sweet face. Most happy they!
For over them was seen a free display
Of outspread wings, and from between them shone
The face of Poesy.

("Sleep and Poetry" 389–94, italics mine)

Though Keats writes unconcernedly of Petrarch's inability to "wean his eyes" from Laura's face (thus evoking once again the connection between the beloved and the lost mother), Ariosto, Tasso, and Spenser all meet the temptations of *atra voluptas* warily, even with hostility. In Spenser's case, the poetry of *atra voluptas* is abandoned, to be replaced with an elegiac mode that refuses to batten on "aching Pleasure." But as this poem already indicates, Keats's attitude seems to be that "art . . . is worth any risk, even the risk of alienation and desolation. The ecstasy of the beautiful lady's 'kisses sweet' and 'language strange' is more than worth the starvation and agony to come."[8]

Harold Bloom has suggested that the Romantic poet "takes the patterns of quest-romance and transposes them into his own imaginative life."[9] I would expand this claim by saying that since these patterns are those of love-melancholy, the Romantic poet's turn inward is marked by an engagement precisely with the "plague of phantasms" that proves so deadly to Orlando, Tancredi, and numerous outlying figures in *The Faerie Queene*. This internalization of certain romance patterns is beautifully illustrated by the relationship between Keats's sonnet "On a Dream after Reading of Paolo and Francesca in Dante's Inferno," his own narrative of the dream that produced the sonnet, and the central scenario of *La Belle Dame*. The continuity between these three pieces is borne out by the fact that they all appear in the same letter; the sonnet and its inspiring dream together in fact constitute a fascinating gloss on the ambiguous nature of the belle dame's allure.[10] There are a number of tonal and verbal similarities between the sonnet and the ballad. Both deal with an encounter with a sweet but mysterious figure in an otherworldly realm; in the case of the sonnet, the woman is Francesca, from Dante's *Inferno*, and this realm is "that second circle of sad Hell." The landscape in the ballad certainly has a hellish cast, and some critics have even divined rather detailed references to the classical underworld in the eerily silent Lake where "no birds sing."[11]

The erotic encounter in the sonnet has a sweet but haunted quality reminiscent of the encounter between the knight and his belle dame:

> Pale were the sweet lips I saw,
> Pale were the lips I kiss'd, and fair the form
> I floated with, about that melancholy storm.

In the ballad, kisses also seem to connote a loss of the real world, this time in exchange for the "wild" world of the "elfin grot" ("And there I shut her wild wild eyes / With kisses four," 32), and paleness is the index of a fatal thralldom ("Pale warriors, death pale were they all," 38).

But the lover in the sonnet is not only a first-person speaker rather than a knight; he is quite clearly the poet himself, whose own dream is the inspiration for the poem. The dream/sonnet thus dramatizes the transposition of a particular topos of quest-romance—the dream or dreamlike encounter with a mysterious lady—into the poet's own imagination. For Keats experiences precisely the kind of dream (of Angelica, Clorinda, or the faerie queene) that prompts the quest romance, not as narrator/spectator but as the lover himself. Whereas Dante stands by and watches as Paolo and Francesca whirl ceaselessly around the "black air" of the second circle, Keats both sees and kisses the lips of the beautiful figure he encounters in his dream. This encounter thus seems to stage precisely the mind's engagement with—seduction by—its own phantasms that is at the heart of love-melancholy. *La Belle Dame*, when considered in its epistolary context, reads like a third version (after the narrative and the sonnet) of the original dream. Such a reading supports the intuition shared by many readers that the knight is a figure for the artist who cultivates the pleasures of the imagination—what Petrarch would call the *dolce error* of imaginative withdrawal—over the harshness of reality. In the ballad the real world is cold and desolate beside the memory of the sensuous "elfin grot"; and although the second circle of sad Hell would seem an unlikely candidate for a *locus amoenus*, the speaker of the sonnet willingly flees the restrictive sounding "dragon-world" for the "melancholy storm" below.

In this newly internalized context, the poet's attitude toward the "melancholy storm" is clearly quite different from that of Dante or of his early modern successors. Though Dante's pilgrim is struck by both the sweetness and the pain of the lovers' plight, he swoons from pity at the end of the episode *as a dead body falls* ("come corpo morto cade," 5.142).[12] The comparison of Dante's body to a corpse seems to sound a warning note precisely against the temptation to identify with Francesca and to become, as she has, a carnal sinner who "submit[s] reason to desire" ("che la ragion sommettono al talento," *Inferno* 5.39). We might also usefully recall Ariosto's deployment of this canto in his description of Atlante's palace, where the lovers wander helplessly ("di su di giù va il conte Orlando e riede" [Count Orlando goes up and down and returns], *OF* 12.10). As D. S. Carne-Ross points out, this structure ("di su di giù / di qua di là) seems to allude to Dante's description of the souls in the second circle, blasted in different directions by the hellish winds ("di qua, di là, di giù, di sù li mena" [hither, thither, downward, upward, it drives them], *Inferno* 5.43). Though Ariosto's is a metaphorical and not a literal hell, there is no question but that the despair that erotic obsession creates in these knights is comparable to that of Dante's sufferers. But in Keats's poem the suffering is greatly lessened, as Dante's "hellish hurricane" ("bufera infernal," 5.31) is transformed into a more pleasurably painful "melancholy storm" in which the speaker "floated"—a gentle verb evoking an altogether gentler experience than in either of Keats's Italian precursors.

The voluptuous pleasure we perceive in the sonnet is unambiguously stated in Keats's own commentary in the letter on the dream-source of the poem. "The dream was one of the most delightful enjoyments I ever had in my life—I floated about the whirling atmosphere as it is described with a beautiful figure to whose lips mine were joined at it seem'd for an age—and in the midst of all this cold and darkness I was warm—even flowery tree tops sprung up and we rested on them sometimes with the lightness of a cloud till the wind blew us away again . . . o that I could dream it every night."[13] Keats's ready submission to the lugubrious pleasures of this dream seems to indicate a willful engagement with the kind of *atra voluptas* (dark pleasure) from which Petrarch cannot tear himself away—the dark pleasure that constitutes a source of both spiritual torment and poetic inspiration. The image of the poet with his lips joined to those of his beautiful (but nameless) companion "as it seem'd for an age" recalls both Petrarch's own eroticized language of feeding and Keats's vision of a Petrarch who, like Du Laurens's melancholic lovers, cannot "wean" himself from the object of his passion. In view of these associations, the intense pleasure that this dream-image produces in the dreamer suggests a regression to a primitive source of satisfaction at the mother's breast. If we turn once again to la belle dame from this dream-narrative, we are likely to feel even more strongly that the knight is "lulled . . . asleep" by a maternal ghost for whom the world is willingly abandoned.

The landscape of Keats's dream suggests that Dante's hell may have passed through a Miltonic revision before it reaches Keats. Eve's dream of Satan in book 5 takes place in a seductive landscape in which Eve finds herself lifted up above the trees (no neutral "flowery tree tops" here, but the "tree / Of interdicted knowledge"):

> [H]e drew nigh, and to me held,
> Even to my mouth of that same fruit held part
> Which he had plucked; the pleasant savory smell
> So quickened appetite, that I, me thought,
> Could not but taste. Forthwith up to the clouds
> With him I flew, and underneath beheld
> The earth outstretched immense, a prospect wide
> And various: wond'ring at my flight and change
> To this high exaltation.
>
> (*Paradise Lost* 5.82–90)

Keats's comfort with his dream of hell suggests an acceptance of what Milton here rejects as a satanic temptation of the imagination. At any rate, Keats's transformation of Dante's descent into the second circle of hell into "one of the most delightful enjoyments" he had ever experienced indicates that Petrarch's *atra voluptas* is no longer a sin to be avoided (the *acedia* of the *Secretum*), but a source of both sensuous pleasure and poetic inspiration. Not surprisingly, perhaps, this reevaluation of the moral status of *atra voluptas* entails a reevaluation of the melancholic patterns of romance. Dante's carnal sinners are led by their reading of the romance of Lancelot into their fateful embrace, and Dante's text suggests that the romance is complicit in their fall: "Galeotto fu 'l libro e chi lo scrisse" (A Gallehault was the book and he who wrote it, *Inferno* 5.137). But Keats's dream suggests no such turning away from its sources in romance, and unlike Eve, who awakens chastened and shaken, relieved to find her dream "but a dream" (5.93), Keats wishes rather that he could "dream it every night."

This dream of Francesca/la belle dame represents a delightful balance between the literary and the psychological; though the dream is presumably "real" and not fictional, it also belongs in a literary history of fictional dreams in which a beautiful but mysterious muse figure entices the lover into an otherworldly realm. It is precisely the value—aesthetic, as well as moral—of that otherworldly realm that is open to question in the early modern romances. Does the dream reveal a kind of "truth" toward which the knight must forever strive (as in Spenser's poem)? Or, as in Ariosto's poem and more ambiguously in Tasso's, does the dream or vision represent a sensual temptation of the imagination that can lead only to madness? The answer to these questions shapes, as we have seen, each author's response to the affiliations between romance and the psychological patterns of love-melancholy. Keats's own dream slips away from him, escaping the structure of the poem that he prepares for it—"I tried a Sonnet upon it—there are fourteen lines but nothing of what I felt in it."[14] In the early modern romances we have read, the evanescence of dreams is one symptom of their profound ontological and epistemological instability. The dream appears frequently as a figure for romance "error" precisely because it is associated with the *dolce error* of illusion. At the crucial moment in his trials, when Tancredi must choose between the "errors" of romance (the phantom Clorinda) and the duties of epic, he is compared to a sick man who dreams of monsters and cannot dispel the illusion (13.44). In both Ariosto's and Tasso's poems, giving in to the dream—with or without any certainty of its truth—is a sure sign that the dreamer is committing an "error" that will lead him further into the dangers of *atra voluptas* and the obsessions that accompany that melancholy pleasure. I will return again presently to the exception of Spenser's use of the dream, in which the dream's epistemological uncertainty is countered by a mystical immanence that converts the romance narrative into an elegiac one. If the belle dame is in some sense a dream figure, a version indeed of Keats's internalized Francesca, it will be useful to consider more narrowly the ballad's treatment of the dream in the context of other crucial moments of awakening in the romance/epic tradition that inform this one.

We are told that at the end of the knight's erotic idyll the lady lulls her knight to sleep in her "elfin grot," whereupon he dreams of hellish figures warning him of his danger:

> I saw their starved lips in the gloom,
> With horrid warning gaped wide,

And I awoke and found me here,
On the cold hill's side.

(41–44)

This cold awakening into a world now utterly changed and no longer sweet and wild seems to be responsible for the knight's melancholic appearance: "And this is why I sojourn here / Alone and palely loitering." In view of the disillusionment that accompanies this awakening—the belle dame is now mysteriously, though definitively, absent—we might wonder about the status of the erotic experience that preceded the dream. Is the dream of warning a "true" sign of the illusoriness of the love that the lady promises? Is the knight, like Spenser's luckless Red Crosse, deluded by a Duessa-like creature and warned in vain by previous lovers as Fradubio warns Red Crosse? In a letter to Benjamin Bailey, Keats famously asserts the truth of the imagination precisely by comparing it to a dream that was found to be in some sense "real": "The Imagination may be compared to Adam's dream—he awoke and found it truth."[15] But the truth of the knight's experience remains ambiguous: when he awakens on the "cold hill's side," we are inclined to wonder whether the whole experience has been a deceptive dream. His awakening reminds us perhaps less of Adam's awakening than of Orlando's, at the close of his traumatic dream of losing Angelica. In Ariosto's poem, the narrator reminds us that the dream material is profoundly unreliable:

A questo orribil grido risvegliossi,
e tutto pien di lacrime trovossi.

Senza pensar che sian l'imagin false
quando per tema o per disio si sogna,
de la donzella per modo gli calse,
che stimò giunta a danno od a vergogna,
che fulminando fuor del letto salse.

[At this horrible cry he awoke and found himself all wet with tears.

Without considering that images may be false when one dreams in fear and in desire, he was so anxious about the maiden who he thought had come to harm or to disgrace, that he leapt from his bed like lightning.]

(OF 8.84–85)

As we saw earlier, it is Orlando's troubled leap from dream to waking action that leads him directly into "l'amorosa inchiesta" (9.7) that structures this romance.

Even the scene of Adam's awakening, as Geoffrey Hartman has pointed out, "skirts . . . traumatic loss."[16] Adam sees "as in a trance" (8.462) the creation of Eve, but his enjoyment of the "spirit of love and amorous delight" (8.477) that Eve exudes is cut short by her sudden disappearance:

> She disappeared, and left me dark, I waked
> To find her, or for ever to deplore
> Her loss, and other pleasures all abjure:
> When out of hope, behold her, not far off,
> Such as I saw her in my dream.
>
> (*Paradise Lost* 8.478–82)

Just at the moment of Eve's disappearance in the dream, Adam wakes *to find her*, but as Hartman suggests, "[T]he caesura's slight suspension [waked / To find her], mimicking expectancy, also insinuates a 'wake / To lose her.'"[17] Milton's syntax also conspires to continue the suspense, as the unexpected alternative "or for ever to deplore / Her loss" distracts us from the more hopeful outcome. Her sudden appearance seems, indeed, too good to be true, and she remains touched by the uncertainty of the dream ("such as I saw her in my dream"). Milton appears to respond in this episode to the losses that characterize romance in particular—the loss of the beloved lady who appears in dream or vision, and more generally the loss of the dreamworld whose power and beauty cannot be recovered. When Eve reappears, Milton hints that in her absence (the romance scenario) Adam would have become a romance lover, bereft but fixated on the lost beloved ("for ever to deplore / Her loss, and *other pleasures all abjure*"). The creation of Eve within the dream evokes the central image that organizes the romances, the "secret wound," as though this dramatic visionary moment will heal the loss at the heart of erotic experience from Lucretius to Freud:

> Mine eyes he closed, but open left the cell
> Of fancy my internal sight, by which
> Abstract as in a trance methought I saw,
> Though sleeping, where I lay, and saw the shape

> Still glorious before whom awake I stood;
> Who stooping opened my left side, and took
> From thence a rib, with cordial spirits warm,
> And life-blood streaming fresh; *wide was the wound,*
> *But suddenly with flesh filled up and healed.*
>
> (*Paradise Lost* 8.460–68, italics mine)

This "wide . . . wound" transforms the figurative "secret wound" of love into a literal wound, one that appears at first to be destructive and dangerous ("life-blood streaming fresh"). But whereas Lucretius's lovers are caught up in a phantasmic world of their own making, Adam is witness here to a dream that is sanctified and guaranteed by its divine author. This dream does not delude, therefore, and the wound itself is made only to be instantly "with flesh filled up and healed."

Milton appears in this scene to banish the specter of loss in Adam and Eve's triumphant reunion by sanctifying the activity of the imagination and thus allowing its full realization in the world. Adam wakes to find that the "creature . . . lovely fair" whom he sees with his "internal sight" is in fact present in the world. The world is consonant with the delights of the imagination—but only because Adam participates "in that celestial colloquy sublime" (8.455) whose aftereffect is the dream of Eve that is no mere dream. Nonetheless, we can hardly forget that Adam in a sense remains wounded, as do all his fallen heirs, and Keats's knight certainly belongs to a distinctly postlapsarian world in which the fantasy of Eve can be nothing more than a fantasy. In the context of this much darker awakening, Keats's claim for the special truth of the imagination seems to mean something different from what it means in Milton's paradise. The knight's awakening into a cold, indifferent world suggests not perhaps that the experience with the belle dame was false, but that its particular "truth" is incommensurate with the real world, just as her "language strange" is untranslatable. Though—as Keats puts it elsewhere in the same letter to Bailey—Adam's dream indicates a perfect consonance between "Imagination and its empyreal reflection," such consonance may be the happy product of the divine Authorship of that particular dream.[18] The knight in the ballad is after all finally left "for ever to deplore / Her loss, and other pleasures all abjure" (*PL* 480) as Adam is not.

In a sense, then, Keats opens up the space of romance loss that Milton's poem deftly skirts, and in doing so he returns us to Spenser's version of a dream encounter that at first blush seems much closer to Keats's own. In the first book of Spenser's *Faerie Queene*, Arthur wakes from his delightful dream to experience the pain of loss that Adam is spared; unlike Adam, Arthur wakes into a newly empty world "for ever to deplore" this loss. It is precisely the absence of the faerie queene that inspires a quest that veers dangerously toward the more overtly melancholic quests of Red Crosse and Timias. The fairy queen seems to promise her love to Arthur in terms that anticipate those of Keats's belle dame:

> Most goodly glee and lovely blandishment
> She to me made, and bad me love her deare,
> *For dearely sure her love was to me bent,*
> As when just time should appeare.
> But whether dreames delude, or true it were,
> Was never hart so ravisht with delight,
> Ne living man like words did ever heare,
> As she to me delivered all that night.
>
> (*FQ* 1.9.14, italics mine)

> And *sure in language strange* she said—
> "I love thee true."
>
> (*BD* 27–28, italics mine)

> And there she lulled me asleep
> And there I dream'd—Ah! Woe betide!
> The latest dream I ever dreamt
> On the cold hill side.
>
> (*BD* 33–36)

But whereas the equivocation of the faerie queene's assertions ("no living man like words did ever heare") is countered, as I have argued, by the figural structure of the narrative ("as when just time should appeare"), the belle dame's statements remain undecidably ambiguous. As Susan Wolfson argues, the claim "sure in language strange she said . . ." only "accentuates the gap between the strangeness of the signs and their proposed translations."[19] The carefully structured episode in *The Faerie Queene*, in which the "nine monthes" of Arthur's quest delivers figurative fruit in his conversation with Una (in the book's ninth canto) reinforces the significance of this dream narrative in the poem's overarching figural structure. But there is no suggestion in Keats's poem that the knight's situation at the end of his telling is any different from what it was at the beginning, as the haunting repetition of the poem's opening lines suggests.

Spenser's description of the "place devoyd" in the grass where the faerie queene had lain in Arthur's dream beautifully distinguishes this moment of awakening from Keats's revision of it:

> When I awoke, and found her place devoyd,
> And nought but pressed gras, where she had lyen,
> I sorrowed all so much as erst I joyd,
> And washed all her place with watry eyen.
>
> (*FQ* 1.9.15)

The place of the faerie queene is empty, and there will be no Miltonic turn toward a newly discovered Eve. But the "pressed gras, where she had lyen" converts this elegiac moment into the purposiveness of the quest; the contours of the faerie queene provide the figural structure that contains and modifies an otherwise "errant" romance quest. Keats's knight awakens into a different world:

> And I awoke and found me here,
> On the cold hill's side.
>
> (*BD* 43–44)

Unlike Spenser's "pressed gras," this "cold hill's side" presents an obdurate blankness to the knight, a blankness realized in the silence and circularity of the poem's ending in the hellish landscape where "no birds sing." Keats's empty hill's side is surely closer to the Petrarchan landscape that may also have served as the inspiration for Spenser's "place devoyd":

> O caduche speranze, o penser folli!
> *vedove l'erbe* et torbide son l'acque
> *et voto et freddo 'l nido in ch'ella giacque,*
> nel qual io vivo et morto giacer volli.

[Oh short-lived hopes, oh mad cares! The *grass is bereaved* and the waters troubled, and *empty and cold is the nest where she lay*, where I have wished to lie living and dead.]

(*Rime Sparse* 320, italics mine)

The "bereaved grass" and "empty and cold . . . nest" are signs, like the "place devoyd," of an absence that promotes the creation of poetry.[20] But while Arthur submits himself to the "sad remembraunce" (1.9.18) of an elegiac quest structured by figural revelation, Petrarch's speaker, like Keats's knight, remains suspended in the melancholic stasis of *atra voluptas*. As in Keats's ballad, there is no movement away from the "place devoyd" by the end of Petrarch's poem, as the opening lines of the following poem reveal: "E' questo 'l nido in che la mia fenice / mise l'aurate et le purpuree penne…?" (Is this the nest where my phoenix / put on her gold and purple feathers…?)

Keats's return to the "aching Pleasure" of loss in his poem indicates a deliberate reopening of the wound of love that Milton takes such pains to heal in his poem. If Milton's revision of romance suggests that the melancholic tendency toward *dolce error* is potentially demonic, Keats's dream dramatizes a willing embrace of that demonic potential. Such an attitude also necessarily estranges him from Spenser's reinvention of romance, which insists on using the figural potential of the "place devoyd" as an antidote to the deadly despair that it also threatens. Keats's poem returns us instead to the phantasmic, hellish worlds of Ariosto and Tasso, and beyond these to Petrarch's powerfully ambivalent portrayal of *atra voluptas*. But whereas these poets clearly recognize the dangers of *atra voluptas* as a spiritual disorder, Keats turns repeatedly to the "plague of phantasms" that accompanies love-melancholy as the deepest source of poetic inspiration. The weeping, sighing song of the nightingale that echoes through Tasso's troubled poem constitutes in that poem a dangerously seductive, if beautiful, appeal from a ghostly maternal figure. As we saw in chapter 4, this song comes to represent in Tasso's poem the ultimately invincible power of romance patterns that are deeply associated with the imperfectly mourned mother. But if Tasso remains clearly ambivalent both toward the lingering power of his *flebil canto* and the maternal figure that it disinters, Keats's portrayal of the belle dame suggests that the ambiguous pleasures she offers are unarguably worth the withering of the world.

Julia Kristeva has written of the "sad voluptuousness" that afflicts the melancholic in his or her awareness that we are "doomed to lose our lives."[21] Though she makes few overt references to the early medical writing on melancholia, this formulation captures quite precisely the fundamental connection we have noted in writers from Petrarch to Spenser between a self-indulgent *atra voluptas* and a revolt against the "vaine and transito-rie" nature of the world. The refusal to mourn the lost object—linked, as Kristeva also argues—to a refusal to *speak* of the lost object, is the primary symptom of what early modern writers call love-melancholy. All the early modern poets we have read acknowledge the roots of romance in the melancholic complex that acquires perhaps its definitive literary form in Petrarch's *dilectoso male*. Spenser's romance, as the latest inheritor of this complex literary/medical tradition, provides the most powerful and coherent revision of the genre's melancholic structure. The "sad voluptuous-ness" that threatens Orlando, Tancredi, and even Arthur and Britomart at times is explicitly rejected; it is the source of Busirane's house of phantasms and Scudamour's "loathed layes" (3.12.44, 1590), but not of the magisterial poem that contains them. In its stead the romance protagonist discovers the force of "sad remembraunce" (1.9.18) as the engine of his or her quest, a process of mourning that permits the substitutive work of the poem's "figural consolation." But Keats's glorification of "Veil'd Melancholy" in the *Ode on Melancholy* suggests that, close reader of Spenser's poem though he undoubtedly is, he will turn away from Spenser's attempt to extricate romance from its roots in melancholic love. As the means for securing (in Kristeva's terms) a "sublimatory hold" over the lost maternal object (the Thing), the melancholy *flebil canto* remains the uncontested source of Keats's most distinctive poetic style. And as the "Ode to a Nightingale" beautifully demonstrates, his pursuit of that song includes a willing submission to the deadly *atra voluptas* that attends it:

> [F]or many a time
> I have been half in love with easeful Death,
> Call'd him soft names in many a mused rhyme,
> To take into the air my quiet breath;
> Now more than ever seems it rich to die,
> To cease upon the midnight with no pain,
> While thou art pouring forth thy soul abroad
> In such an ecstasy!
>
> (*Ode to a Nightingale* 51–58)

Baudelaire said of Delacroix that he was the foremost "modern" paint-er of his time and thus perforce a Romantic. According to Baudelaire, the aspect of Delacroix's style that made him "the true painter of the nineteenth century" (and thus the true romantic), was "the unique and persistent melancholy with which all his works are imbued."[22] The same claim could be made for Keats within the context of romantic poetry; his poetry is also imbued with a "persistent melancholy" that has come to seem the quintessence of Romanticism. Yet reading Keats in the context of early modern romance allows us to see his version of Romanticism as the last stopping place (in our story) of a tradition of love, melancholy, and resistance to loss that is as old as Western medicine itself. But unlike the early modern poems we have studied, where medicine's view of love-melancholy as a deadly illness brings romance into tense but productive dialogue with epic and elegy, Keats's ballad allows the romance world to subsume all others. There is no escape, now, from the Tassoan wood, and the nightingale's song holds both lover and reader alike "in thrall."

Reference Matter

Notes

INTRODUCTION

The passage from Mullen and Pathé is quoted in Ian McEwan's novel *Enduring Love*, 259, which treats what in the sixteenth century would have been called "love-melancholy" in terms of our modern discourse of "stalking."

1. My own investigation of the history of love-melancholy is indebted to a number of studies. Mary Wack's *Lovesickness in the Middle Ages* offers a groundbreaking study of the earliest medieval translations of Arabic writing on lovesickness and their cultural context. Her book is particularly helpful in that it includes new editions and translations of several key texts, including Constantine's *Viaticum* and a number of commentaries on that work. I draw frequently on these editions in chapters 1 and 2. For an earlier seminal work on lovesickness, see Lowes, "Loveres Maladye of Hereos." In the discussion that follows, I have also frequently consulted Ferrand, *Treatise on Lovesickness*; Jacquart and Thomasset, *Sexuality and Medicine in the Middle Ages*; Arnaldus, *Tractatus de amore heroico*; Agamben, *Stanzas*; Heffernan, *Melancholy Muse*; and Schiesari, *Gendering of Melancholia*.

2. Du Laurens, *Discourse of the Preservation of Sight*, 118.

3. Indeed, this disease demonstrates precisely that interdependence of mind and body that strikes Robert Burton as characteristic of melancholy: "[A]s the body works upon the mind, by his bad humours, troubling the spirits, sending gross fumes into the brain, and so disturbing the soul . . . with fear, sorrow etc., which are ordinary symptoms of this disease: so, on the other side, the mind most effectually works upon the body, producing by his passions and perturbations miraculous alterations" (*Anatomy of Melancholy*, 217).

4. Du Laurens, *Discourse of the Preservation of Sight*, 118.

5. Michael McVaugh gives a useful account of this process as it is de-

scribed by Arnaldus, *Tractatus de amore heroico*, 26. See also Gerard of Berry's (ca. 1236) analysis of the etiology of the disease, in Wack, *Lovesickness in the Middle Ages*, 201.

6.   Some authors suggest that melancholy causes the disease; see, e.g., Ferrand: "[T]he melancholy humor, hot and dry through the adustion of yellow bile, blood or natural melancholy, is the principal cause of erotic melancholy or erotic mania, for which reason Aristotle in his Problems says that 'melancholiacs are subject to incessant sexual desire'" (*Treatise on Lovesickness*, 250). Earlier writers tend to see melancholia as a later stage of the disease, following a period of frustrated, anguished desire. See, e.g., Constantine's *Viaticum*, text and translation in Wack, *Lovesickness in the Middle Ages*, 188–89. I discuss the important shifts in the relationship between lovesickness and melancholy in chapter 1.

7.   De Clérambault (1872–1934) was a French psychiatrist who first diagnosed a particular kind of delusional love, now called de Clérambault's syndrome or erotomania. The sufferer is usually a woman who believes herself to be the love-object of a man (normally a man of higher standing) who is personally unknown to her.

8.   Ferrand, *Treatise on Lovesickness*, 238.

9.   Text and translation of Peter of Spain in Wack, *Lovesickness in the Middle Ages*, 219. Wack dates the composition of Peter of Spain's two commentaries on the *Viaticum* between 1247 and 1261 ("New Medieval Medical Texts," 289).

10.   For a full discussion of the *Determinatio*'s relation to Peter of Spain's text, including its use of Aristotelian philosophy, see Wack, "New Medieval Medical Texts." Wack dates the *Determinatio* at some time after 1335.

11.   Wack, "New Medieval Medical Texts," 292.

12.   Fradenburg, *Sacrifice Your Love*, 2. With the usual caveats, Fradenburg dates the rise of this "amorous subjectivity" to the flowering of courtly love in the twelfth century.

13.   Lawrence Babb writes: "There are many melancholic lovers in Elizabethan tradition whose despondencies and debilities are sufficiently explained by literary precedents. Even if one is content to account for them thus, however, he does not exclude an indirect scientific influence. . . . Such a mutual influence probably operated throughout the long and parallel histories of the literary and scientific concepts of lovesickness" (*Elizabethan Malady*, 156–57).

14.   See Chaucer's *Knight's Tale* (*Riverside Chaucer*, 1369 ff.).

15.   See the list of names in the *General Prologue*'s description of the

Physician, l. 429–43. Among other figures, Chaucer mentions Constantine, whose *Viaticum* became a seminal text on lovesickness for doctors in the west. But as Carol Falvo Heffernan notes in her discussion of this passage, it is not certain that Chaucer had firsthand knowledge of these writings, though many of them were available to him. See her chapter "The Book of the Duchess: Chaucer and the Medieval Physicians," in *Melancholy Muse,* 38–66.

16.   The frequency with which Bernard of Gordon finds himself writing "et de hoc ovidius" in his discussion of the cures for love-melancholy is perhaps the most striking illustration of the blurring of the lines between the medical and the literary discourses. See the section titled "cura" in chapter 20, "Amor qui hereos dicit," in *Lilium medicinae.*

17.   Valleriola, *Observationum medicinalium libri VI,* especially 188–90.

18.   I engage in this book with two important earlier studies of melancholia and early modern literature: Schiesari, *Gendering of Melancholia,* and Enterline, *Tears of Narcissus.* But this book focuses less on the disease of melancholia proper than on the intersecting disease of love-melancholy. I also examine, as these works do not, the specific relationship between the medical discourse of love-melancholy and the development of romance as a genre in the early modern period.

19.   The term *assidua cogitatio* belongs to Arnaldus of Villanova: "amor talis (videlicet qui dicitur hereos) est vehemens et assidua cogitatio supra rem desideratam ("this kind of love [that is, that which is called 'hereos'] is a vehement and assiduous thought about the desired object" (Arnaldus, *Tractatus de amore heroico,* 47).

20.   On the importance of *De amore,* Schiesari writes: "Probably Ficino's most influential work, *De Amore* was widely received and admired throughout the European aristocratic court milieu, and its ideas spawned the Neoplatonic poetry so predominant in that milieu from the late fifteenth through the mid-seventeenth centuries" (*Gendering of Melancholia,* 115).

21.   Stephen Greenblatt's essay "Psychoanalysis and Renaissance Culture" has been at the center of a heated critical debate about the applicability of psychoanalytic criticism to early modern texts. See my comments on this debate at the end of chapter 1.

22.   I also benefit here from the excellent studies of the relationship between mind and body in Paster, *Body Embarrassed;* Maus, *Inwardness and Theater in the English Renaissance;* Sawday, *Body Emblazoned;* Stallybrass, *"Patriarchal Territories";* and Paster, Rowe, and Floyd-Wilson (eds.), *Reading the Early Modern Passions.*

23.   Schoenfeldt, *Bodies and Selves in Early Modern England,* 12. The texts

I consider draw on the Neoplatonic/Stoic concept of pneuma, or spirit, to describe the fine substance that mediates between mind and body, and on the basically Aristotelian notion of a quasi-material "phantasm," without which no thought is possible. I am particularly indebted in my discussion of this material in chapter 1 to Giorgio Agamben's useful discussion of what he calls this "pneumo-phantasmology" (*Stanzas,* 90–101).

24. The primary source of my title is Arthur's "secret wound" as it is described in *The Faerie Queene,* book 1, canto 9. In response to Arthur's description of his love-wound in literal terms as a "fresh bleeding wound, which day and night / Whilome doth rancle in my riven brest" (1.9.7), Una replies by turning the wound inward: "Ah curteous knight (quoth she) what secret wound / Could ever find, to grieve the gentlest hart on ground?" (1.9.7). Lucretius also uses the image of a hidden wound in his medicalized discussion of *furor:* "usque adeo incerti tabescunt volnere caeco" (in such uncertainty do they waste away with an unseen wound) (*De rerum natura,* 4.1120). Numerous other figures suffer from hidden wounds that are often described as literal bodily ones: Angelica, whose wound appears as she soothes Medoro's actual wound; Timias, whose bodily wound heals at the hand of Belphoebe, only to be replaced by a figurative wound of the heart: "O foolish Physick, and unfruitfull paine, / That heales up one and makes another wound: / She his hurt thigh to him recur'd againe, / But hurt his hart, the which before was sound, / Through an unwary dart, which did rebound / From her faire eyes and gracious countenance" (*Faerie Queene,* 3.5.42). This last passage reveals the influence of Ficino's theory of fascination, in which he transforms the Lucretian *vulnus caecum* into a literal, internal wound of the heart caused by the blood-borne "infection" passing through the lover's eyes. See *De amore* 7.5.

25. See my more detailed analysis of the etiology of love-melancholy in chapter 1. The term "strange imagination" comes from Du Laurens again, who admits (after a long scientific discussion of melancholia) that something in the disease may be beyond the reach of science: "[W]e observe and find such strange imaginations in some melancholike men, as cannot be referred either to the complexion of the bodie, or to their condition of life: the cause thereof remaineth unknowne, it seemeth to be some secret mysterie" (*Discourse of the Preservation of Sight,* 98).

26. Ibid., 123.

27. Constantine, *Viaticum* 1.20.27–30. Text and translation in Wack, *Lovesickness in the Middle Ages,* 188–89.

28. Jacquart and Thomasset, *Sexuality and Medicine in the Middle Ages,* 86.

29. Burton, *Anatomy of Melancholy*, 657.

30. Burton (*Anatomy of Melancholy*, 154) refers to love-melancholy as "Knight melancholy." On the Platonism of the poems, see, e.g., Tasso's interpretation of love in his *Allegory of the Poem:* "The love that causes Tancred and the other knights to act foolishly, and alienates them from Godfrey, and the wrath that diverts Rinaldo from the enterprise, signify the tension between the rational faculty and the concupiscent and irascible faculties, and the rebellion of these two" (*Jerusalem Delivered*, 471, trans. Nash). Though the disjunction between Tasso's superimposed allegorical reading and the poem's actual treatment of these issues is well known, his recourse to a Platonic model of the soul is a telling means of rationalizing some of the poem's unruly matter. Spenser's Platonism is more fully integrated into the structure of his allegory, which emphasizes the figural relationship between material entities and ideal, abstract forms. I thus agree with C. S. Lewis's hypothesis that in the poem's finished form "Glory would have been spiritualized and Platonized into something very like the Form of the Good, or even the glory of God" (*Allegory of Love*, 336).

31. Staten, *Eros in Mourning*, 3

32. The Arabic concept *'ishk*, which can denote both a melancholic love for a person *and* a striving towards the divine, may have contributed to the idealization of "heroic love." See my remarks on *'ishk* in chapter 1, and Wack, *Lovesickness in the Middle Ages*, 35–38.

33. Johannes Afflacius, *Liber de heros morbo*, circa 1100. Edited and translated in Wack, "The *Liber de heros morbo* of Johannes Afflacius," 328.

34. Burton, *Anatomy of Melancholy*, 657. Mary Wack discusses the similarities and differences between the medical conception of "amor hereos" and the "noble love" of the courtiers ("Noble Love," in *Lovesickness in the Middle Ages*, 50–73).

35. Socrates's allegory of the soul in which reason (the charioteer) is threatened by the appetitive part of the soul (the bad horse) suggests how the soul might succumb to love of the body: "[H]is fellow [the bad horse], heeding no more the driver's goad or whip, leaps and dashes on, sorely troubling his companion and his driver, and forcing them to approach the loved one and remind him of the delights of love's commerce" (Plato, *Phaedrus*, 254 b).

36. Du Laurens, *Discourse of the Preservation of Sight*, 118.

37. I am suggesting not that there are no significant differences between troubadour poetry and Petrarch's lyric sequence, but rather that, as Gordon Braden has argued, "Petrarch writes of possibilities already acknowledged, explored, and graced with the sanction of tradition. His novelty is to some

extent the clarification of that tradition, the definitive exclusion of other possibilities" (*Petrarchan Love and the Continental Renaissance*, 23).

38. The phrase *dolce error* occurs in canzone 129.49.

39. See the section below "*Atra voluptas:* The Dark Pleasures of Poetry" for a fuller discussion of this concept.

40. Staten, *Eros in Mourning*, 11.

41. Ibid.

42. Ibid., 84.

43. Ibid., 90.

44. Jaeger, *Ennobling Love*, 109

45. Wilhelm, *Lyrics of the Middle Ages*, 69.

46. Jaufre Rudel's celebration of the psychological martyrdom of *amor de lonh* prompts Stephen Jaeger to interpret such love as a force that "hallows" the object whose own nobility it strives to emulate: "[T]he lost love of the woman hallows desire. Love ends and is perfected in desire" (*Ennobling Love*, 123).

47. See Wack, *Lovesickness in the Middle Ages*, 62 ff., for a detailed analysis of the similarities and differences between the *De amore* and particular medical writings on love.

48. Staten, *Eros in Mourning*, 76.

49. As Jacquart and Thomasset note: "Medicine constantly underlined the danger represented by an obstacle placed in the way of a natural function" (*Sexuality and Medicine in the Middle Ages*, 174).

50. Giorgio Agamben also notes the disjunction between the medical account of "amor hereos" and the "exaltation of amorous joi so characteristic of the poetry of the troubadours": "We find almost all the elements that characterize the noble love of the poets in the gloomy syndrome 'similar to melancholy' that the physicians outlined under the rubric of amor hereos, but with a negative connotation." *Stanzas* 114—15. But rather than seeing the medical tradition as developing in parallel with, and providing a corrective to, the literary erotic tradition, he sees this poetry as undertaking a "self-conscious reversal of, and defiant challenge to," the recommendations of the physicians. *Stanzas*, 114. But is also surely possible to read the medical "therapies" as offering a corrective to what the doctors perceived as an unhealthy exacerbation of erotic desire in the lyric poems. I would argue therefore that the proximity of the two discourses gradually alters the way the obsessive love of the poets was understood. Certainly by the time we get to Orlando's brutal madness or Timias's degrading "melancholie," the poetic conception of melancholic love seems to be in substantial agreement with the medical one. Mary Wack's

discussion of Capellanus seems to support the idea that medicine was used to undercut the tenets of courtly love: "Andreas appropriates medicine in order to unmask courtly pretensions, to lay bare the libido masquerading as refined love. The thrust of the *De Amore* is anti-courtly, and the blunt realities of medicine are meant to drive the point home" (*Lovesickness in the Middle Ages*, 62).

51.   See Giorgio Agamben's celebration of this *joi d'amor* as the concept that "constitutes the sole coherent attempt in Western thought to overcome the metaphysical fracture of presence" (*Stanzas*, 130). Agamben's acknowledgment that the "essential textual tension of Romance poetry will displace its center from desire to mourning" (129) to recover the love object as already lost comes closer to recognizing the fracture already present in the troubadours' *joi*.

52.   See chapter 1, pp. 26–28, for a detailed discussion of the role of pneuma in the body.

53.   Agamben, *Stanzas*, 23.

54.   Ciavolella, "Eros and the Phantasms of Hereos," 80.

55.   Certain contemporary psychoanalytically oriented writers recognize the striking continuities between modern conceptions of fantasy and the medieval-early modern theory of spirit and phantasm. See, e.g., Slavoj Žižek, whose book *The Plague of Fantasies* takes its title from a phrase used by Augustine in Petrarch's *Secretum*: "pestis illa fantasmatum" (*Secretum*, 64). Augustine's point is that Petrarch's mind is disturbed and distracted by phantasms that block his access to the Platonic/Christian Good, the "summum lumen" (*Secretum*, 66). Žižek undertakes a Lacanian interpretation of the "plague of phantasies" that dominates contemporary culture, focusing on the relationship between fantasy, ideology, sexuality, and cyberspace.

56.   Sarah Kay's Lacanian analysis of courtly love also emphasizes the phantasmic nature of desire as it is expressed in the poetry: "[W]hen medieval poets emphasize how truly unobtainable the love object is, they admit the impossibility of filling the space of the object of desire with anything other than an illusion" (*Courtly Contradictions*, 311).

57.   Laplanche, *Life and Death in Psychoanalysis*, 88.

58.   Beecher and Ciavolella offer this helpful commentary on the psychic state of the lover in Ferrand, *Treatise on Lovesickness*, 150.

59.   See Wack (*Lovesickness in the Middle Ages*, 15–18) for a discussion of the most popular of these stories about incestuous love. Du Laurens duly retells the story: "By all these tokens the great Phisition Erasistratus perceived the disease of Antiochus the sonne of Seleucus the king, who was ready to die for

the love of Stratonica his mother in law. For seeing him to blush, to waxe pale, to double his sighes, and change his pulse so oft at the very sight of Stratonica, he deemed him to be troubled with this eroticke passion" (*Discourse of the Preservation of Sight*, 118–89).

60. Du Laurens, *Discourse of the Preservation of Sight*, 96.

61. Schiesari notes Ficino's emphasis on loss: "Marsilio Ficino is important for having foregrounded the sentiment of lack and loss as the subjective condition of melancholia" (*Gendering of Melancholia*, 111). More interesting for the present study is the specific connection Ficino makes between love-melancholy and *grief*, which he establishes through his use of the story of Artemisia.

62. See Ficino, *De amore* 7.6.

63. I consult primarily Freud, "Mourning and Melancholia," Abraham and Torok, *Shell and the Kernel*, and Kristeva, *Black Sun*.

64. See Julia Reinhard Lupton and Kenneth Reinhard's discussion of melancholia and object loss: "Freud describes the melancholic's desire to devour the lost object as a regression to an earlier object-choice; it is also a regression to an early object-loss, to an infantile experience of mourning. A feeling of unpleasure is projected as external, to be refigured, as Melanie Klein will argue, as the absent, lost mother" (*After Oedipus*, 21).

65. Though I certainly agree with Staten's reading of Plato, I resist his terminology. Because he regards Plato's philosophy as obviating the need to suffer the loss of a mortal beloved, he sees it as advocating the doctrine of what he calls "anti-mourning." He expresses the heart of his argument as follows: "The fundamental terms of the classical problematic of eros are simple, though the logical and dialectical possibilities these terms open up are endless: one may love mutable, contingent beings as such, in which case one is subject to limitless mourning; or one may love such beings as a step on the way to the true, ultimate, and unfailing object of love, in which case mourning is mastered or at least mitigated by a movement of transcendence" (*Eros and Mourning*, 7). More useful for the purposes of this book is the distinction between mourning and melancholia, in which mourning encompasses precisely a "working through" of the loss of a beloved individual in an attempt to "transcend" that loss, and melancholia, by contrast, is the result of a stubborn refusal to do so. Thus, Plato's doctrine represents a "mournful" response to human loss, while the attitudes recorded in the medical discourse on love-melancholy express a melancholic resistance to the transcendence of the object.

66. Quoted in Nelson, *Renaissance Theory of Love*, 87. I am indebted to Staten's discussion of Platonism and Neoplatonism for drawing this reference to my attention. See his reference to Ebreo's dialogue (*Eros in Mourning*, 2).

67. Freud, "On Transience," 288.

68. I use the edition of "Daphnaïda" in Spenser, *Shorter Poems*.

69. Alcyon's attitude is interestingly echoed in Freud's essay "On Transience," which begins to formulate the ideas about mourning and melancholia that eventually appear in the essay of that name. Remarking on a young poet's inability to enjoy the natural beauty before him on a walk, he comments: "The poet admired the beauty of the scene around us but felt no joy in it. He was disturbed by the thought that all this beauty was fated to extinction, that it would vanish when winter came, like all human beauty and all the beauty and splendour that men have created or may create. . . . The idea that all this beauty was transient was giving these two sensitive minds a foretaste of mourning over its decease" (287–88).

70. Boitani, "Petrarch's *Dilectoso Male* and Its European Context," see especially 308–11.

71. The history of *acedia* is extremely complex, since the term undergoes multiple transformations from its earliest usage. See in particular chapters 1 and 2 in Wenzel, *Sin of Sloth*.

72. Petrarch, *Secretum*, 106.

73. *Petrarch's Secretum*, 84.

74. Wenzel discusses the relationship between melancholia and acedia (*Sin of Sloth*, 59 and 191–92).

75. Ibid., 158–59.

76. George McClure comments: "In unifying these types of emotional experience Petrarch was breaking important ground in the history of ideas and emotion. In fusing 'love sorrow' and 'life sorrow' he introduced possibilities for philosophers, literati, and theologians to explore more fully the anatomy of sorrow" (*Sorrow and Consolation in Italian Humanism*, 26).

77. Petrarch, *Secretum*, 156.

78. *Petrarch's Secretum*, 114.

79. See Boitani, "Petrarch's *Dilectoso Male*," 309.

80. Petrarch, *Secretum*, 140.

81. *Petrarch's Secretum*, 106.

82. Petrarch, *Secretum*, 164; *Petrarch's Secretum*, 119.

1. FROM AMOR HEREOS TO LOVE-MELANCHOLY

"Love is a sickness of the mind in which the spirit wanders through emptiness, mixing joy with frequent sorrows." The text and translation of Peter of Spain's *Questions on the Viaticum* are found in Wack, *Lovesickness in the Middle Ages*, 232–33.

1.   I use throughout Sears Jayne's edition of the text of *De amore* (*Commentarium Marsilii Ficini Florentini in convivium Platonis de amore*), and his translation of the text in *Commentary on Plato's Symposium on Love*.

2.   See Ciavolella, "Eros/Ereos?."

3.   For the text and translation of Dino del Garbo's commentary see Bird, "Commentary of Dino del Garbo on Cavalcanti's Canzone d'Amore" (1940, 1941). I use this text and Bird's translation throughout, unless otherwise indicated. This passage occurs in the 1941 essay, p. 130.

4.   See Ciavolella ("Eros/Ereos?," 43–44) for a discussion of previous interpretations of the poem.

5.   The *Viaticum* is an adaption of al-Jazzār's (d. 979) work titled *Kitāb Zād al-musāfir wa-qūt al-hādir* (Provisions for the traveler and the nourishment of the settled). See Wack, *Lovesickness in the Middle Ages*, 34–35 for a discussion of this text, and my brief remarks below, pp. 30–31.

6.   For an essential discussion of the origin and development of the term, see Lowes, "Loveres Maladye of Hereos," 31–34. See also Wack, *Lovesickness in the Middle Ages*, 182–84.

7.   Lowes, "Loveres Maladye of hereos," 34.

8.   I owe this observation to Wack, "*Liber de heros morbo*," 337–38.

9.   Wack, "*Liber de heros morbo*," 338.

10.   Text and translation in Wack, *Lovesickness in the Middle Ages*, 202–3. Agamben (*Stanzas*, 117) argues that the term *amor hereos* clearly derives from a conflation of *heros* and *eros*, while Lowes ("Loveres Maladye of Hereos," 31–33) maintains that it derives primarily from a corruption of the Greek *eros*.

11.   Tasso treats this etymological link quite seriously in his dialogue *Il Messaggiero*: "[I]l nome d'eroe è nome ch'in greca favella deriva da 'amore', perché il vicendevole amore fra l'iddio e l'uomo è stato cagione ch'egli sia nato" (*Prose*, 55). See Ficino's own play on the etymological derivation of hero from eros (*De amore* 6.5).

12.   For the dating of Arnaldus's treatise, see McVaugh's discussion, introduction, 11.

13.   Wack discusses the cultural implications of this aspect of lovesickness in some detail: "Set against the idealization of the beloved object, which is a narcissistic mirroring of the noble lover in the ennobled object . . . there is a loss of inner control and governance in the noble subject, a degradation of the mental faculties expressed in the infantilization or feminization of the lover's body and behavior" (*Lovesickness in the Middle Ages*, 72).

14.   See Arnaldus, *Tractatus de amore heroico*, 50–51. Wack observes that Johannes Afflacius's (ca. 1100) text, the *Liber de heros morbo*, also establishes

this love as a "heroic" force that subjects the lover as though to a lord and master: "The suggestive juxtaposition of loyalty toward a lord and intense sexual love offers an intriguing parallel to the literary convention of love figured as feudal service" ("*Liber de heros morbo*," 338). But although the literary trope of abject love service to the beloved and this medical conception of *amor dominalis* resemble each other, I nonetheless hesitate to agree that "by intimating a connection between the most intense form of secular love and the nobility, the Liber de heros morbo might have contributed to the idealization of passionate love" (Wack, "*Liber de heros morbo*," 344). Although the *Liber* contains notably Neoplatonic passages concerning the "delight of the rational soul in the beautiful object," it also insists on the harmful effects of this passion on the soul of the lover: "The more the soul plunges into these sorts of thoughts [i.e., the 'incessant thoughts' about the beloved], the more its actions and the body's are damaged. . . . If therefore the obsessive thoughts of the patients of heros are not removed, they necessarily fall into melancholy" (trans. in Wack, "*Liber de heros morbo*," 328–29). The medical discourse seems to suggest rather the potential peril to the lover's soul and thus at least to problematize this conception of "nobility."

15.   See my later discussion of the relationship between love-melancholy and hysteria in chapter 6, and Wack, who argues that Peter of Spain's placement of the disease in the sexual organs rather than in the brain "may help to account for its transformation from a 'heroic' malady to a 'hysteric affliction'" (*Lovesickness in the Middle Ages*, 123).

16.   I use the translation of the *Symposium* in Plato, *Collected Dialogues*, 526–75.

17.   See Michael McVaugh on the importance of the Arabic doctors in establishing love-melancholy as a distinct disease (introduction, 14).

18.   Klibansky et al., *Saturn and Melancholy*, 17.

19.   Ibid., 16.

20.   Ficino, *Three Books on Life*, 116–17, italics mine. For an excellent study of the transmission of ancient theories of melancholia into later Renaissance and modern theories of melancholy and depression, see Jackson, *Melancholia and Depression*.

21.   As Klibansky notes, "It was an essentially Platonic thought . . . that *theía manía* in its 'fourth' (erotic) form transcends the prophetic, religious and poetic forms, and becomes the universal power which raises souls to the vision of ideas" (*Saturn and Melancholy*, 17 n. 49). Socrates presents this theory in the *Phaedrus*: "Mark therefore the sum and substance of all our discourse touching the fourth sort of madness—to wit, that this is the best of all forms

of divine possession, both in itself and in its sources, both for him that has it and for him that shares therein—and when he that loves beauty is touched by such madness he is called a lover" (249 e).

22. Klibansky et al., *Saturn and Melancholy*, 18.

23. Petrarch adopts Bellerophon as a figure for melancholic love in both the *Canzoniere* (poem 35) and the *Secretum*; see my discussion in the introduction. Tasso borrows this Petrarchan Bellerophon for his own portrayal of melancholia in his *Il Messaggiero* (see chapter 4).

24. These Greek terms appear in Klibansky et al., *Saturn and Melancholy*, 22 and 24 respectively.

25. For a discussion of the emergence of a biological psychopathology among the "philosophers of nature," see Roccatagliata, *History of Ancient Psychiatry*, chap. 1. He emphasizes the role of Anaximenes (600–530 BC), "who thought that air was the noblest part of matter. It was the breath of life and the principle of existence, and coordinated the organism according to a preordained plan. . . . Later the value of this vitalistic approach was stressed by Diogenes of Apollonia, Praxagoras, and Hippocrates. It had its practical realization in the idea of pneuma, a substance that was the basis of mental life and thereby, through its pathological modifications, the origin of psychiatric disturbances" (85). See also Heinrich von Staden's discussion of the Stoic version of the theory of pneuma: "Thoroughly blended with the body throughout the ensouled entity, this psychic pneuma renders the body capable of sentience, impression, impulse, and in the case of humans, also capable of rational thought" ("Body, Soul, and Nerves," 102).

26. Harvey, *Inward Wits*, 5. I am indebted to Harvey's meticulous monograph for this section on pneuma.

27. Constantine (ca. 864–923), quoted in Harvey, *Inward Wits*, 37. Harvey also notes that the line Constantine draws between the immaterial soul and the material spirit is extremely fine, so that at times he "allows spirit to usurp the functions of the soul" (38).

28. See Harvey, *Inward Wits*, 28.

29. Ficino, *De amore* 6.6

30. Klibansky's description is effective: "In this pneuma there dwells a singularly stimulating driving-force which sets the whole organism in a state of tension (ὄρεξις), strongly affects the mind and tries, above all in sexual intercourse, literally to 'vent itself'; hence both the aphrodisiac effect of wine and the lack of sexual restraint, proper, in the author's view, to the man of melancholic temperament" (*Saturn and Melancholy*, 30).

31. Ibid., 21–22.

32. Ibid., 24.

33. Tasso, *Prose*, 18.

34. Ferrand, *Treatise on Lovesickness*, 251.

35. Du Laurens, *Discourse of the Preservation of Sight*, 119–20.

36. Ibid., 98.

37. Wack notes that although Galen classifies love as a disease of the soul rather than the body, "in Galenic medicine the operations of the soul are a function of the body's humoural composition, so that his view of love is ultimately somatic" (*Lovesickness in the Middle Ages*, 8).

38. See McVaugh: "Antiquity seems not to have reified the condition [i.e., lovesickness] as a 'disease,' or to have focused attention upon it as such; this was done only by Arabic physicians, and it was from their works that the Latin Middle Ages built up an understanding of the condition" (introduction, 14).

39. For a full discussion of Galen's treatment of this case study in the context of its implications for the field of psychophysiology, see Mesulam and Perry, "Diagnosis of Love-Sickness," 548–49.

40. Ferrand, *Treatise on Lovesickness*, 273.

41. As a disciple of Epicurus, Lucretius emphasizes the materiality of the mind and its consequent vulnerability to the sickness of the body: "[M]ust we not admit that mind and spirit are bodily?" (*On the Nature of the Universe*, 3.166, ed. Don Fowler, trans. Ronald Melville).

42. Beecher emphasizes the somatic origins of the disease: "[W]hile the disease could originate with sollicitudo, the determining factor was the constitution of the body, for it was observed that only certain persons, in accordance with the individual temperament, actually succumbed to amorous frenzy or despair" ("Lover's Body," 4).

43. Burton, *Anatomy of Melancholy*, 657.

44. See Wack, *Lovesickness in the Middle Ages*, 34–35 for a fuller discussion of this text. Numerous earlier Arabic doctors comment on excessive love, among them Rhazes (al-Rāzī). Lowes ("Loveres Maladye of Hereos," 17–27) discusses the influence of his work on love (in the *Liber medicinalis Almansoris*), focusing on the commentary by Gerardus de Solo (c. 1330–40). Since I am primarily concerned with later developments in the history of the disease, and thus with the texts that wielded the greatest influence in the West, I cannot do justice here to the full complexity of the Arabic tradition.

45. Lowes notes that a Greek translation of the Arabic text was also available by the time Constantine produced his Latin version, suggesting that he may have consulted both texts in preparing his own. For details, see Lowes, "Loveres Maladye of Hereos," 25–26. More recent philological studies argue

that this is unlikely. See McVaugh's comments, introduction, 14. For my information on Ibn al-Jazzār's text, I am relying on the Greek translation, which is reprinted in Daremberg and Ruelle, *Les Oeuvres de Rufus d'Ephèse*, 582.

46. Wack, *Lovesickness in the Middle Ages*, 186–87.

47. Ibid., 188–89. As Klibansky notes, Rufus's influence on the Arabic doctors—in particular as an interpreter of *Problem 30*—is considerable (*Saturn and Melancholy*, 49 ff.).

48. Ibid., 188–89.

49. The Greek version of the Arabic original is even more clearly Platonic than Constantine's translation: this text refers to the ἐπιθυμία σπεύδουσα, the "striving desire" that grips the lover when he observes the beautiful object (Daremberg and Ruelle, *Oeuvres de Rufus d'Ephèse*, 582). Perhaps this is an argument for the idea that Johannes Afflacius's more overtly Platonizing translation also drew on the Greek text.

50. See Wack, "*Liber de heros morbo*," 328, for the text and translation of the *Liber*.

51. Wack, *Lovesickness in the Middle Ages*, 39.

52. Quotation from Wack, *Lovesickness in the Middle Ages*, 190–91.

53. Agamben, *Stanzas*, 114. See also Introduction, note 50.

54. Wack, *Lovesickness in the Middle Ages*, 188–89.

55. For a discussion of the influence of Arabic medicine (in part via Gerard's translations) on Western culture, see Siraisi, *Medieval and Early Renaissance Medicine*, 14, 188.

56. Avicenna, *Liber canonis*, bk. 3, fen I, tractatus IV, cap. 23. The Latin passage is quoted in Lowes, "Loveres Maladye of Hereos," 22; the translation is mine.

57. Wack (*Lovesickness in the Middle Ages*, chaps. 4 and 5) discusses Peter of Spain and Gerard of Berry's assimilation of Avicennian doctrine. See also McVaugh's discussion of the same issue (introduction, 22–24).

58. Bird, "Commentary of Dino del Garbo" text (1940), 169; trans. (1941), 129.

59. John of Gaddesden, *Rosa Anglica*, 149.

60. Ibid.

61. Gerard of Solo, *Commentum super nono Almansoris*, 34.

62. Du Laurens, *Discourse of the Preservation of Sight*, 119.

63. Daniel Sennertus, quoted in Jackson, *Melancholia and Depression*, 358.

64. Burton, *Anatomy of Melancholy*, 657.

65. Ibn al-Jazzār uses this term in his *Kitāb Zād al-musāfir*, but, presum-

ably because Avicenna's *Canon* became known in its own right via the Latin translation of Gerard of Cremona, it was Avicenna's usage that fixed *illishi* or *ilisci* as a technical term in Latin. As Wack reports, Constantine and Avicenna "were considered the standard authorities on the subject of lovesickness in the thirteenth and fourteenth centuries" (*Lovesickness in the Middle Ages*, 49). Constantine's more ambiguous *eros* was less useful in distinguishing the disorder from other kinds of love. See Siraisi, *Medieval and Early Renaissance Medicine*, chap. 1, for a fuller account of the formation of Western medicine from Arabic texts.

66. See Ioan Couliano's discussion of the relationship between *al-'ishq*, *amor hereos*, and the ennobling love of the courtly poets (*Eros and Magic*, 21–22).

67. Wack, *Lovesickness in the Middle Ages*, 35.

68. Avicenna, *Treatise on Love*, 212–13.

69. Wack, *Lovesickness in the Middle Ages*, 35–38. Maria Menocal's work on the origin of Western conceptions of love in Arabic philosophy and literature is a crucial resource here: see in particular her chapter on courtly love in *The Arabic Role in Medieval Literary History*, 71–91. There are countless examples from Andalusian lyric of lovers exhibiting the symptoms of what came to be known as the medical disorder of love-melancholy. Thus, e.g., the poem by Ibn Zaydun (d. 1070):

> Wishings of passion, save me!
> At my back is death's shade.
>
> Keep the oath that I, by God,
> won't be the one to betray.
>
> Console a mournful lover
> sorrow thinned away,
>
> His nights sickness, sighs,
> worry, and care.
>
> Love wasted him and he became
> too thin to see.

This poem is quoted and discussed in Sells, *Literature of Al-Andalus*, 128.

70. See my discussion below (pp. 41–43) for a fuller account of the estimative faculty.

71. The question as to which power of the soul the disease of love belongs becomes quite technical and varies from author to author. Wack notes the importance of Peter of Spain in clarifying this point: "Peter's answer is that lovesickness is a disease of the imaginative faculty in its beginnings and

initial motion, but in its complete form, is a disease of the estimative power, that is, of the psychological function that determines whether an object is to be pursued or avoided" (*New Medieval Medical Texts*, 290). In any case, as is clear from Avicenna's account of the powers of the mind, the imaginative and estimative powers collaborate very closely.

72. Beecher and Ciavolella, introduction, 151.

73. The work of the imagination is sometimes split between two distinct powers and two regions of the brain. Avicenna's influential account places what he calls the "imaginatio" in the first ventricle, and gives this power the role of receiving sense impressions from the "sensus communis." The imaginative faculty ("imaginative" or "cogitative") in the second ventricle combines and orders these images under the direction of the estimative faculty. See Harvey, "Inward Wits," 44–45.

74. Arnaldus of Villanova, *Tractatus de amore heroico*, 47.

75. Interestingly, contemporary versions of "lovesickness" tend to see the "disorder" of love as primarily a female condition. Thus in a recent review of contemporary theories of lovesickness, Peele notes: "Tennov (1979) developed the proposition that the deficiency was an inbred, bio-chemical trait that made women 'limerent'—or unusually predisposed to form desperate, unrequited attachments to inappropriate men. Liebowitz (1983) explicated the biochemistry of the phenomenon as an inadequate regulation of neurotransmitters (again one that strikes women almost exclusively) which leads to an affective disorder (as per DSM III) requiring antidepressant drug treatment" (*Psychology of Love*, 166). This feminization of love-melancholy supports the view proposed in chapter 6: the gradual somaticization of love-melancholy draws it away from the "masculine" disease of melancholia and toward the "feminine" disease of hysteria.

76. Beecher, Wack, and McVaugh all note the significance of this commentary. See Beecher and Ciavolella, introduction, 71–76, and Wack, *Lovesickness in the Middle Ages*, chap. 3. McVaugh notes: "It may well be that in Gerard's commentary we are seeing the first attempts by the medical community of the early thirteenth century to assimilate the new medical translations of Gerard of Cremona [i.e., translations of Arabic works] to the Constantinian writings that had so long been the staples of the schools" (introduction, 22).

77. Gerard of Berry, *Notule super Viaticum*, text and trans. Wack, *Lovesickness in the Middle Ages*, 198–201, italics mine.

78. Beecher and Ciavolella, introduction, 72.

79. Ibid.

80. Avicenna, *De viribus cordis* 1.5, quoted in Harvey, *Inward Wits*, 26.

81. Ciavolella provides a helpful discussion of this process: "This process of physiological disruption [i.e., the overheating of the estimative faculty and the drying of the imaginative faculty] causes the growth of the melancholic humour—dry and cold—which, once it overflows into the cavities of the brain, fixes the image of the object of desire in the organ of imagination and memory, polarizing the attention of thought itself. Thus the image perceived by the senses remains the only datum present to the consciousness of the lover" ("Eros and the Phantasms of Hereos," 80).

82. I use the edition of the *De anima* in Aristotle, *Basic Works*, 535–607.

83. Giorgio Agamben (*Stanzas*, 76 ff.) quotes this passage and discusses its importance for medieval psychology. Later chapters in his book make it clear that the phantasm itself is the object of the love melancholic's obsession.

84. Emily Michael provides this synopsis of Pomponazzi's argument, quoting his radical conclusion: "'But the human soul is unqualifiedly the act of a physical and organic body, since it has no operation in which it does not depend in some way on the body; and if not as subject, at least as object; when it receives something from that body'" ("Renaissance Theories of Body, Soul, and Mind," 155).

85. I am particularly indebted in this section to Ruth Harvey's clear and detailed exposition of Avicenna's faculty psychology (*Inward Wits*, 43 ff.).

86. As Agamben notes, Plato uses the metaphor of a wax tablet inscribed with images in an influential passage in the *Theaetetus* (191 d-e) (*Stanzas*, 75).

87. Avicenna, *De anima* 1.5.48–53; trans. in Harvey, *Inward Wits*, 45, with some emendations.

88. For a detailed discussion of Avicenna's *De anima* and its reception, see Hasse, *Avicenna's De anima in the Latin West*. Hasse quotes *De anima* 3.8 on estimation: "Estimation presents the form to the soul through the mediation of the cogitative or imaginative faculty. There [at estimation] ends the transmission of the sensible form" (138).

89. Hasse, *Avicenna's De anima in the Latin West*, 132.

90. Peter of Spain describes the process succinctly: "[I]n lovesickness, the estimative faculty judges some woman or some other thing to be better or more beautiful than all the rest, even though it might not be so, and then it orders the cogitative faculty to plunge itself in the form of the thing (tunc inperat virtuti cogitative ut profundet se in formam illius rei) . . . and then the imaginative faculty imagines that thing and sends it to the irascible and concupiscible faculties, which are faculties located in the heart that control

movement. And then these controlling faculties order the faculty of movement, which is in the nerves, to move the limbs in pursuit of that thing"
(Wack, *Lovesickness in the Middle Ages*, 217).

91. I draw here on McVaugh's analysis of the role of the phantastic and
estimative faculties in Arnaldus' *Tractatus* (introduction, 23–24).

92. "Et ex hoc ulterius necessario sequitur quod propter hoc rei desiderium vehemens eius *formam impressam fantastice fortiter retinet* et memoriam
faciendo de re continue recordatur" (*Tractatus de amore heroico*, 46–47, italics mine). See McVaugh (introduction, 26 ff.) for a more detailed analysis of
Arnaldus's account of the mechanism of lovesickness.

93. Bird, "Commentary of Dino del Garbo" (1941), 135.

94. Ciavolella, "Eros and The Phantasms of Hereos," 80.

95. Cf. Agamben's useful perception that "the imaginary loss that so obsessively occupies the melancholic tendency has no real object, because its funereal strategy is directed to the impossible capture of the phantasm" (*Stanzas*,
25).

96. Ciavolella, "Eros and the Phantasms of Hereos," 80.

97. Paster's description of the humoral body suggests the compatibility
of humoral medicine and the "spiritual" psychology I am considering here:
"[F]or the humoral body, all boundaries were threatened because they were
porous and permeable" (*Body Embarrassed*, 13).

98. Agamben, *Stanzas*, 94.

99. "In this curious little book [*De insomniis*] can be found, already for-
mulated at least in its general outlines, the complex of doctrine that, by iden-
tifying the interior image of Aristotelian phantasmology with the warm breath
(the vehicle of the soul and of life) of Stoic-Neoplatonic pneumatology, would
so richly nourish the science, speculation, and poetry of the intellectual renaissance from the eleventh to the thirteenth centuries. The synthesis that results
is so characteristic that European culture in this period might justly be defined
as a pneumophantasmology" (ibid., 94).

100. See Synesius, *De somniis*, 134–40.

101. See Agamben, *Stanzas*, 94.

102. The notion of the spirit as *copula* between body and soul, of course,
returns us to much older theories of pneuma, noted briefly earlier.

103. Del Garbo agrees that melancholic love overturns the body's natural
equilibrium:

> For this passion can alter the body so much that it often causes death which is
> the most terrible of things. But the way love causes death is stated by Guido
> in, *se forte la vertu fosse impedita*, by which he means that love kills when it is

so vehement that it impedes the work of the vegetative or vital virtues of the soul, which conserve life and its operation in the human body. Thus we see that those, who are excessively in love and cannot satisfy their desire, dry up until they are consumed away and are dead; this however happens not only to those in love but to all having a vehement cogitation (*vehementi cogitatione*) and solicitude of the soul. For they thereby have their vital virtues impeded, which are said to help the contrary way, i.e., which conserve life which is the contrary of death. (Bird, "Commentary of Dino del Garbo" [1941], 123–24)

104.   Couliano writes that the "phantasmic vampire has devoured the soul," and the subject is no longer a subject (*Eros and Magic*, 31).

105.   Couliano remarks similarly: "Metaphorically, therefore, it can be said that the subject has been changed into the object of his love" (ibid., 31).

106.   See, e.g., Ferrand, *Treatise on Lovesickness*, 230.

107.   In his discussion of the impact of the "one-sex" model on cultural conceptions of gender, Thomas Laqueur notes the fear that excessive love of women could make a man effeminate: "Men's bodies too could somehow come unglued. 'Effeminacy' in the sixteenth century was understood as a condition of instability, a state of men who through excessive devotion to women became more like them" (*Making Sex*, 123).

108.   Beecher and Ciavolella, introduction, 93.

109.   Valleriola, *Observationum medicinalium libri VI*, 204.

110.   Du Laurens, *Discourse of the Preservation of Sight*, 118.

111.   Ferrand, *Treatise on Lovesickness*, 233.

112.   Giorgio Agamben also regards this remark as a crucial piece of Ficino's theory of love: "The erotic intention that unleashes the melancholic disorder presents itself as that which would possess and touch what ought merely to be the object of contemplation, and the tragic insanity of the saturnine temperament thus finds its root in the intimate contradiction of a gesture that would embrace the unobtainable" (*Stanzas*, 17–18).

113.   "[T]hen from that body of a younger man it shines out, especially through the eyes, the transparent windows of the soul. It flies onward, through the air, and penetrating the eyes of an older man, pierces his soul, kindles his appetite, then leads the wounded soul and the kindled appetite to their healing and cooling, respectively, while it carries them with it to the same place from which it had itself descended, step-by-step indeed, first to the body of the beloved, second to the Soul, third, to the Angel, and finally to God, the first origin of this splendor" (Ficino, *De amore* 6.10).

114.   See Staten (*Eros in Mourning*, 3) on this tension.

115.   Ciavolella, "Saturn and Venus," 175.

116. Ficino, *Three Books on Life*, 115.

117. Ficino, *De amore* 9.6, p. 121.

118. Arnaldus, *Tractatus de amore heroico*, 47.

119. I therefore disagree with Juliana Schiesari's interpretation of the similarity between the two accounts; for her, both passages (the one in *De amore* as well as the one in *De vita*) indicate that melancholia is always associated with the heavenly Venus or with Saturn (*Gendering of Melancholia*, 128). But in fact the passage from the *De amore* (Jayne ed., 121) continues just beyond Schiesari's excerpt by saying unequivocally that "these things are accustomed to happen to those, who, having abused love, converted what is a desire for contemplation into a desire for embrace" (*De Amore* 6.9). The similarity between the two passages thus reveals, as I argue here, a fundamental discrepancy within Ficino's thought that arises from the dual nature of melancholia itself.

120. Couliano notes the relationship between Ficino's phantasmic theory of desire and Jung's psychology: "We do not love another object, a stranger to ourselves, Ficino thinks (*Amore* 6.6), thus anticipating the analytic psychology of Carl Jung. We are enamored of an unconscious image" (*Eros and Magic*, 31).

121. Fink, *Lacanian Subject*, 95, discusses the Freudian concept of *das Ding* as a forerunner of Lacan's *objet a*.

122. For an account of the "hypothetical mother-child unity," see Fink, *Lacanian Subject*, 59–60 and 94. Jacobus uses this formulation in the spirit of critique. Her sympathies are with precisely the "mother-identified" psychoanalytic texts that reassess the symbolic role of the mother. See her *First Things*, iv.

123. Laplanche, *Love and Death in Psychoanalysis*, 88.

124. Agamben, *Stanzas*, 25.

125. Kristeva, *Black Sun*, 63.

126. Ibid.

127. Greenblatt argues for this incompatibility not on the grounds of anachronism but, more bizarrely, on the basis that psychoanalysis is causally belated: "If psychoanalysis was, in effect, made possible by (among other things) the legal and literary proceedings of the sixteenth and seventeenth centuries, then its interpretive practice is not irrelevant to those proceedings, nor is it exactly an anachronism. But psychoanalytic interpretation is causally belated, even as it is causally linked: hence the curious effect of a discourse that functions as if the psychological categories it invokes were not only simultaneous with but even prior to and themselves the causes of the very phenomena of which in

actual fact they were the results" ("Psychoanalysis and Renaissance Culture," 221). Several writers have ably responded to Greenblatt's critique of psychoanalysis. For responses to Greenblatt, see in particular Skura, "Understanding the Living and Talking to the Dead"; and Enterline, *Tears of Narcissus*, 325 n. 31. Schiesari's psychoanalytic reading of melancholia in the early modern period offers a robust challenge to Greenblatt's thesis, since she both historicizes psychoanalysis and suggests, as I do, a continuity between psychoanalysis and earlier theories of mind: "If, as Greenblatt states, the Renaissance is that period that undertakes the 'prepsychoanalytic fashioning of the proprietary rights of selfhood' that makes the later invention of psychoanalysis possible, then psychoanalysis is indeed capable of shedding some light on the literature of that period. Moreover, the psychoanalytic reading of such texts—also and necessarily—transforms the very theory that carries out the interpretation through contact with those texts that seem to prefigure psychoanalytic categories" (*Gendering of Melancholia*, 25).

128. Greenblatt, "Psychoanalysis and Renaissance Culture," 216.

2. VULNUS CAECUM

1.   Stanley Jackson does note a shift toward acknowledging the relationship between grief and melancholia at the beginning of the seventeenth century. He cites Felix Platter's assertion that "'Sadness or vehement Grief lasting long' could 'beget a Melancholick Perturbation of the Mind'" (*Depression and Melancholia*, 317). One exception to this rule is Ishāq ibn 'Imran, who, as Jackson observes, does include grief as a possible cause of melancholia. Constantine's *De melancholia* (based on 'Imran's text) reproduces this connection: those, he says, "rem preciosam quam restaurare non possunt" (who have lost some precious thing that they cannot restore) are inclined to fall into melancholia ("*De melancholia, libri duo*," 284).

2.   Kristeva, *Black Sun*, 12. The most significant psychoanalytic texts for the purposes of this discussion are Freud, "Mourning and Melancholia"; Kristeva, *Black Sun*; Abraham and Torok, *Shell and the Kernel*.

3.   See introduction, p. 12, and note 66.

4.   Quotations and translations, unless otherwise noted, are taken from R. Brown, *Lucretius on Love and Sex*.

5.   I am indebted here to Don Fowler's very useful summary of this Epicurean doctrine in his introduction to Lucretius's *On the Nature of the Universe*, xxi–xxiii.

6.   As we noted at the end of chapter 1, there are clear points of contact between this conception of desire (as a displaced form of orality) and psycho-

analytic theories of desire. For Laplanche, as we have seen, all sexual desire is "propped" on the craving for food, and is thus both doomed to disappointment and essentially phantasmic in nature: "In the very act of feeding, the process of propping may be revealed in a culminating satisfaction that already resembles orgasm; but above all, in an immediately subsequent phase, we witness a separation of the two, since sexuality, at first entirely grounded in the function, is simultaneously entirely *in the movement which disassociates it* from the vital function. . . . Henceforth, the object is abandoned, the aim and the source also take on autonomy in relation to the activity of feeding and the digestive system." Laplanche goes on to interpret this understanding of sexuality as follows: "[I]t means that *on the one hand there is from the beginning an object, but that on the other hand sexuality does not have, from the beginning, a real object.* It should be understood that the real object, milk, was the object of the function, which is virtually preordained to the world of satisfaction. Such is the real object which has been lost, but the object linked to the autoerotic turn, the breast—become a fantasmatic breast—is, for its part, the object of the sexual drive" (*Life and Death in Psychoanalysis*, 18–20).

7.   Virgil attributes *dira cupido* to Dido, and his development of her deadly passion in fact owes much to these Lucretian passages.

8.   François Valleriola, who is a remarkably close reader of Ficino, seems to intuit precisely this convergence. In his *Observationum* (1588) he revises Ficino's incorporation of Lucretius, replacing the lines on the *simulacrum* that make the identification between the *simulacrum* and the phantasm clear:

> Quod Lucretius scite admodum libro de rerum natura quarto explicasse est visus, inquiens:
>
> > *Hinc illae primum veneris dulcedinis in cor*
> > *Stillavit gutta, et successit fervida cura.*
> > *Nam si abest quod ames, presto simulachra tamen sunt*
> > *Illius, et nomen dulce obversatur ad aureis.*
>
> Qua vero spiritalis ille vapor a sanguine elaboratissimo genitus, et dulcis quoque ipse est, sanguinis unde manavit natura referens: ea sane ratione *fit ut viscera quodamodo pascat*, foveat, atque oblectet. quo fit, ut amantium desiderium atque; cupiditas inde mira excitetur, quum *amans amatae appetat corpus.* (Valleriola, *Observationum*, 201–2, italics mine)

9.   R. Brown, *Lucretius on Love and Sex*, 21.

10.   Ibid., 24.

11.   As we saw in chapter 1 (pp. 47–51), Ficino's theory of the penetration of the mind by the spirits applies not only to the obvious "infection" of vulgar

love, but also more controversially to the erotic ascent of divine love (see *De amore* 6.10).

12. Ficino, *De amore* 7.13, italics mine.

13. Schiesari (*Gendering of Melancholia*, 131) notes Ficino's pervasive distrust of mourning.

14. Valleriola, *Observationum*, 200.

15. See Beecher and Ciavolella's comment on this tendency in Jacques Ferrand's treatise: "[W]hile Ferrand concerns himself with men driven mad by their erotic impulses, by their corrupted spirits and perverted judgments, he also understands that their symptoms are synonymous with those described in the lyrics of the love poets. Perhaps the line may be drawn between the eroticized fanatic who loses touch with reality in a riot of mind and the erotic visionary who revels in the anxieties of verse, but in Ferrand's terms that demarcation is nearly invisible. The Italian love poets had taught him to accept the witness of the poets concerning the sweet misery of an unattainable love as an accurate transcription of the melancholy mind" (*Treatise on Lovesickness*, 150–51).

16. Petrarch, *Secretum*, 164; *Petrarch's Secretum*, 119.

17. See Staden, "Body, Soul, and Nerves," 99.

18. Martha Nussbaum, *Therapy of Desire*, 177, italics mine.

19. See note 1 for the source of the "precious thing" of my subtitle.

20. Freud, "Mourning and Melancholia," 174. The second use of the figure of the wound occurs at the end of the essay: "The conflict in the ego, which in melancholia is substituted for the struggle surging around the object, must act like a painful wound which calls out unusually strong anti-cathexes" (179).

21. Ibid., 173.

22. Ibid., italics mine.

23. Freud, "On Transience," 287–90.

24. Ibid., 288. Julia Kristeva sees in the essay a tentative theory of the sublimation of grief: "[B]y linking the themes of mourning, transience, and beauty, Freud suggested that sublimation might be the counterpoise of loss, to which the libido so enigmatically fastens itself. Enigma of mourning or enigma of the beautiful? And what is their relationship?" (*Black Sun*, 98).

25. For an interesting discussion of Freud's essay in the context of earlier treatments of melancholia (including those of Aristotle and Ficino), see Schiesari, *Gendering of Melancholia*, 36–63.

26. Freud, "Mourning and Melancholia," 164. The notion that mourning, unlike melancholia, is teleological is underscored in the earlier essay:

"Mourning, as we know, however painful it may be, comes to a spontaneous end. When it has renounced everything that has been lost, then it has consumed itself, and our libido is once more free (insofar as we are still young and active) to replace the lost objects by fresh ones equally or still more precious" ("On Transience," 290).

27. Freud, "Mourning and Melancholia," 166.

28. Ibid., 171.

29. Ibid., 170.

30. "Along with the demolition of the Oedipus complex, the boy's object-cathexis of the mother must be given up" (Freud, "Ego and the Super-Ego," 32). Sacks writes interestingly of the analogy between successful Oedipal resolution and mourning: "At the core of each procedure is the renunciatory experience of loss and the acceptance, not just of a substitute, but of the very means and practice of substitution" (*English Elegy*, 8). See also Ferguson's discussion of the relationship between a defensive identification with the mother during the Oedipal crisis and melancholia (*Trials of Desire*, 123–24).

31. "We have come to understand that this kind of substitution has a great share in determining the form taken by the ego and that it makes an essential contribution towards building up what is called its 'character'" (Freud, "Ego and the Super-Ego," 28). See also Lynn Enterline's useful discussion of Freud's second thoughts on melancholia (*Tears of Narcissus*, 21–23).

32. Freud, "Ego and the Super-Ego," 29. Jonathan Lear's discussion of the role of melancholia in psychic formation is useful here: "[T]he identificatory processes by which the it's loves are abandoned and re-created in the developing I involve a 'desexualization.' It is not just that the love-object has been given up; libidinal energy has been transformed into psychic structure. Love's compensation to humans for living in a world of distinct love-objects is to fuel the process by which they develop into individual I's. One might thus think of psychic structure as *structured love*" (*Love and Its Place in Nature*, 165).

33. Lear, *Love and Its Place in Nature*, 161.

34. Freud, "Ego and the Super-Ego," 29.

35. Though she does not discuss Lucretius' analysis of love and sex, Theresa Krier provides an interesting account of the pervasive images of maternity elsewhere in Lucretius' poem (*Birth Passages*, esp. 172–82. Her focus on a narrative of "nostalgia for an archaic mother" (20) is certainly relevant to my argument in this book.

36. Enterline emphasizes the implications of the continuing identification with the mother for masculinity: "If consolidation of masculine identity turns, as Freud argued, on a son's obeying the father's command to renounce love

for his mother, then his analysis of melancholia in *The Ego and the Id* suggests that such giving up would operate only when the son identifies with precisely the woman he is to renounce. He identifies, that is, with the woman who will be signified to him as lacking parts, as a mutilated version of himself" (*Tears of Narcissus*, 22).

37.   Freud, "Ego and the Super-Ego," 32.

38.   For Freud, of course, this degradation is largely a result of the subject's own self-denigration, while for Ficino the melancholic lover's sexual obsession causes him to "sink back to the nature of beast" (*De amore* 7.12).

39.   Freud, "Ego and the Super-Ego," 30. Freud notes the centrality of the transformation of sexual-object libido into narcissistic libido for all sublimation: "The transformation of object-libido into narcissistic libido which thus takes place obviously implies an abandonment of sexual aims, a desexualiza-tion—a kind of sublimation, therefore. Indeed, the question arises, and deserves careful consideration, whether this is not the universal road to sublimation, whether all sublimation does not take place through the mediation of the ego which begins by changing sexual object-libido into narcissistic libido and then, perhaps, goes on to give it another aim" (30).

40.   Lear, *Love and Its Place in Nature*, 163.

41.   Abraham and Torok, *Shell and the Kernel*, chap. five.

42.   Abraham and Torok quote from Ferenczi's formulation of this distinction: "'I described introjection as an extension to the external world of the original autoerotic interests, by including its objects in the ego. . . . In principle, man can love only himself; if he loves an object he takes it into his ego. . . . I used the term 'introjection' for all such growing onto, all such including of the loved object in, the ego" (ibid., 112).

43.   "It is not at all a matter of 'introjecting' the object, as is all too commonly stated, but of introjecting the sum total of the drives, and their vicissitudes as occasioned and mediated by the object. According to Ferenczi, introjection confers on the object, and on the analyst, the role of mediation toward the unconscious . . . introjection transforms instinctual promptings into desires and fantasies of desire, making them fit to receive a name and the right to exist and to unfold in the objectal sphere" (ibid., 113).

44.   Ibid.

45.   Ibid, 114.

46.   "Like a commemorative monument, the incorporated object betokens the place, the date, and the circumstances in which desires were banished from introjection: they stand like tombs in the life of the ego" (ibid.).

47.   Ibid., 113.

48. Kristeva, *Black Sun*, 41.

49. Abraham and Torok, *Shell and the Kernel*, 128.

50. Kristeva, *Black Sun*, 12.

51. See also Shoshana Felman, who emphasizes that the Symbolic is "a network of equations between . . . substitutes. Language is, precisely, a relation between substitutes. . . . Thus . . . introjection is not simply the symmetrical displacement of an object from the outside to the inside, but a movement from the outside to the inside of an object's name, that is, the assumption by the ego of a relation between a named object and a system of named objects. Introjection, says Lacan, is always a linguistic introjection, in that it is always the introjection of a relation" (*Jacques Lacan and the Adventure of Insight*, 115).

52. Kristeva, *Black Sun*, 53.

53. Felman, *Jacques Lacan and the Adventure of Insight*, 115.

54. For a succinct account of the relationship between the Imaginary and Symbolic, see Felman, *Jacques Lacan and the Adventure of Insight*, 104.

55. Du Laurens, *Discourse of the Preservation of Sight*, 96, italics mine.

56. Valerius Maximus, *Factorum et dictorum memorabilium libri novem*, quoted in Beecher and Ciavolella, introduction, 48–49.

57. Wack, *Lovesickness in the Middle Ages*, 154.

58. Mary Wack also suggests that various childrearing practices might have contributed to the medieval medical portrayal of lovesickness: "[T]he medieval aristocracy, the class most subject to lovesickness, was exposed to significant disruptions of the affectional bonds between children and their attachment figures, whether mothers or wetnurses. As a consequence, anxiety, anger, and hostility toward maternal figures may well have complicated their feelings of love" (ibid., 161).

59. Paster, *Body Embarrassed*, 261.

60. "The universally-recognized symptom of lovesickness in the Middle Ages, wasting from failure to eat, is associated . . . with the feminine and the maternal" (Wack, *Lovesickness in the Middle Ages*, 151). Freud also notes a refusal of food as a symptom of melancholia and links this to the broader pattern of self-destruction occasioned by the subject's covert identification with a loved/hated object: "This picture . . . is completed by sleeplessness and refusal of nourishment, and by an overthrow, psychologically very remarkable, of that instinct which constrains every living thing to life" ("Mourning and Melancholia," 167).

61. Krier, *Birth Passages*, 13.

62. Ibid. As we shall see in chapter 4, Tasso's portrayal of Tancredi's eroti-

cized battle with Clorinda demonstrates especially clearly a failure to acknowledge separation from the mother. As Krier argues, "It is in not acknowledging parturition that fantasies of fusion with an archaic mother arise" (13).

63. Wack, *Lovesickness in the Middle Ages*, 201–2.

64. Cited in Wack, *Lovesickness in the Middle Ages*, 302, italics mine. The translation is mine.

65. Bernard of Gordon, *Lilium Medicinae*, 1486, 49; my translation. Bernard lifts this passage almost verbatim from Gerard of Berry's *Glosses on the Viaticum*, ca. 1236.

66. Burton, *Anatomy of Melancholy*, 722.

67. Wack, *Lovesickness in the Middle Ages*, 190–91, italics mine.

68. Michael Schoenfeldt demonstrates how central the notion of temperance was for Galenic medicine: "In its emphasis on temperance as a central strategy for the maintenance of physiological and psychological health, locating both at the mid-point of unhealthy extremes, Galenic physiology provides a compelling model of just how good health could emerge from good living" (*Bodies and Selves*, 7).

69. Klibansky et al., *Saturn and Melancholy*, 21.

70. Heinrich von Staden's discussion of pneuma mentions one theory (attributed to Chrysippus) in which "the same kind of psychic pneuma [extends] like the tentacles of an octopus or like a spider's web from the ruling part of the psyche, in the heart, to its local organs such as the eye, ear, nose, *tongue, larynx*, genitals, etc." ("Body, Soul, and Nerves," 103, italics mine). In a similar vein, Giorgio Agamben has noted the inclusiveness of the doctrine of pneumatic circulation in Aristotle and the Stoic medical writers: "Thus one single pneumatic circulation animates the intelligence, the voice, the sperm, and the five senses" (*Stanzas*, 92).

71. Agamben draws attention to the importance of Aristotle's link between voice and phantasm: "The semantic character of human language is thus explained by Aristotle in terms of the psychological theory that we know, with the presence of a mental image or phantasm, so that, if we wish to transcribe into Aristotelian terms the algorithm now usually used to represent the notion of sign (S/s, where s is the signifier and S the signified), it would be configured as follows: P/s, where s is sound and P the phantasm" (*Stanzas*, 125).

72. Smith, *Acoustic World of Early Modern England*, 100.

73. Crooke, *Microcosmographia: A Description of the Body of Man* (1616), quoted in Smith, *Acoustic World of Early Modern England*, 100.

74. Agamben notes this distinction between medical and poetic treatments of love; as he notes, the poets often seem to deploy the various therapies

advanced by the doctors (such as walking in a *locus amoenus*) as ways of further exalting their love (*Stanzas*, 114–15).

75. See in particular chapter 4, the section entitled "Il Flebil Canto."

76. Agamben (*Stanzas*, 114) refers to this passage in Valescus's text to suggest that the poets lifted their inspiration for the trope of the *locus amoenus* from the doctors' very different usage of it. As I argue in chapter 1 (p. 33), the literary-medical influence seems to me to flow in both directions.

77. Wack, *Lovesickness in the Middle Ages*, 64.

78. Kristeva, *Black Sun*, 65. Kristeva develops her notion of the semiotic in conjunction with Freud's concept of primary processes: "This modality [the semiotic] is the one Freudian psychoanalysis points to in postulating not only the facilitation and the structuring disposition of drives, but also the so-called primary processes which displace and condense both energies and their inscription" (264 n. 24).

79. Kristeva, *Black Sun*, 53, italics mine.

80. Ibid., 51.

81. Ibid., 22.

82. Ibid., 62.

83. Ibid., 264 n. 24.

84. Burton, *Anatomy of Melancholy*, 722.

85. Kristeva, *Black Sun*, 97.

86. Ibid., 64.

87. I use throughout Durling's edition and translation of Petrarch's *Rime Sparse*. I refer interchangeably to the *Rime Sparse* and the *Canzoniere*.

88. See my introduction, pp. 13–16, and Piero Boitani, "Petrarch's *Dilectoso Male* and Its European Context."

89. Text in *Prose, Secretum*, 106; translation in *Petrarch's Secretum*, 84.

90. Kristeva, *Black Sun*, 42.

91. Ibid., 53.

92. I owe this observation to Boitani, Petrarch's *Dilectoso Male* and Its European Context," 309.

93. I use throughout the text and translation of Ovid's *Metamorphoses* in the Loeb Classical Library edition.

94. Greene, *Light in Troy*, 123.

95. I use the Loeb Classical Library edition of Virgil's *Georgics*.

96. Greene, *Light in Troy*, 123.

97. Lupton and Reinhard, *After Oedipus*, 171.

98. Petrarch, *Secretum*, 64–66, translation mine, quoted with discussion in Wenzel, *Sin of Sloth*, 156.

3. SOLVITE ME

1.   Of the many critical readings that deal with Atlante's palace, the most important for my argument are Quint, "Figure of Atlante"; Parker, *Inescapable Romance*, 16–53; Carne-Ross, "One and the Many" (1976); and Ascoli, *Ariosto's Bitter Harmony*, 37–38.

2.   An important exception to this statement is Elizabeth Jane Bellamy's psychoanalytic reading of the poem. She argues that "the aggressive search for the object becomes the principle of psychic organization for the vast economy of narcissism that constitutes Ariosto's labyrinthine narrative" (*Translations of Power*, 86–87). While I find much of what Bellamy has to say about the poem intuitively plausible, I situate the psychodynamic structure of the poem in historically contemporary conceptions of mind, reading Orlando's "search for the object" in terms of a melancholic obsessiveness (the pursuit of the internalized phantasm) rather than a Freudian narcissism.

3.   See, in particular, Parker's discussion of the aesthetic and epistemological consequences of the "errant" structure of Ariosto's poem: "'Error' is not only a romance pun, sign of the interplay between mental and geographical 'wandering'; it is also the concept which connects the diverse aspects of a long and complex poem" (*Inescapable Romance*, 20). For contemporary accounts of the formal qualities of Ariostan romance, see Weinberg, *History of Literary Criticism*, vol. 2, esp. 954–1073. D. S. Carne-Ross offers an influential early discussion of the meaning of "error" in the poem: "The different senses of *errare*, or *errore*—intellectual misjudgment, emotional enslavement, physical movement—are all present in canto 1 and indeed govern its narrative content. . . . And the conduct of almost every character in the canto involves 'error' in one or more of the three senses of the word" ("One and the Many" [1966], 200).

4.   Critical discussions of Orlando's madness usually remain quite general, referring broadly to classical conceptions of love-madness. See in particular Ascoli, *Ariosto's Bitter Harmony*, 355–56. My contention is that Orlando's madness is rooted in a conception of love as a melancholic disease, and that the etiology and trajectory of his *furor* reflect their origins in the tradition of erotic melancholia. Jane E. Everson's account of Orlando's madness is typical in not distinguishing between classical portrayals of *furor* and Ariosto's deployment of a *furor* inflected by the complex early modern medico-philosophical conception of love-melancholy that passed through Ficino and others: "[I]n respect of love Ariosto in fact returns this theme to a classical foundation with his equation of love as madness, *furor*, always and in everyone. . . . Ariosto's

lovers exemplify as fully as any in Ovid's *Metamorphoses* this most ambivalent and irresistible emotion" (*Italian Romance Epic in the Age of Humanism*, 347). Elissa Weaver provides a useful summary of the features shared by three stories of love madness in Ariosto's poem (those of Orlando, Bradamante and Rodomonte), but again without exploring the contemporary medical understanding of this madness ("Reading of the Interlaced Plot," 131–36).

5. For more details, see note 10. For a comparison of the variations among the 1516, 1521, and 1532 editions of the poem, I consult *Orlando Furioso*, edited by Santorre Debenedetti and Cesare Segre.

6. I use the edition of Virgil's *Eclogue* in Loeb Classical Library: *Eclogues, Georgics, Aeneid.*

7. The significance of the allusion to the *Eclogue* has to a large extent eluded readers of the Italian poem; indeed, critics have searched for alternative sources for the allusion in an effort to make clearer sense of its force in this new context. Some critics have noted a possible reference to Seneca's *Hercules Furens* here, e.g., Parker, who notes the relevance of the line referring to the cure of Hercules' madness (*HF* 1063): "solvite tantis animum monstris" (*Inescapable Romance*, 248). Ascoli picks up this cue and argues for the importance of the Senecan drama as a source for this moment as well as for the shape of Orlando's madness more broadly (*Ariosto's Bitter Harmony*, 60). The language of the allusion, however, is that of Virgil's text, and though I do not discount the obvious relevance of *Hercules Furens* (for the title of Ariosto's text, among other things), it is from Virgil's mysterious Lucretian mini-epic that Orlando's cure draws its significance.

8. Quint, "Figure of Atlante," 87. The relationship between epic and romance elements in Ariosto's poem has been of concern to critics since the poem's first appearance. Contemporary critical accounts of the issue include Patricia Parker's influential insistence that epic closure is continually subverted by romance (*Inescapable Romance*, 38–39), a reading seconded by Ascoli (*Crisis and Evasion*, 363–64). David Quint maintains that epic permanently overmasters romance after the destruction of Atlante's palace, but his argument differs considerably from mine in its claim that this turn toward epic is presented as unambiguously positive: a move away from the avoidance and procrastination of romance ("Figure of Atlante," 77–91). My argument also takes issue with Daniel Javitch's contention that romance and epic strains are deliberately juxtaposed and harmonized in the poem: "Ariosto's fusion of Virgilian and medieval romance elements was an effort to demonstrate how these two narrative strains could be effectively united to produce a new sort of heroic poetry whose originality lay in this very syncretism" ("Grafting of Virgilian Epic in *Orlando Furioso*," 72).

9.   This reading is supported by the fact that, as Parker points out, Atlante was frequently allegorized as "Amore" (*Inescapable Romance*, 21).

10.   D. S. Carne-Ross notes these changes, suggesting that the palace represents a development of the dream vision: "In the original version of the poem, published in 1516, this [the dream] was immediately followed by the scene in Atlante's palace which developed his dream vision of Angelica in danger, even though the distressed figure he saw there was not Angelica herself but only a phantom resembling her" ("One and the Many" [1976], 147). Peter Marinelli recognizes the allegorical import of the connection between the dream and the palace, though without placing his observation in the context of contemporary (to Ariosto) conceptions of mind: "In both the 1516 and 1521 editions, Orlando no sooner deserts Paris at midnight to seek Angelica than he falls, ineluctably, into the gilded trap of Atlante's Palace of Illusion, where he is 'housed' with a number of other mad boiardan desirers like himself. . . . By such devices does Ariosto 'place' utter single-mindedness, the monopolistic nature of human craving" (*Ariosto and Boiardo*, 25).

11.   I agree with Carne-Ross's intuition ("One and the Many" [1976], 162) that although the palace is ostensibly created for Ruggiero (to avoid his fated death), the "palace has greater bearing on Orlando's quest." As Carne-Ross argues, the "palace provides the most comprehensive image of the Quest that the poem has yet provided" (163).

12.   Unless otherwise noted, I use the Italian text of the *Furioso* edited by Marcello Turchi and translation by Allan Gilbert.

13.   Carne-Ross, "One and the Many" (1976), 161.

14.   Ibid.

15.   On the close relationship between the madness of the characters in the poem and the madness Ariosto claims for himself, see Durling, *Figure of the Poet*, 161.

16.   See, e.g., Arnaldus's account of this psychophysiological process, in which the hot spirits from the heart dry out the imaginative faculty, causing the unnatural retentiveness of the phantasm (McVaugh, introduction, 26).

17.   Beecher and Ciavolella, introduction, 151.

18.   Du Laurens, *Preservation of Sight*, 120.

19.   Ferrand, *Treatise on Lovesickness*, 235.

20.   Carne-Ross, "One and the Many" (1976), 162.

21.   Donato, "Per Selve e Boscherecci Labirinti," 47.

22.   See Ferrand, *A Treatise on Lovesickness*, 229. Mary Wack discusses this feature of the disease: "[T]he symptoms 'unman' the lover. As a patient he is passive, helpless and vulnerable. The signs of lovesickness . . . connote feminine and infantile behavior" (*Lovesickness in the Middle Ages*, 151).

23.   Mary Wack records Isidore of Spain's remark in his etymologies that "love beyond all measure among the ancients was called 'womanly love' (femineus amor)" (13). See also my discussion, chapter 1, p. 23, and chapter 6, pp. 221–24.

24.   Thomas Laqueur, *Making Sex*, 123. Jacques Ferrand also discuss gender lability as a symptom of love-melancholy, though he focuses on the masculinization of women: "[I]t is quite plausible that the genitals of a girl, overheated by the fury of love, would be pushed outside the body, because those parts are the same as the male parts reversed according to the same physician [Galen]" (*Treatise on Lovesickness*, 230).

25.   Quint argues by contrast that "the labyrinthine palace of Atlante is, in fact, a critical rewriting of the labyrinth-prison of Morgana" ("Fortunes of Morgana," 22). The two influences need not be mutually exclusive, of course, but the episode as a whole seems to me closer to the Dragontina episode, for the reasons I outline here. Jo Ann Cavallo notes the relationship between Circe, Dragontina, and Angelica in "Tasso's Armida and the Victory of Romance," 79.

26.   See for instance Boiardo, *Orlando Innamorato* 1.10.7, and 1.14.39.

27.   See Ficino, *De amore* 6.6, and my discussion of this passage in chapter 1, p. 47.

28.   Piero Boitani writes very interestingly of the melancholic self-division of Troilus, who, after his sighting of Crisyede "gan make a mirour of his mynde / In which he saugh al holly hire figure" (*Troilus*, 1.365–66, *Riverside Chaucer*, 478). This inward reflection leads in turn to the translation and adaptation of Petrarch's "S'amor non è," a poem in which "[Troilus'] divided mind emerges fully" (*Petrarch's Dilectoso Male*, 312). Boitani sees this moment of interior reflection as a crucial literary development: "The lyrical pause of the Canticus Troili creates for the first time the image of a meditative, divided, potentially melancholic hero. Is it by chance . . . that Petrarch's *dilectoso male* lies at the very root of this which we must consider the first interior monologue of the Troilus and perhaps of English Literature?" (314). Orlando's situation is similar to Troilus's, in that he speculates on an internal vision of the beloved and is thereby drawn into a melancholic self-division that leads to his literal loss of self: "non son, non sono io quel che paio in viso" (23.128).

29.   Text and translation of Boiardo's poem in *Orlando Innamorato*, translation by Charles Ross. This passage contains a minor emendation.

30.   Agamben, *Stanzas*, 25.

31.   This literal draining of the lover's spirits in love-melancholy seems to symbolize the figurative emptying out of the self into the internalized image of the lost Other. In her discussion of Chaucer's *Book of the Duchess*, Cyndy

Hendershot describes the Man in Black's identification with White as "vampirically drain[ing] his masculine ego" from within ("Male Subjectivity, Fin Amor, and Melancholia," 13). Spenser's Alcyon also describes his lost beloved Daphne as "she that did my vital powres supplie" (*Daphnaïda*, l. 437). See my discussion of both poems, Chapter 5, pp. 187–90.

32. My reading of this moment therefore differs somewhat from that of Thomas Greene, for whom the *ombra* is a sine qua non of the poetry itself: "Sgombra means conventionally 'clears out' or 'removes'; here the context and the rhyme oblige one to make out a meaning something like 'dis-shadows.' It is precisely this act of dis-shadowing, of correcting his hallucinated vision, that empties the speaker of his being, and with it his creative gift" (*Light in Troy*, 134).

33. See, e.g., canto 24.3 for a self-conscious reflection on the narrator's own sickness.

34. Thus although Albert Ascoli interestingly compares the destructiveness of the storm to the "deconstructive power" of the magic ring on Alcina's enchantments, the salient comparison seems to be rather the destructive force of Orlando's own *furor* (*Ariosto's Bitter Harmony*, 309).

35. G. Resta entertains the Freudian interpretation, but shrewdly realizes that the dream is in fact "autopunitivo": "Il sogno di Orlando, preceduto da pensieri 'acuti ed irti' (8.79), avendo nell'ultimo parte un contenuto spiacevole, dando luogo ad un risveglio in stato di ansia si può considerare autopunitivo" ("Il Sogno di Orlando," 147).

36. For Bartlett Giamatti, the point of the destruction of the grove is not so much that Petrarchanism is inherently self-destructive, but rather that it must be destroyed because it represents "traditions and conventions that take us out of ourselves, that give us assumptions about life and the world that are false, and that the world does not or cannot sustain" ("Headlong Horses, Headless Horsemen," 69).

37. See Ascoli, *Ariosto's Bitter Harmony*, 309, for a brief reference to the significance of this allusion.

38. Ibid.

39. Lear, *Happiness, Death, and the Remainder of Life*, esp. 90–105.

40. Ibid., 93, italics mine.

41. Ibid., 92.

42. Ibid., 95.

43. Ibid., 94, italics mine.

44. Paul Fédida, quoted in Phillipe Bonnefis, "Melancholic Describer," 145, italics mine.

45. Quint, "Figure of Atlante," 81.

46. See Valeria Finucci's Freudian reading of Angelica for an elaboration of this idea (Lady Vanishes, 111 ff.). I find her interpretation of Angelica as the "textual archetype of an obscure, inaccessible, longed-for, and yet seemingly easy to obtain Madonna" (111) interesting, though she does not explore some of the deeper sources of this psychological pattern, including the symbolic conflation of the beloved and the maternal figure that we have traced in both early medical and literary texts and modern psychoanalytic ones.

47. Fink, *Lacanian Subject*, 94.

48. Wack (*Lovesickness in the Middle Ages*, 159) turns to the invectives against women in Capellanus's *De amore* to illustrate her point.

49. Quoted in Radden, *Nature of Melancholy*, 84. Mary Wack also notes the relevance of Hildegard's comment (*Lovesickness in the Middle Ages*, 162), which she interprets as foreshadowing "Freud's understanding of the connection between anger and melancholy."

50. See my brief discussion of this issue at the beginning of this chapter (n. 7).

51. Segal, "Virgil's Sixth Eclogue," 304 ff.

52. Ibid, 304.

53. Segal comments, "Pasiphae's tale receives both more space and a more dramatic coloring than any other single episode" ("Virgil's Sixth Eclogue," 315).

54. This passage is found in Peter of Spain's *Questiones super Viaticum* (Wack, *Lovesickness in the Middle Ages*, 232–33). This arresting description is also found verbatim elsewhere; see, e.g., Valescus de Taranta, *Philonium* (1418), 19.

55. Padel, *Whom the Gods Destroy*, 14.

56. Hershkowitz, *Madness of Epic*, 30.

57. See note 7 above.

58. Peter Marinelli shrewdly observes that Boiardo's Orlando laments his knowing selection of the wrong course of action in Medea's words: "[I]o vedo il meglio ed al peggior m'appiglio" (I see the better and choose the worse, *OI* 1.1.31). As Marinelli comments, Boiardo borrows Petrarch's translation of Medea's lament at *Metamorphoses* 7.20–21. He also notes—and this is particularly relevant for my argument—that Medea's "story since medieval times has been a chief monitory emblem of the destructiveness of love-passion" (*Ariosto and Boiardo*, 22).

59. Hershkowitz, *Madness of Epic*, 37.

60. Gordon Williams notes the crucial importance of the verb *solatur*:

"[T]he link with what has gone before is contained in *solatur*, and the consolation which Silenus gave is that he told in his song how Pasiphae herself found consolation in the love of a bull" (*Tradition and Originality*, 245).

61. Elaine Fantham argues that "Roman epic introduces the public collective lament as a narrative movement, providing closure or renewed resolution" ("Role of Lament," 222).

62. Although Pallas is not literally married or engaged, he does occupy the symbolic space of the bridegroom, as the mythic story on his baldric suggests (the fifty bridegrooms murdered by the Danaids). He is also feminized by his association with Dido, as I discuss in more detail later.

63. Williams, *Tradition and Originality*, 247; Segal, "Virgil's Sixth Eclogue," 323.

64. Segal emphasizes the contrast between the Apolline order of poetry and restraint and the uncontrolled *furor* of Pasiphae's love. For Segal, the fusion of Silenus's and Apollo's songs represents the fusion of art and passion ("Virgil's Sixth Eclogue," 324–25).

65. David Quint notes the association between Achilles/Patroclus, Aeneas/Pallas, and Orlando/Brandimarte. He suggests further that Brandimarte's death clearly anticipates Orlando's own, in his last stand at Roncevaux ("Death of Brandimarte," 79).

66. Fantham notes that the use of elegiac ritual in epic becomes conventional in Roman epic; see note 61 above.

67. My reading of *furor* in the Aeneid is influenced by and indebted to a series of conversations with the late Don Fowler, Fellow and Tutor in Classics, Jesus College, Oxford.

68. I owe this observation about the verb *obnubuit* to Don Fowler.

69. I owe this comparison to Pyrrhus to Don Fowler.

70. It will be apparent that although I do agree with David Quint that "the impetus towards closure of the *Furioso* reveals an authentic human temporality . . . [which] affirms the reality of death" ("Figure of Atlante," 84), I also maintain that this movement is not the neutral or even positive one that Quint's reading suggests. The poem's treatment of epic *furor* is such that it does not seem adequate to say with Quint that "mortality is one unassailable fact in a world where everything else human is illusion and madness" (ibid.). Epic madness may occur on a battlefield among real persons rather than phantasms, but it is madness all the same.

71. Daniel Javitch notes that the ending of Fiordiligi's story is explicitly connected to the genre of romance by its echoes of earlier romances: "[F]or

those who may not appreciate the romance ending, [Ariosto] highlights it by rewriting a prior version of it in the well-known Roman de Palamède" ("Grafting of Virgilian Epic," 73). However, my interpretation of Ariosto's intention here is quite different from Javitch's. He maintains that Ariosto's intercutting of "epic" and "romance" strains, and in particular the movement from the Virgilian passages describing Brandimarte's funeral to the "romance" ending of Fiordiligi, establishes a seamless continuity between the two genres: "Ariosto's imitations of Virgil, standing out as they did because of the romance context surrounding them, aimed to make us admire his ability to master and conjoin two different generic codes" (74). My reading of this moment suggests that the shift between the epic funeral and the romance entombment is designed to jar the reader into an assessment of the implications (psychological, moral, and cultural) of the differences between these two modes and to imply, furthermore, that they are radically incompatible.

72. For an excellent study of the figurative identification of the death of youthful warriors with defloration, see Don Fowler, "Vergil on Killing Virgins." My thinking on this subject is influenced by this essay and by conversation with Don Fowler.

73.   [U]t flos in saeptis secretus nascitur hortis,
             ignotus pecori, nullo convulsus aratro,
             quem mulcent aurae, firmat sol, educat imber,
             multi illum pueri, multae optavere puellae:
             idem cum tenui carptus defloruit ungui,
             nulli illum pueri, nullae optavere puellae:
             sic virgo dum intacta manet, dum cara suis est;
             cum castum amisit polluto corpore florem,
             nec pueris iucunda manet nec cara puellis.

[As a flower springs up secretly in a fenced garden, unknown to the cattle, torn up by no plough, which the winds caress, the sun strengthens, the shower draws forth, many boys, many girls, desire it; when the same flower fades, nipped by a sharp nail, no boys, no girls desire it: so a maiden, whilst she remains untouched, so long is she dear to her own; when she has lost her chaste flower with sullied body, she remains neither lovely to boys not dear to girls.] (Catullus 62.39–47, trans. Loeb)

74. Giamatti records the bleakness of this ending but sees a ray of hope in Ruggiero's display of self-control at the end: "[T]his resolution—momentary, tenuous—and the story of Orlando, who learned how a man becomes headless and runs away, beside himself, into the forests of despair, and how he can come back, is the paradigm of man's excesses and for the self-imposed limita-

tions that will be his salvation" ("Headlong Horses," 75). But since Ariosto's Virgilian model emphasizes precisely Aeneas's *loss of control* to the domination of *furor*, it seems to me rather that Ariosto closes, as Virgil does, with a grim vision of inhuman rage. For although Ariosto does try to emphasize Ruggiero's greater self-control, he is in the end forced to kill Rodomonte in a particularly violent way, burying his dagger several times in Rodomonte's face.

75.   Gian Biagio Conte gives a full philological analysis of Virgil's description of Pallas's baldric, showing how the myth of the Danaids brings together two distinct types of youthful death: untimely death and death before marriage (*Rhetoric of Imitation*, 185–96).

76.   Quint, "Death of Brandimarte," 79. Quint also notes that Orlando's lament parallels the lament that Orlando's uncle Charlemagne makes over Orlando's body in a fourteenth-century version of the Roncevaux story (82).

4. IL PRIMO ERROR

1.   Bruno Basile, for example, calls Tasso's poetic style "la poetica dell' alienazione malinconica" (*Poëta melancholicus*, 46). See also Petrocchi, *I fantasmi di Tancredi*; and Schiesari, *Gendering of Melancholia*. Schiesari locates Tancredi's melancholia primarily in his inability to act in the enchanted wood: "It is because of his incapacity to act in the face of such simulacra that Tancredi has been heralded as the melancholic character of the *Gerusalemme Liberata*" (206–7). Though I do not disagree with this reading, I regard Tancredi's fixation and paralysis as symptoms of a more broadly conceived erotic melancholy.

2.   Ferguson, *Trials of Desire*, 127. Ferguson's use of the term "melancholia" is basically Freudian, and while there are, as I have shown, significant points of contact between early modern and psychoanalytic uses of the term, I ground my reading of Tancredi's melancholy in the medieval and early modern medical tradition.

3.   Enterline, *Tears of Narcissus*, chaps. 1 and 2.

4.   "As a figure for the author who tries and fails to read himself as the origin of his own text, Tancredi dramatizes the disruptive potential of allegory as a poetic version of the phantasms of dubious origin that fill his author with 'infinite melancholy'" (ibid., 82).

5.   Tasso himself notes in various places the existence of love as an illness. In "La molza overo de l'amore," the speaker canvasses the different kinds of love, coming finally to the medical opinion that love is a kind of malady: "[S]e [vorrò parlarne] con altri medici, conchiuderò che sia una sorte di malatia" (*Dialoghi*, 747). Later in the same dialogue the speaker classifies what he calls

love as *infirmita* as the second of six types of love, the first of which is Platonic desire (750). In *Il Messaggiero* he refers to the well-known story of Lucretius's death-for-love as an instance of deadly melancholy: "Lucrezio s'uccise per maninconia" (*Prose*, 18).

6.   Elizabeth Bellamy's assertion that Clorinda is a "marvel" who "leaves in her wake an image that, in Tancredi's imagination, takes on a life of its own" responds precisely to the poem's representation of the phantasmic hold of love-melancholy (*Translations of Power*, 169).

7.   Tasso argues against those who consider love too "light" a subject for the heroic poem: "I have always been of the opposite opinion, holding that all beautiful things are suitable to the heroic poem, and love is indeed beautiful, as Phaedrus says in Plato" (*Discourses*, 45). See Jo Ann Cavallo ("Tasso's Armida," 106–9) for an excellent discussion of Tasso's inclusion of love in his heroic ethos.

8.   Though Tasso argues that "we may regard actions performed for the sake of love as beyond all others heroic," the love that overcomes Tancredi clearly draws him away from the "epic" center of the poem and seems to dramatize the dark, somatic aspect of "heroic love" that we examined in chapter 1 (*Discourses*, 47).

9.   Tasso, *Prose*, 17. Ferguson puts the problem succinctly in her discussion of Tancredi's inability to shake off the false visions in the wood: "Analyzing both the symptoms and the causes of a malady he clearly shares with his hero, Tasso returns, once again, to the question that preoccupied him throughout his life: "how does one know the difference between a 'simulacrum' and a 'true form'?" (*Trials of Desire*, 129).

10.   Tasso, *Prose*, 18. Juliana Schiesari writes perceptively about the significance of the term *soverchia maninconia*, arguing that "this ferocious brand of melancholy, soverchia maninconia, turns the work of mourning into a perpetual labor, a more-than-Herculean task, one whose excessive—or rather infinite—production of its own loss comes to define the ego precisely in terms of its loss as the condition of its selfhood: a self forever mourning the loss of its own self" (*Gendering of Melancholia*, 201–2). The term *soverchia maninconia* is Tasso's own: in *Il Messaggiero*, he reflects on the nature of his *nova pazzia* (new madness). His remarks on melancholy follow the pseudo-Aristotelian (and Ficinian) tradition of associating melancholy with greatness of mind: "Forse è soverchia maninconia, e i maniconici, come afferma Aristotele, sono stati di chiaro ingegno ne gli studi de la filosofia e nel governo de la republica e nel compor versi; ed Empedocle e Socrate e Platone furono maniconici; e Marato poeta ciciliano allora era più eccelente ch'egli era fuor di sé" (Perhaps it

is an excess of melancholy, and melancholics, as Aristotle asserted, were quick witted in the study of philosophy and government and the writing of poetry; and Empedocles and Socrates and Plato were melancholics; and the Sicilian poet Marato was the more outstanding the more beside himself he was (*Prose*, 18, trans. mine). Tasso relies in this section in some detail on the Aristotelian account of melancholia and its causes that we discussed in chapter 1.

11.   Schiesari, *Gendering of Melancholia*, 198–99.

12.   Petrarch, *Secretum*, 156; *Petrarch's Secretum*, 114.

13.   Bellamy, *Translations of Power*, 177. We may wish to consider Erminia's "healing" of Tancredi as a kind of resolution, but as I argue later, the poetics of this scene suggest a deeper implication in—because fantasized fulfillment of—Tancredi's melancholic condition.

14.   Unless otherwise stated, I use the following translation of Tasso's poem throughout this chapter: *Jerusalem Delivered: An English Prose Version*, trans. and ed. Ralph Nash. Quotations from the Italian text are taken from the edition of the poem by Lanfranco Caretti.

15.   Ferguson, *Trials of Desire*, 58.

16.   Ibid., 58.

17.   See my discussion, chapter 1, p. 45.

18.   "The vision of the beatified lady is retrospectively defined by the bleeding tree episode as a text which must compete for authority with the one jointly created by the pagan magician and by the hero's own guilty memories and desires" (Ferguson, *Trials of Desire*, 126).

19.   According to the medical authorities, as we have seen, the too-adherent phantasm skews the judgment of the estimative power and transforms love into a melancholic disorder. See my discussion of the structure of obsession, chapter one, pp. 37–44.

20.   This poem begins with an evocation of the speaker's wandering and distracted thoughts: "Di pensier in pensier, di monte in monte / mi guida Amor" (From thought to thought, from mountain to mountain / Love guides me). But it is especially focused on the power of the mind to project its own fantasies on the world: "Ove porge ombra un pino alto od un colle / talor m'arresto, et pur nel primo sasso / disegno co la mente il suo bel viso" (Where a tall pine or a hillside extends shade, there I sometimes stop, and in the first stone I see I portray her lovely face with my mind, ll. 27–29).

21.   Beecher and Ciavolella, introduction, 150.

22.   Bellamy, *Translations of Power*, 156. Margaret Ferguson writes interestingly of Tasso's vision of the Virgin Mary, uneasily interpreted by him as a miracle rather than a fantasy generated by his *maninconia infinita*: "The epis-

temological doubts generated by Tasso's experience of 'maninconia infinita' led him to approach, uneasily, the territory Freud explored in his discussions of religion as a phantastic cultural version of the family romance. . . . Tasso, I think, anticipates Freud's theory that the human consciousness never fully liberates itself from primal memories and that its journey forward in time is also a return to the past. In this double journey, the authorial psyche wages war with a host of phantasms which it both loves and hates, believes in and distrusts" (*Trials of Desire*, 59). This reading of Tasso's ambivalent engagement with a phantasmic netherworld will be relevant for my discussion of Tancredi's love-melancholy, though my emphasis is on contemporary pneumo-phantas-mology. Lynn Enterline discusses the same vision, interpreting Tasso's uncertainty regarding its validity as a crucial commentary on his aesthetic practice: "[L]a fantasia and i fantasmi mark a liminal point for Tasso, a point called 'melancholia,' between the poetic faculty, signs, and madness. Fantasy and phantasms mark that uncertain threshold where Tasso sometimes finds it impossible to designate the origin of a sign with certainty, and thus to grasp intuitively the distinction between interior and exterior, or between what he would then call false and true" (*Tears of Narcissus*, 61).

23. Agamben, *Stanzas*, 23.

24. Bellamy makes a similar point on different grounds, arguing that the marvelous constitutes a kind of "poetic other" in the poem. The effort to harmonize the *maraviglioso* with the *verisimile* thus reveals an anxious desire for "a guarantee that [Tasso's] narrative cannot be subverted by the potentially psychic play of fantasy" (*Translations of Power*, 147). See also Enterline on the confusion of inner and outer (*Tears of Narcissus*, 61).

25. Marilyn Migiel notes the importance of this picture—and the organizing trinity of knight-monster-virgin—to the story of Clorinda as a whole (*Gender and Genealogy*, 33–37). See also David Quint's discussion of the political implications of Clorinda's "overlapping and contradictory identities" (*Epic and Empire*, 244).

26. See in particular Migiel: "Here, as in an earlier encounter, he turns as if to stone upon seeing Clorinda (6.27; 3.23), suggesting that Clorinda is a figure around whom are concentrated the horrifying and reassuring feelings excited by the vision of the Medusa herself" (*Gender and Genealogy*, 21). See also Bellamy: "Transformed to virtual stone by the sight of Clorinda . . . Tancredi reacts as if he were glimpsing Medusa's head itself" (*Translations of Power*, 171).

27. Bellamy notes that Tancredi persistently treats Clorinda "as an image" (*Translations of Power*, 171 ff.), and Migiel even refers repeatedly to Clorinda

as a "phantasmatic image" to which Tancredi is bound by desire (*Gender and Genealogy*, 21); but neither critic ties Clorinda's problematic ontology to contemporary psychiatric conceptions of Tancredi's melancholic disorder.

28. Tasso, "La Molza Overo de l'amore," 748, italics mine.

29. See my discussion of the historically contemporary indications that the beloved object of melancholic love was frequently cast as a maternal figure, chapter 2, pp. 79–81.

30. See Lynn Enterline's discussion of the "fissured" nature of masculinity: "When Freud speculates that melancholia illuminates the 'common and typical' process of substitution by which the ego acquires its character he is also, then, engaging in a discussion that crucially suggests how that ego achieves a (composite, fractured) sexual 'identity' and disposition" (*Tears of Narcissus*, 23).

31. Migiel, *Gender and Genealogy*, 44.

32. Ibid.; Tasso, *Gerusalemme Liberata*, 376.

33. Caroline Walker Bynum, *Holy Feast and Holy Fast*, 269–73.

34. Ibid., 270.

35. For useful psychoanalytic readings of the *Canzone*, see Enterline, *Tears of Narcissus*, 119 ff.; Ferguson, *Trials of Desire*, 74–77; and Schiesari, "Victim's Discourse."

36. For a more detailed account of the story, see Schiesari, "Victim's Discourse," *Gendering of Melancholia*, 174; and Solerti, *Vita di Torquato Tasso*, vol. 1, chap. 1.

37. I am grateful to my colleague Natasha Chang for some helpful suggestions about this translation.

38. Lynn Enterline argues that the language of the maternal-filial relation in the *Canzone* is also echoed in the embrace between Rinaldo and Armida: "Both Rinaldo and the lyric speaker find themselves forcibly separated from a loving breast in the shade, but where in the 'Canzone' Tasso laments that he can no longer lie 'face to face' with his mother, in the epic the narrator pauses to describe in some detail how Rinaldo lies 'face to face' with Armida ('volto a volto' in both cases, l. 36 and XVI.18)" (*Tears of Narcissus*, 120). Although Schiesari does not note the similarity between the two passages in the *Canzone* and the *Liberata*, she does observe the erotic nature of the *nodi tenaci* that bind mother and son: "The knots represent a corporeal loss since they are the knots of the mother's embrace; they call attention to a morbidly erotic bond even as they devalue the specificity of her loss and victimization" (*Gendering of Melancholia*, 184). See also her discussion of the "nodi tenaci" in the Canzone in "Victim's Discourse," esp. 194–96. Margaret Ferguson also argues that "Tas-

so's biography offers rich material for associating Clorinda with the beloved mother Tasso lost as a child" (*Trials of Desire*, 62).

39. Schiesari, *Gendering of Melancholia*, 182.

40. Ferguson, *Trials of Desire*, 74.

41. Ibid., 74.

42. For a general discussion of the Morgana/Ventura/Fortuna figure, see Quint, "Fortunes of Morgana," 29.

43. Freud, *Mourning and Melancholia*, 170.

44. "Therefore will you be surprised if blood imprinted with a certain likeness has impressed that likeness on parts of the body, so that eventually Lysias will seem to have become like Phaedrus in some colors, or features, or feelings, or gestures?" (Ficino, *De amore* 7.8).

45. Ficino's comment on the subject is remarkably close to Freud's: "Who would not hate one who took his soul away from him?" (*De amore* 6.10).

46. Freud, *Mourning and Melancholia*, 165. As we will see in the next chapter, Scudamour's "self-revilings" would seem to fit Freud's diagnosis of melancholic self-hatred extremely closely.

47. Wack, *Lovesickness in the Middle Ages*, 162.

48. In stanza 12.75, the antecedent of "tu" is Tancredi's own hand: "tu, ministra di morte empia ed infame"; in 12.83 it is himself; and in 12.79 it is the "amate spoglie," Clorinda herself.

49. Abraham and Torok, *Shell and the Kernel*, 113.

50. Ibid., 114.

51. This ambiguous space of feminine enclosure that is both womb- and tomblike reinforces Margaret Ferguson's suggestion that the "haunted romance landscape" is one in which "the cradle and the sepulchre lie side by side" (*Trials of Desire*, 75).

52. Abraham and Torok, *Shell and the Kernel*, 114.

53. Lynn Enterline, *Tears of Narcissus*, 79.

54. Ibid., 79.

55. Ferrand, *Treatise on Lovesickness*, 235.

56. Agamben, *Stanzas*, 24.

57. Schiesari also notes—though not in relation to the Tancredi/Clorinda relationship—the eroticization of the maternal knots evoked in the *Canzone*. See note 38 above.

58. See, e.g., Ascanius's words to the Trojan women at *Aen.* 5.670: "'[Q]uis furor iste novus? quo nunc, quo tenditis?'" (What new madness is this? Where now, where are you heading?).

59. Giamatti, "Headlong Horses, Headless Horsemen," 295.

60. Ibid.

61. Sacks, *English Elegy*, 72.

62. In his discussion of canzone 129, Thomas Greene rightly emphasizes the importance of the word *ombra* and its cognates in Petrarch's lyrics: "The verb derives from the latin adumbrare—to shade in, to sketch (whence adumbratus—sketched, hence imperfect, shadowy, unreal). In this canzone [129], the phantasm of the beloved, which is said to outshine all stars, is only adumbrated, shadowed forth; it belongs to that shadow world of definition which is here all the speaker's being" (*Light in Troy*, 133). The relevance of this account to Tancredi's vision of the phantasmic Clorinda in the shadowy wood is clear and provides important insight into the poetic significance of Tancredi's experience.

63. Plato, *Phaedrus*, 210 d.

64. Schiesari, *Gendering of Melancholia*, 183–84. For a further exploration of Tasso's appropriation of the mother's position, see Schiesari's essay "Victim's Discourse."

65. See Lynn Enterline's reading of the import of this grieving voice (*Tears of Narcissus*, 74–79). For Enterline, the point of the scene is "the hero's inability to read allegorically, to decipher the hidden 'meaning' of signs, in part because his reading is interrupted by the sound of many 'indistinct' voices moaning in lamentation" (79). Allegory, in this reading, stands "as a poetic version of the phantasms of dubious origin that fill his author with 'infinite melancholy'" (83).

66. This enchanted space filled with the song of birds—and especially of the nightingale—recalls the *locus amoenus* prescribed by Valescus de Taranta (and many others) for the cure of love-melancholy. However, as in Ariosto's poem, the *locus amoenus* here clearly exacerbates Tancredi's condition.

67. Lynn Enterline discusses Tasso's interest in quasi-human voices in relation to the birdsong in Armida's garden. The "empty voice" of both the bird and the phantasmic Clorinda dramatize for Enterline "a momentary evacuation of personal agency in language" (*Tears of Narcissus*, 115) that she associates with Tasso's doomed "search for an author's informing, grounding presence to allegorical signs" (114). My reading of the sudden incursion of these mournful voices is that they represent a return to the prelinguistic speech patterns that Kristeva associates with melancholia. This incursion is identified, partly through its association with the mother, with the shift away from epic/allegory to romance.

68. See my earlier discussion of Kristeva's theory of melancholic discourse, chapter two, pp. 86–90.

69. Lynn Enterline reads the melancholic strain of this episode quite differently. For her, the crucial feature of the scene is Tancredi's inability to tell whether the marvels he sees exist independently of his own imagination or are instead figments of his imagination: "As a figure for the author who tries and fails to read himself at the origin of his own text, Tancredi dramatizes the disruptive potential of allegory as a poetic version of the phantasms of dubious origin that fill his author with 'infinite melancholy'" "*Tears of Narcissus*, 82). Though I agree with both Enterline and Ferguson that Tasso's "acute awareness of his own 'frenetic' mental processes led him to suspect that even divine revelations might really be products of human *fantasia*" (Ferguson, *Trials of Desire*, 58), the medical discourse of love-melancholy provides an essential theoretical framework for understanding Tasso's representation of this fear. Melancholy is characterized, as we have seen, by a radical ontological instability that undoes the boundary between the mind and the world in quite literal ways: the flow of the spirits into and out of the lover facilitates alterations in the mind and in the world such that no clear distinction between the "mental" and the "material" holds true.

70. See my translation above, p. 151.

71. Ferguson emphasizes the falsity of this Clorinda—she is a "delusion the Christian should resist" (*Trials of Desire*, 131). Presumably, the similarity between the maternal figure and Clorinda suggests that the mother has also become in retrospect a dangerous phantasm.

72. For a discussion of Erminia as a quintessential romance agent, see Kristen Olson Murtaugh: "Perhaps more than any other single character, Erminia, 'la bella Erminia,' brings the perspective and dynamic of romance into the Gerusalemme Liberata" (*Erminia Delivered*, 1).

73. Lynn Enterline explores the relationship between Erminia's tears and her development as a lyric poet. She argues that Erminia's stance resembles that of the grief-stricken speaker in the *Canzone* (*Tears of Narcissus*, 138).

74. See Caretti's comment in Tasso, *Gerusalemme Liberata*, 196, note to *GL* 7.4.

75. See Enterline's interesting reading of the death of Orpheus in Virgil and Ovid (*Rhetoric of the Body*, 73–74). She also emphasizes the role of breath and voice: "Vergil's tour de force of sounding and resounding voices is not one that Ovid, captivated with the idea of animated nature voice, and 'fugitive breath' ('anima fugiente vocabat'), would be likely to forget" (73). Enterline

suggests that Ovid appropriates the *vox ipsa* as a trope for his own poetic voice: "Ovid competes with Vergil, in other words, by assuming the extraordinary poetic voice that Vergil records only second-hand" (74).

76. Tasso, *Prose*, 18.

77. Margaret Ferguson emphasizes the important distinction between Tasso's use of the bleeding tree episode and similar episodes in Vergil and Ariosto: "Tasso's echo marks a crucial difference between his hero and Virgil's. Like Aeneas, Tancredi wounds a tree not once but repeatedly; the voice Tancredi hears, however, unlike the one Aeneas hears, brings him knowledge that the epic narrator defines as false" (*Trials of Desire*, 127).

78. Ibid., 128.

79. Murtaugh, "Erminia Delivered," 12.

80. Jo Ann Cavallo's reading of the return of Armida at the end of the poem suggests, in her view, the triumph of romance over epic ("Tasso's Armida and the Victory of Romance"). I shall return to her argument later.

81. Lynn Enterline notes the striking echoes between Tasso's description of Armida and the description of his own mother in the *Canzone*: in both texts, for example, the protective female figure bestows kisses, tears, and holds the male figure *volto a volto* (*Tears of Narcissus*, 120).

82. Cavallo, "Tasso's Armida," 107.

83. Ibid., 108.

5. REWRITING ROMANCE

1. See my discussion in the introduction, pp. 14–16.

2. David of Augsburg, *Formula novitiorum*, 50: "Prima [species accidiae] est quaedam amaritudo mentis. . . . Haec aliquando nascitur . . . ex praedominantibus melancholicis humoribus" (Bigne, XXV, 893, quoted in Wenzel, *Sin of Sloth*, 191).

3. Petrarch, *Secretum*, 64–65.

4. Patricia Parker also notes the similarity between the two dreams, though her reading of this similarity suggests that its primary purpose is a kind of slippery parody: "[T]he relation of real form to parody in Spenser's poem is often no more predictable than that of fable to its allegorical meaning" (*Inescapable Romance*, 85). My view is that the linguistic similarity between the two episodes is part of the larger story Spenser is telling about the relation between mourning and melancholia in the poem.

5. William Perkins describes the subversion of the imagination by melancholy in terms that apply directly to Red Crosse: "There is no humour, yea

nothing in mans bodie, that hath so straunge effects, as this humour hath, being once distempered. The effects are of two sorts. The first, is in the braine and head. For this humour being corrupted, it sends up noysome fumes as cloudes or mists which doe corrupt the imagination, and makes the instrument of reason unfit for understanding and sense. Hence followes the first effect, strange imaginations, conceits and opinions, framed in the minde" (*Cases of Conscience*, 1.12.188). Of the three kinds of temptation, or what Perkins calls "seducement," that lead, according to Perkins, to despair, one is the corrupted imagination, one the sufferer's knowledge of his own sins, and the third is the influence of the devil (1.7.88). All three kinds of "seducement" seem to be in operation in this scene.

6.   Susan Snyder ("Left Hand of God," 33) notes Spenser's subtle characterization of Red Crosse as melancholic, suggesting that his melancholy allegorizes in part his role as fallen man struggling toward salvation. In this reading, then, despair has in part a physiological origin, and melancholy has spiritual connotations. This interpretation is supported by the close medieval association between melancholy and the fall. Thus Hildegard von Bingen writes: "Bile is black, bitter, and releases every evil, sometimes even a brain sickness. It causes veins in the heart to overflow; it causes depression and doubt in every consolation so that the person can find no joy in heavenly life and no consolation in his earthly existence. This melancholy is due to the first attack by the devil on the nature of man since man disobeyed God's command by eating the apple" (cited in Radden, *Nature of Melancholy*, 81).

7.   "For Spenser, sadness—not joy—is the exact opposite of melancholy" (Trevor, "Sadness in The Faerie Queene," 241). It is perhaps notable that Trevor quotes only the phrase "solemne sad" in relation to Red Crosse, and not the more problematic "*too* solemne sad." It seems to me that Red Crosse's sadness is from the beginning a sign of a spiritual vulnerability.

8.   See my discussion of this concept, pp. 41–44.

9.   Douglas Trevor's view that the poem "reaffirms the transcendence and incorruptibility of a spiritual dominion demarcated by sadness" ("Sadness in The Faerie Queene," 252) is problematized not only by what I see as the continuity between Red Crosse's "sadness" and the spiritually inflected love-melancholy that he later endures, but also by Spenser's depiction of Britomart. Though Trevor does not refer at all to Book 3, the portrayal of Britomart's noble quest as deeply "engraffed" (3.3.18) within her procreative womb and significantly conditioned by physiological forces runs counter to his sense of the poem as profoundly hostile to a Galenic reading of the mind-body re-

lationship. I therefore agree with his sense of the "difficulty of reconciling Spenser's renunciation of melancholy with his support of non-humoral sorrow" (250), but for reasons quite opposed to his own.

10.   This is not to say that Archimago does not also allegorize the role of satanic forces in Red Crosse's departure from the true way. The causal confusion implicit in Spenser's allegory (are these melancholy visions the result of the pressure of an internal, humoral disorder, or are they the devil's work?) reflects a similar confusion in the medieval and early modern literature on despair. Thus Robert Burton, for instance, asserts that the effective cause of despair is the devil, but that his instrument is melancholy: "The principal agent and procurer of this mischief is the Devil; those whom god forsakes, the Devil, by his permission, lays hold on. . . . His ordinary engine by which he produceth this effect, is the melancholy humour itself, which is the Devil's bath; and as in Saul, those evil spirits get in, as it were, and take possession of us. Black choler is a shoeing-horn, a bait to allure them, insomuch that many writers make melancholy an ordinary cause, and a symptom of despair, for that such men are most apt by reason of their ill-disposed temper, *to distrust, fear, grieve, mistake, and amplify whatsoever they preposterously conceive, or falsely apprehend.* A scrupulous conscience comes of a natural defect, a melancholy habit (saith Navarrus). *The body works upon the mind, by obfuscating the spirits and corrupted instruments*" (*Anatomy of Melancholy*, 939, italics mine). If Archimago is, like Despaire, a "man of hell" who insinuates himself into Red Crosse's dreaming mind and "abuses" his fantasy through the "shoeing-horn" of melancholy, Spenser's allegory seems to illustrate the interplay between a theory of melancholy as "possession" of the mind by demonic forces and a medical theory that emphasizes the physiological conditioning that supports such possession. Certainly Red Crosse becomes a dreamer who distrusts, fears, and amplifies what he preposterously conceives and falsely apprehends. Sleep itself is a hellish state that absorbs the fantasy and "tormenteth" the sufferer, as Du Laurens argues, with all manner of phantasms. Burton's remark that "the body works upon the mind, by obfuscating the spirits and corrupted instruments" (*Anatomy*, 939) raises precisely the kind of epistemological dilemma we have found throughout the medical writing on melancholy and love-melancholy.

11.   Cheney, *Spenser's Image of Nature*, 29.

12.   See Hamilton's note on 1.1.36, *Faerie Queene*.

13.   Du Laurens, *Discourse of the Preservation of Sight*, 82, italics mine.

14.   Agamben, *Stanzas*, 5.

15.   Ibid.

16. The relationship between despair and melancholy is complex. Susan Snyder ("Left Hand of God," 38–39) suggests that the dryness of melancholy was thought to leave a person vulnerable to despair (this is Robert Burton's view); she also points out that for Richard Hooker melancholy was a cause of despair.

17. See Wenzel, *Sin of Sloth*, 191, for a list of passages illustrating the association between melancholy and *acedia*.

18. See note 2.

19. Agamben, *Stanzas*, 9.

20. Quoted in Snyder, "Left Hand of God," 46.

21. Agamben, *Stanzas*, 6.

22. Burton, *Anatomy*, 867.

23. See Hamilton, *Faerie Queene*, 68. Golding's commentary on Ovid's story of Salmacis and Hermaphroditus makes a similar connection, suggesting that "idlenesse / Is cheefest nurce and cherisher of all voluptuousnesse" (*Epistle*, ll. 113–14).

24. Agamben (Stanzas, 9) notes the frequent anguished references to uncontrollable "cogitationes" in the *Lives of the Fathers* (Patrologia Latina). The term "cogitatio," as Agamben notes (*Stanzas*, 9), "refers [in medieval terminology] always to the phantasy and to its phantasmatic discourse."

25. Radden, *Nature of Melancholy*, 83–84.

26. See Hamilton's comment in *Faerie Queene*, 40.

27. The narrator later refers to his suffering as "a sicknesse / That I have suffred this eyght yere. / And yet my boote is never the nere, / For there is phisycien but one / That may me heale" (*BD* 36–40). The nature of this mysterious "sicknesse" is somewhat controversial, but in context it makes sense to understand it as lovesickness, the "one physicien" perhaps the lady herself. See, in particular, Steven Kruger's excellent analysis of the significance of melancholy/lovesickness in the poem, in "Medical and Moral Authority"; and Cyndy Hendershot, "Male Subjectivity, Fin Amor and Melancholia."

28. Rambuss, "'Process of Tyme,'" 662.

29. Ibid.

30. "In this situation, the energy that should be assigned to the work of mourning is instead invested in the task of keeping secret (even to oneself) the unacceptable fact of loss" (Rambuss, "'Process of Tyme,'" 668). Rambuss notes Freud's view of melancholy as "in some way related to an object loss which is withdrawn from consciousness" (667).

31. Rambuss, "'Process of Tyme,'" 668.

32. Ibid., 678.

33. Like the narrator of *The Book of the Duchess*, the narrator of this poem also nurses his own sorrow, which receives only the most ambiguous description: "There came into my mind a troublous thought, / Which dayly dooth my weaker wit possesse" (*Daphnaïda*, 29–30). Critics suggest that this may be a reference to Spenser's first wife, but the salient point seems rather to be the deliberate obscurity of the stanza. See Oram's note, in Spenser, *Shorter Poems*, *Daphnaïda*, n. 29.

34. Freud, "Mourning and Melancholia," 165.

35. See Wack ("Lovesickness in the Middle Ages," 162): "[T]he depression and self-abasement characteristic of melancholy—or lovesickness—is nothing other than hostility toward the object redirected to the self."

36. Discussing the relationship between melancholia and the masculine self, Cyndy Hendershot writes: "The Man in Black's identification with White thus vampirically drains his 'normal' masculine ego in an attempt to transform it into an undead corpse" ("Male Subjectivity, Fin Amor and Melancholia," 13). This account accords well with the medical understanding of the threat posed to the subject by the phantasm of the beloved, which as it were takes the lover over from within. See Couliano's account of the work of the phantasm as a "vampiric" process (*Eros and Magic*, 31), and my discussion of this process in chapter 1, pp. 49–50.

37. Cyndy Hendershot notes in addition that "identification with the woman in fin 'amor is always a potential for the male subject because it recalls a former position occupied by him—the infantile identification with the feminine" ("Male Subjectivity, Fin Amor and Melancholia," 16).

38. Perkins, *Cases of Conscience*, 1.12.188, italics mine.

39. Snyder, "Left Hand of God," 20–21.

40. Perkins refers to "the changeable condition of our life in this world, whereby it comes to passe, that we are always in a fleeing and transitorie state. For we are (as Saint Peter speaketh) but strangers and Pilgrimes, that wander to and fro in the earth" (*Cases of Conscience*, 1.9.142).

41. See introduction, p. 12.

42. See Sacks: "[A] healthy work of mourning . . . requires a withdrawal of affection from the lost object and a subsequent reattachment of affection to some substitute for that object" (*English Elegy*, 6).

43. For a discussion of the relationship between Arthur's quest and this scene in Despair's cave, see Thomas Roche, "Menace of Despair and Arthur's Vision."

44. As we shall see in the next chapter, Terwin's "wallowing" stance anticipates Scudamour's very similar wallowing outside the house of Busirane; both
figures represent a crossing of despair with love-melancholy.

45. Valleriola's schematic rendering of the course of *insania amoris* predicts
exactly the end suffered by Sir Terwin: "[S]ibiipsi iniecisset manus, ni suorum
vi prohibitus fuisset" (*Observationum*, 185).

46. See chapter 1, pp. 38–44.

47. Skulsky, "Spenser's Despair Episode."

48. Ibid., 234–35.

49. Ibid., 237.

50. Ibid., italics mine.

51. Andrew Hadfield provides a dark reading of Arthur's vision, arguing
that it reflects on, and sharply critiques, Elizabeth's failure to provide an heir:
"Arthur's barren union is mirrored in Elizabeth's barren virginity: she has led
suitors nowhere . . . just as the Faerie Queene has led Arthur on" ("Spenser
and the Death of the Queen," 30–31). But to say that the Faerie Queene has
"led Arthur on" is to deny the difference—that I take to be crucial—between
the truly errant quests of an Orlando or a Tancredi, and Arthur's quest, ty-
pologically secured to an unfolding truth. As the remainder of this chapter
makes clear, I argue that while Spenser is acutely aware of the dangers of the
"melancholic" quest, with its attendant drift into Petrarchan *atra voluptas*, he
goes out of his way to recuperate the structure of romance. Willy Maley offers
yet another very different reading of this episode. Though he does broadly
accept a typological account of the dream's significance, he also suggests that
the absence of this visionary faerie queene figures the queen's absence from her
colonial subjects in Ireland: "A ghost is someone who isn't there, and in Ireland
the status of the prince was necessarily ghostly. What haunts the pages of *The
Faerie Queene* is the spectre of sovereignty without the presence of a sovereign"
(*Salvaging Spenser*, 112). Though I find this tightly localized and historicized
reading intriguing, it does seem clear to me that the poem's philosophical
ambitions extend further than this reading suggests. By the same token, while
Maley reads the episode as in part a critique of Elizabeth's absenteeism (117),
the poem's carefully structured unfolding of "veritas" within the quest structure suggests rather a broader elegiac reflection on the absence of full truth and
knowledge from human existence.

52. This motto is exhaustively discussed in Fritz Saxl's "Veritas Filia
Temporis."

53. Saxl, "Veritas Filia Temporis," 203.

54. Ibid., 208–9.

55.   See Erich Auerbach's classic essay "Figura": "[T]hey [the *figurae*] point to something which is in need of interpretation, which will indeed be fulfilled in the concrete future, but which is at all times present, fulfilled in God's providence, which knows no difference of time. *This eternal thing is already figured in them*" (59, italics mine). For an excellent discussion of typology in literature (and especially in Milton), see also Madsen, *From Shadowy Types to Truth*, and N. Frye, *Great Code*.

56.   Auerbach, "Figura," 34.

57.   David Lee Miller notes the relevance of the motto to the figural structure of *The Faerie Queene* in *The Poem's Two Bodies*, 123 ff. My reading differs from his on the fundamental point of the effect of this motto on the structure of Arthur's quest for self-knowledge: "[T]he figure of Time as a revealer is shifted from Una to Gloriana, where instead of hailing the emergence of Truth it reconciles Arthur to an indefinite delay" (127). Similarly, writing of the various fulfillments figured by the *veritas filia temporis* motto (moral, historical, and anagogical), Miller writes: "None of these fulfilments is imminent in the poem as we have it, though: they remain mirages of a condition in which the subject would recover oneness of being with the source of life—a sublime projection of the infantile fusion of self with the maternal breast" (141). My view, of course, is that the typological structure provides a perspective from which Truth, like Glory, is not imminent but *immanent*, and gives shape and meaning to the "endlesse worke" of the poem. See also Susan Frye, *Elizabeth I*, 43 ff., who provides an interesting cultural reading of Elizabeth's use of this motto.

58.   Patricia Parker's subtle reading of the figural structure of the poem is particularly relevant: "Spenser's poem . . . becomes a kind of 'old testament,' a text still within the realm of the figure" (*Inescapable Romance*, 79). Though she acknowledges the implied presence of "'Glory' in its full theological sense," she finds the revelatory power of Spenser's figures compromised by the poem's "movement towards multiplication and refraction": "shadow is often suspect, multiplicity is often the source of potential variance, and refraction into 'mirrours more than one' may be the centrifugal counterpart of 'erring'" (80). As I argue here, this account does not do justice to the significance of the immanence of Glory in Spenser's text: the "pressed gras where she had lyen" delineates precisely the difference between the true, though ungraspable vision, and the false visions that appear to parody and undermine it.

59.   Auerbach, "Figura," 59.

60.   Parker, *Inescapable Romance*, 79.

61.   Bellamy, *Translations of Power*, 121. Miller, *Poem's Two Bodies*, 139.

62. Tyndale, *Works*, 1.346.

63. "The cataleptic impression is said to have the power, just through its own felt quality, to drag us to assent, to convince us that things could not be otherwise. It is defined as a mark or impress in the soul" (Nussbaum, *Love's Knowledge*, 265).

64. Ibid., 265.

65. See Kruger ("Medical and Moral Authority," 52) for a discussion of this term in medieval poetry.

66. Skulsky, "Spenser's Despair Episode," 235. For a broad account of these issues, see also Popkin, *History of Skepticism from Erasmus to Descartes*.

67. Skulsky points to Spenser's use of Archimago's successful machinations as evidence that the poem accepts this skeptical argument. He abuses Red Crosse's fantasy by "simulat[ing] one of the Academics' favorite counterexamples to the notion of the phantasia kataleptike: a twinning so perfect that even 'the maker selfe for all his wondrous witt / Was nigh beguiled with so goodly sight'" ("Spenser's Despair Episode," 239).

68. Ibid., 240.

69. Thomas Roche makes a similar observation for different reasons: "Despair intervenes when human love is not returned (Terwin) or when divine love is not apprehended (Red Crosse). Only Una and Arthur escape the menace of despair, because their love is faith both in the loved one and in love itself" ("Menace of Despair," 91).

70. Skulsky, "Spenser's Despair Episode," 241.

71. Nussbaum, *Love's Knowledge*, 267.

72. Spenser's response to skepticism is indebted to Calvin's position on what he took to be human beings' innate tendency to believe in God. As Alvin Plantinga has argued, this position survives in what is now called Reformed Epistemology. He quotes from the nineteenth-century Dutch theologian Herman Bavinck, whose description of "spontaneous testimony" is remarkably close to the notion of cataleptic impressions: "The so-called proofs are by no means the final grounds of our most certain conviction that God exists: This certainty is established only by faith; i.e., by the spontaneous testimony which forces itself upon us from every side" (Plantinga, "Reformed Objection to Natural Theology," 330).

73. Stanley Cavell, *Claim of Reason*, 412.

74. On the psychology of melancholia, Agamben writes: "[M]elancholia offers the paradox of an intention to mourn that precedes and anticipates the loss of the object" (*Stanzas*, 20).

75. Auerbach, "Figura," 59.

76. Ibid.

77. I derive this information about the theological significance of glory from Leopold Sabourin, "Glory of God."

78. David Lee Miller also discusses the imagery of birth here: "Arthur makes a womb of his imagination; inseminated with glory by his visionary copulation with the fairy queen, he gestates and gives birth to the noble deeds that constitute a comprehensive exemplum of magnificence" (*Poem's Two Bodies*, 129). He also notes the relevance of the ninth canto (129).

79. Sacks, *English Elegy*, 6.

80. Ibid., 7.

81. Wack, *Lovesickness in the Middle Ages*, 64.

82. See my discussion of this passage in chapter 2, p. 86.

83. See Parker, *Inescapable Romance*, 78–80, for a discussion of the implications of Spenser's use of *figurae*.

84. Auerbach, "Figura," 59.

85. Bishop Richard Hurd, *Letters on Chivalry and Romance*, 107–8, italics mine.

86. Ibid., 113.

87. Patricia Parker also notes the function of the *Tale of Sir Thopas* in drawing attention to the endlessness of romance. "The Tale of Sir Thopas may be Spenser's native *Orlando Innamorato*, the unfinished predecessor whose example bespeaks the difficulty of bringing this errant form to any satisfactory ending" (*Inescapable Romance*, 83). Unlike Parker, though, I argue that Spenser deploys this model of romance only to change it radically from within through the deliberate evocation of a typological structure.

88. Note the difference between this reading and that of Parker, who argues that Spenser's poem remains an "Old Testament" text in its deployment of shadowy figurae (*Inescapable Romance*, 79).

6. "THE LOVE-SICKE HART"

1. Glauce's attempts to cure Britomart suggest that she is following the medical guidelines for the cure of lovesickness; these emphasize herbal cures and the efficacy of counsel, or *confabulatio*: "Full many wayes within her troubled mind, / Old Glauce cast, to cure this Ladies griefe: / Full many waies she sought, but none could find, / Nor herbes, nor charmes, nor counsell, that is chiefe / And choisest med'cine for sicke harts reliefe" (3.3.5).

2. Edward Jorden, whose 1603 text on the condition called "suffocation of the mother" I shall discuss in detail later, refers to the common ascription of

symptoms such as Britomart's to "either . . . diabolicall possession, to witch-craft, to the immediate finger of the Almightie" (*Disease of the Suffocation*, 1).

3. Schoenfeldt, *Bodies and Selves*, 1.

4. The connection between love-melancholy and the hysterical disorders remained controversial, but the family resemblance between the symptoms of these disorders encouraged their connection. Ferrand confirms the connection in chapter 12 of his *Treatise on Lovesickness*, 263–65.

5. The uterine symbolism of this episode is central to Elizabeth Bellamy's psychoanalytic reading of Britomart's viewing of herself in the mirror: "The circumference of Merlin's 'glassie globe' (21.1) is described as 'round and hollow shaped' (19.8)—in effect, a simulacrum of vaginal or intrauterine enclosures. Merlin's mirror, then, becomes an uncanny anticipation of Luce Irigaray's privileged trope of the speculum. . . . As sure as the concave configuration of the surgeon's speculum penetrates female bodily cavities, so also does the signifiying space of Merlin's 'hollow shaped' speculum 'penetrate' Britomart's unconscious, representing her divided 'selfe' to herself" (*Translations of Power*, 207). Though I find Bellamy's reading of the episode in the light of Lacan's analysis of "specular méconnaissance" plausible, it is not necessary to reach forward to contemporary psychoanalysis to explain Spenser's use of specular imagery here. Giorgio Agamben aptly draws attention to the proliferation of images of reflection in medieval accounts of cognition. In Averroës he argues, "the whole cognitive process is . . . conceived as speculation in the strict sense, a reflection of phantasms from mirror to mirror. . . . To know is to bend over a mirror where the world is reflected, to descry images reflected from sphere to sphere: the medieval man [or woman] was always before a mirror, both when he looked around himself and when he surrendered himself to his own imagination" (*Stanzas*, 81). As we saw in chapter 1, (self-)reflection within the internal spirits of the subject is also central to Ficinian theories of cognition, which grow directly out of the medieval context discussed by Agamben.

6. Wofford, "Gendering Allegory," 8. Interestingly, Spenser also uses the closet to figure the inner source of male inspiration ("Deepe in the closet of my parts entyre, / Her worth is written with a golden quill: / that me with heavenly fury doth inspire, / and my glad mouth with her sweet praises fill" [*Amoretti*, 85, in Spenser, *Shorter Poems*, 652]).

7. Wack, *Lovesickness in the Middle Ages*, 109. Among Wack's examples is Boccaccio's Lisa (*Decameron* 10.7), whose melancholy condition threatened her very life: "[B]eing unable to endure it any longer, the beautiful Lisa fell ill and began to waste visibly from one day to the next, like snow in the rays of

the sun" (109). This description, of course, reminds us of Spenser's description of Britomart:

> Ne ought it mote the noble Mayd avayle,
> Ne slake the furie of her cruel flame,
> But that she still did waste, and still did wayle,
> That through long langour, and hart-burning brame
> She shortly like a pyned ghost became,
> Which long hath waited by the Stygian strond. (3.3.52)

8. Debra Hershkowitz (*Madness of Epic*, 20) notes that that Sappho is singled out by Longinus in his *Peri Hypsous* as an example of ἐρωτικαῖς μανίαις. I also argue (chapter three, pp. 123–24) that love-madness in classical literature seems in general to have been closely associated with women.

9. Sappho, fr. 9, in *Lyrics in the Original Greek*. Hershkowitz discusses this passage, pointing out that it "was considered in antiquity to be an exemplary treatment of the sufferings of erotic madness" (*Madness of Epic*, 20).

10. Longinus, *On the Sublime*, 10.3.

11. See Wack, *Lovesickness in the Middle Ages*, chapter 6.

12. Ferrand, *Treatise on Lovesickness*, 229, italics mine.

13. Helen King notes that "it would be fair to say that, in Hippocratic gynecology, all diseases are hysterical" ("Once upon a Text," 13).

14. Wack, *Lovesickness*, 123. Massimo Ciavolella also accounts for the paradoxical claim that women are both cooler than men and more subject to the emotional and physical disorder of lovesickness by pointing to the assocation between lovesickness and hysteria: "Le seule façon de réconcilier la froideur des femmes avec leur évidente extrême sensibilité et leur propension a l'erotomania consistait à associer la maladie avec le refoulement des sens et l'hystérie" (The only way to reconcile the coldness of women with their evident extreme sensitivity and propensity for lovesickness is to associate the disease with suppression of judgment and with hysteria) ("Métamorphoses sexuelles et sexualité féminine durant la Renaissance," 14).

15. The need to distinguish clearly between male and female forms of erotic melancholy is clearly allied to this conceptual shift. As Jacquart and Thomasset put it in their analysis of "the hysterical malady," "the hysterical malady was entirely 'rationalized' by doctors: female nature was sufficient to explain it, because of woman's unbridled sexual appetite and the imperfection of the substances she produced. It is thus hardly any cause for astonishment that writers did not retain the possibility of a male 'hysteria,' although this was suggested by Galen" (*Sexuality and Medicine in the Middle Ages*, 177).

16. Schoenfeldt, *Bodies and Selves*, 12.

17. For an interesting discussion of the ramifications of this feminization of love-melancholy for later periods, see Helen Small, *Love's Madness*. Small notes that "the feminization of love-madness is often taken to be a phenomenon of the late eighteenth and early nineteenth centuries, but in the case of love-madness that gender shift occurs nearly 100 years earlier" (7). As we have seen, in fact, this shift occurs considerably earlier than this, and certainly by the sixteenth century. Small goes on to argue that this shift "paved the way for the eighteenth century's primary emphasis on women as the typical sufferers from debility of the nerves" (7).

18. Beecher, "Lover's Body."

19. Jorden, *Disease of the Suffocation*, 2, italics mine.

20. See Wofford, "Gendering Allegory," 9. In general, critics who address the graphic nature of Britomart's descriptions tend to be medically vague. James Broaddus's account comes closest to locating Britomart's condition within the medical tradition: "The episode cannot be adequately understood apart from the inescapable physiology of the time: the Galenic theory of bodily humors, in which both male and female seed were humors or fluids concocted by the testicles from blood, one of the four humors" (*Spenser's Allegory of Love*, 26). Though noting the inadequacy of purely Neoplatonic accounts of Britomart's love, he remains vague on the specific nature of her complaint: "Britomart thinks she is suffering from something like stomach cancer but actually describes symptoms, both psychological and physiological, of her newly awakened and powerfully aroused sexuality. . . . This is no merely periodic flow that she experiences; she is describing a malaise from which she gets no relief and she does not exaggerate. Her words express her not to be discounted sense of her new psychophysiological state" (28).

21. McCracken, *Curse of Eve*, 5.

22. Jacquart and Thomasset, *Sexuality and Medicine*, 175.

23. Schoenfeldt, *Bodies and Selves*, 13.

24. Jorden, *Disease of the Suffocation*, 20, italics mine.

25. Jorden, *Disease of the Suffocation*, 16. Glauce's attempts to treat Britomart suggest that she is attempting to purge Britomart of "excremental" blood. For a full and fascinating discussion of the uses of herbs for contraception and abortion in this period, see Riddle, *Eve's Herbs*. The herbs that Glauce chooses ("rew, and savine, and the flowre / of Camphora, and Calamint, and Dill" (3.2.49) were commonly held to regulate female fertility. According to early printed herbals, calamint "stimulate[s] menstruation," while rue and

artemisia also "stimulate menstruation and expel a dead fetus" (*Eve's Herbs*, 140). Savin, according to Riddle, was thought to "provoke menstruation better than any medicine" (140), and for this reason was recommended as an abortifacient. Rue, similarly, "destroys the ability to get children if used in the long term." Riddle points out that such herbal regulation of female fertility was regarded with extreme suspicion in the period, and midwives who possessed this information were commonly thought to be witches. The odd ritual that Glauce carries out in order to "undoe her daughters love" also associates her with the practice of witchcraft: "That sayd, her round about she from her turned, / She turned her contrarie to the sunne" (3.2.51). Riddle describes a ritual performed by a certain Jean Sprot, a sixteenth-century woman thought to be a witch: "She practised a ritual known to promote fertility when done in the sun, but she went 'against the sun' when performing the ritual, an indication of evil intention" (*Eve's Herbs*, 118).

26. As Ferrand makes clear, blood plays a key role in the development of nonpathological passionate love: "[A] copious amount of blood of a good temper and rich in spirits through the constant influence of the heart is a true antecedent cause of love as a passion of the soul because blood is the material cause of seed" (*Treatise on Lovesickness*, 250).

27. Ferrand clarifies that in love-melancholy the heart is not the diseased part itself (the brain is the diseased part) but is "the seat of the cause of the disease" (ibid., 257).

28. Ibid., 256, italics mine.

29. Bellamy, *Translations of Power*, 197.

30. Jacquart and Thomasset outline the debate over whether female seed existed: Aristotle states unequivocally that "the female does not contribute any semen to generation," while Hippocrates, followed by the Arabic doctors, claims that the embryo was formed from the union of male and female seed. (*Sexuality and Medicine*, 61–66). Western doctors, by and large, accept the existence of female seed.

31. See, e.g., Ferrand, *Treatise on Lovesickness*, 250.

32. "Solubility" in this context amounts to the healthy flow—through digestion and excretion—of essential bodily fluids. Schoenfeldt argues cogently that the centrality of this conception of the self speaks against a Bakhtinian notion of the enclosed, or "classical" body: "This critical link between health and flow urges revision of the account of the ideal classical body we have inherited from Bakhtin's compelling work on Rabelais. Under the Galenic regime of the humors, which imagines illness as an imbalance among the four nutritive

fluids produced by digestion, soundness of mind and body is achieved not by immuring bodily fluids but rather by carefully manipulating them" (*Bodies and Selves*, 14).

33. Jorden, *Disease of the Suffocation*, 20, italics mine.

34. See my discussion of pneuma in chapter 1, pp. 26–27.

35. Arisotle, Problem 31,. sect. 4, quoted in Ferrand, *Treatise on Lovesickness*, 414 n. 5.

36. Constantinus Africanus, *Opera Ysaac*, bk. 6, chap. 11, quoted in Jacquart and Thomasset, *Sexuality and Medicine*, 174.

37. The misogyny implicit in the interpretation of female blood and seed as potentially disease-causing is evident: "[T]hat the disease was caused by the retention of menstrual blood or of seed could only reinforce a belief in the harmfulness of these substances. While the sexually active woman could contaminate man without herself suffering . . . the chaste woman lost her immunity: the venom turned against her organism and led her to the verge of madness or death" (Jacquart and Thomasset, *Sexuality and Medicine*, 174). Massimo Ciavolella also notes the misogyny that underlies treatment of the disease; since coitus was recommended as the treatment for "hysterical" young women, asylums known as "carneficina" promoted this so-called therapy at the discretion of the doctors ("Métamorphoses sexuelles," 15).

38. Ferrand, *Treatise on Lovesickness*, 230.

39. Ciavolella notes the casual misogyny underlying these claims: "[L]a possibilité même de ce processus d'éversion . . . est chargée de la notion de l'Autre, le 'monstrum'; mais aussi de la source et du produit monstrueux des transformations anormales—la pervertie et la pervertisseuse" (Even the possibility of this process of inversion . . . is infused with the notion of the Other, the monster; but also with the notion of the depraved and depraving woman as the source and monstrous product of these transformations) ("Métamorphoses Sexuelles," 19).

40. Bellamy, *Translations of Power*, 206.

41. Jorden, *Disease of Suffocation*, 14.

42. Ferrand, *Treatise on Lovesickness*, 264.

43. Du Laurens, *Treatise of the Preservation of Sight*, 97, italics mine.

44. Ibid., 96, italics mine.

45. Ibid., 97.

46. Ferrand, *Treatise on Lovesickness*, 280, italics mine.

47. Ibid., 270.

48. Compare Spenser's very similar description of the Petrarchan lover, Scudamour:

What equall torment to the grief of mind,
And pyning anguish hid in gentle hart,
That inly feeds it selfe with thoughts unkind,
And nourisheth her own consuming smart?
. . . .
Such was the wound that Scudamour did gride;
For which Dan Phebus selfe cannot a salve provide. (4.6.1)

49. Numerous critics have noted the ubiquitous wound imagery in book 3. Elizabeth Jane Bellamy (*Translations of Power*) and Jonathan Goldberg (*Endlesse Worke*) in particular read the wound in terms of a metapsychological exploration of trauma (Bellamy) and subjectivity (Goldberg). Bellamy's remarks are representative: "The wound, of course, is a recurring trope throughout *The Faerie Queene*; much of the epic would appear to be Spenser's investigation of a metapsychology of trauma and the extent to which it serves as the beginning of consciousness itself. Significant episodes throughout the narrative are particularly devoted to a virtual epistemology of the wound and its relationship to a narcissistic subjectivity" (*Translations of Power*, 197 n. 13). Although these critics are certainly correct in noting a relationship between the wound and an exploration of subjectivity in the poem, the bleeding, internal wound, like Lucretius's *vulnus caecum*, gains its full meaning only from the medical discourse of love that emphasizes a radically material conception of selfhood.

50. Spenser's representation of Britomart also supports Michael Schoenfeldt's more general claim that in this period "the purportedly immaterial self is constituted as a profoundly material substance" (*Bodies and Selves*, 10).

51. Jacquart and Thomasset, *Sexuality and Medicine*, 176. The quotation is taken from John of Gaddesden's *Rosa Anglica*.

52. Ferrand, *Treatise on Lovesickness*, 333.

53. We might compare Glauce's activities with those of the actual witch whose son is in love with Florimell; frightened by the strength of his grief when Florimell disappears, she struggles to quench his "brutish lust": "All wayes she sought, him to restore to plight, / With herbs, with charms, with counsell, and with teares" (3.7.21). The love of this "chorle" is characterized as "brutish lust, that was so beastly tind" (3.7.15) and perhaps suggests how Britomart's "franticke" love might develop under Glauce's misguided tutelage.

54. Elizabeth Story Donno defines the epyllion as "the erotic-mythological verse narrative" (*Elizabethan Minor Epics*, 60).

55. "Through its indulgence in peripheral sexualities and its exploitation of eroticism, the epyllion promotes what is marginal and even what is transgressive" (Brown, *Redefining Elizabethan Literature*, 106). Brown also argues

that "the genre provides an experimental intellectual space in which to explore the ways marginality and transgression interact with sexuality and gender" (106). This point seems especially relevant to Spenser's exploration of a (potentially transgressive) sexual quest that begins in untutored eroticism and progresses to a steadier conception of marital sexuality.

56. Padel, *Whom the Gods Destroy*, 15. See my discussion of female love-madness in classical literature, chapter 3, pp. 123–24.

57. Brown, *Redefining English Literature*, 168.

58. Virgil, *Aeneid* 12.64–9.

59. *Petrarch's Secretum*, 84.

60. Agamben, *Stanzas*, 5.

61. Ibid., 8.

62. Ibid., 5.

63. Rancor and impatience are often considered to be features of, or related to, *acedia*. See Wenzel, *Sin of Sloth*, 191 ff.

64. See in particular Maureen Quilligan: "Busyrane's instrument of torture is his lyric pen, and a profoundly reverberating pun on this word insists on the sterile, prisonlike effect of his art" (*Milton's Spenser*, 198). Lauren Silberman also reads the House of Busirane as Spenser's critical investigation of Petrarchan poetics: "[I]n the Petrarchan discourse here subjected to critique, female desire is construed as a function of male desire" (*Transforming Desire*, 61).

65. See Agamben's discussion of the iconography of *acedia*: "This desperate sinking into the abyss that is opened between desire and its unobtainable object was fixed by medieval iconography in the type of acedia, represented as a woman who desolately lets her gaze fall to earth and abandons her head to the support of her hand" (*Stanzas*, 7).

66. As we noted earlier (introduction, p. 11, we might compare this long tradition of the melancholic "turn" inward with Jean Laplanche's analysis of sexuality as a phantasmic derivation from the "vital function" of feeding: "[F]or sexuality, it is the reflexive (*selbst* or *auto*) moment that is constitutive: the moment of turning back towards the self, an 'autoerotism' in which *the object has been replaced by a fantasy, by an object reflected within the subject*" (*Life and Death in Psychoanalysis*, 88, italics mine).

67. It is significant that the fantasy is associated in Spenser's poem with women and children as well as lovers. In Phantastes's chamber, "idle fantasies . . . flit" in the minds of "fooles, lovers, children, Dames" (2.9.50), and here in the house of Busirane the poet refers to the "phantasies" that occur "in waver-

ing wemens wit" (3.12.26). The melancholic lover, as we have seen, suffered from symptoms that during this time period "connote feminine and infantile behavior" (Wack, *Lovesickness in the Middle Ages*, 151).

68. Aristotle, *Nicomachean Ethics*, 1150b25.

69. Ficino, *De amore*, 6.9.

70. Spenser seems to use the word "abuse" in a similarly Ficinian context at *Proem* 4.2: "Such ones ill iudge of love, that cannot love, / Ne in their frosen hearts feele kindly flame: / for thy they ought not thing unknowne reprove, / Ne naturall affection faultlesse blame, / For fault of few that have abusd the same."

71. John Watkins suggests rather that "Busirane's spectacles metaphorically mirror aspects of [Britomart's] continually frustrated longing for Arthegall" (*Specter of Dido*, 171). But the point seems to be that Britomart, unlike Scudamour, has distanced herself from her erotic melancholy sufficiently both to enter the house and ultimately to destroy it. The entrapment of Amoret cannot be attributed to Britomart, but clearly results from Scudamour's obsessive desire for her.

72. "In the context of Scudamore's account, denay has the sense of 'to say 'no' to the claims of' (OED s.v. 'deny' 2). That is to say, Busirane continues to torment Amoret because she will not deny her commitment to Scudamore. However, another meaning of 'denay' as 'to withold anything desired' (OED s.v. 'deny' 3.5) suggests that Amoret is tormented by Busirane because she will not deny anything to her lover Scudamore" (Silberman, *Transforming Desire*, 65).

73. Nussbaum, *Therapy of Desire*, 177, italics mine.

74. Freud, "Mourning and Melancholia," 172.

75. Schiesari, *Gendering of Melancholia*, 110–12.

76. Ibid., 112.

77. For accounts that address the negative overtones of the hermaphrodite image, see in particular Cheney, "'Spenser's Hermaphrodite' and the 1590 Faerie Queene," and Berger, *Revisionary Play*, 191–94.

78. Watkins, *Specter of Dido*, 172.

79. Ibid.

80. Agamben, *Stanzas*, 6.

81. Wofford, *Choice of Achilles*, 259; Watkins, *Specter of Dido*, 173–74.

82. Watkins, *Specter of Dido*, 173.

83. Ibid.

CONCLUSION

1.   McEwan's 1997 novel *Enduring Love* depicts the obsessive love of Jed Perry for a virtual stranger, the science writer Joe Rose. The novel's appendices discuss this love in light of the psychiatric disorder known as De Clérambault's syndrome, an illness presenting as a delusional love for a stranger.

2.   Mario Praz notes the affinity between Keats's poem and Baudelaire's remark (*Oeuvres Posthumes*, 319): "La mélancolie, toujours inséparable du sentiment du beau" (Praz, *Romantic Agony*, 30).

3.   Gilbert and Gubar, *Madwoman in the Attic*, 574.

4.   Kristeva, *Black Sun*, 61. See my discussion of these Kristevan terms in chapter 2, pp. 87–90.

5.   Krier, *Birth Passages*, 13; see also my discussion of these issues in chapter 2, especially pp. 79–81.

6.   Kristeva, *Black Sun*, 42.

7.   See my discussion of *Rime Sparse* 23 (which contains the phrase "estrania voce," l.63), chapter 2, p. 92.

8.   Gilbert and Gubar, *Madwoman in the Attic*, 574.

9.   Bloom, "Internalization of Quest Romance," 15.

10.   The letter is dated April 16, 1819 (no. 159), in *Letters of John Keats, 1814–1821*, 2:91.

11.   See Utley, "Infernos of Lucretius and of Keats' La Belle Dame," 108–9.

12.   Text and translation of Dante's poem come from *The Divine Comedy*, trans. and with commentary by Charles S. Singleton.

13.   Keats, *Letters*, 2:91.

14.   Ibid.

15.   Keats, *Letters*, 1:185.

16.   Hartman, "On Traumatic Knowledge," 555.

17.   Ibid.

18.   Keats, *Letters*, 1:185.

19.   Wolfson, "Language of Interpretation in Romantic Poetry," 37. Patricia Packer (*Inescapable Romance*, 85) notes that Spenser's "Dearely sure" is "at least potentially as ambiguous" as Keats's "sure in language strange."

20.   Gordon Braden notes in passing the possible connection between these Spenserian and Petrarchan moments (*Petrarchan Love and the Continental Renaissance*, 82).

21.   Kristeva, *Black Sun*, 5.

22.   Baudelaire, *Art in Paris*, 65. See also 52 ff. for a discussion of Delacroix as a modern "romantic."

Bibliography

Abraham, Nicolas, and Maria Torok. *The Shell and the Kernel: Renewals of Psychoanalysis*. Translated and edited by Nicholas T. Rand. Chicago: University of Chicago Press, 1994.

Agamben, Giorgio. *Stanzas: Word and Phantasm in Western Culture*. Translated by Ronald L. Martinez. Minneapolis, MN: University of Minnesota Press, 1993.

Ariosto, Ludovico. *Orlando Furioso*. Translated by Allan Gilbert. 2 vols. New York: S. F. Vanni, 1954.

———. *Orlando Furioso*. Edited by Santorre Debenedetti and Cesare Segre. Collezione di Opere Inedite o Rare, vol. 122. Bologna: Commissione per i Testi di Lingua, 1960.

———. *Orlando Furioso*. Edited by Marcello Turchi, with a critical essay by Edoardo Sanguineti. 2 vols. Milan: Garzanti Editore, 1974.

Aristotle. *The Basic Works of Aristotle*. Edited by Richard McKeon. New York: Random House, 1941.

Arnaldus de Villanova. *Tractatus de amore heroico*. Edited by Michael R. McVaugh. In *Opera medica omnia*, III. Barcelona: Universidad de Barcelona, 1985.

Ascoli, Albert. *Ariosto's Bitter Harmony: Crisis and Evasion in the Italian Renaissance*. Princeton, NJ: Princeton University Press, 1987.

Auerbach, Erich. "Figura." Chap. 7 in *Scenes from the Drama of European Literature*. New York: Meridian Books, 1959.

Avicenna. *Liber canonis*. Venice, 1507.

———. *Liber de anima seu sextus de naturalibus*. Edited by S. Van Riet. 2 vols. Louvain: Editions orientalistes; Leiden: E. J. Brill, 1968–72.

———. "A Treatise on Love." Translated by Emil Fackenheim. *Medieval Studies* 7 (1945): 208–28.

Babb, Lawrence. *The Elizabethan Malady: A Study of Melancholia in English Literature from 1580 to 1642*. East Lansing, MI: Michigan State University Press, 1951.

Basile, Bruno. *Poëta melancholicus: Tradizione classica e follia nell'ultimo Tasso*. Pisa: Pacini Editore, 1984.

Baudelaire, Charles. *Art in Paris 1845–1862: Salons and Other Exhibitions*. Translated and edited by Jonathan Mayne. London: Phaidon, 1965.

———. *Oeuvres posthhumes*. Paris: Mercure de France, 1908.

Beecher, Donald. "The Lover's Body: The Somatogenesis of Love in Renaissance Medical Treatises." *Renaissance and Reformation* 24, no. 1 (1988): 1–12.

Beecher, Donald, and Massimo Ciavolella. Introduction to *A Treatise on Lovesickness*, by Jacques Ferrand. Syracuse, NY: Syracuse University Press, 1990.

Bellamy, Elizabeth. *Translations of Power: Narcissism and the Unconscious in Epic History.* Ithaca, NY: Cornell University Press, 1992.

Berger, Harry. *Revisionary Play: Studies in the Spenserian Dynamics.* Berkeley: University of California Press, 1988.

Bernard of Gordon. *Practica dicta Lilium medicinae.* N.p., 1486.

Bird, Otto. "The Commentary of Dino del Garbo on Cavalcanti's Canzone d'Amore." *Medieval Studies* 2 (1940): 150–203.

———. "The Commentary of Dino del Garbo on Cavalcanti's Canzone d'Amore." *Medieval Studies* 3 (1941): 117–60.

Bloom, Harold. "The Internalization of Quest Romance." Chap. 2 in *The Ringers in the Tower: Studies in the Romantic Tradition.* Chicago: University of Chicago Press, 1971.

Boiardo, Matteo Maria. *Orlando Innamorato.* Translated by Charles Stanley Ross. Foreword by Allen Mandelbaum. Berkeley: University of California Press, 1989.

Boitani, Piero. "Petrarch's *Dilectoso Male* and Its European Context." In *Zusammenhänge, Einflüsse, Wirkungen: Kongressakten zum Tübingen Symposium des Mediävistenverbandes,* edited by Karl Heinz Göller, Joerg Fichte, and Bernhard Schimmelpfennig, 299–315. Berlin: De Gruyter, 1986.

Bonnefis, Phillipe. "The Melancholic Describer." *Yale French Studies* 61 (1983): 145–75.

Braden, Gordon. *Petrarchan Love and the Continental Renaissance.* New Haven, CT: Yale University Press, 1999.

Bright, Timothy. *Treatise of Melancholie.* Reproduced from the 1586 edition printed by Thomas Vautrollier. New York: Facsimile Text Society, Columbia University Press, 1940.

Broaddus, James. *Spenser's Allegory of Love: Social Vision in Books III, IV, and V of the Faerie Queene.* Madison, NJ: Fairleigh Dickinson University Press, 1995.

Brown, Georgia. *Redefining Elizabethan Literature.* Cambridge: Cambridge University Press, 2004.

Brown, Peter, ed. *Reading Dreams: The Interpretation of Dreams from Chaucer to Shakespeare.* Oxford: Oxford University Press, 1999.

Brown, Robert D. *Lucretius on Love and Sex: A Commentary on the De Rerum Natura IV, 1030–1287 with Prolegomena, Text, and Translation.* Leiden: E. J. Brill, 1987.

Burton, Robert. *The Anatomy of Melancholy.* Edited by Floyd Dell and Paul Jordan-Smith. New York: Tudor, 1927.

Bynum, Caroline Walker. *Holy Feast and Holy Fast: The Religious Significance of Food to Medieval Women.* Berkeley: University of California Press, 1987.

Carne-Ross, D. S. "The One and the Many: A Reading of *Orlando Furioso.*" *Arion* 5, no. 1 (1966): 195–234.

———. "The One and the Many: A Reading of the *Orlando Furioso.*" *Arion,* n.s., 3 (1976): 146–220.

Catullus. "The Poems of Gaius Valerius Catullus." Translated by F. W. Cornish. In *Catullus, Tibullus, Pervigilium Veneris*. Loeb Classical Library. Cambridge, MA: Harvard University Press, 1976.

Cavallo, Jo Ann. "Tasso's Armida and the Victory of Romance." In Finucci, *Renaissance Transactions*, 77–111.

Cavell, Stanley. *The Claim of Reason: Wittgenstein, Skepticism, Morality, and Tragedy*. Oxford: Oxford University Press, 1979.

Chambers, Jane. "'For Love's Sake': Lamia and Burton's Love Melancholy." *Studies in English Literature* 22 (1982): 583–600.

Chaucer, Geoffrey. *The Riverside Chaucer*. Edited by Larry D. Benson. 3rd ed. Boston, MA: Houghton Mifflin, 1987.

Cheney, Donald. "Spenser's Hermaphrodite and the 1590 Faerie Queene." *PMLA* 87 (1972): 192–200.

———. *Spenser's Image of Nature: Wild Man and Shepherd in the Faerie Queene*. New Haven, CT: Yale University Press, 1966.

Ciavolella, Massimo. "Eros/Ereos? Marsilio Ficino's Interpretation of Guido Cavalcanti's 'Donna me prega.'" In *Ficino and Renaissance Neoplatonism*, edited by Konrad Eisenbichler and Olga Zorzi Pugliese, 39–49. Ottawa, ON: Dovehouse Editions, 1986.

———. "Métamorphoses sexuelles et sexualité feminine durant la Renaissance." *Renaissance and Reformation* 12, no. 1 (1988): 13–20.

———. "Eros and the Phantasms of Hereos." In *Eros and Anteros: The Medical Traditions of Love in the Renaissance*, edited by Donald Beecher and Massimo Ciavolella, 75–80. University of Toronto Italian Studies. Toronto: Dovehouse Editions, 1992.

———. "Saturn and Venus." In *Saturn from Antiquity to the Renaissance*, edited by Massimo Ciavolella and Amilcare A. Iannucci. University of Toronto Italian Studies 8. Toronto: University of Toronto Press, 1992.

Constantinus Africanus. *De melancholia, libri duo*. In *Opera omnia*, 280–98. Basel, 1536.

———. *Opera Ysaac*. Lyon: B. Trot and J. Platea, 1515.

Conte, Gian Biagio. *The Rhetoric of Imitation: Genre and Poetic Memory in Virgil and Other Latin Poets*. Ithaca, NY: Cornell University Press, 1986.

Couliano, Ioan. *Eros and Magic in the Renaissance*. Chicago: University of Chicago Press, 1987.

Dante, Alighieri. *The Divine Comedy*. Translated by Charles S. Singleton. Bollingen Series 80. Princeton, NJ: Princeton University Press, 1970.

Daremberg, Charles, and Emile Ruelle, eds. *Oeuvres de Rufus d'Ephèse*. Paris: Imprimérie Nationale, 1853.

Donato, Eugenio. "'Per Selve e Boscherecci Labirinti': Desire and Narrative Structure in Ariosto's *Orlando Furioso*." In *Literary Theory/Renaissance Texts*, edited by Patricia Parker and David Quint, 33–63. Baltimore, MD: Johns Hopkins University Press, 1986.

Donno, Elizabeth Story. *Elizabethan Minor Epics*. New York: Columbia University Press, 1963.

Du Laurens, André. *A Discourse of the Preservation of Sight: Of Melancholike Diseases; of Rheumes, and of Old Age*. London: Felix Kingston, 1599.

Durling, Robert. *The Figure of the Poet in Renaissance Epic*. Cambridge, MA: Harvard University Press, 1965.

Enterline, Lynn. *The Tears of Narcissus: Melancholia and Masculinity in Early Modern Writing*. Stanford, CA: Stanford University Press, 1995.

———. *The Rhetoric of the Body from Ovid to Shakespeare*. Cambridge: Cambridge University Press, 2000.

Everson, Jane E. *The Italian Romance Epic in the Age of Humanism: The Matter of Italy and the World of Rome*. Oxford: Oxford University Press, 2001.

Fantham, Elaine. "The Role of Lament in the Growth and Eclipse of Roman Epic." In *Epic Traditions in the Contemporary World*, edited by Margaret Beissinger, Jane Tylus, and Susanne Wofford, 221–35. Berkeley: University of California Press, 1999.

Felman, Shoshana. *Jacques Lacan and the Adventure of Insight: Psychoanalysis in Contemporary Culture*. Cambridge, MA: Harvard University Press, 1987.

Ferguson, Margaret. *Trials of Desire: Renaissance Defenses of Poetry*. New Haven, CT: Yale University Press, 1983.

Ferrand, Jacques. *A Treatise on Lovesickness*. Translated and edited by Donald A. Beecher and Massimo Ciavolella. Syracuse, NY: Syracuse University Press, 1990.

Ficino, Marsilio. *Commentarium Marsilii Ficino Florentini in Convivium Platonis de amore*. Edited by Sears Jayne. New York: Columbia University Press, 1944.

———. *Commentary on Plato's Symposium on Love*. Translated by Sears Jayne. Dallas: Spring Publications, 1985.

———. *Three Books on Life*. Edited and translated by Carol V. Kaske and John R. Clark. Medieval Texts and Studies 57. Renaissance Society of America Renaissance Text Series 11. Tempe, AR: Arizona Center for Medieval and Renaissance Studies in conjunction with the Renaissance Society of America, 2002.

Fink, Bruce. *The Lacanian Subject: Between Language and Jouissance*. Princeton, NJ: Princeton University Press, 1995.

Finucci, Valeria. *The Lady Vanishes: Subjectivity and Representation in Castiglione and Ariosto*. Stanford: Stanford University Press, 1992.

———, ed. *Renaissance Transactions: Ariosto and Tasso*. Durham, NC: Duke University Press, 1999.

Fowler, Don. "Vergil on Killing Virgins." In *Homo Viator*, edited by Michael Whitby, Philip Hardie, and Mary Whitby, 185–98. Bristol: Bristol University Press, 1987.

Fradenburg, Louise. *Sacrifice Your Love: Psychoanalysis, Historicism, Chaucer*. Minneapolis: University of Minnesota Press, 2002.

Freud, Sigmund. "The Ego and the Super-Ego." In vol. 19 of *The Standard Edition of the Complete Psychological Works of Sigmund Freud*, translated by James Strachey, 28–39. London: Hogarth Press, 1953–74.

———. "Mourning and Melancholia." In *General Psychological Theory: Papers on Metapsychology*, edited by Philip Rieff, 164–80. New York: Macmillan, 1963.

———. "On Transience." In *Art and Literature*, 283–90. Penguin Freud Library 14. London: Penguin, 1990.

Frye, Northrop. *The Great Code: The Bible and Literature*. New York: Harcourt Brace Jovanovich, 1982.

Frye, Susan. *Elizabeth I: The Competition for Representation*. Oxford: Oxford University Press, 1993.

Gerard of Solo. *Commentum super nono Almansoris*. Venice, 1505.

Giamatti, A. Bartlett. "Headlong Horses, Headless Horsemen: An Essay on the Chivalric Epics of Pulci, Boiardo, and Ariosto." In *Exile and Change in Renaissance Literature*, 33–76. New Haven, CT: Yale University Press, 1984.

Gilbert, Sandra M., and Susan Gubar. *The Madwoman in the Attic: The Woman Writer and the Nineteenth-Century Literary Imagination*. New Haven, CT: Yale University Press, 1979.

Goldberg, Jonathan. *Endlesse Worke: Spenser and the Structure of Discourse*. Baltimore, MD: Johns Hopkins University Press, 1981.

Golding, Arthur. "Epistle," in *Shakespeare's Ovid, Being Arthur Golding's Translation of the Metamorphoses*. Edited by W. H. D. Rouse. London: De La More Press, 1904.

Greene, Thomas M. *The Light in Troy: Imitation and Discovery in Renaissance Poetry*. New Haven, CT: Yale University Press, 1982.

Greenblatt, Stephen. "Psychoanalysis and Renaissance Culture." In *Literary Theory/Renaissance Texts*, edited by Patricia Parker and David Quint, 210–25. Baltimore, MD: Johns Hopkins University Press, 1986.

Gregerson, Linda. *The Reformation of the Subject: Spenser, Milton, and the English Protestant Epic*. Cambridge: Cambridge University Press, 1995.

Guillory, John. *Poetic Authority: Spenser, Milton, and Literary History*. New York: Columbia University Press, 1983.

Hadfield, Andrew. "Spenser and the Death of the Queen." In *Imagining Death in Spenser and Milton*, edited by Elizabeth Jane Bellamy, Patrick Cheney and Michael Schoenfeldt, 28–46. Hampshire and New York: Palgrave Macmillan, 2003.

Hartman, Geoffrey. "On Traumatic Knowledge and Literary Studies." *New Literary History* 26 (1995): 537–63.

Harvey, E. Ruth. *The Inward Wits: Psychological Theory in the Middle Ages and the Renaissance*. London: Warburg Institute, 1975.

Hasse, Dag Nikolaus. *Avicenna's De anima in the Latin West: The Formation of a Peripatetic Philosophy of the Soul 1160–1300*. London: Warburg Institute, 2000.

Haverkamp, Anselm. "Mourning Becomes Melancholia—A Muse Deconstructed: Keats's *Ode on Melancholy*." *New Literary History* 21.3 (1990): 693–706.

Heffernan, Carol Falvo. *The Melancholy Muse: Chaucer, Shakespeare and Early Medicine*. Duquesne Studies Language and Literature Series 19. Pittsburgh, PA: Duquesne University Press, 1995.

Hendershot, Cyndy. "Male Subjectivity, Fin Amour, and Melancholia in *The Book of the Duchess*." *Mediaevalia* 21 (1996): 1–27.

Hershkowitz, Debra. *The Madness of Epic: Reading Insanity from Homer to Statius*. Oxford: Clarendon Press, 1998.

Higashinaka, Itsuyo. "Spenser's Use of the Idea of Love Melancholy in The Faerie Queene." *Studies in English Literature* (Japan) (1972): 129–50.

Hurd, Bishop Richard. *Letters on Chivalry and Romance*. London: Printed for A. Millar, 1763.

Jackson, Stanley. *Melancholia and Depression: From Hippocratic Times to Modern Times*. New Haven, CT: Yale University Press, 1986.

Jacobus, Mary. *First Things: The Maternal Imaginary in Literature, Art, and Psychoanalysis*. New York: Routledge, 1995.

Jacquart, Danielle, and Claude Thomasset. *Sexuality and Medicine in the Middle Ages*. Princeton, NJ: Princeton University Press, 1995.

Jaeger, Stephen. *Ennobling Love: In Search of a Lost Sensibility*. Philadelphia: University of Pennsylvania Press, 1999.

Javitch, Daniel. "The Grafting of Virgilian Epic in *Orlando Furioso*." In Finucci, *Renaissance Transactions*, 56–77.

John of Gaddesden. *Rosa Anglica*. Augsburg, 1595.

Jorden, Edward. *Disease of the Suffocation of the Mother*. 1603. Edited by Michael Macdonald. Reprint, New York: Routledge, 1991.

Kay, Sarah. *Courtly Contradictions: The Emergence of the Literary Object in the Twelfth Century*. Stanford, CA: Stanford University Press, 2001.

Keats, John. *Complete Poems and Selected Letters*. Introduction by Edward Hirsch. New York: Modern Library, 2001.

———. *The Letters of John Keats 1814–1821*. Edited by Hyder Edward Rollins. 2 vols. Cambridge, MA: Harvard University Press, 1958.

King, Helen. "Once upon a Text: Hysteria from Hippocrates." In *Hysteria beyond Freud*, edited by Sander L. Gilman, Helen King, Roy Porter, G. S. Rousseau, and Elaine Showalter, 3–91. Berkeley: University of California Press, 1993.

Klibansky, Raymond, Erwin Panofsky, and Fritz Saxl. *Saturn and Melancholy: Studies in the History of Natural Philosophy, Religion, and Art*. New York: Basic Books, 1964.

Krier, Theresa M. *Birth Passages: Maternity and Nostalgia, Antiquity to Shakespeare*. Ithaca and London: Cornell University Press, 2003.

Kristeva, Julia. *Black Sun: Depression and Melancholia*. Translated by Leon S. Roudiez. New York: Columbia University Press, 1989.

Kruger, Steven. "Medical and Moral Authority in the Late Medieval Dream." In Brown, *Reading Dreams*, 51–84.

Laplanche, Jean. *Life and Death in Psychoanalysis*. Translated by Jeffrey Mehlman. Baltimore, MD: Johns Hopkins University Press, 1976.

Laqueur, Thomas. *Making Sex: Body and Gender from the Greeks to Freud*. Cambridge, MA: Harvard University Press, 1990.

Lear, Jonathan. *Happiness, Death, and the Remainder of Life: The Tanner Lectures on Human Values*. Cambridge, MA: Harvard University Press, 2000.

———. *Love and Its Place in Nature: A Philosophical Interpretation of Psychoanalysis*. New Haven, CT: Yale University Press, 1998.

Lewis, C. S. *The Allegory of Love: A Study in Medieval Tradition*. Oxford: Oxford University, Press, 1958.

Longinus. *On the Sublime*. Translated by James A. Arieti and John M. Crossett. Texts and Studies in Religion, vol. 21. New York: Edwin Mellen Press, 1985.

Lowes, John Livingston. "The Loveres Maladye of Hereos." *Modern Philology* 11 (1914): 491–546.

Lucretius. *De rerum natura*. Loeb Classical Library. Cambridge, MA: Harvard

University Press, 1975.

———. *On the Nature of the Universe*. Introduction and notes by Don and Peta Fowler. Translated by Ronald Melville. Oxford: Oxford University Press, 1977.

Lupton, Julia Reinhard, and Kenneth Reinhard. *After Oedipus: Shakespeare in Psychoanalysis*. Ithaca, NY: Cornell University Press, 1993.

Madsen, William. *From Shadowy Types to Truth*. New Haven, CT: Yale University Press, 1968.

Maley, Willy. *Salvaging Spenser: Colonialism, Culture and Identity*. London: Macmillan Press, 1997.

Marinelli, Peter. *Ariosto and Boiardo*. Columbia: University of Missouri Press, 1987.

Maus, Katharine Eisaman. *Inwardness and Theater in the English Renaissance*. Chicago: University of Chicago Press, 1995.

McClure, George. *Sorrow and Consolation in Italian Humanism*. Princeton, NJ: Princeton University Press, 1991.

McCracken, Peggy. *The Curse of Eve, the Wound of the Hero: Blood, Gender, and Medieval Literature*. Philadelphia: University of Pennsylvania Press, 2003.

McEwan, Ian. *Enduring Love*. New York: Anchor Books, 1997.

McVaugh, Michael R. Introduction to *Tractatus de amore heroico*, by Arnaldus of Villanova. In *Opera medica omnia*, vol. 3, 11–39. Barcelona: Universidad de Barcelona, 1985.

Menocal, Maria. *The Arabic Role in Medieval Literary History: A Forgotten Heritage*. Philadelphia: University of Pennsylvania Press, 1987.

Mesulam, Marek-Marsel, and Jon Perry. "The Diagnosis of Love-Sickness: Experimental Psychophysiology without the Polygraph." *Psychophysiology* 9 (1972): 546–51.

Michael, Emily. "Renaissance Theories of Body, Soul, and Mind." In Wright and Potter, *Psyche and Soma*, 147–73.

Migiel, Marilyn. *Gender and Genealogy in Tasso's "Gerusalemme Liberata."* Lewiston, NY: Edwin Mellen Press, 1993.

Miller, David Lee. *The Poem's Two Bodies: The Poetics of the 1590 Faerie Queene*. Princeton, NJ: Princeton University Press, 1991.

Momigliano, Attilio. *Saggio sull' 'Orlando Furioso.'* Bari: Laterza, 1928.

Mullen, P. E., and M. Pathé. "The Pathological Extensions of Love." *British Journal of Psychiatry* 165, no. 5 (1994): 614–23.

Murtaugh, Kristen Olson. "Erminia Delivered: Notes on Tasso and Romance." *Quaderni d'Italianistica* 3, no. 1 (1982): 12–25.

Nelson, John Charles. *Renaissance Theory of Love: The Context of Giordano Bruno's Eroici furori*. New York: Columbia University Press, 1958.

Nohrnberg, James. *The Analogy of the Faerie Queene*. Princeton, NJ: Princeton University Press, 1976.

Nussbaum, Martha C. *Love's Knowledge: Essays on Philosophy and Literature*. Oxford: Oxford University Press, 1990.

———. *The Therapy of Desire: Theory and Practice in Hellenistic Ethics*. Princeton, NJ: Princeton University Press, 1994.

Ovid. *Metamorphoses.* Translated by Frank Justus Miller. Revised by G. P. Goold. 2 vols. Loeb Classical Library. Reprint, Cambridge, MA: Harvard University Press, 1994.

Padel, Ruth. *Whom the Gods Destroy: Elements of Greek and Tragic Madness.* Princeton, NJ: Princeton University Press, 1995.

Parker, Patricia A. *Inescapable Romance: Studies in the Poetics of a Mode.* Princeton, NJ: Princeton University Press, 1979.

Paster, Gail Kern. *The Body Embarrassed: Drama and Disciplines of Shame in Early Modern England.* Ithaca, NY: Cornell University Press, 1993.

———, Katherine Rowe, and Mary Floyd-Wilson, eds. *Reading the Early Modern Passions: Essays in the Cultural History of Emotion.* Philadelphia: University of Pennsylvania Press, 2004.

Peele, Stanton. "Fools for Love: The Romantic Ideal, Psychological Theory, and Addictive Love." In Sternberg and Barnes, *Psychology of Love,* 159–91.

Perkins, William. *Cases of Conscience.* Cambridge: John Legate, 1606.

Petrarch, Francesco. *Petrarch's Lyric Poems: The Rime Sparse and Other Lyrics.* Translated and edited by Robert M. Durling. Cambridge, MA: Harvard University Press, 1976.

———. *Petrarch's Secretum.* Edited and translated by Davy A. Carozza and H. James Shey. American University Studies 12, Classical Languages and Literature 7. New York: Peter Lang, 1989.

———. *Secretum.* Edited by E. Carrara. In *Francesco Petrarca, Prose,* edited by G. Martellotti et al. La Letteratura Italiana 7. Milan: Riccardo Ricciardi Editore, 1955.

Petrocchi, Giorgio. *I fantasmi di Tancredi: Saggi sul Tasso e sul Rinascimento.* Caltanisetta: Salvatore Sciascia, 1972.

Plantinga, Alvin. "The Reformed Objection to Natural Theology." In *Philosophy of Religion: Selected Readings,* edited by Michael Peterson, William Hasker, Bruce Reichenbach, and David Basinger, 327–41. Oxford: Oxford University Press, 2001.

Plato. *The Collected Dialogues.* Edited by Edith Hamilton and Huntington Cairns. Bollingen Series 71. Princeton, NJ: Princeton University Press, 1961.

Popkin, Richard. *The History of Skepticism from Erasmus to Descartes.* Assen: Van Gorcum, 1964.

Praz, Mario. *The Romantic Agony.* Translated by Angus Davidson. London: Oxford University Press, 1933.

Quilligan, Maureen. *Milton's Spenser: The Politics of Reading.* Ithaca, NY: Cornell University Press, 1983.

Quint, David. "The Death of Brandimarte and the Ending of the *Orlando Furioso.*" *Annali d'Italianistica* 12 (1994): 75–86.

———. *Epic and Empire: Politics and Generic Form from Virgil to Milton.* Princeton, NJ: Princeton University Press, 1993.

———. "The Figure of Atlante: Ariosto and Boiardo's Poem." *Modern Language Notes* 94 (1979): 77–91.

———. "The Fortunes of Morgana: From Boiardo to Marino." In *Boiardo in America,* edited by Jo Ann Cavallo and Charles Stanley Ross, 17–29. Medieval and Renaissance Texts and Studies no. 183. Ithaca, NY: Cornell University Press, 1998.

Radden, Jennifer. *The Nature of Melancholy from Aristotle to Kristeva*. Oxford: Oxford University Press, 2000.

Rambuss, Richard. "'Process of Tyme': History, Consolation, and Apocalypse in *The Book of the Duchess*." *Exemplaria* 2, no. 2 (1990): 659–83.

Resta, G. "Il sogno di Orlando." In *I metodi attuali della critica in Italia*, edited by M. Corti and C. Segre, 144–53. Turin: ERI/Edizioni RAI, 1970.

Riddle, John M. *Eve's Herbs: A History of Contraception and Abortion in the West*. Cambridge, MA: Harvard University Press, 1999.

Roccatagliata, Giuseppe. *A History of Ancient Psychiatry*. New York: Greenwood Press, 1986.

Roche, Thomas. "The Menace of Despair and Arthur's Vision, *The Faerie Queene* 1.9." *Spenser Studies* 4 (1983): 71–93.

Sabourin, Leopold. "Glory of God." In *The Oxford Companion to the Bible*, edited by Bruce M. Metzger and Michael D. Coogan. Oxford: Oxford University Press, 1993.

Sacks, Peter M. *The English Elegy: Studies in the Genre from Spenser to Yeats*. Baltimore, MD: Johns Hopkins University Press, 1985.

Sappho. *Lyrics in the Original Greek*. Translated by Willis Barnstone. New York: Anchor Books, 1965.

Sawday, Jonathan. *The Body Emblazoned: Dissection and the Human Body in Renaissance Culture*. London: Routledge, 1995.

Saxl, Fritz. "Veritas Filia Temporis." In *Philosophy and History: Essays Presented to Ernst Cassirer*, edited by Raymond Klibansky and H. J. Paton, 197–222. Oxford: Clarendon Press, 1963.

Schiesari, Juliana. *The Gendering of Melancholia: Feminism, Psychoanalysis, and the Symbolics of Loss*. Ithaca, NY: Cornell University Press, 1992.

———. "The Victim's Discourse: Torquato Tasso's 'Canzone al Metauro.'" *Stanford Italian Review* 5, no. 2 (1985): 189–205.

Schoenfeldt, Michael. *Bodies and Selves in Early Modern England: Physiology and Inwardness in Spenser, Shakespeare, Herbert, and Milton*. Cambridge: Cambridge University Press, 1999.

Segal, Charles. "Virgil's Sixth Eclogue and the Problem of Evil." Chap. 13 in *Poetry and Myth in Ancient Pastoral: Essays on Theocritus and Virgil*. Princeton, NJ: Princeton University Press, 1981.

Sells, Michael. *The Literature of Al-Andalus*. Cambridge: Cambridge University Press, 2000.

Sennertus, Daniel. *Practical Physick*. 2 vols. London: Peter Cole, 1662–64.

Silberman, Lauren. *Transforming Desire: Erotic Knowledge in Books 3 and 4 of "The Faerie Queene."* Berkeley: University of California Press, 1995.

Siraisi, Nancy. *Medieval and Early Renaissance Medicine: An Introduction to Knowledge and Practice*. Chicago: University of Chicago Press, 1990.

Skulsky, Harold. "Spenser's Despair Episode and the Theology of Doubt." *Modern Philology* 78, no. 3 (1981): 227–42.

Skura, Meredith. "Understanding the Living and Talking to the Dead: The Historicity of Psychoanalysis." In *The Uses of Literary History*, edited by Marshall Brown, 93–107. Durham, NC: Duke University Press, 1995.

Small, Helen. *Love's Madness: Medicine, the Novel, and Female Insanity, 1800–1865*. Oxford: Clarendon Press, 1996.

Smith, Bruce. *The Acoustic World of Early Modern England: Attending to the O Factor*. Chicago: University of Chicago Press, 1999.

Snyder, Susan. "The Left Hand of God: Despair in the Medieval and Renaissance Tradition." *Studies in the Renaissance* 12 (1965): 18–59.

Solerti, Angelo. *Vita di Torquato Tasso*. Turin: Ermanno Loescher, 1895.

Spenser, Edmund. *The Faerie Queene*. Edited by A. C. Hamilton. London: Longman, 1977.

———. *The Yale Edition of the Shorter Poems*. Edited by William A. Oram, Einar Bjorvand, Ronald Bond, Thomas H. Cain, Alexander Dunlop, and Richard Schell. New Haven, CT: Yale University Press, 1989.

Staden, Heinrich von. "Body, Soul, and Nerves: Epicurus, Herophilus, Erasistratus, the Stoics, and Galen." In Wright and Potter, *Psyche and Soma*, 79–117.

Stallybrass, Peter. "Patriarchal Territories: The Body Enclosed," in *Rewriting the Renaissance: Discourses of Difference in Early Modern Europe*, edited by Margaret Ferguson, Maureen Quilligan, and Nancy Vickers, 123–44. Chicago: Chicago University Press, 1986.

Staten, Henry. *Eros in Mourning: Homer to Lacan*. Baltimore, MD: Johns Hopkins University Press, 1995.

Sternberg, Robert J., and Michael L. Barnes, eds. *The Psychology of Love*. New Haven, CT: Yale University Press, 1988.

Synesius. *De somniis*. Translated by Marsilio Ficino. 1549.

Tasso, Torquato. *Dialoghi*. Edited by Ezio Raimondi. 3 vols. Florence: Sansoni, 1958.

———. *Discourses on the Heroic Poem*. Translated by Mariella Cavalchini and Irene Samuel. Oxford: Clarendon Press, 1973.

———. *Gerusalemme Liberata*. Edited by Lanfranco Caretti. Turin: Einaudi, 1971.

———. *Jerusalem Delivered: An English Prose Version*. Translated and edited by Ralph Nash. Detroit: Wayne State University Press, 1987.

———. "La Molza overo de l'amore." In *Dialoghi*, 745–60.

———. *Prose*. Edited by Ettore Mazzali. Introduction by Francesco Flora. Milan: Ricciardi, 1959.

Trevor, Douglas. "Sadness in The Faerie Queene." In *Reading the Early Modern Passions*, edited by Gail Kern Paster, Katherine Rowe, and Mary Floyd-Wilson, 240–53. Philadelphia: University of Pennsylvania Press, 2004.

Tyndale, William. *The Works of the English Reformers: William Tyndale and John Frith*. Edited by Thomas Russell. 3 vols. London: Ebenezer Palmer, 1831.

Utley, Francis Lee. "The Infernos of Lucretius and of Keats' La Belle Dame Sans Merci." *English Literary History* 25, no. 2 (1958): 105–21.

Valescus de Taranta. *Philonium*. Lyons, 1526.

Valleriola, Francois. *Observationum medicinalium libri VI*. Lyons, 1588.

Virgil. *Eclogues, Georgics, Aeneid*. Edited by G. P. Goold. Translated by H. R.

Fairclough. Loeb Classical Library. 2 vols. Reprint, Cambridge, MA: Harvard University Press, 1994.

Wack, Mary Frances. "The *Liber de heros morbo* of Johannes Afflacius and Its Implications for Medieval Love Conventions." *Speculum* 62, no. 2 (1987): 324–44.

———. *Lovesickness in the Middle Ages: The Viaticum and Its Commentaries*. Philadelphia: University of Pennsylvania Press, 1990.

———. "New Medieval Medical Texts on *Amor Hereos*." In *Zusammenhänge, Einflüsse, Wirkungen: Kongressakten zum Tübinger Symposium des Mediävistenverbandes*, edited by Karl Heinz Göller, Joerg Fichte, and Bernhard Schimmelpfennig, 288–98. Berlin: De Gruyter, 1986.

Watkins, John. *The Specter of Dido: Spenser and the Virgilian Epic*. New Haven, CT: Yale University Press, 1995.

Weaver, Elissa. "A Reading of the Interlaced Plot of the Orlando Furioso: The Three Cases of Love Madness." *In Ariosto Today: Contemporary Perspectives*, edited by Donald Beecher, Massimo Ciavolella, and Roberto Fedi, 126–54. Toronto: University of Toronto Press, 2003.

Weinberg, Bernard. *A History of Literary Criticism in the Italian Renaissance*. 2 vols. Chicago: University of Chicago Press, 1961.

Wenzel, Siegfried. *The Sin of Sloth: Acedia in Medieval Thought and Literature*. Chapel Hill, NC: University of North Carolina Press, 1960.

Wilhelm, James J., ed. *Lyrics of the Middle Ages: An Anthology*. New York: Garland, 1990.

Williams, Gordon. *Tradition and Originality in Roman Poetry*. Oxford: Clarendon Press, 1968.

Wofford, Susanne. *The Choice of Achilles: The Ideology of Figure in the Epic*. Stanford, CA: Stanford University Press, 1992.

———. "Gendering Allegory: Spenser's Bold Reader and the Emergence of Character in *The Faerie Queene* III." *Criticism* 30 (1988): 1–21.

Wolfson, Susan. "The Language of Interpretation in Romantic Poetry." In *Romanticism and Language*, edited by Arden Reed, 22–50. Ithaca, NY: Cornell University Press, 1984.

Wright, John P., and Paul Potter, eds. *Psyche and Soma: Physicians and Metaphysicians on the Mind-Body Problem from Antiquity to Enlightenment*. Oxford: Clarendon Press, 2000.

Žižek, Slavoj. *The Plague of Fantasies*. London: Verso, 1997.

Index